DATE OF RETURN
UNLESS RECALLED BY LIBRARY

PLEASE TAKE GOOD CARE OF THIS BOOK

D1465350

LIVE
FROM
THE
BATTLE

PETER
ARNETT

A Touchstone Book
Published by Simon & Schuster

FIELD

From Vietnam to Baghdad
35 Years in the World's
War Zones

New York   London   Toronto   Sydney   Tokyo   Singapore

TOUCHSTONE
Rockefeller Center
1230 Avenue of the Americas
New York, New York 10020

Copyright © 1994 by Peter Arnett

All rights reserved
including the right of reproduction
in whole or in part in any form.

First Touchstone Edition 1995
TOUCHSTONE and colophon are registered trademarks
of Simon & Schuster Inc.

Designed by Deirdre C. Amthor

Manufactured in the United States of America

1   3   5   7   9   10   8   6   4   2

Library of Congress Cataloging-in-Publication Data
Arnett, Peter, 1934–
Live from the battlefield : from Vietnam to Baghdad: 35 years in
the world's war zones / Peter Arnett.
p.   cm.
Includes index.
1. Arnett, Peter, 1934–   War correspondents—New Zealand—
Biography.   3. Journalists—New Zealand—Biography.   I. Title.
PN5596.A76A3   1994
070.4′333′092—dc20
[B]   93-33817
                                                                                    CIP

ISBN 0-671-75586-2
ISBN 0-684-80036-5 (pbk)

A leatherbound signed first edition of this book has been published by
The Easton Press.

Acknowledgments

My daughter, Elsa Arnett, contributed more to this book than I can adequately credit. Elsa put her own promising journalism career on hold to help me tackle the project. Without the intuition, the discipline and the encouragement of the daughter, the father would have drowned in the minutiae of his reporting life—and never completed this account of it.

The Gulf War was the most controversial story of my life and I am indebted to my fiancée, Kimberly Moore, for encouraging me to go to Baghdad in the first place and urging me to stay on during the bombing. Kimberly has been invaluable in proofreading both the hardcover and paperback editions of this book.

Old friends weighed in with indispensable support. Not only did David Halberstam defend my controversial television reporting while I was in Baghdad, but on my return home he introduced me to the skilled literary agent Lynn Nesbitt. She secured me this book contract with Simon & Schuster, where editor Alice Mayhew took me in hand, testing the skills she had honed in twenty-five years of nurturing reporter-authors and overcoming their shortcomings. Alice and editor Eric Steel brought the project to fruition and I owe them both my heartfelt gratitude. Nina Arnett was encouraging from the beginning, and with her family helped me try to unravel the tangled threads of the Vietnam experience.

I am appreciative of Ted Turner and Tom Johnson of CNN for unhesitatingly granting me two years' leave to write this book, and for the support that they and other CNN executives have given me,

Acknowledgments

including Ed Turner, Bob Furnad, Eason Jordan, Lou Dobbs, Bill Headline and Lisa Dallos. CNN staffers also contributed their help: Reid Collins, David French, Frank Sesno, Vito Maggiolo, Charles Jaco, Robert Wiener, Nic Robertson and the other Boys of Baghdad, Bernard Shaw and John Holliman, as well as the CNN library staff in Atlanta, and Stacy Jolna.

For my early years, I am indebted to the still vivid memories of my ninety-one-year-old mother, Jane Arnett, in Bluff, New Zealand; the staff of the Wallace County Pioneers museum at Riverton; and Mick Hesselin, Brent Procter, Jim Valli and the New Zealand ambassador to Washington, Dennis McLean. Myrtle McKenzie Haidar was generous with her recollections of Southeast Asia thirty years ago, as were Tony and Bobbie Yared.

Colleagues from the Associated Press related their memories of Vietnam, particularly George Esper, Ed White, Horst Faas, Eddie Adams, Bob Ohman and Wes Gallagher. Lou Boccardi obligingly gave me access to office correspondence and approved my extensive use of AP material on the war. Others who helped recall Vietnam experiences were Mike McGrath, Dr. Tom Durant, George Gaspard, Michel Renard, Marvin Wolf and Steve Stibbens. I owe much to those who worked with me in later years and shared their memories, including Gerlind Younts, Paul Roque, Ted Kavanau, Stu Loory and Chuck DeCaro.

I was also heartened by friends and colleagues who spoke out and wrote on my behalf during the Gulf War, despite the hostility of those who wanted to trash the First Amendment right to freedom of speech. Among those many supporters were Paul Dean, Charles Kuralt, Bob Greene, Meg Greenfield, Walter Cronkite, William Prochnau, Bill Monroe, Arnaud de Borchgrave and the late Harrison Salisbury.

I received numerous letters of backing from CNN viewers during the controversy. Alice Zimmerman of Oakhurst, California, enclosed in her moving letter an American flag that she had flown in memory of her firefighter husband's fallen comrades. She concluded her letter: "In many ways journalists such as yourself represent and portray the freedom the flag symbolizes even more than the military personnel who fight to preserve it."

To my colleagues in the field
who routinely risk their lives
to cover the news.

Contents

Contents

10

Preface

I HAVE a rule never to do anything dangerous for fun. I thought of that rule as our helicopter pilots defied the laws of aeronautics, bucking and bouncing in the air drafts of Afghanistan's Panjsher valley as they negotiated windswept ravines and straddled sharp mountain ridges at 180 miles per hour. To calm my beating heart, I reasoned that the risk was worth it for the dramatic view of the debris of war below us, even though a few months earlier an American reporter had been killed in a neighboring valley in just such a helicopter outing.

The next evening I bent my rule again. After interviewing Islamic fundamentalist leader Gulbuddin Hekmatyar at his field headquarters outside Kabul, we decided to make the trip back to the capital. As dangerous as the trip promised to be, it was more dangerous to spend the night. We were assigned a van of soldiers to escort us to the last Hezb-i-Islami checkpoint. It was well after dark when we drove out the gate past the security guards sitting at a candlelit table. The nearby mountains were gray shadows against the blackness of the night. Outside the gates we saw our taxi driver, Amir Shah, in our headlights, signaling for us to stop. He handed CNN producer Peter Bergen a hastily scrawled note from our colleague in Kabul, Richard Mackenzie, warning us not to drive back to the capital. "On no account come back tonight. It is too dangerous. Your lives are more valuable than leaving early in the morning," Mackenzie had written. Our cameraman, Peter Jouvenal, impatient to leave the uncertain security of the war zone, insisted we proceed and climbed into Amir Shah's taxi. Bergen briefly considered the alternative, which was bedding down

Preface

with a platoon of unwashed soldiers and using nature's toilet in the trees. Our rooms at the German Club in the city were only forty minutes away. We drove off behind our escort.

The danger was not in Hezb territory but beyond, the two-mile stretch of no-man's-land that separated the belligerents in the outer suburbs of Kabul, an expanse rarely traversed at night. There were three layers of sentinels to pass, the first a mercenary force based at the old fort of Bala Hissar. We drove slowly beyond the last Hezb checkpoint with the vehicle lights our only illumination. A soldier materialized at my window with a submachine gun. He was a Hezb and waved us on. Further on in the glow of the headlights of the taxi ahead I saw the snout of a rifle grenade launcher bobbing toward us past some overturned cargo containers. I heard Jouvenal's voice shouting urgently in Dari, the local language, "Foreign journalists, foreign journalists." The grenade launcher was joined by an automatic rifle and pistol in the hands of three soldiers who peered into our vehicles and let us proceed. Jouvenal walked back to our car. "I think they were Dustan's men, but I'm not sure," he said, naming the local warlord. "Just go very slowly and listen for rifle shots and stop when you do."

We slowed down to three miles an hour. I could have walked faster. A match flickered in a building to my right and I could see the outlines of a soldier at a machine gun lighting his cigarette. To our left appeared the bulky outlines of Bala Hissar. Ahead was a checkpoint where the soldiers asked Amir Shah for money before we drove on. Now we were in the three city blocks controlled by the Kabul garrison. The city power was off again. I could barely make out the gaunt remains of businesses destroyed in the civil war. I thought we had made it safely. But even here, relatively early in the evening, there was no traffic in the streets, no movement whatsoever. I remembered a local official telling me, "Don't ever go out at night. After dark, everyone in Afghanistan is a bandit."

Peter Arnett
New York
October 1993

Part I
1934–1962

School Days

I LIVED MY YOUTH in Bluff, a gale-lashed town at the bottom end of New Zealand, which is at the bottom end of the world. Bluff was named after the wooded headland that overlooks the seaport, and from its windy summit I could look south across Stewart Island toward Antarctica, the vast land mass in that direction. The ice floes and wastelands were far beyond my sight, 1,600 miles distant, but I could often sense their presence. Antarctica was in the waves that washed across the stony beaches carrying the chill of melting ice; and in the short-tempered yellow-eyed penguins that nested along the rocky out-croppings of the shoreline flapping to their full height in anger and towering over me when I, as an inquisitive child, would disturb their nests.

New Zealand lies in the region of the Roaring Fifties, the southern latitude where the great oceans of the world become one, the Great Southern Ocean. Today, oceans are to yawn over while flying between great cities. But when I was a youth, the age of the steamship had followed the age of the sail, and the jet age was yet to arrive. The past hung heavily over the town where I grew up. Bluff was born of the Great Southern Ocean, or more correctly of the mammalian life that thrived there: the seals and whales riding the eddying and flowing sea currents that swirled around New Zealand and washed the con-tinental shores on the east and west sides of the Pacific.

It was from the same soaring headland I climbed in my youth that whale spotters a hundred years earlier cocked their eyes, searching for the telltale waterspouts and dark shapes of the black whales as they passed through Foveaux Strait in the months from May to August, seeking sheltered waters in which to calve. A sighting would prompt the shout, "There blows, blows, blows," and a runner would pass the message to the whaling station in the scrubland behind the beach in the harbor below. The signal would prompt a flurry of activity: six or eight oarsmen would launch the long, cedar-wood whaleboats into the light surf, boats built for speed with their tapered bows and sterns. In the open sea beyond Stirling Point, the crews' big oars would dig deeply into the ocean swell, driving the slim craft to a fatal rendezvous with the lumbering giants of the sea that sometimes measured fifty or sixty feet long, twice the length of the longboats and of course immeasurably heavier. The black whales were big, but docile, lurching along at walking speed, sometimes with their young in tow. According to the legends of the town, the black whales were easy pickings for the harpooners, but the task of towing the carcasses into shore was backbreaking.

I first heard these whaling tales from the grizzled Bluff fishermen who drank beer with my dad on Saturday afternoons. The rusting remains of what they said was the old whaling station were visible on the shore of Bluff Harbor. In my youth, whales were a rare sight off the coast, a consequence, in part, I later learned, of the indiscriminate killings of the previous century.

The whaling boom lasted less than a decade, but in that time the region was the focus of an emerging industrial world that needed oil for its machinery. There were old-timers when I was young who claimed to recall when Bluff Harbor was jammed with the three-masted, square-sterned, blunt-bowed whaling ships out of faraway Nantucket and New Bedford, the two greatest whaling ports in history. But this was before a series of circumstances ended the whaling days: the American Civil War saw the last of the New England whaling ships blasted out of the Pacific Ocean by Confederate gunboats; the California and Australia gold rushes led to a prohibitively high number of desertions from whaling ship crews; the opening of the American West attracted the young adventurers who had previously gone to sea for excitement; and the first oil well was sunk in Titusville, Pennsylvania, in 1859, providing a stiff and finally fatal competitor to whale oil in industry.

One hundred years after the first hardy whalers ventured across the Pacific Ocean to the anchorage in Bluff Harbor, the community had stabilized into a prosperous port. The memory of its stormy whaling days and later settlement were embodied in the names of the townspeople: Christiansens and Johansens from Scandinavian stock, Jamiesons and McDonalds from Scotland, Goldsworthies, Andersons, Arnetts from England, and the Waitiris and Tipenes, descendants of the original Maori inhabitants.

Tradition might also have accounted for the hard drinking and wenching of some of Bluff's fishermen and oystermen, the mainstay of the population. It was said the early whalers "drank their rum, and drank it neat." The whaling era was long over, but my neighbors still put out to sea in ships, working the dangerous waters sometimes weeks at a time to bring in substantial catches of grouper, blue cod, lobster and sacks of Bluff oysters, which were the gourmet delight of the country. Nature was demanding of those who would brave the deep, but was bountiful, too.

As a child I watched many of the seafaring men celebrating their return home, reeling in and out of the town's several pubs spaced half a block apart along Main Street, dissipating their considerable paychecks in formidable boozing exploits.

My father, Eric, was a light beer drinker who confined his pub socializing to Saturday afternoons. He carried his occasional inebriation well, unsteadily climbing the concrete steps up to the back door of our hillside home after the pubs had closed, and heading early to bed. My mother rarely accompanied him to the pub, but she was tolerant. He was a gentle man with an amiable disposition who worked long hours during the week as a builder, paid the bills of his young family on time, and was building up an adequate savings nest egg in those post-Depression days.

While I admired the tough men who braved the seas, I was never comfortable with Bluff's boisterous reputation. I was more thrilled that it was home to "the southernmost lamppost in the world," so certified by a sign at Stirling Point, where the waters of the Pacific Ocean and the Tasman Sea met, crashing against the worn-smooth rocks. Nailed to the lamppost were distance and directional signs to the rest of the world painted in black on yellow wood: London, 12,608; New York, 10,005; Hamburg, 12,198; Tokyo, 6,389. Those signs mesmerized me as the Pied Piper bewitched the children of Hamelin. I would follow those signs and my dreams to the far reaches of the world.

While I claim Bluff as my hometown, I was born in Riverton, on November 13, 1934—a small community fifteen miles to the west. Many of our relatives lived at Riverton, and my mother, Jane, spoke of it fondly as the place she, her mother and grandmother once lived.

17

Along with Bluff, Riverton was one of the first of the few, small European bay whaling settlements in New Zealand, located along the coasts of the North and South Islands in the early nineteenth century. They were established half a century after Lieutenant (later to be Captain) James Cook's first expedition had rediscovered the legendary, remote southern lands, virtually forgotten to the world after the Dutch explorer Abel Tasman found them in 1642. L. S. Rickard said in *The Whaling Trade in Old New Zealand* that the whaling settlements were bawdy, anarchic locales made up "of a motley collection of whalers, fugitive convicts and seamen, grog sellers, traders and the like who went about their often doubtful business untroubled by the missionaries, or a so-called British Resident totally lacking in authority." Early New Zealand history is redolent with wild tales of dissolute living in the Bay of Islands settlements and elsewhere along the coast at the beginnings of the nineteenth century.

My family history as passed down over the years portrays Riverton in a somewhat different light, a whaling community much more respectable than the others, well organized and law abiding, a fitting locale for our ancestral roots. The family progenitor was James Leader, from Eastbourne, Sussex, then an important English port handling the Pacific trade. Young Leader was drawn to New Zealand waters by the opportunity for adventure and achievement, twin goals sought by many underprivileged Englishmen of his time.

Leader sailed with Captain John Howell on his flagship, the ten-gun schooner the *Eliza,* in 1834, with a commission to set up a shore whaling station at a locality known as Jacob's River near the mouth of the Aparima River. Two other ships, the *Postboy* and the *Frolic,* joined them in the expedition. They arrived offshore in the late afternoon, their passengers gazing with approval at the sheltered beaches washed by the Aparima River, which poured into the sea through a narrow channel. Beyond were a succession of gentle slopes, with open land or bush that ran into the interior.

The pioneers anchored their vessels in the sheltered harbor on a gray winter day, lowering their whale boats into the blue-black waters and rowing ashore. The sixty Englishmen introduced themselves at a small Maori settlement called a Kaik, extending along the flat eastern shore of the riverside. They had been advised in advance that the natives at the Aparima River were extremely wild. But in fact the Maoris, from the Ngati Mamoe tribe, were the remnants of what once had been a proud, fierce people, their potential for combat destroyed by disunity and past vendettas. James Leader and the others quickly won their friendship. They treated the Maoris as equals, and the natives became valued helpers around the whaling station.

At that time in New Zealand there were more than a hundred thousand Maoris, most of them grouped in tribes in the North Island. James Leader and his fellow pioneers numbered no more than a thousand throughout the country, but the impact of foreigners had already undermined the traditional Maori way of life, further hastened by the enthusiastic proselytizing of Christian missionaries. As James Leader and the others cleared the flat land behind the towering sand dunes to build their first homes, they began finding evidence of the grim social history of the area. There were signs of a bloody battle that had been fought a decade earlier along the riverbank. Eventually, someone found an old Maori oven dug into the ground, complete with charred human bones, grim enough evidence of the practice of cannibalism. Much later government investigations asserted that the settlement was the site of the last white-man cannibalistic feast in New Zealand, according to F. W. G. Miller in *West to the Fiords*. The victim who had gone ashore from a passing ship was "a foreign violinist in the early days, who was discovered by some braves on the beach near the Waimatuku, and deported to the Kaik as a treasure trove, and being in fair condition, was incontinently roasted and devoured with much apparent relish."

The unsavory culinary history of the locality did not deter the bay whalers. They persevered, clearing the land and erecting their huts made of tree fern plastered with clay, or dwellings of wattle and daub, simple houses crude in appearance but comfortable enough in winter and cool in summer. The pioneers' main task, the building of the shore whaling station, was soon accomplished. They erected tall, wooden shears on the hard sandy beach, a hoisting apparatus of two upright spars fastened together at the upper ends with tackle for lifting the slaughtered whales out of the water to better carve them up for the try-works. The fires from the furnaces burned all day and night during the spring and summer whale season as the try-pots rendered the yellow blubber into oil.

But the harvest of black whales was abundant for only half a dozen years. The great mammals either altered their seasonal migratory patterns or were so diminished in numbers by the killings that they ceased to provide sufficient livelihood for the bay whalers. But unlike most other temporary communities that quickly withered and became New Zealand's first ghost towns, the bay whaling station at Riverton survived. The expedition chief, Captain Howell, saw great agricultural potential in the area, and encouraged James Leader and others in his party to settle on the rich land in the foothills above the bay. This was the first permanent European settlement in the South Island of New Zealand, and its bay whalers were some of the founding fathers of the country.

The founding mothers were the Maori women from the neighborhood. South Seas visitors had long been attracted to the large-eyed, light-brown-skinned Polynesian women with their dark glossy hair and submissive ways, and the bay whalers usually made seasonal arrangements with the local tribes for female companionship. For the girls' relatives, this connection was a useful one because it gave them some access to the bounty of the bay whaling stations. From such casual relationships a nation was born.

Captain Howell set a more legitimate standard for the Riverton whaling station by marrying a Maori girl named Koi Koi Patu, the young chieftainess of Center Island. The marriage cemented the ties between the natives and the settlers and guaranteed racial harmony. With Howell's encouragement, James Leader followed his example, taking for his wife a cousin of Koi Koi named Mere Wehikore. My great-great-grandmother moved into the unfamiliar surroundings of the whaling station, agreeing as was the custom of the time to be faithful, to rise before dawn to prepare her husband's food, and to keep the house clean and mend his clothes. Leader was required to treat her kindly, dress her adequately, and support the interests of her relatives and tribe.

Bishop George Augustus Selwyn, who visited Riverton in 1844, agreed to marry them officially in a brief service at Captain Howell's house, a sturdy four-roomed cottage built of Australian gum timber that still stands in Riverton today. The fact of the marriage was relevant in my family history; to my close relatives it differentiated us from neighbors whose ancestors failed in the earliest days to legitimize their unions with their Maori wives. "Never forget that James Leader was legally married," my grandmother used to tell me, and I was young enough then to believe that it really mattered.

There were three children from the marriage, James Jr., Lisa and Elizabeth, my great-grandmother, born in 1848. To support his growing family as the days of productive whaling waned, James Leader turned his boat-building skills to other undertakings, and as a carpenter and general handyman he helped his fellow settlers raise the new community of North Riverton. Leader also had his eyes on the land, the vast hinterland of rolling native bush and open spaces left fallow by the Maoris and beckoning to those who wished to farm it. Captain Howell had received fifty thousand acres of prime property as his wedding dowry from his Maori bride. James Leader's bequest was more modest, several thousand acres of fertile land along both banks of the Aparima River a dozen miles inland from the settlement. He built a small family house on the eastern bank of the river, planting potatoes as a food crop. And he cleared the bush on the other side of the river for a pig farm, letting the animals feed for themselves off the fern roots. His farm flourished and his health was fine, but his teeth were bad and he eventually acquired the nickname "Gummy." His farm became known then, as it is now, as Gummy's Bush.

The Aparima is a tidal river and treacherous, fed by swift streams from the snow-caked Rimutaka Mountains. James Leader was in the habit of crossing the river each day to tend his pigs, choosing low tide, when the waters were comparatively safe. Drowning was a known hazard in early New Zealand; the water was so cold and swift, the force of the current could roll an unwary man over and over like a barrel before he sank to the bottom. Drowning in those days was known as "the New Zealand death." One evening before dinner Leader crossed the river at low tide on farming chores. But his return was delayed and he tried to get back to the other side of the now swollen river even though he was a poor swimmer. The New Zealand death swallowed him up.

His grieving wife returned to her tribe after Captain Howell insisted on taking the three fatherless children as his wards. They moved into his Riverton home, which had pictures of Lord Nelson, Admiral Collingwood and other British naval heroes on the walls, and the children participated fully in Howell family life. They were educated by the family governess and encouraged to master their native tongue. The captain eventually had three wives and nineteen children, a not unusually large number of progeny for those pioneering times, but he never did forget his commitment to the offspring of his friend and fellow pioneer James Leader.

My great-grandmother sent her children to be educated in the new grade school built on the site of the Maori earth oven where the unfortunate kidnapped musician had been roasted. My great-grandfather, John Arnett, was a chairman of a surveying team mapping the South Island, in preparation for full British settlement, and he gave his name to several small rivers and promontories. Captain Howell gave the couple a gift of farm stock as their wedding present and they led an uneventful life in the untroubled, prosperous rural community, part of the full-fledged British colony of New Zealand.

When I was born, Elizabeth was nearly ninety years of age and in poor health. She died two years later and I have no memory of her. Her death severed our direct ties to the romantic, adventuresome past. Hanging on a wall in the cluttered Wallace County Pioneers' Museum in Riverton today is a splendid photograph of her at the turn of the century, her waist corseted in a full-length formal velvet gown, long hair tucked under a feathered Victorian hat, her dark, mischievous eyes challenging the world. The strong-willed Elizabeth outlived her two husbands by twenty years and by all accounts she was a smart, polished woman, accomplished in riding to the hounds in what passed for gracious colonial society in those days, and proud of her status as a daughter of a pioneer.

The New Zealand where I was born had been vastly transformed in the hundred years since James Leader had stepped ashore. On the beach where I played as a child in summertime, the old whaling station had long rotted away, and the towering sand dunes had been removed to make room for the expanding town. The native forests in the hinterland were but distant memories; artificially sown pasture and modified tussock grassland for sheep and cattle cloaked much of the country, including the rolling hills around Gummy's Bush.

I was not as troubled by the squandering of the once beautiful landscape of which I had no memory, as much as I was by the growing realization that I was culturally unanchored, disoriented by my mixed heritage. My elder brother, John, younger brother, David, and I—our Polynesian blood enfeebled by intermarriage—looked like all the other white kids in the neighborhood. As a small child I thought little of my cultural allegiances but as I grew older I wrestled with the pressing issue of who I was. Inside our home I was the inheritor of an exotic tradition that portrayed a New Zealand that was created by the Pacific god Maui who dragged up the ocean, using the jawbone of an ancestress as the hook and his own blood the bait. Outside the house I lived in a land that hundreds of thousands of settlers had turned into a mirror-image of England, ignoring the existence of most Maori tradition.

My parents were lovingly insistent that I brush my teeth, eat my greens and keep practicing the piano. I turned to the classroom when my short stature and lack of physical coordination drove me from the sports field, my nose broken both in boxing and in cricket. I was so eager to prove my academic prowess that I won the Bluff Anglican Church's Bible study prize five years in a row, admittedly against a weak field. I joined the Sea Scouts and earned a score of skill badges that I wore proudly on the arms of my navy blue sweater. I received certificates of special merit throughout the World War Two years from the New Zealand Education Department for my victory gardens grown in the backyard of our quarter-acre property, planted and weeded by my maternal grandmother, Nana (Elizabeth and John's daughter), but always attributed to me.

When the American Liberty Ships came to port to load up cargoes of mutton, beef and butter to feed the war effort, I was often the first aboard ship to beg for Juicy Fruit gum and Camel cigarettes. To celebrate Victory over Japan Day in 1945 I stole a whole case of soft drinks from the doorway of greengrocer Willie Wong's store. To prove my manhood to Johnny Jamieson and Owen McQuarrie I became the best apple thief in the neighborhood, the terror of orchard owners everywhere.

As the years went by, I realized that I was a loner, not a leader, maybe because I was too selfish to share the glory or too insecure to risk rebuke from my peers. Marlon Brando became my idol and in my early twenties I took to wearing the black jacket, black-striped shirt and white tie he favored as the gambler Sky Masterson in *Guys and Dolls*. I got along fine with the guys; I struggled with the dolls.

.   .   .

My parents were not privy to my rapidly expanding life experience, but they knew the tough town well enough to get me out of there before I grew up too early. My father was as loyal to Bluff as any resident, served on the volunteer fire brigade for years, and helped found the local Lions Club. But he planned to educate his children to a higher level of achievement than anyone in the family or the town before. He chose one of the most select private schools in the country, Waitaki Boys High School, located at Oamaru on the northeast coast of Otago Province. With its ivy-walled campus and cedar-lined driveways, Waitaki was a New Zealand version of an exclusive British public school, a South Island Eton.

My father's resolve to start us on the path to higher education came after his own attempts to escape the bonds of a predictably uneventful life crashed, along with the stock market, in the late 1920s. He was born in the country town of Mataura in 1903, and in his mid-twenties he made his way to the capital of Wellington, where he bought a small shop and went into business selling candy and other inexpensive items. Forced back home by the Depression, he married my mother in 1929 and settled in Riverton. Through the Depression years, my father scraped together a living with the carpentry and bricklaying skills he had learned as a trade apprentice. Business recovered as New Zealand's dairy produce became important to a worrying Europe on the verge of World War Two and the building boom improved my family's fortunes. We moved into a solid concrete showcase home in Bluff that my father designed and helped to build, with a bold exterior stairway leading up to a wide, open porch where my brothers and I preferred to sleep in stormy weather because it was like camping out. My father stayed home from the war because of a bad heart but he served in the town home guard. I loved standing on watch with him on Bluff Hill keening our eyes for Japanese submarines, the way the whalers had watched for their prey a hundred years earlier. My father had his wooden rifle at the ready; the real ones were all at the war front. By war's end he was sending off his children for the education he never had.

Though I dearly loved them both I had no regrets leaving my parents, to set off in my brother's footsteps, on a long train ride to Oamaru and four years of boarding school with high hopes for my future. I was thirteen. My mother complained that I didn't cry at the train station as John had when he left.

Waitaki Boys High was run like a boot camp for unruly children. The school attracted a clientele both of genteel parents anxious to give their heirs a helping hand up the social ladder, and successful businessmen and farmers who were seeking a superior education for their sons. It fielded a competent, generally sympathetic staff; the classrooms and sport fields were first-rate. But the pretty English gardens and handsome sandstone facade hid a repressive authority determined to go to great lengths to rein in and reign over youthful excess. This outlook enlivened the novel *Tom Brown's Schooldays,* but to read about it is not to live it.

I remember the darker side of my boarding school days intensely. The record will show that most students survived the experience, indeed are convinced that it made them better men and citizens; they regret the ending of the disciplinary traditions in recent years. I don't. In a sports-mad school, my lack of such skills limited my overall performance, even though I did in my last year captain the Don House rugby team and win the championship after a mild flu epidemic had felled most of the opposing players. But I made friends, kept getting

A's, took Latin and French, and expanded my horizons with classical music studies. I graduated from Waitaki High School at the end of my third year and moved into the sixth form for pre-university study. I was all set to sit for my university entrance examinations, when I was kicked out of school.

Her name was Dawn, and I broke the rules by dating her. When I dragged my bags off the train and arrived home, my father looked thunderstruck.

In the News Business

THE *SOUTHLAND TIMES* was on our breakfast table every morning except Sunday for as long as I can remember. Like most New Zealand newspapers in those days it was modeled after *The Times* of London, with small advertisements packed on the front and back pages and mostly local political and sports news inside. It was a model of rectitude with balanced, unsensational reports of the day's news; no bylines. There was one exception—the sports column called "Onlooker" written by Albie Keast, one of the few media personalities in the area. Albie covered the rugby internationals played by his beloved All Blacks, treating each game like the Second Coming. But he was the rogue elephant of rugby writers, and it was said that an unkind mention in Albie's column could kill the future prospects of an up-and-coming player.

My brother John had taken a reporting job on the newspaper after leaving high school. Though my father complained that reporters sat around at town meetings and drank too much beer, he telephoned Albie Keast, who was also the chief reporter of the *Times,* and said he had another son in the pipeline if the newspaper was interested. The networking paid off and I scored an appointment with Jack Grimaldi, the editor in chief, who asked me directly in his gravelly voice if I was willing to obey orders and follow instructions. He had clearly been on the phone to the Waitaki High School rector and I feared for the worst. Grimaldi smiled at my discomfiture and as he hired me said I could date as many girls as I wished but not on company time. I started work on January 7, 1951, and I still remember the joy of riding the bus up from Bluff along the winding country road to Invercargill, where the newspaper was published. I strode along sunlit Dee Street past the whitewashed war memorial and through a shopping arcade to the red-brick, three-story office building and introduced myself to the staff.

It turned out that I had a knack for the job, and when I finally started regular reporting duties, my note pad and pencil fit me like a glove.

I covered my share of cat shows, backyard brush fires, minor sports events and lots of anniversaries and committee meetings of the most obscure organizations. This was a local paper after all and everyone in the community wanted to see his name in print. Albie Keast was a man of meticulous routine but little imagination, and he kept a folio-sized assignment book in which each evening he scribbled our tasks for the following day. Veterans swore you could interchange the books year for year and not miss an assignment.

I respected the man who had given me my first job. But I kept my distance. The trouble with Albie, as a colleague once observed, was that he treated his staff like galley slaves, pushing them to the limit in their six-day-a-week jobs. Then he'd turn the screw further by taking out the pain of his failed endeavors on the poor inkstained wretches who worked for him.

When I began reporting, Albie would add assignments to my work-load late in the day that had me scrambling to fulfill them. I often pulled late-night duty and he would peer over my shoulder and mutter as I pecked away at a story on my typewriter. He would complain that I wrote too slowly, and I would respond that he gave me such lousy assignments I had to be creative to make them interesting. He chatted congenially with my father on the phone, but he treated me like a blockhead who had stumbled into a job I had no good reason to have.

The *Southland Times* hired me for thirty shillings a week; the room I shared with a portly old gentleman at a bed-and-breakfast place near Queen's Park was forty shillings, so I needed support from my father for the first year or so. Money was not too important to me because my needs were small. I usually ate after work at the local pie cart, a curbside restaurant on wheels that dispensed crusty mystery meat pies, with side orders of sloppy mashed potatoes and greasy peas splashed on top. My friends were junior reporters from the newspaper, like-minded youths similarly freed from the constraints of school and home and anxious to make their way in the news industry in the time-honored apprenticeship tradition, working first as menial cadet reporters, then rising in the ranks over four or five years to become general reporters, akin to graduating with a degree from a community college and guaranteeing your future career.

I was busy but I was restless. It was not just that Albie Keast was making my working life miserable. I could already sense that journalism was a ticket to a ride around the world and I was at a dead stop in Invercargill. I applied for a reporter's job on *The Standard,* the trade union movement's weekly newspaper published in Wellington. I got the job—I was the only applicant. I did not miss Albie. He had a room at Deschler's Hotel across the street from the newspaper and years afterward I visited him. He had long retired and he could barely stand to greet me, I learned, because he was arthritic and had gained a lot of weight. My father told me Albie had spoken well of me in the years following my departure, but he was surly when I met him. How could I tell such a man that his ornery ways had shaped me into a functioning professional journalist, and given me the grit to face down characters far more venal than he would ever dream of being.

Albie Keast was a blessing for my future employers. No one who ever gave me orders again could surpass his bullying, and for that I am grateful.

.   .   .

The Standard was in a five-story building in the center of Wellington. The lanky editor, Sid Pickering, was volubly friendly. Not only was I the only applicant, he informed me, I was the weekly's only reporter and was responsible for dealing with the Federation of Labour and the Labour Party's shadow government, which had been out of power for three years but was favored to win the next election. He gave me my own office and a telephone near the subeditor's enclosure. It was all heady stuff to me but I was smart enough to realize that *The Standard* was a rag by any definition, a propaganda sheet for the working man tacked together each week by an underpaid, skeletal staff. I was required to make so many visits to the august halls of Parliament House to interview Labour Party leader Walter Nash and other Labour Party officials that I may as well have hung a party membership card around my neck.

I did have a foot in the other camp; one of the government cabinet members, the minister of health, Ralph Hanan, was the brother of my Invercargill dentist, Roy Hanan, and on the strength of what he called "past associations" he granted me interviews and slipped me little tips on things happening around town that gave me some political balance.

I joined the Esperanto Club to meet girls but found it even more difficult to communicate with them in a foreign tongue. I tried out for the Thespian Society and I joined the Wellington Jazz Club and began playing basketball and some badminton, but the pickings were equally slim and I kept running into male friends from Invercargill also in unsuccessful pursuit of romance. I did enjoy the perks of being a reporter in the nation's capital, the dinners at Parliament House for the visiting deputy prime ministers, the private movie screenings at the Japanese Embassy and the cocktail parties given by others in the diplomatic corps.

The Standard editor burned with the fire of a social reformer; he championed the disadvantaged and composed fiery editorials and urged me to be a crusader. When I was writing about the ruling National Government shelving a set of new safety regulations for high tension power linesmen, Pickering watched over me as I typed the article; deadline was approaching and he was urging me toward increasingly extreme description. By the time my article went to press, we had charged the minister of public works with a capital crime. A lurid page one headline rubbed the allegation in: "The Charge Is Murder: The Verdict Must Be Guilty." The minister was upset and brought a criminal libel suit against *The Standard,* the first case of its kind in the British Commonwealth since the late nineteenth century. I was too young to appear in court. We won the case on a technicality.

In January of 1956, I made my annual two-week visit to the bleak Waiouru area in the center of North Island. Compulsory military training was a requirement for all young men. I was in a mortar battery that was equipped with rusting weapons of an early vintage that frequently misfired and I feared ever going into combat with them. Our group assembled at a tent camp at Baggush, eight miles into the desert. We remained in that landscape of rugged hills, tussock, wind and dust for two weeks. A team of hard-nosed military instructors endeavored to put us through our lethargic paces with little success, even though they warned we might be seeing action in Malaysia, where the British were trying to suppress a communist insurgency. I vowed to myself that I would never go to war for any reason because I thought the military was inept. Even at this brief exercise we were on short rations for no good reason, the hygiene was awful and someone came down with polio. It was such a depressing place and the morale so low that

I decided to write a story about it for *The Standard,* but when I returned to Wellington a Major Healey from the military public relations bureau phoned me to warn that any uncleared story "will be a breach of military security" and that I would be dealt with under the Espionage Act. I felt compromised by the military and fed up with *The Standard.* In midwinter of 1956 I left the newspaper and headed off for a new start in Australia.

.   .   .

When the MV *Wanganella* berthed at Sydney Harbor on July 16, 1956, she was eleven hours overdue because a southerly buster had blown us off course. The city had a raw reputation. New Zealanders felt about Australia as Canadians do about the United States: it's an elephant that's liable to crush you when it stirs. I walked five city blocks to the offices of the *Sydney Sun* newspaper, on Broadway along streets lined with the first skyscrapers I'd ever seen in my life. With nothing to lose, I boldly told the managing editor's secretary that I wanted a job. The editor was not available so I waited for an interview in the corner of a newsroom that could have accommodated all of the *Southland Times,* printing presses included. The *Sun*'s offices stretched across a block-long floor, with glass-doored management offices and a score of desks where reporters and editors were busily preparing material for the upcoming edition. Shouted commands punctuated the din of clacking teleprinters and ringing telephones. The *Sun* was a breezy tabloid that published half a dozen new street editions during the course of the day in deadly competition with its rival, the *Sydney Daily Mirror.*

I was hired on the spot for six Australian pounds a day. Australian editors favored young New Zealanders who had survived the demanding Albie Keast–style school of journalism. Jack Tuohy, the news editor, put me to work on the crisis of the day, the chase for a suspected hatchet murderer running loose on the streets of Paddington.

I raced downstairs and jumped into a staff car with a photographer and we sped to the scene. The photographer guessed that I had not done this sort of thing before, and when I concurred he exclaimed, "Oh, shit," gazing out the window as we passed a tangle of slummy streets with bars and pawnbroking shops into the Paddington section. Our driver slammed on his brakes at an intersection where a crowd was gathering.

"He's there," shouted a frightened woman, pointing to a storefront across the street. The pavement was smeared with blood; there were no police at the scene. I knew I had to jump on the story, but I blanched at the prospect of facing an axe murderer on my first day at work. Before I could move in, three police cars arrived, sirens blaring, and the detective kicked me off the street because I had no press credentials.

I borrowed a phone and called the newsroom with what little information I had, but when I got back to the office Jack Tuohy was severe. "Son, what the hell were you doing out there?" He held up the latest edition of the hated *Daily Mirror*. It featured a full confession by the axe murderer allegedly given to a *Mirror* reporter at the bloody scene. I protested that the *Mirror* wasn't even there, that the whole thing was made up. The news editor wagged his forefinger at me: "Son, if you're to make it in the news business around here you've got to learn how to compete."

I never did get the chance to redeem myself at the *Sun,* even though they kept me on the staff for the next three months and paid me more than a living wage. I was that kid who had let the axe murderer get away. Eventually, a pink slip came with my pay and I was on the street without a job.

My friends consoled me, assuring me it was all for the better. I was not so sure; the news business in Sydney was going through one of its cyclical slowdowns. Many journalists were out on the streets. I had moved out of the Salvation Army hostel to a house at 29 Arcadia Street at Coogee Beach with two roommates. We each had a bed in a corner of the large room, the fourth corner reserved for a hot plate.

For several months I worked as a temporary laborer. I had the back and arms for it, but not the attitude and outlook. Thankfully, the Sydney job market improved. I got occasional day work on the four local newspapers. On a blind date I met a Doris Day look-alike named Myrtle Mackenzie. One of my roommates purchased an ancient Model T Ford and all of us drove down to Melbourne to the 1956 summer Olympic Games. When I returned to Sydney I was hired by an entrepreneur who was starting a TV weekly. The Sydney *TV Preview* magazine listed programs for the infant television industry and featured long interviews with stars. One afternoon I drove out to Kingsford Smith Airport to attend a press conference given by Mike Todd and Elizabeth Taylor to promote the blockbuster movie *Around the World in 80 Days*. They talked little about the movie and argued with each other over personal matters most of the time.

I realized I was getting bored in Sydney, that it was not the grand adventure I had yearned for when I left New Zealand. I was remembering the books of exciting ventures written by the reporting stars of Fleet Street and I was tempted to try and join them. But then, I couldn't even corner an axe murderer. Myrtle came up with an idea. She was from England and had traveled some. She had learned that an obscure Dutch shipping company carried freight and passengers on their slow boats to the Orient. We could just afford to make the trip. I have always been a pushover for a strong-willed woman.

En Route to Asia

IN MARCH 1958, after I cadged the money to pay for the journey from my parents, and vowed that this would be the last occasion I would raid the family coffers, Myrtle and I embarked on a slow boat to Asia. As our ship, the SS *Silindoeng,* an old tub of a Dutch tramp steamer, pulled out from the docks, we roamed the deck hand in hand and watched the waves rippling across the harbor surface.

In keeping with the proper appearances of the time, Myrtle would not share a cabin with me because we were not married, and refused to consider my spirited objections. I was allotted a cabin with a Thai student named Phongthep who was returning home to Bangkok after completing his accountancy exams in Melbourne. He promised to invent discreet absences to allow me some intimacy with Myrtle, but Phongthep was a poor sailor and was barely able to leave the cabin at all during the whole trip. Myrtle's cabin partner was an Australian woman named Elaine who took a dislike to me and proved unwilling to play Cupid. Consequently, the dreamed-of romantic possibilities for our journey were rarely realized. At dinner the first night, Myrtle proved the wisdom of her moral stance: the passenger list included two Christian missionary couples bound for Borneo who quizzed us relentlessly about our personal lives.

The voyage of the *Silindoeng* was the bargain route to Asia via a dozen ports of call in remote locales in the western Pacific that were little known then and even less known now. Sorong, Manakwari, Biak, Morotai are hardly names to light up a résumé. It seemed to me the end of the world. Most ports were too little for us to enter, located in small, palm-fringed bays along mountainous coasts, or inside coral reefs dangerous to navigate. So we usually lay offshore at anchor, unloading our cargo of consumer goods and appliances into sampans and taking on the copra and hemp they brought back; watching the Chinese messboys fishing for fresh food in waters infested with the deadly yellow-banded krait sea snakes that wrapped around the fishing lines and slithered up the sides of the ship. In one grubby harbor we saw locals carve up the carcasses of a large school of hammerhead sharks that had gotten stranded on an inshore sandbank, and blood washed the beach a dark red color as the villagers shared the unexpected harvest.

The circuitous route of the *Silindoeng* took us not only through nature's playground, but also into the forgotten past and to the edge of the pressing future. With no privacy of our own, Myrtle and I spent much time on the bridge with Captain Mueller and he was glad for the company, sharing his pots of thick Sumatran coffee. One afternoon as we passed through a channel between two volcanic Moluccan islands, he pointed to the ruins of once great mansions in the thick foliage. They reminded him of the spice wars that had raged in those waters in the sixteenth century when ships manned by the Dutch, Portuguese, British and Spanish fought to control the islands and the trade in nutmeg and cloves. All the competing European nations eventually secured a piece of Southeast Asia and grew rich, until World War Two. Captain Mueller clearly identified with the Dutch colonialists whose blood ran in his veins and he mourned the declining days of Holland's rule in Indonesia. He deplored what he sarcastically called President Sukarno's "experiment in socialism."

At the palm-fringed port of Morotai, two young English women begged for transportation to Borneo. Mueller allowed them to board the ship though both were broke. They brought news of an insurgency against the Indonesian government by a band of discontented right-wing military men who had taken over most of the neighboring island of the Celebes. Captain Mueller and his officers listened with rapt attention over dinner as the women recounted their adventures with the rebels. I was less interested in the account of the insurrection than I was in the messengers; both were unkempt but wore a confident air, indifferent to their ragged appearance. They said they were freelance journalists stringing for Fleet Street papers, the *News of the World* and the *Daily Sketch,* sensationalist rags. But I was impressed with the boldness of the reporters and was eager to find out how they had gotten their jobs. Before I could study them to my satisfaction, we had arrived at the Borneo port of Jesselton, where they landed to file their stories and make their way back to the war zone.

The emerging political struggle in Southeast Asia of the late 1950s was news to me as I sailed guilelessly into its midst. The Korean War had alerted Australia and New Zealand to the challenges further north of an emerging communist China and its partners, and both nations at the request of the United States contributed forces to the war effort. At age seventeen I had been uncomfortably poised for combat myself, drafted to serve in the army and put on alert as a gunner on a mortar team. At the last moment an artillery unit was sent in our place to my enormous relief: our weapons were so ancient they would have been of questionable utility in modern war, and I frankly had no stomach for the real dangers of military action.

Always more fearsome than the communists, in the New Zealanders' mind, was the thought of a resurgent Japan, bent on reclaiming the island territories it had conquered in World War Two, and using these stepping stones through the South Pacific to invade us. In Australia the specter of the "yellow peril" inflamed political campaigning to an embarrassingly racist degree. The Pacific island battles of World War Two were seen as a holy crusade against the Asian heathens, so it was with a sense of pride and wonder that I watched from the deck of the *Silindoeng* as we downed anchor at the coral-fringed harbor of Biak Island off the northern coast of Dutch New Guinea and Captain Mueller pointed to the World War Two mementos arrayed on the seaside cemetery that was the beach. There were the rusting carcasses of Japanese tanks, their guns curled toward the sky; the blackened, twisted remains of destroyed trucks buried in the sands, garlands of bougainvillea vines threading through the visible wreckage.

The ship's officers told us there was much more to see ashore so we loaded up a picnic basket with a lunch of sandwiches and beer and took it with us. The Japanese stronghold on Biak had been attacked by General MacArthur's Forty-first Infantry in an invasion on May 27, 1944, and fighting continued until August that year. The island stronghold was expected to fall in a week but the intelligence preparation was inaccurate: there were nearly three times the number of defenders on Biak than the Americans estimated and they fought fanatically and died to the last man. The operation cost the United States nearly five hundred deaths and 2,400 wounded.

We walked through the narrow streets of the small tropical port and out to the weed-fringed airstrip, the main objective of the American assault. The battle had taken place fourteen years earlier but much was left of the refuse of war. There were stacks of steel helmets, some neatly punctured with bullet holes, others partly melted from the intense heat of the flamethrowers. Webbing from belts and harnesses was rotting on the damp ground, along with rusting cartridge shells and mangled rifle stocks. We discovered piles of human bones in the caves and ravines where we searched. Bleached human skulls stared at us from mossy crevasses and dark places in the rocks. To my horror, I learned that all twelve thousand Japanese soldiers killed on Biak either lay in the jungle where they died, or had been bulldozed into the caves for sanitary purposes. The Japanese government was embarking on an accounting of the Pacific War dead but was still far from examining the distant island battlefields.

We bade farewell to the *Silingdoeng* and our Dutch hosts at Bangkok. I stepped lightly ashore. I felt I had learned much since embarking on the voyage forty days earlier. I felt physically sturdy, well fed from the ship's abundant galley and deeply tanned for the first time in my life from the hot tropical sun; and as a regular at the captain's table I had been privy to hours of boisterous adult conversation that ranged across a whole spectrum of new and interesting subjects.

I had become friends with my cabin-mate Phongthep and he prepared me for our arrival by teaching me a few words of his native language. Phongthep was a gentle, responsive person with a wide smile and an ardent desire to please. I was to discover those were the national traits, that the Thais were capable of showing great generosity toward people they valued, though their generosity was laced with cunning. The Thai kingdom had survived the colonial era intact by playing off the covetous Western powers against one another, maintaining its independence while neighboring Burma, Laos, Cambodia, Vietnam and Malaysia were swallowed up. It had similarly survived the ire of the West for allying with Japan in World War Two by agreeing to anchor the regional strategy against the new enemy, communism. With leaders of suave assurance, and blessed with rich agricultural lands and a languid tropical climate, the Thai people were self-indulgent and successful. Before I learned these truths I had already made an instinctive judgment in my first hours ashore: it was love at first sight.

My upbringing did not prepare me for the startling sensations of the Orient. My education had been aimed at inoculation against the destructive temptations of strange cultures, but in that it failed miserably. If New Zealand was gray-green and wrapped up against the cold and smelling of damp earth and sheep dip, then Thailand was red-yellow and sweat-stained T-shirts and stinking of overripe fruit and wild hibiscus. If mealtimes back home were boiled meats and steamed vegetables and baked breads, now they were gang tom yam lemon grass soup and gaeng phet hot curry and sticky rice and man-goes. I roamed Bangkok's back alleys bewitched by the street life and the pungent odors leaking from the stalls of the legal opium dens, with Thailand's resplendent Buddhist Temple of Dawn towering like a porcelain vision over the Chao Phraya River.

If at home I was a short, ordinary-looking bloke competing with my contemporaries for a place in the sun, here in Bangkok I felt taller and exotic among the diminutive Thais, accorded deference for being different and for just being there. I noticed when Myrtle and I boarded a chaotic public bus for a trip out of town the driver insisted we sit in the choice seats next to him. At roadside restaurants small groups of locals would gather in the vicinity and chat about us. At the little hotels in Tak and Lop Buri and Chieng Mai where Myrtle finally agreed to share a room "for protection," we would sometimes discover that small crowds were listening outside our window in the morning, gig-gling and pointing in our direction when we emerged.

Myrtle and I just kept going until our money ran out, staying in dollar-a-night hotels, riding the dusty roads and eating fried noodles and pri kee noo. On a whim we rode a bus to Mae Sot on the Burmese border, traveling a winding highway that crossed a wooded mountain range where a snow leopard snoozed on the roadside in the afternoon sun. The bus driver reached for his rifle but the sleek animal slipped away into the underbrush.

When we arrived, one of the three policemen who could speak a little English convinced us to travel overland with him by a jungle route to the northern city of Chieng Mai to visit his sister. We set off on foot across dry, rutted rice fields, climbing up through a forest of mountain beech trees to a village where we spent the night in houses built on high posts to protect against marauding tigers. Our week-long trek grew arduous on the third day along a steep rockbound mountain ridge, and we appealed for horses to make the journey easier. By evening our policeman friend had borrowed two mud-caked working elephants from a small sawmill and in this manner, poised uncomfortably on the backs of the compliant beasts, we lurched and bumped over the jungle trails that led us most of the remaining way to Chieng Mai.

We were to discover the hard way that the charm of the Thai people was unique to the region. The success of our travels emboldened us to visit the legendary Khmer ruins of Angkor Wat buried deep inside the jungles of Cambodia, and we embarked on the border train with hopes for high adventure. At Poipet the Cambodian border guards hassled us over our visas, claiming the required port of entry was at the capital, Phnom Penh, and that we could not proceed, and to make things worse, the immigration official professed to be ignorant of the existence of my homeland of New Zealand and was not anxious to accept my passport.

Our explanations in bad French failed to convince him but I saw to my relief a large wall map of the world in a neighboring room and I dragged him there, proudly splashing my finger into the South Pacific Ocean only to find that the world ended at Australia; it was an Air France route map and the airline did not fly to New Zealand. We eventually resolved our differences and were on our way and had time to lunch at Sisophon.

We purchased tickets to Phnom Penh, splurged our remaining dollars on a weekend in Saigon, riding a taxi bus along Route 1 and across a somber Vietnamese countryside of guard posts, military barracks and patrolling soldiers. Already I was yearning for the gentle assurance of our new Thai friends, a sensation reinforced in Saigon by the aggressiveness of the shopkeepers and the hotel staff. I looked up the Reuters correspondent, Bruce Russell, who took us to lunch at the Hotel Continental and endeavored to explain the political situation but I wasn't listening. All I wanted to do was to get back to Bangkok.

Bangkok World

MYRTLE CAME TO MY HOTEL several days after we returned to Bangkok. "I've got a job with a United Nations agency, ECAFE, as a secretary. I'm staying, I like it here," she informed me. I asked about our plans to go on to London, to Fleet Street, "the street of adventure." She shrugged dismissively, fanning herself with a magazine because the tiny room was sweltering. I looked at her blonde hair tied back in a ponytail and her bright, determined smile and I knew my destiny was still rooted with hers; I put Fleet Street on hold and went job hunting.

Each morning at a newsstand outside the railway station I purchased the *Bangkok World* newspaper for two baht. The newspaper had only a dozen pages, the thick typeface wore an unfinished look, and the ink came off in my hands. The *World* was one of two English language dailies in town catering to the Western community and educated Thais, so I ventured there first, riding a pedicab through the city to the address on Larn Luang Road, stopping outside a gray two-story wooden building with a noodle shop next door. A Thai attendant ushered me up a narrow, dingy flight of stairs to the newsroom; it was cavelike, cluttered with desks and chairs and battered typewriters. A cramped adjoining space was a chaos of tables loaded with trays of typefaces; the *Bangkok World* was wholly set by hand, a practice abandoned even in New Zealand by that time.

A solitary figure was sitting at a desk in the newsroom, an American in his late twenties. He introduced himself as Jack Shidler, an associate editor, and when I told him I was looking for a job, he answered, "You can have mine." I expressed a measure of disbelief at this wind-fall opportunity but he explained that he was fed up with Thailand, was owed vacation time by the newspaper, and was anxious to leave. Then he cleared out his desk drawer, wished me the best of luck and proceeded down the stairs with me in hot pursuit, but he was gone. I waited at his desk until someone arrived.

An hour later, a florid man in an outsize, loud sports shirt swept up the stairs, mopping abundant sweat from his face and blurting out a welcoming "sawadi" as he grasped my outstretched hand. He was the owner and publisher of the newspaper, Darrell Berrigan. "Damn him," he exclaimed when I revealed the reason for my presence. Then he assembled a broad smile. "Can you do this sort of thing?" he asked, waving a copy of that morning's paper. This sort of thing included putting headlines on wire service stories and pasting up the page layouts, and writing local stories. The pay was sixty dollars a week. The job was mine.

My rendezvous with Darrell (call me Berry) Berrigan and the *Bangkok World* staff was one of those fortuitous encounters that number at best half a dozen over a lifetime. The self-assured expatriate provided me with an introduction to the unfamiliar byways of American journalism. And his small but attentive, urbane staff helped in my rites of passage from credulous country boy to knowing maturity. I found parallels with mine in Berrigan's life. Years earlier, bored in Bakersfield, California, he had begun roaming the world as a freelance writer, washing up in Shanghai at the beginning of World War Two. Now he was an old Asia hand with a newspaper of his own in a ripening political hotspot; he was a touchstone for all American journalists who were passing through the Orient and needed an experienced brain to pick and hospitable company to enjoy. Sitting at my desk writing headlines, I looked up once to see Bill Lederer with a bundle of galley proofs of a book he had co-authored with Eugene Burdick, *The Ugly American,* for Berrigan to peruse, and I sneaked a preview read of this influential appraisal of American policy in Southeast Asia.

At another time the white-haired Edgar Snow came by to visit; Teddy White and Berrigan swapped stories about the moral corruption of old Shanghai with the zeal of men who missed it; Keyes Beech, Robert "Pepper" Martin, Tillman Durdin— the list of visiting contemporary journalists was long and Berrigan assured me they were all important to get to know if I wanted to go anywhere in this business.

It was not difficult to believe that consequential journalism revolved around the *Bangkok World* and Berrigan, particularly when a *New York Times* correspondent became so dependent on him that he moved into the accommodations closest to the office, a brothel across the street, and stayed there for nine weeks during a local political crisis.

Among his many commitments, Berrigan was the stringer for the *New York Times,* and when the publisher of the newspaper and his wife were arriving for a week at the Erawan Hotel, they cabled that they needed a masseuse in daily attendance. Berrigan told me to handle it. I turned to the only source I knew. I telephoned the Starlight nightclub and ordered a massage girl. When Berrigan learned of my selection he exploded in outrage. "By God, she's a whore. They're all whores at the Starlight. This will be terribly offensive to the Sulzbergers." But it was too late; the visitors had already been in town a night, and Berrigan went to lunch with them with grave foreboding. Later that evening he shook my hand. "They're delighted. The old man says that she uses a delicate touch system, very effective. They're keeping her on all week."

Berrigan's preoccupation with his friends kept him out of the office much of the time, and gave him little choice but to tolerate my ignorance of the United States. Once I spelled out the initials "Pa" in a wire service news story as Pasadena, as in Pittsburgh, Pasadena. "PA is an abbreviation for Pennsylvania," Berrigan was shouting at me as he mounted the narrow stairway to the office the next day, waving the newspaper in his fist.

My margin of error was magnified by my unfamiliarity with Thailand's sensitive social and political system, making me dependent on three Indian co-editors and the fresh-faced young Thai university students Berrigan brought in to translate. In a land where house servants routinely approached their masters on their knees, the possibility of offending the ruling class was considerable, and made worse because their foreign language of choice was English.

We were allowed to use pictures of young King Phumiphon and Queen Sirikit only above the fold on page one, never inside. The political leaders of the nation were always to be shown decorously and if not smiling, at least in solemn repose. I was preparing page one on the night of a military overthrow of the government in October 1958, and I cautiously selected a photograph of the coup leader Field Marshal Sarit Thanarat visiting his victorious troops assembled at the captured Parliament building on Rajadamnern Avenue. The picture of the burly, uniformed Sarit covered three columns at the top of page one under a heavy black headline announcing his tough new policies.

At the end of a long day I grabbed a fresh copy of the edition from the old flatbed press downstairs and went home to sleep. I was met at the office next morning by my colleague Sam Krishniah, who was wearing a wicked grin, his forefinger jabbing at the front page picture. "He's pissed himself. Goddamn it, he's pissed himself," Sam began howling with glee.

I was uncomprehending until I looked closely at the picture. There indeed was a large dark stain the size of two fists over the crotch of the general's uniform trousers. The excitement of the moment had revealed a weakness in strongman Sarit, but the pressure of publishing had also rushed me into a questionable choice of pictures. I had not noticed the stain the previous night. Berrigan arrived, his shirt flapping, slapping his sweating forehead. "They're gonna close us down, I know it," he said, "everyone in town is talking about it, this is ruining us." He turned to me and muttered cruelly, "This is worse than Pittsburgh, Pasadena."

Berrigan's concern was fueled by his awareness of the checkered history of the *World*. The newspaper had been founded the previous year by police chief General Phao Sriyanond, whom Berrigan had exposed in a magazine article as Thailand's drug kingpin. The general had in a cunning move appointed Berrigan editor of the paper in the belief that a man with such contacts among the country's lowlife would be ideally suited for the job. General Phao was exiled later in the year in a political shake-up, but from his base in Switzerland he kept funneling funds to Bangkok to keep the *World* going. These shady antecedents could well have worked against Berrigan in this crisis, but apparently Strongman Sarit's reading habits did not include the *Bangkok World*. One of my chores each day was to debrief our two Thai reporters and write carefully worded accounts of the various political and business events they covered. One hazard was that they spoke little English, passing the time downstairs in the noodle shop drinking Mekong whiskey while awaiting our early-evening sessions. Sometimes the interpreter didn't show up, requiring me to proceed alone. Thomsat or Phrapat would sit beside me, sweating profusely and breathing liquor fumes in my face.

The clarity of our reporting was less important than its inoffensiveness. Berrigan did not intend for the *World* to be more than an information and entertainment sheet, at its best an up-to-date rendering of the day's international news. Competition amongst wire services and syndicates cut prices so low that for its 3,500 readers the *World* provided AP and UPI news, along with the elite American journalism of the time: political columns by Walter Lippmann and Joseph Alsop, the satire of editorial cartoonist Herblock, the humor of Art Buchwald, and Pogo and Steve Canyon comic strips. At its worst the *World* was a mouthpiece for the U.S. government and its aid enterprises in Thailand, which we covered in great detail, along with gossip from the American and other Western embassies. We followed the dominant local political line slavishly, fearing to offend those who could have closed us down with a telephone call.

Berrigan's energetic championing of American foreign policy was not the exception but the rule for foreign correspondents. It was widely accepted that the resident *New York Times* correspondent in an Asian nation ranked immediately after the ambassador in the social pecking order. Journalists would round off their reporting trips with a cordial visit to the embassy political officer for policy guidance. It became clear to me that American reporters enjoyed a status far beyond Australians and New Zealanders. But even as a callow reporter on the *Bangkok World,* I, too, was privy to the spoils of office, eagerly accepting invitations to embassy parties and to the home of the amiable American ambassador, Alexis Johnson.

Bangkok was also my finishing school for sensual experience. The rich colors and smells and sounds were an intoxicant that liberated the libido; everyone in Bangkok seemed to be living on a hot tin roof. When I began my job I moved into a small room on a side street near the office that turned out to be famous for its prostitutes and where at night red lights lit up every window. Under these circumstances Myrtle was reluctant to visit very often. And she was still unwilling to share a house with me and moved into the home of a Thai girlfriend from ECAFE. To improve my situation I rented a small bungalow built on stilts on Wireless Road opposite the American Embassy, and shared it with John Cantwell, an Australian friend from Sydney.

My relationship with Myrtle shrank away in the hot days and the torpid evenings, and the social temptations she faced in a Bangkok as seductive for a woman as for a man. My new friends at the *Bangkok World* were eager to induct me into their profligate lifestyle. One of our reporter-translators, Thamnoon Mahapaurya, led me on my first adventure, offering me a blind date "Thai style."

On the appointed hour a black, chauffeured sedan pulled up at the office and I was greeted by a smiling young woman whose lack of English was compensated by her affectionate smile. We drove to her small bungalow, where she showed that the most intimate of human relations is possible without the need of verbal communication.

On my return to the office later that day Thamnoon greeted me conspiratorially and revealed that I had been given a signal honor. He asserted that my paramour was a favorite wife of General Sarit who was bored with him and desperate for adventure. Thamnoon revealed he was having an affair with yet another wife, one of the fifty that the aging general was rumored to have accumulated. My ardor quickly waned. At that time Sarit was personally enforcing the law of the land. He had recently ordered all opium dens closed, supervised the gathering of all smoking paraphernalia, and watched it pile up at the Pramane Ground, before setting the torch to the huge stack of pipes, oil lamps and raw opium. And he was campaigning for city cleanliness: on road patrol Sarit had followed a Danish woman who was throwing orange skins out her car window, accosting her at her driveway and fining her on the spot for littering. I was not eager to find out what punishment the strongman would inflict on an adulterous wife and her lover.

My friends justified their frequent whoring as traditional behavior for young males, and in their company I visited bordellos, bars and exhibition halls. I was often accompanied by my pal John Cantwell, who was younger than I and who kept falling in love with the impossibly pretty girls who eagerly sold their favors to us. I learned that they bloomed only briefly, like the blossoms of the tropical hibiscus, and would soon succumb to tuberculosis or venereal diseases. My moral doubts were not strong enough to persuade me to join Myrtle, who had surfaced from her own Bangkok adventures and was heading home to London. As I waved her farewell from Don Muang Airport I felt

I was waving away my own past and false dreams. I was sure now my destiny lay in the dazzling, feverish landscape of Southeast Asia that was enveloping me in its potent embrace.

.   .   .

Berrigan gave me my wings as a writer, opening up the pages of his newspaper and daring me to fly with them, and I did so with frantic abandon. I wrote about the institutions that hid behind the acronyms of the era, the SEATOs, the ECAFEs, the UNESCOs and the USOMs; I wrote an automobile column every week, and rode the rickety public buses for stories on backwood shrines and remote towns; I covered the many festivals of Bangkok, the water-throwing, the kite-flying, the banana-boating, the rice-plowing festivals; I researched stories on the farm culture, the fish culture, the religious culture. I once wrote a twenty-four-page supplement on local sports preoccupations ranging from Thai boxing to horned beetle fighting. I wrote about aged British writer Somerset Maugham, who stayed three months at the Erawan Hotel on his last visit to the Far East and told me through his wrinkled, pencil-thin lips in a hoarse, wheezing voice of his inspiration for *The Moon and Sixpence* and *East of Suez* and his other haunting tales of the British colonial era.

Still, the man at the next desk teased me that I was not producing serious journalism. "Basically what we're doing here is bullshit," Sam Krishniah would sometimes tell me in frustration, usually when he was trying to edit the daily social column from a diplomat's wife who tended to gush all over him as he fine-tuned her anecdotes of the embassy world. Sam would have preferred to be traveling and writing but his editing and management skills anchored him to the office. Sam seemed carved from ebony, with thick black hair to match, and a resonant voice. He was a Tamil Indian, broad-shouldered, handsome and intellectual, but I began to get the impression that life had been rough with him and that this newspaper job, however unsatisfying professionally, was a necessary port in a storm. He was reticent about his past but hinted at a university education in England.

One afternoon he brought in an edition of an Oxford collection of modern verse and shyly pointed to his two-page contribution to it, an idyll in iambic pentameter of an expatriate in London. Sam preferred to emphasize his virility over his sensitivity, and enjoyed recounting tales of bacchanalia in London where the whores used the back seats of taxis for tricks and would exhort him as they sped around Piccadilly

Circus, "Hurry up, can't you, the meter's running." It was the phenomenon of the British colonial system that brought Sam and me comfortably together in language and culture even though we were born in far distant parts of the world. It was as natural for an ambitious Sam Krishniah in his youth to yearn for London where its Royal Family presided over his world, as it was for me to head in the same direction.

Sam was living in Bangkok with a pretty French woman named Jeannette, an accountant at an export firm, but he had an Indian wife and four growing children back in his home city of Madras and he was totally committed to their support. Sam's association with Berrigan went back many years and he knew facts about the editor and publisher that I preferred not to hear. Soon after I joined the paper, Sam told me gravely, "Berry's gay, you know. Henri Cartier-Bresson told me he watched him bugger a boy through the window of the bedroom of his Paris house." Sam offered the information not in reproach but as analysis of Berrigan's character, and I was pleased to discover that I was not shocked as I might have been a year or so earlier. "Did he get pictures?" I quipped. Six years later Darrell Berrigan was murdered on the streets of Bangkok by four young men to whom he had offered a ride home. The Thai language press treated the terrible incident as a homosexual scandal, but his friends didn't let him down and his funeral was attended by those of high and low station.

Sam Krishniah did not let his exasperation bite the hand that fed him, and in middle age, with his dreams discarded, a wife and dependents in India and a mistress to comfort in Bangkok, he labored as industriously as I did. He enjoyed joshing me about my assembly-line feature writing, but he was unwilling to challenge the conventional wisdom that any truthful accounting of the corrupt politics of Thailand would close our newspaper down. He preferred talking up a storm rather than writing it. I saw the daily news grind as basically the need to fill the gaps in the pages left after the advertising layout had been pasted up; the filler material needed to be accurate and topical, and if you could make it interesting then all to the good. I hadn't matured yet to take my responsibilities more seriously.

Sam offered me a solid education in the politics of Southeast Asia. India had nurtured the region's culture a millennium earlier, and Sam viewed the political gamesmanship of her wards with a proprietary interest. I listened to only a part of what he said; I was so far out of his league in experience and insight. I was comfortable with the knee-

43

jerk anticommunism of every Westerner in the city. I was happy to cast my lot with the high-spirited Americans I was meeting, and comfortable under the military umbrella of SEATO.

When the Associated Press correspondent, David Lancashire, offered me a stringing job early in 1959 I snapped it up, earning an extra fifty dollars a month filing brief political and economic stories when he was out of town. And the *London Daily Express,* for which I filed stories on the misfortunes of British travelers or failed business interests in Thailand, boldly rewrote my dispatches to match the inventive headlines they stretched across the pages. The *Express,* one of the most popular newspapers on Fleet Street, was edited by Hugh Cudlip, who wrote the defiant autobiography *Publish and Be Damned,* which I had admired a few years earlier.

The *World* was prospering and I felt I could pull myself free of Berrigan's gravitational pull and I was mulling over a job offer from a more exotic quarter, the editorship of a weekly newspaper in Laos. The title sounded great but meant less than it seemed: I would be the whole masthead, from editor to copyboy. And Kaye Ando, the entrepreneur pitching the position, didn't inspire much confidence. He was another of the wondrous cast of characters from Berrigan's theater of life who entered and exited with regularity; he did all his negotiating over a bottle of Mekong whiskey in the noodle shop downstairs. Kaye Ando stuttered, was pinch-thin and stooped, and wore gold rings on fingers stained with cigarette tar. He had British citizenship and claimed Japanese and Malaysian ancestry, yet his wispy beard reminded me of Ho Chi Minh or a Confucian scholar, and his droopy mustache was a duplicate of Fu Manchu's. Kaye was the sole distributor in Laos for *Time* and *Newsweek* magazines and the *Bangkok World* newspaper. He proposed to me that I move to Vientiane, Laos, and put together a weekly news supplement that would attract local advertising and that could be folded into the *Bangkok World* that was distributed in Laos. Berrigan supported the project, but Kaye Ando told me privately that his real intention was to compete with Berrigan's newspaper.

I was still naive enough to leap before I looked, and I joined forces with my unlikely sponsor. Berrigan was understandably furious when he realized that we were planning to compete, intimidating us with his towering rage. He forced us to sign a joint venture agreement drawn up by a law firm, "for the purpose of engaging in the business of publishing, editing and distributing a new newspaper in Vientiane, in the Kingdom of Laos." Berrigan was named publisher, I was editor, and Kaye Ando was executive director. It was all impressively legal and I signed the agreement with the confident flourish of the twenty-five-year-old genius that I thought I was. By year's end the document would be all that was left of the venture.

The City of the Moon

LAOS WAS AT THE END of the line, north of the great Mekong River. It was easy to romanticize Laos if you hadn't been there; the king characterized his people as knowing only "how to sing and to make love," and the guidebooks of the time called it "the land of the million elephants and the white parasol," suggesting a place of harmony, a sanctuary, an Asian El Dorado.

After a long railway journey through red-clay scrublands, I crossed the broad, silver-muddy Mekong River on a shabby barge from the Thai border town of Nong Khai. Laos in 1960 was a place that time had forgotten. I scrambled up a rutted dirt track gouged into the steep banks of the river to the border post at Tha Deua, a wooden shack where a tired immigration officer stamped my visa and wished me adieu. At the customs shed a young official glanced at my two battered suitcases and dismissed me.

Aboard a small van marked taxi I bumped the fifteen miles into Vientiane, a name that translates into the City of the Moon, and checked in at the Hotel Constellation on Sam Sene Thai Street, with the promise of unlimited credit from the owner, Maurice Cavellerie, who by his generous gesture confirmed his reputation in press circles as the most understanding hotelkeeper in Indochina. Maurice became my family in Laos, and the man I turned to for political insights. He had inexhaustible patience and sympathy yet was a clever businessman who controlled the import of many foreign goods, including beer, and had the political connections to stay out of trouble. He was trim and olive-skinned and handsome, of Tibetan and French descent, which gave him an advantage in business in colonial Laos. He spoke English, and was a bridge between the Lao, the French and the Americans, who were coming in increasingly large numbers.

My introduction to the Lao people came through Dr. Puvong No-savan, an acquaintance of Kaye Ando, who had agreed to be partner and play frontman for our newspaper. Dr. Puvong was a member of a privileged family from the small Lao middle class, and had been permitted educational opportunities the colonial authorities had denied most others. He had a degree in engineering from a French university but he had long ago given up that career and was now engaged in enlarging the family fortunes through his connection with General Phoumi Nosavan, his nephew, and the man chosen by the Eisenhower administration to maintain a free Laos in the camp of the Western world.

And it was through General Phoumi that the inevitable, formidable red tape was unscrambled, allowing us to publish our weekly. For these efforts, the Nosavan family earned three hundred dollars a week and a promised share of the profits, modest by itself but because they had similar arrangements with a score of other enterprises in Vientiane at the time, their position was ultimately quite lucrative.

While Dr. Puvong never bothered to visit our office, he was a sociable partner and sometimes had me over to gatherings at his large bungalow on Phai Nam Street. General Phoumi was sometimes at the house, heavyset and smiling, sipping hot tea and sneaking confident, sidelong glances at his uniformed bodyguards lounging on the balcony outside. General Phoumi spoke poor English and if Dr. Puvong was unavailable to interpret, I communicated in my poor French, or in Thai, a language similar to Lao, that I butchered to the amusement of all assembled. At the time, I saw no conflict of interest being in business with such a gang. I saw only opportunity.

It was through Dr. Puvong's family that I met Prince Boun Oum, a bulky, charismatic aristocrat, one of the Three Princes of Laos who sat atop the powerful political forces shaping the country's destiny—the left-wing communists, the neutralists and the right-wing militarists. The florid, congenial Boun Oum was the right-winger of the three, a former King of Champasak in the southern region of the country, who had renounced his throne to permit the creation of a unified Laos after the Japanese withdrawal and the reluctant departure of the French. In return, he was named Inspector General of the Kingdom for life, an agreeable sinecure that allowed him to retain his great estates and much of his power in the south. The middle-aged prince was a favorite of the American Embassy, not just because of his appropriate political views. He was also the éminence grise behind General Phoumi, and as a political heavyweight he gave legitimacy to the ambitions of his military protégé.

Boun Oum attended the fancy Lao wedding of Dr. Puvong's daughter Siriphand. I watched him display his celebrated charms with a series of female partners, bowing first and then sliding forward and backward to the traditional lam wong dance, never touching hands but sighing audibly as the music of the bamboo kaens and strings pulsated in intricate rhythm. Boun Oum encouraged me to try the dance, then tut-tutted when I lost balance and accidentally steadied myself on the arm of my partner. Seeing that I needed training in the social graces, he invited me to a party he was throwing the following week, and later insisted that I attend.

I was flattered by his invitation but flustered when Dr. Puvong informed me the party would be a three-day affair in distant Pakse, a celebration of the incarnation of the Buddha at Wat Phou, a moldering tenth-century limestone temple on a jungled hill. I traveled to the gathering by airplane, cyclo and motor sampan, and arrived a day late to discover that the party was turning into one of the social events of the year, with senior members of the diplomatic corps in attendance along with prominent Lao officials.

There were Thai boxing, cockfights, dancing and religious ceremonies, but I heard rumbles of discontent from the assembled guests. This was a remote place in a remote country; our accommodations were in newly erected white, round tents, billowing like giant mushrooms across a field below the temple. Boun Oum's staff was hard pressed to provide the niceties of life, setting up army cots with thin blankets half a dozen to a tent. The diplomatic wives teamed up for slumber parties and their husbands were forced to do the same.

Boun Oum enjoyed the party much more than we did. He arrived in regal style on the third day, dressed in his flowing royal robes and mounted upon a golden palanquin carried by a pinkish white elephant. He waved enthusiastically to the disheveled crowd now yearning to go home.

There was a bounce to Lao society that resisted the gravitational pull of social and political change. It was powered by the Buddhist religion, embodied in the voluptuous, golden-spired pagodas that embellished the cities, and in the yellow-robed monks who walked the streets begging for their food. For the Lao Buddhist the reward for doing right was not eternal life but a gentle death and freedom from the successive reincarnations prescribed by the competing religion of Hinduism. To buttress the faith, the Buddhist authorities encouraged religious and harvest festivals that enlivened the social calendar. I particularly enjoyed the Bang Fai, the most jubilant celebration of the year, when crude wooden rockets thirty to forty feet long manufactured by the monks are assembled to commemorate Visakha Puja—the birth, enlightenment and death of the Buddha. The pyrotechnic skills of the monks at the That Luang pagoda in particular were legendary: the shrine's great central tower and surrounding sharp stupas gave the appearance of a missile battery poised to fire.

Buddhism was a natural ally for the Americans, just as opposed to the ideology of Godless communism as the most vehement congressional red-baiters. The mellow public serenity of the religious hierarchy concealed their fears that the communist powers emerging in the east could easily sweep them away. I carried with me to Laos a copy of *Life* magazine. On the cover a circle of shaven, yellow-robed monks surrounded a tall, confident American named Hank Miller inside Wat Sisaket. The picture confirmed the status of Buddhism's new ally: Miller ran the United States Information Service programs in Laos, trying to improve the image of the central government, a thankless task in a land where telephones barely reached beyond the capital, and where most of the two million population were illiterate and living in simple villages far from the beaten paths.

Hank also handled the visiting press correspondents and I often made my way to his office on Avenue Lan Xang seeking story ideas, daunted by his imposing six-foot-six-inch frame and his imperious manner. Since he had access to the biggest overseas aid program per capita that the United States was then spending, perhaps his manner was understandable. Hank enjoyed critiquing my newspaper, laughing at the typos and the turns of phrase. I don't believe that he ever took me seriously as a journalist, because in the pages of the *Vientiane World* there were many stories acclaiming American aid programs that he had provided me, stories that I used because I was eager to please, and also because of the unavoidable requirement to fill the columns on time.

One May morning in 1960, Hank Miller pulled up in his jeep at the street-side end of the bar of the Constellation Hotel and shouted, "Have they caught Soupy yet?" Soupy was the Americans' nickname for Souphanouvong, the leftist "Red Prince" of the triumvirate, who had been locked up at Phone Kheng police camp on the outskirts of Vientiane, along with his senior political and military aides. Souphanouvong had spent ten years in the jungle fighting the Japanese and had later emerged to lead the communist Pathet Lao resistance movement. The conditions of the Geneva settlement for Laos required that he be included in a new government, but during a border crisis in 1959 he and his followers were arrested by the right-wing military and incarcerated.

Hank Miller was astounded that I was not aware that the Red Prince had escaped that very morning, a setback for American policy. He drove off in disgust without giving me further information. Normally I would have already called on Hank for a news briefing, but I was suffering the consequences of a late night with innkeeper Maurice Cavellerie's brandy-laced reminiscences. I tottered to my feet and ran in haste to the nearby American Embassy on Bartolini Street, burdened with guilt and heavy journalistic responsibilities.

I was being paid ninety dollars a month to be the AP stringer in Laos, but in addition I had quietly agreed to fill in for an absent UPI reporter who was visiting Bangkok. I had also agreed to help out the Reuters Saigon correspondent, Bruce Russell, who was fruitlessly seeking a replacement for a departed stringer. I knew that the Agence France-Presse news agency reporter was on leave. I was the only journalist left in the whole country, and I felt even more irresponsible.

The embassy political staff sketched out the sorry details of the story with some embarrassment: the communist leader had escaped through the early-morning monsoons with all his jailers joining him and there was no clue to his immediate whereabouts.

My next stop was the telegraph office on nearby Sethathirat Street, where I arrived out of breath but with a clear plan of action in mind. My first obligation was to the AP because that organization had hired me in good faith. On a cable form I carefully wrote in long hand an urgent news bulletin addressed to the agency's headquarters in Tokyo, conveying the facts of the dramatic escape. I passed it over to the waiting telex operator and as he punched the message into his machine I wrote a dispatch for UPI; their correspondent, Arthur Dommen, had agreed to pay me fifty dollars. To that report I added a few extra details of the search for the Red Prince and handed it over to the operator before proceeding with the Reuters version of the story. I added additional material to the telegraphed accounts of the escape during the day and by evening was resting content that I had passed muster on my first serious international news story, thankful that the professional Agence France-Presse man, who would have shown me up as an incompetent, was out of town.

The next day Cavellerie handed me a sheaf of cables. The first was from the AP and it congratulated me on being eight minutes ahead of all others with the escape story. The next was from UPI, which complained that I lagged on the initial story break but amply made up with better detail. The third was from Reuters thanking me for helping them out. I didn't have the courage to brag of my triumph to Hank Miller.

It was in Miller's office that I met Bob Burns, a fast-talking bear of a man with an easy smile and American moral certitude. Burns was officially attached to USIS as a communications technician, helping to organize an Information Ministry, and trying to convince the Lao of the need to compete in the propaganda war in the distant provinces. As part of his operation, he provided scores of informational movies and projectors for secluded communities that had never heard a radio.

Burns bossed his Lao subordinates around, giving a first impression that he was one of those Ugly Americans. But I warmed toward him when I realized that his subordinates responded to his commands more with impish insouciance than proper respect. Beneath his tough exterior was a soft heart. I amused him and he introduced me around to the American community, and sometimes joined me at the bar of the Constellation Hotel for a drink.

Even though I grew to know him well, Bob was never candid with me about what I began to see as the real crisis in Laos: a privileged class of entrepreneurs in the cities was getting richer at the expense of the impoverished in the countryside. Burns rarely tolerated my criticisms, particularly when I would suggest that the movie projectors he was sending into the provinces were winding up in the living rooms of Lao officials in the capital.

Burns was a pal of Dr. Tom Dooley, the founder of Medico, a charitable organization that operated small hospitals in remote parts of Laos. For a time, Dooley was a household name in America, a symbol of the Free World's decency and self-sacrifice. In articles and books, especially his *Deliver Us from Evil,* he managed to connect medical care with anticommunism. In his second best-seller, *The Edge of Tomorrow,* Dr. Dooley went further, likening communism to serious disease and presenting himself as a Dr. America, and solidifying his popularity as a crusading medical superstar. When Dooley underwent surgery for melanoma at Memorial Hospital in New York City in 1959 he was the subject of an hour-long prime-time CBS News documentary.

To many Americans Tom Dooley was all they knew about Laos, but in Laos the doctor was the subject of quiet ridicule by the local and foreign community. Burns would hear none of it, exclaiming to me one day, "Better a Tom Dooley as a hero for the American people than an Elvis Presley." Burns had helped Dooley set up his new hospital at Muang Sing in northern Laos on the Chinese border the year before.

My own experience with Dr. Dooley had begun during my editing days with the *Bangkok World*. At Berrigan's orders, I routinely threw Medico press releases into the wastepaper basket: the vivid tales of jungle medicine may play in Bangor, Maine, Berrigan would say, but not in Bangkok, where the doctor's flair for personal publicity was well known.

In person, at Burns's house in Vientiane one evening, Dooley looked skinny and hollow-cheeked but was genial and witty, like Ensign Pulver in a road show of the play *Mister Roberts*. Later in the evening he grew more somber and talked of his American lecture tour, and told us that at the University of Notre Dame a nun had shouted to him from the crowd, "Jesus was your age when he did his greatest works." Next day I asked Burns if Dooley had walked across the Mekong River. Enraged, he declared that I would be more respectful if I knew just how sick the young doctor was, still recovering from the operation for melanoma "that left great holes in his upper body and thighs."

The real impact of Dooley's medicine was welcome but minuscule. What rankled his critics in the American community was that Dooley reduced the war against communism to a hypodermic needle and a bottle of aspirin. *Life* magazine, which had collaborated on his rise to fame over the years, sent another writer for yet another article on him. Scott Leavitt, however, picked up on the negative vibrations and Dooley's faults were aired for the first time: his arrogance toward his medical staff, his brimming ego, and the essential impermanence of the small hospitals he was building and then turning over to local untrained medical staff. Burns told me melodramatically that Dooley was heartbroken by the article and that it may have worsened his already bad health.

I saw the story in a different perspective. *Life*'s challenging of the Dooley myth gave me my first real sense of the media as an instrument of power for conveying accuracy, for correcting the record. I was not yet practicing such bold journalism in my puny news sheet but the example was there to emulate.

Bob Burns was the visible peak of a clandestine world that tried to pull the political strings in Laos. He enjoyed telling strangers that he was just a typist in the Army of the Lord, though he had told me a few weeks after we met that he actually worked in military intelligence.

I did not press him further on the subject because any talk about such activities was taboo, along with any public acknowledgment of the service connections of the plainclothes American military men who moved around town.

Years later, Lieutenant General John Heintges complained to me that a reporter had blown his cover in Laos by revealing his military affiliation, and I reminded him that even when he wore civilian clothes we sometimes saw the young, crew cut men who often crowded the street-side bar of the Constellation Hotel jump smartly to their feet and salute him whenever he walked by. Because of the troublesome requirements of the Geneva Agreements, much of American policy and personnel had gone underground in Laos. Though the United States had agreed to limit their involvement, hundreds of military advisers and CIA agents poured in under clumsy cover.

But by the time I had settled in town, the communist Pathet Lao, and the nationalist neutralists, had been frozen out of the coalition government, their leaders in flight or in jail. That summer of 1960, America was administering a Laos colony in fact if not in name. What looked like a fait accompli on paper, though, was a theater of the absurd.

There were many doors to the CIA. Bob Burns had the keys to most of them and often took me through. Access to the CIA was not so difficult if they knew you wouldn't write about them. Few reporters did. My New Zealand nationality did not even get in the way. Burns pointed out one evening to a group of assembled operatives that I was a dope, "but our dope." Beyond the obvious coverup in Laos were more extraordinary secrets that amazed me. Air America, an airplane company run by the CIA, was flying support for the hill tribes' opium-growing operations, secretly transporting the raw product to rich markets in Bangkok and Saigon.

The *Vientiane World* was first published on April 9, 1960, and was for sale on the streets the next day; only one thousand copies of the six-page tabloid were printed and most of those were inserted into the Sunday *Bangkok World* like a supermarket throwaway. I catered to the American community with the full awareness that the paper's success rested there. A column on page three gave a sympathetic account of an unsuccessful tiger shooting foray to the Bolovens Plateau by Ambassador Horace H. Smith, and an accompanying story noted the visit to Laos of the television and radio star Arthur Godfrey on his way to Tom Dooley's hospital at Muang Sing.

The lead article on page one gave the status of the upcoming general elections, alongside stories on local drownings and the plight of a fire-ravaged village. Across the top of the back page I ran a picture of my friends in the band at one of the city's favorite nightclubs, and underneath was the first of a regular gossip feature called "Cocktail Party Time." The few advertisements included pitches from the competing White Rose and White Lotus massage parlors, notorious for the sexual tricks of their hostesses. The *Vientiane World* was a modest effort but it was mine; the requirement each week to fill its twenty-five columns with local news consumed me.

I had no plan for the *World* to become involved in the crucial political and social issues of the time because, frankly, I was not competent to provide that journalistic service. Yet events pressed me forward. I explored the environs of the city each week for suitable material and in the course of these activities I discovered that empty news columns were a vacuum that sucked in information.

The official American community looked upon my efforts as a convenient public relations vehicle. Some Lao officials saw the newspaper in a different light, as a place to float their ideas independent of the backroom policy-making at the American Embassy. Military strongman General Phoumi took a swipe at neighboring Cambodia in the paper's second issue, calling me in for an "interview" and declaring that while Laos believed in neutrality, such a policy should be backed by a strong army, "a real neutrality not like that practiced by other countries such as Cambodia." In the following week Khampan Panya, an influential member of the anticommunist Committee for the Defense of National Interests, which had won the elections, told me for publication the name of their choice for future prime minister, Tiao Somsanith, a candidate the American Embassy disliked. I continued to rely on USIS handouts to fill the columns of the newspaper, and I entertained hopes that the *Vientiane World* would become more than a supermarket tabloid and attain a credibility that the *Bangkok World* never achieved.

The Coup

I WAS LOOKING over proofs of Saturday's copy of the *Vientiane World,* which had arrived from the printing office in Bangkok, with a picture of a working elephant, dragging logs in Sayaboury Province, on the front page, along with stories on Laos agreeing to join the World Bank, and a renewed drive by government information officers to penetrate the remote provinces.

It was Monday, August 8, 1960, and I had four days to make the upcoming edition more interesting. The pickings were slim. On my desk was an invitation from the British ambassador to a dinner for a departing embassy staffer; another summoned me to a cocktail party for the new USIS director. Maybe I could pick up some diplomatic gossip there. Tom Dooley was arriving back midweek after another emergency medical trip to the United States, and I planned to meet with him for an interview. But nothing was doing politically: the whole cabinet was out of town to make final arrangements for the ceremonial cremation of the late King Sisavang Vong. He had been lying in state, embalmed on a sandalwood bier, since last October, awaiting a propitious time for his funeral.

In the evening I walked over to the Constellation Hotel, threw the Cameroons dice in a game against Maurice Cavellerie, and watched the evening parade on Sam Sene Thai Street—the cyclo drivers, the bar hostesses, the food vendors and the diplomats. I visited the Vien Rattri nightclub, a gloomy barn known locally as the green latrine, where I was romancing the singer in the Thai band, a comely young lady popular for her impassioned rendering of "I Left My Heart in Bangkok, Thailand." The dance floor was quiet perhaps because the lively young members of the Lao cabinet who danced every night with the Vietnamese bar girls were absent. I later joined the singer in her hotel room and the night passed uneventfully until the early hours when she insisted on listening to music on Radio Vientiane.

She roused me with a push to the shoulder and began chattering about a broadcast she was hearing. My bar Thai was as bad as her bar English, but she made it clear that the Lao announcer was criticizing Americans and the United States in the most savage language. I dozed off for an hour or so until I was awakened by the grinding of metal treads on pavement. I pulled aside the curtains and two stories below several Patton tanks were driving by, their Lao crews sprawled over the guns and on the steel turrets, calling out to one another in evident joy and waving opened bottles of beer and swigging on them. I knew that the Lao were not early-morning drinkers; I dressed hurriedly and ran to the streets. Something was breaking, and my heart was pumping.

I bumped into squads of soldiers in green and brown camouflage uniforms and red berets lounging at intersections and guarding government buildings. At the Constellation Hotel, Maurice was listening to announcements over Radio Vientiane that declared the Lao Army's Second Paratroop Battalion had assumed full civil and military powers in Laos. I found Burns at the USIS building, and he was distraught, hoping, praying that the whole thing was a joke. He had told me that the previous week, at the request of the Second Battalion, American military advisers had conducted a nighttime exercise to show the unit how to recapture the capital city in the event of communist occupation.

I sat at Burns's desk, borrowed his typewriter, wrote a story for the AP, and ran to the telegraph office. No use. A tank sat at the entrance to the building and a squad of soldiers pushed me away with their rifle barrels. I rushed to appeal to Maurice for help, but he was a veteran of political disorder and had closed the steel shutters of his hotel, waiting for the shooting to start.

The once loyal men of the Second Parachute Battalion now controlled the airport, all the government buildings in the city, and the power station. An armored squadron at the Chainaimo Military Camp with several hundred supporting troops had been won over by the rebels, and were now enjoying the spoils of victory. The leader of this disorder was a short, shy army captain named Kong Le who had earned his promotions at the American-run Camp Vincente Lim in the Philippines. I had met Kong Le earlier in the year at a military awards ceremony where his battalion was decorated. Sometimes, when his unit was on leave in Vientiane, he would drop by the Constellation Hotel bar, wearing his jaunty red beret and paratrooper uniform and practice his English and his beer drinking. I could not imagine what had motivated him to stage this coup and I didn't have time to further find out. This was the biggest news story of my life and I had to find a place, any place, to file it.

My only hope for a news scoop lay on the other side of the mile-wide Mekong River in Thailand. I searched for a boat, only to find that the paratroopers had anticipated this escape route and lined the banks and beaches. I ran along the river road toward the Sala Khok-tane, a boating and swimming club owned by Kaye Ando and favored by the foreign community. There were no boats, but no soldiers either. The manager and staff watched in surprise as I lowered myself into the river from the deck, the waters surging up my chest and neck; the typed AP story, my passport and twenty ten-dollar bills were clamped in my teeth.

The swift, warm current carried me to a sandy bar in the river center where I scrambled and waved and gestured to the opposite side. A sleek motor sampan steered by a Thai police officer came to pick me up and as we landed I noticed army soldiers lying in the bamboo trees, their guns aimed at Vientiane. The Thai authorities were concerned about the political developments on the other side of the river and were reluctant to let me proceed, but I agreed to give them a hand-written copy of my dispatches for their records and I was soon on my way.

I hitched a ride to the nearest telegraph office in Udorn Thani, on a timber truck, cramped in the driver's seat beside two young peasant girls with rice-field mud caked up to their bare thighs and mischievous grins on their faces as we bumped and swerved along the road. At the telegraph office I sent my story collect but handed the operator a hundred dollars to speed its passage, and within a few hours the late-closing AP morning newspapers in the western United States were carrying my story of the coup, some even giving me the courtesy of a byline.

I repeated the journey the next day, carrying not only my own reports but several rolls of film for the AP, eighteen pages of material from Tillman Durdin of the *New York Times* and a story by James Wilde of *Time* magazine, two reporters who had arrived in Laos after the coup. They thought me mad to swim the river but at the time it made sense to me. I had to get the story out as fast as I could.

.　　.　　.

When Captain Kong Le made himself available for interviews he claimed that he had been pushed into making the coup d'etat because he and his men were being abused by an indifferent government, a government that was enriching itself in Vientiane as his men were dying in the jungles. Whatever his motivation, the tiny captain was soon swallowed up by larger forces from the left. One day he called me into his office at the National Palace and announced apologetically that the *Vientiane World* was being closed down because it was financed by the CIA. I did not demur. It was not the case, but the Vientiane I had known was gone.

John Meier, an American who worked as an English language instructor for Laotian soldiers, came to the Constellation Hotel bar for a farewell drink and to ride with me to the airport. I told Meier that I wanted to join the AP, become a real foreign correspondent, make something of myself in the world, and he laughed at me. "Peter, I'm your friend. Listen, you're the wrong nationality. You don't know enough about what they need. You'll never make it with them."

I boarded an old Air Laos C-47 aircraft at Wattay Airport, and I thought about what Meier had told me. I figured he was partly right. I lacked the easy confidence that journalists like Michael Field, of the *London Daily Telegraph,* Tillman Durdin and Bruce Russell had around important officials. I was apt to react too emtionally to events. To me, Kong Le seemed a decent man and a patriot rather than the hotheaded pawn of the communists as portrayed by my colleagues. I was well aware that Kong Le's rash act had collapsed American policy in Laos, but I felt he was responding to critical flaws in that policy. Perhaps my elemental impressions were inadequate in a business that required detached worldliness.

In some ways I had bitten off more than I could chew in Laos; I was somewhat ashamed of my ambiguous association with the Phoumi family and I swore to myself to avoid entangling relationships with entrepreneurs and politicians, to steer clear of both the business enterprises and the mistresses of the power elite. I was out of my depth in my occasional dealings with CIA operatives and was beginning to understand that they inhabited a world where I, as a journalist, did not belong, a place that encouraged deception, a place where misrepresentation and subterfuge were a means to an end. I was much more comfortable with the regular American Embassy staff who were more directly accountable to the press and to the taxpayer.

On the other hand, Laos was the first place that I had ever regretted leaving. I had been invited to join an entertaining cast of characters in an international political black comedy, but now the show was over.

Jakarta

DESPITE JOHN MEIER'S PESSIMISM, the Associated Press hired me to be its correspondent in Jakarta, Indonesia, in 1961. In the complex pecking order of the American news organization I was one of the littlest beaks in the roost. The pay was accordingly modest, $87.50 a week, and I had to barter my way from Bangkok to Jakarta by writing three travel articles promoting Thai International Airlines in exchange for tickets.

My boss was Don Huth, an old Asia hand who wore his white hair in a spiky crew cut and had worked as a newsman in India and the Philippines before taking executive duty in Singapore. New York headquarters had suggested he hire an Asian reporter for the job, someone who would be more attuned to the galloping political changes. But Don thought I would be more help, and no more expensive to employ than an Asian. I was what he called "a self-starter" with the get-up-and-go that he required. "Pedro," he instructed me when I stopped over in Singapore on my way to Jakarta, "the name of the game is production, lots of stories. The AP is a competitive organization. Get out there and kick butt, I know you can do it."

I tried to fulfill the expectations of the Associated Press in Indonesia the only way I knew, by outhustling everyone else. In my daily rush, I picked up items from PIA and Antara, the Indonesian government news agencies, and from the local newspapers, and I wrote numerous stories about every oddball topic that I could come up with, from the art of wayang puppeteering and Balinese temple mysticism to tea planting ceremonies in Bogor. I interviewed visitors from aging movie great Charlie Chaplin to Borscht Belt entertainer Joey Adams. I sent out my daily gleanings through the Jakarta post office, located in an old Dutch colonial building that, like much of the city, had seen better days. Communications were antiquated; the operators were still using Morse key transmitters, and they would grow pale at my sheafs of material, which represented hours more of torturous tape punching for them. Later I learned that AP editors in Tokyo and New York threw away more than half of my stuff from Indonesia: they thought it was trash. From the truncated versions of my stories that appeared in Asian newspapers, it was clear that my freewheeling writing style was not surviving the editor's pencil. It took months to strip my writing of its rambling embellishments to the bare-bones wire service style that honors the basic declarative sentence above all literary skills.

Jakarta was overcrowded and desperate. There were some fine outer suburbs, but many people lived in bamboo and mat huts along the canals, breeding grounds for disease. At night the main streets were aglow with candles and brazier fires where vendors prepared foodstuffs for passers-by. Parts of grand old Dutch Batavia were still standing, the ceremonial gates and cannons a mute affront to the misery that four hundred years of colonialism had brought upon the Indonesians. I lived in a decrepit lodging house called the Wisma Lokantara run by the government for visiting press people. It was all I could afford: fifty dollars a month for a tiny bedroom, a toilet that I shared with the Middle East News Agency correspondent from Morocco, and the use of the phone in the dining room that was usually out of order. It was a ten-block walk to the office along streets of knee-high grass or sidewalks of ankle-deep mud.

I thought I had solved my transportation problems by purchasing a Japanese motor scooter from the departing *New York Times* correspondent, but it had a proclivity to break down, leaving me stranded on distant suburban roads. I became dependent on the betjas, the motorized rickshaws that dueled recklessly with trucks and cars on the rutted streets and delivered their passengers to their destinations coated with dust or mud.

The AP bureau was located in a dilapidated wooden house on a dingy side street off Djalan Gadjah Mada and behind the old Hotel Des Indes, which was once a colonial showplace but had fallen on hard times. The office manager was a Bengali Hindu named K. R. Ramanath, a vegetarian who clucked with disapproval when I brought food into the office from sidewalk vendors. Ramanath had run the operation alone for two years, reporting to Don Huth in Singapore, and he saw me as a threat to the status he had built up with government officials and the local community. He punished me in little ways; delaying cash advances until I was almost reduced to begging for money, neglecting to tell me of important press conferences and then covering them himself, throwing my invitations into the wastepaper basket, and sneaking off to diplomatic parties. I was disconcerted by Ramanath but I did not fight him; he was one of the great army of underpaid, unsung locals whose consistent output in political crisis and natural disaster allowed the Associated Press to claim the title of the greatest wire service in the world.

I had nowhere to go but up, but Ramanath had nowhere to go. He was under fire for his loose management style, aggravated by a directive that our operation be financially self-sufficient in the very poor Jakarta market. To generate some income, a small staff typed up the incoming AP international news report, mimeographed it twice each day and sent out the stapled sheets to a hundred or so diplomatic and business subscribers. It wasn't Ramanath's fault that the local delivery man, who used a bicycle for the job, sometimes tossed whole bundles of his precious cargo into the canal.

Ramanath was also required to trade money in the black market to pay office expenses, a questionable practice not asked of the American staff. One day he showed me a bundle of letters sent to him on Singapore bureau letterhead with the most shocking racist slurs and loathsome criticisms. None of the missives were signed. I was struck into dumb silence by the evil I was seeing, perpetrated by my own AP superiors, a crude attempt to bully the man.

My role in the Jakarta bureau was never officially defined and even though Ramanath continued to be suspicious of me, he saw I was sympathetic to him and helped me get the stories covered. The outgoing Eisenhower administration had disapproved of the political direction Indonesia was heading after it had broken free of Dutch colonial rule. In 1958 the CIA had launched the covert operation Archipelago, which provided support for a military rebellion aimed at overthrowing President Sukarno, whose "democratic" leadership had slipped much closer to dictatorship. The venture had collapsed when a CIA pilot Allan Lawrence Pope was captured after the rebel B-26 aircraft he was using to bomb a crowded village marketplace in Ambon was shot down, alerting the world to the secret American role. The failure of the rebellion had strengthened Sukarno's domestic standing and his credibility as a leader of the then significant neutralist bloc at the United Nations. The Kennedy administration may have been more interested in Vietnam and Laos, but it saw this most populous of Southeast Asian nations as worth courting. There was suddenly a demand for news from Indonesia.

Our news output centered on Sukarno. The middle-aged president cut a dazzling figure on the world stage with his military tunic, swagger stick and black pitjik perched jauntily on his head. President Kennedy called Sukarno "the George Washington of Indonesia" and presented him with a helicopter for his personal use. The pendulum of American foreign policy had certainly swung.

I covered Sukarno's every public move, particularly his appearances at political gatherings, which were always good for a headline story. With his noisy nationalism, studding his remarks with quotations from Karl Marx, Thomas Jefferson and the U.S. Constitution, he drove crowds to a frenzy. They roared "hidup Bung Karno" in fevered response. Sukarno enjoyed taking his show on the road and the small international press corps was invited on the grand tours of his far-flung island domain, but like the diplomatic corps we were often required to play straight man to his comedic whims.

American Ambassador Howard Palfrey Jones was an object of Sukarno's jests and was frequently called upon to perform duties on the road above and beyond those normally required of a senior diplomat from the world's preeminent power. The white-haired, aristocratic Jones favored the song "The Red River Valley" and would warble it at parties as Sukarno's assembled courtiers tittered and averted their eyes. At Atjeh, after he had been ordered to dance in shirt sleeves on the hot sands, I asked the ambassador if he had been adequately prepared for his Indonesian assignment, and he answered with a degree of impatience as the sweat dripped off his brow, "If you don't think I'm serving my country, I'd like to know what I'm doing."

On these journeys we reporters would stock up on anecdotes about Sukarno's love life for use on the cocktail party circuit. In keeping with the press mores of the time we wrote nothing for publication about the Indonesia leader's legendary amatory escapades. At Atjeh we were invited into one of the huge festive tents and found Sukarno shirtless and prostrate on a makeshift bed, his bulging belly being massaged by a team of nubile young women dressed in hip-hugging, ankle-length Kebayas. The president raised himself on an elbow, inquired about our health and then ordered us into the ocean. Richard Myerscoff of Reuters and I were the first to strip down to our skivvies and plunge into the warm surf, followed by most of the president's female retinue.

John Henderson, the American deputy chief of mission, told me that the sixty-year-old Sukarno bragged he was "a very physical man who needed sex every day," and that the embassy was scandalized when it learned that during his visit to Washington in 1961 Sukarno had, unsuccessfully, demanded that the State Department provide him call girls. Sukarno's fixation on sex became even more clear during an official visit by Robert and Ethel Kennedy in February 1962. The Indonesian leader quickly took a liking to Ethel and enjoyed calling her name at the official gatherings, but he deliberately and gleefully pronounced it in an accent that in the Bahasa Indonesia language turned the name Ethel into common slang for the female genitalia, bringing knowing smirks to the faces of his aides.

Robert Kennedy's visit to Indonesia generated considerable interest in AP headquarters. Jakarta was blanketed with "Kennedy Go Home" signs painted on the sides of buildings, and the American Embassy was stoned by hostile demonstrators. Extra security was in place for the visit and armed soldiers were all over town. The Singapore bureau cabled detailed instructions to me on how to deal with the story and sent down a photographer, Fred Waters. He was a professional who had covered wars and revolutions in Asia for more than a decade, long enough to answer to and enjoy the nickname Mizu, his surname in the Japanese language, and long enough to learn all the ropes. Waters had taken me under his wing briefly in Laos, and here he was again, on the eve of my biggest story in Indonesia, offering a helping hand.

The Kennedys' first public appearance was at the University of Indonesia, where Robert Kennedy faced a turbulent student body with humor, bluntness and charm. The burning issue of the day was the demand for the Dutch to turn over its colony of West New Guinea to Indonesia. Kennedy counseled restraint and boldly declared, "We have been a friend of the Dutch for a long time and we have no apology to make for it. The Dutch were among the first to come and settle in our country and they founded our biggest city, New York, which they called New Amsterdam. But we do have a close friendship with the people of Indonesia."

There were murmurs of disagreement in the student body and some debate about what happened next, but not in my mind. From my perch at the edge of the stage, I watched a slim youth push his way through the crowd and let fly with an object that struck the surprised Kennedy on the nose, stopping him in midspeech. The security men closed in and hustled the youth away, giving time for the shaken speaker to regain his composure and resume his presentation.

When I returned to the office Fred Waters was in the darkroom developing his pictures of the assailant being dragged off by the police, and it was sometime later before he looked over the story I had filed and exclaimed loudly, "What the hell is this about?" My account began, "Robert Kennedy, the president's brother, was hit on the face with a cold fried egg as he opened his week-long tour of Indonesia today with a speech at a crowded university auditorium."

Fred did not have pictures of the incident because it had happened so unexpectedly, nor did anyone else. But the specificity of my report cried out for photo documentation and Fred knew that he would be held accountable. He pressed me for details, contending that some believed the projectile was a piece of fruit, and I explained that I had seen the remains of the eggy mess on the stage behind Kennedy, and that I had attached the modifying adjective for the kind of telling detail that would invite newspapers to choose my account over UPI's.

Sure enough, messages from New York next morning confirmed the popularity of my story; there was also a demand from the photo department: "Need pics soonest of cold fried egg hitting Kennedy." Fred could not deliver, and suggested I should have downplayed the specifics. The best way to survive overseas, he said, was a team effort not only to beat the competition but also to avert the wrath of the head office. It was a "cover your ass" concept that made sense to me, and I tried as best I could to accommodate Fred's wishes.

We achieved a satisfactory working relationship for the rest of the week as Kennedy barnstormed through Java, and we were on the home stretch in Bali when it happened again. I rode into the capital, Denpasar, in the Kennedy entourage and joined my press colleagues in a rush to the small post office to file our stories, as Fred and the other photographers followed the VIPs.

I began my account, "Robert and Ethel Kennedy ended their tour of Indonesia today with a quick visit to fabled Bali island where bare-breasted peasant girls waved to their motorcade from rice fields alongside the highway." On our return to Jakarta that evening there was a message from New York waiting for Fred: "Need pics of bare-breasted Balinese welcomers immediately," and he confronted me again in indignation. He did not have pictures of the peasant girls; he had been to Bali often and presumably did not regard them as newsworthy. I had seen them in the fields waving, not in organized demonstrations of welcome but in spontaneous reaction to the impressive motorcade passing by. As a reporter I felt that the juxtaposing of the two circumstances was justified. I had never worked with a photographer before and I had clearly wounded Fred. My vivid written accounts left him looking lacking.

I tried to apologize but he was unforgiving and sent a message to New York that there were no bare-breasted beauties waving at Robert Kennedy and defied me to argue the point. Fred had been a champion army light heavyweight boxer and still worked out at the gym and could have had me for breakfast. He also had fifteen years seniority on me in the AP, so I gracefully conceded the point. Fred was not one to carry a grudge and we parted company amiably several days later.

The smear on my credibility rankled me, however, and after Fred was out of town I flew to Bali and with my old Rolleiflex camera photographed Balinese women in various stages of undress. At the Denpasar market I snapped women selling piglets that they were breast-feeding to improve the animals' weight; on the road leading to the new beach hotels I photographed scores of young female laborers, their upper garments neatly folded on the side of the road to avoid soiling them, busily swinging hammers to crack stones for road construction; and in the rice fields the comely young women posed with becoming immodesty. I packaged up the three rolls of film and shipped them off to New York.

.   .   .

After a year, the AP gave me a fifty-dollar-a-month raise. In the weekly log, of January 4, 1962, I was "introduced" to the rest of the staff around the globe.

"This week, meet Peter Arnett, who has been touring the Celebes with Indonesia's President Sukarno, reporting his campaign to take over Dutch New Guinea and winning 81 percent of competitive play. A highlight was a beat [by] more than two hours on the bomb explosion at Makassar. Arnett is a born optimist, enthusiastic and eager. As a colleague says, 'Pete put the zeal in New Zealand,' his native land. He's wiry, medium height, and his nose is slightly crooked as a memento of more athletic (but not more active) days."

I was glad for both the raise and the recognition and prepared to go to great lengths to gain more. While visiting the American-sponsored charity hospital ship the *Hope* at Lombok Island I came down with a high fever; my Indonesian photographer also claimed he was ill and blood was drawn from both of us. The medical staff assured me I was fine but that my photographer was suffering from hepatitis. I rushed him back to his family in Jakarta, all the time feeling increasingly worse myself, and it soon turned out that he was well and I was sick, that the hospital staff mixed up the blood samples. Instead of the comparative luxury of the modern hospital ship *Hope,* I rotted six weeks in a Jakarta hospital trying to get well before I was rescued by Don Huth and taken to Singapore to convalesce, dreadfully thin and yellow-skinned.

In my journeys to the remote islands of the archipelago, I had no choice but to eat at the local restaurants, and was thus unavoidably and frequently stricken with amoebic dysentery. I was willing enough to pay this tax on my health in return for the opportunity to chase exotic adventures, but to protect myself I accumulated a medicine chest filled with store-bought and borrowed cures and potions that I guzzled with regularity. One of these concoctions was a yellow sulfur compound in tablet form reputed to help stomach upsets. I swallowed the pills constantly until one afternoon, while riding a betjak to the American Embassy, I suffered the most excruciating pains in my stomach and I cried out in agony. The attending Chinese physician at the Rumah Tjikini Protestant hospital informed me gravely that I was suffering from some kind of kidney blockage and that I would need to be restricted to the minimum of liquids to avoid generating fatal amounts of nitrogen in my body.

Two days later, in the stuffy, un-air-conditioned ward, he told me that the nitrogen content in my blood was rising alarmingly because of my inability to urinate, and that to save my life he was contemplating a kidney transplant, an operation never before successfully performed anywhere in the world. My mouth was parched and my body was drained of liquid; I felt I would die of thirst long before any other cause, but the medical staff was adamant that I drink no more than the spoonful of sweetened water they rationed me.

One afternoon, a young orderly came through the ward with a cart of large glasses of fresh orange juice for the more fortunate patients. I beckoned her over and begged. With no regard to the consequences, I gurgled the cool liquid with unworried pleasure, and when she returned with several other glasses of untouched juice on her cart, I drank those, too. I felt my body absorbing the liquid and as cool beads of perspiration formed on my face I fell asleep.

I awakened with a compelling need to urinate and searched for the enamel basin under my bed. The liquid flowed with abandon; the juice had flushed the sulfur crystals from my kidneys, depositing a mound an inch deep in the bottom of the bedpan. The hospital medical staff had mixed feelings about my unconventional remedy, but I had gambled and won.

Ramanath was happy to see me out of town and encouraged my travels. The authorities now gave me enough rope to hang myself by letting me voyage widely. In June, I made a visit to Timor, a place cloaked in myth and history, the large island at the tip of the Indonesian archipelago half owned and occupied by Portugal. When the local military commander at Kupang refused me transportation to the Portuguese border, I rented a horse and rode several days through the purple valleys even though I had barely ridden in my life. The commander was furious and reported me to his superiors in Jakarta for disregarding his orders.

In October, I visited the northern Celebes and sailed from Bitung in a rented fishing launch for the Spice Islands of Tidore and Ternate two hundred miles across the Molucca Sea. We ran into a southerly storm halfway across and the crew demanded to return home, confronting me in the captain's cabin with their wicked looking copra knives. They appeared scared enough to use them so we turned back. Even though I carried letters of introduction signed by the central military command, I could not convince the local military authorities nor Governor Baramuli of the innocent intentions of my trip to the Spice Islands. They would not let me fly out and made me sit around Manado for more than a week while they claimed they were checking with Jakarta on my status. I sidestepped the problem by hitching a ride to Balikpapan on a Shell oil tanker and from there made my way back home by commercial aircraft. A journey to northern Sumatra and Lake Toba was similarly viewed with the greatest suspicion. The army information chief, Colonel Soenarjo, asked me, "But why do you want to visit the outlying areas? They are difficult to reach and conditions there are hard. We don't go, why should you?"

The AP was getting nervous about my reputation, and the Singapore correspondent, Hal McClure, urged me to exercise "at least momentarily" some caution. The wire service was not eager for a public confrontation over press freedom in a peripheral place such as Indonesia. It was more concerned about building up its coverage for regional clients. My slide into controversy was seen as an avoidable annoyance, a circumstance made worse because I had squandered a special relationship between the AP executive suite and a key member of the Indonesian government, Foreign Minister Subandrio.

The clever, articulate Subandrio was known as the artful dodger of Indonesian politics and diplomacy. He was a dashing international personality, peddling Sukarno's brand of left-leaning neutralism, while at home he ran his spooky Central Intelligence Bureau, keeping tabs on political opponents of the regime. In his rise to power he had met and befriended Stanley Swinton, at one time a foreign correspondent in Southeast Asia and Europe who was now promoted to chief of AP World Services in New York.

The two often dined together when Subandrio was in New York attending sessions of the United Nations. Don Huth had advised me to "get along with Subandrio because he's Stan's buddy," and it was clear the relationship was mutually beneficial. Denied direct diplomat contact with his counterparts in The Hague because Indonesia had broken off relations with the Netherlands in mid-1960, Subandrio had found it convenient to try using the AP wires to convey important initiatives over the West New Guinea issue. Ramanath, who was a regular tennis partner with Subandrio, would sometimes return from their matches carrying government policy statements directed at the Dutch foreign minister, Joseph Luns, which we would write into a news story and send off to the AP. Usually within a few hours Subandrio would be on the phone asking, "Did Luns respond yet? What did he say?" knowing that the AP bureau in The Hague would be pressing the Dutch government for a response.

The traffic got particularly heavy in March of 1962 when the Dutch indicated they were willing to make concessions. The diplomatic negotiating grew intense, with Subandrio's daily statements of give-and-take eventually leading to a settlement favorable to Indonesia. I took to dropping by the foreign ministry to visit Subandrio and his chief spokesman, Garnis Harsono, and I was invited to public and private functions where he was in attendance along with his wife, Hurustiati, a bright, articulate, politically active woman. At times the companionable minister would call with suggestions for improving political analyses I was writing, and correcting what he saw as inaccuracies in my assessments. Our inside track with Subandrio was understandably envied by our press colleagues—and deplored. But where power belonged more to individuals than to government, you cultivated the powerful as best you could.

From my experience in Laos, I knew that such a selective arrangement can become a pact with the devil. I had promised to stick to the straight and narrow, but I guess I couldn't resist.

While the military leadership in Jakarta supported the aggressive foreign policy of the government, the highest officers were looking beyond the aging Sukarno to the future, and to their place in it. They, too, routinely cultivated the press corps, appeared for interviews and were candid in their assessments of the regime. In a January 1962 meeting, the army deputy chief of staff made it clear to me that the military opposed too great a leftward swing in Indonesian politics; he argued persuasively that his commander in chief, National Security Minister General Abdul Haris Nasution, was gathering strength as a leader, and he arranged a background meeting with him for me.

After checking for supporting opinion from the political staff in the American Embassy, I felt emboldened to write a news analysis that was distributed on February 6 to all of the AP's member newspapers, with this paragraph as the lead: "A bitter anticommunist has become virtual heir apparent to President Sukarno and the second most powerful figure in socialist Indonesia because of the West New Guinea dispute. Sukarno has been forced to give vast powers to his national security minister, General Abdul Haris Nasution, to guarantee full support at home for his militant campaign against the Netherlands."

The dispatch fell like a lead balloon upon Subandrio's foreign ministry, where he was seen as the man of the future. And the ministry was responsible for dealing with the foreign press. A spokesman called me in to his office, holding a copy of my story in the *International Herald Tribune,* and announced that my visa would not be extended, "because of incorrect and speculative reporting damaging to us."

Subandrio, furious, called me on the phone, spluttering in his high-pitched voice, "Everyone is united over Irian Barat [West New Guinea]. How can you suggest that the campaign is being used to further the personal ambition of some Indonesians?" His anger had the authority of law.

I had neglected to mention in my story the strong claim that Subandrio had on the leadership, given his international reputation and close association with Sukarno and the Indonesian revolution. I had, exclusively, fostered the chances of his arch-enemy, General Nasution. Even though I was remiss I was stunned that Subandrio would take such personal affront. The analysis was a reading of the political scene by a journalist whose writings could have no influence.

I scrambled to recover by assembling support for my side, winning Ambassador Jones's promise to make unofficial representations for me at the Foreign Ministry. I gained sympathetic vibrations from the military leadership who had floated the story to me in the first place, though no promise of help. It was not until a few days before my visa was to expire that Subandrio seemed to relent, chucking me under the chin at a Foreign Ministry ceremony and joking that I could stay if I volunteered for service in West New Guinea, then the popular method for removing political undesirables from Jakarta.

Two days later I could message Hal McClure in Singapore in triumph, "They're not outkicking me. Foreign Minister Subandrio conveyed this news to the American ambassador, so my visa will be renewed later this month."

McClure responded, "Thanks for the most welcome news about visa renewal. . . . It would have indeed upset Don Huth's plans for Southeast Asia had Arnett been outkicked. For God's sake don't get thrown out—at least until Don gets home."

But I was gathering momentum like a runaway train on a mountain track, destined to self-destruct.

.   .   .

I learned that Subandrio had put a price on his generosity. I would have to toe the government line in all my future reporting or face the consequences if I faltered. "Why does the AP concentrate on writing bad things about Indonesia when there is so much good here?" Subandrio demanded angrily at stories I had written on the famine in central Java. I protested that the information had come from govern-ment news agencies but no one was listening.

Ramanath offered little sympathy. He averted his eyes and muttered under his breath and I got the impression that he was more concerned about losing his special cachet as a tennis partner to the foreign min-ister than losing me as a colleague.

Ramanath cautioned that Subandrio's beef was not with the AP, but with me and my "indiscretions" as a journalist, and that my career was at stake. My heart sinking, I wrote McClure in Singapore, "With the risk of giving you the impression that I have a persecution complex, I'll pass on the latest warning on our news coverage." I concluded, "It is not as though we are on bad terms with the Foreign Ministry; quite the contrary. I personally think we are too close to them. Su-bandrio regards the AP as his personal news agency. When we report something he doesn't like he gets personally offended. Both Reuters and UPI have carried the economic reports we have carried, without any kickbacks."

Subandrio had thrown down the gauntlet. I waited for guidance from headquarters but got none. I was twenty-seven years old and out of my depth and in the end I handled the mess the only way I knew how: I wrote the most uncompromisingly critical analysis story I could accurately assemble: "Indonesia's President Sukarno has spent so much time and money on his militant West New Guinea campaign that near famine has crept across his nation almost unobserved. For months Sukarno has been telling his people that the military campaign against the Netherlands must have top priority no matter what the hardship at home."

The repercussions broke over me in waves. Ramanath was called in and had the riot act read to him. I would be expelled from Indonesia, and the AP in the future should report only what the leadership said publicly. Subandrio was leaving on a visit to Moscow and I had only a brief moment to meet with him and plead my case.

He was not his usual ebullient self: "We welcomed you as a friend and you turned on us. The facts of what you are writing I am not disputing, but what I cannot stand is your persistent disregard of our feelings by presenting such negative information to the whole world."

On May 2, the immigration department officially notified me that my visa was canceled and that I would be escorted to the airport by the police two days hence for my official expulsion. I made a last call on John Henderson, the counselor at the American Embassy. He was sympathetic but reluctant to intercede on my behalf, giving me a lesson in the fine arts of bureaucratic obscurantism by arguing that no purpose would be achieved by taking the matter up with President Sukarno because he had already clearly shown his impatience with the Western concepts of the rights of a free press and would not be likely to change his mind.

My press colleagues had reason to snicker considering the circumstances, but they rallied to my side and organized a series of farewell parties that culminated in a champagne bash at the restaurant at Kemayoran Airport. My police escort stared balefully into the room as we drank. I left Jakarta on the flight to Singapore with a headache and an overpowering sense of failure. I had been seduced by Indonesia's political passions and tropical intrigues, only to lose all these things. I dared not contemplate my professional future after blundering in this first great opportunity.

What I had not counted upon was the fury of a news organization scorned. The AP embraced me as one of its own forsaken flock. Hal McClure had arranged an airport news conference for my arrival, and he wrote the account of the expulsion emphasizing my side of the story. The State Department spokesman, Lincoln White, said the United States "has made clear beyond doubt its attachment to the principle of freedom of the press and in this context it is unfortunate whenever a journalist representing an American wire service is denied access to news." The International Press Institute complained to Sukarno, and the AP president, Frank Starzel, protested my expulsion and declared, "The facts are as he stated them; his dispatches were accurate but the government resented their distribution."

I realized to my relief that my AP career was still on track. I heard that Don Huth was thinking of giving me a return assignment to Laos for a few weeks and then perhaps a tour in Bangkok, my favorite city. When I met Don at the office he said, "Pedro, you think you're tough, huh? I have just the place for you. Vietnam."

Part II
1962–1975

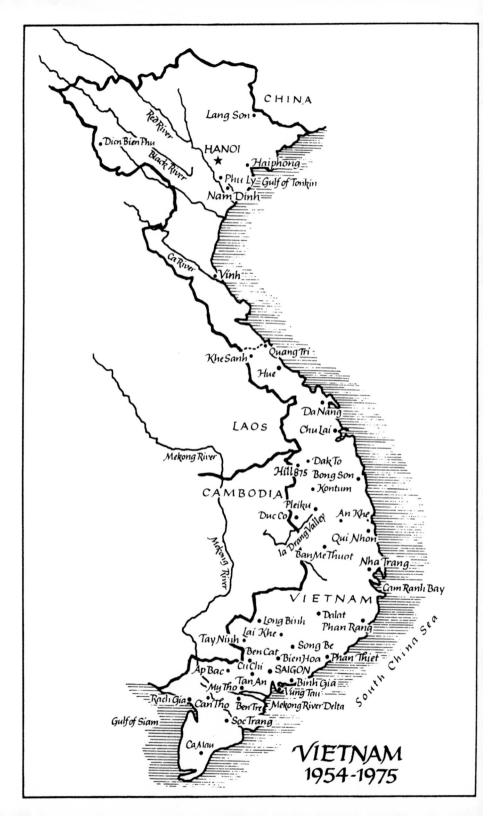

CHINA

Lang Son

Red River

Dien Bien Phu

Black River

HANOI ★

Haiphong

Phu Ly · Gulf of Tonkin

Nam Dinh

Ca River

Vinh

Khe Sanh · Quang Tri

Hue

Da Nang

LAOS

Chu Lai

Mekong River

Dak To

Hill 875 · Bong Son

CAMBODIA

Kontum

Pleiku

Duc Co · An Khe

Ia Drang Valley

Qui Nhon

Ban Me Thuot

Nha Trang

VIETNAM

Cam Ranh Bay

Mekong River

Dalat

Long Binh

Phan Rang

Lai Khe

Tay Ninh

Song Be

Ben Cat · Bien Hoa · Phan Thiet

Ap Bac

Cu Chi

SAIGON

Tan An

Binh Gia

My Tho

Vung Tau

Rach Gia · Can Tho · Ben Tre · Mekong River Delta

Soc Trang

South China Sea

Gulf of Siam

Ca Mau

VIETNAM
1954–1975

Saigon

I BEGAN MY VIETNAM assignment on June 26, 1962, arriving in Saigon from Vientiane on the Tuesday Air Vietnam flight and splashing in from the airport in an ancient airline bus after a late afternoon monsoon downpour had drenched the boulevards. I checked into a room in the Caravelle Hotel with a view overlooking Lam Son Square and the Hotel Continental; the handsome white National Assembly building was below my window.

My circumstances had improved considerably since I had first visited Saigon with Myrtle four years earlier as a penniless tourist. This time I was arriving as a reporter for an international news organization. And I had an expense account. But the four years had taken their toll; I had become a chain smoker and was plagued with a persistent stomach disorder. The constant smoking and the spicy diet wreaked havoc on my teeth, and I looked in vain for decent treatment.

Everything I owned I carried in two battered suitcases: one threadbare dark blue polyester suit, a beige cotton jacket, two pairs of sports trousers, several short-sleeved shirts, along with two cheap souvenir Kris daggers from Indonesia, a fist-sized bronze Buddha head I dug up from the ruins in Ayuthya, the center of an old Thai dynasty north of Bangkok, and a red-tasseled ceremonial tribal sword I bought in Laos that I hung on the wall of my hotel room. I had no intention of staying very long. There was still a desperate quality about the country and its people that I remembered from my first visit, which had unfolded in newspaper headlines since that time: the attempted coups d'etat against the dictatorial family regime, and the ferocious guerrilla insurgency that made the chaotic events I had witnessed in neighboring Thailand, Laos and Indonesia seem mild by comparison. The violence frightened and repelled me; a thousand dead and wounded from the war were being reported each month in 1962. I had seen only one man killed in my life, a prisoner in Vientiane chained from hand to foot who leaped from the back of an army truck and attempted to make his escape across the grounds of the Catholic church, hobbling desperately through the garden shrubs. I watched from the street as a uniformed guard took deliberate aim with his rifle and to my horror pressed the trigger, bringing the man crashing to the ground, his blood splashing across the rose bushes. Such violence was apparently routine in Vietnam; I wondered whether I had the courage to swim in those turbulent waters or match the legendary exploits of the foreign correspondents I had read about.

There was another reason I thought my stay might be short. Rumor had it that the resident AP correspondent Malcolm Browne ran the Saigon bureau like a drill sergeant. Browne had the ear of the AP personnel chief in New York, Wes Gallagher, and was not averse to bending it. His reporting was extraordinary for its detail. On a wire service that was always short of space, he was permitted great length.

Early Wednesday I set off to meet Browne, walking the four city blocks to the bureau at Rue Pasteur, first along Tu Do Street past the Continental Hotel where crew cut young men in shirtsleeves, who I presumed were American military advisers, were having coffee on the terrace. Later I learned it was called the Continental Shelf. The bureau at 158/D3 Rue Pasteur was a ground-floor room in a three-story apartment building, a stone's throw from the Gia Long Palace, where President Ngo Dinh Diem was in residence.

Browne was typing with a two-finger tattoo on his old Remington when I walked in. He didn't look up until I introduced myself to Bill Ha Van Tran, the office manager, a chubby crew cut Vietnamese with an efficient manner. When he heard my name Mal pulled back from his desk, stood up and walked toward me, hand outstretched. He towered over me. "Welcome, another scabby sheep," he exclaimed with a grin. Coming from New Zealand, where there were far more sheep than people, I thought he was being personal, but Mal explained that the local authorities regarded reporters as bearers of contagious diseases and shunned them. There was an intensity about Mal, a blaze in his eyes, a directness that contrasted with the easygoing attitude of the American journalists I had met up to that time.

Mal was a rarity in the AP, an Ivy Leaguer in an organization that favored Southerners and Midwesterners sometimes short on intellectual accomplishment. He tossed me a twenty-four-page pamphlet to read as he turned back to his typewriter, a document that he had written and mimeographed for all visiting staff members titled *A Short Guide to News Coverage in Vietnam,* the gleanings from his year in the Saigon bureau. I had heard of this document on the AP grapevine; the comments were generally disparaging, particularly from veteran reporters who figured they had nothing left to learn.

I sat on a rattan side chair and began reading the introduction. It mentioned that the contents were confidential. "Coverage in Vietnam requires aggressiveness, resourcefulness and at times methods uncomfortably close to those used by professional intelligence units. You can expect very little help from most official sources and news comes the hard way. At the same time, the Vietnamese people are friendly and agreeable and private sources can be cultivated. Because of the political climate it is vitally important to protect sources, particularly those of Vietnamese nationality. Disclosure of sources by several indiscreet newsmen in Vietnam has wrecked careers or worse. American military sources must be similarly protected. Good luck, you'll need it."

The subject matter ranged from health and money matters to field duty and dealings with friends and enemies. "Don't trust information you get from anyone without checking it the best you can, including the information in this booklet. You will find quickly that most 'facts' in Vietnam are based at least in part on misinformation or misunderstandings." Mal advised newcomers to "avoid the crowd. Newsmen and newswomen come to Vietnam by the hundreds and there is a tendency to gather in bunches in bars, in offices, on operations and so forth." He cautioned visitors, "The AP Saigon office is a small, crowded and overworked place. You're always welcome if you want to talk about a story, but if you just want to shoot the breeze you come at your peril. Please do not talk to our hired help when they are grinding out copy or otherwise gainfully employed."

Modeled on the instruction manuals written for military personnel, Mal's booklet provided practical advice on how to cover the war, including a listing of two dozen items required to be carried on military operations, all packed into an infantryman's field pack, which could be purchased on the Saigon black market along with everything else he listed: a camouflage mosquito net, canteen with case, jackknife, assorted canned foods, a rubber air mattress and ground sheet, several changes of underwear and socks, toilet paper, a small flashlight, a light blanket, a first aid pack, water purification tablets, aspirin, a suitable map, money and identification papers, condoms and a pocket pistol, optional.

The need for the pistol was explained. "If you are with a government operation you will be the target of enemy fire, exactly as if you were a combatant. If you are wounded in a convoy or in a position that is overrun, you probably will be shot to death. The Vietcong generally does not take wounded prisoners but shoots them on the spot because of the difficulty of keeping them alive in the jungle. Most war correspondents in Vietnam carry pistols on operations to have some chance of shooting themselves out of this kind of situation if wounded. Personal arms may also be useful if with a small unit under heavy attack in cases where every effective fighter is needed to avoid being swamped. Carrying pistols is not condoned officially either by Vietnamese or American authorities but American officers privately approve of the practice. Under no circumstances try to shoot it out with the Vietcong if you are alone; they always outnumber you and generally pack tommy guns."

The condoms were explained in this way: "In crossing streams, canals and ditches, the correspondent often is neck deep in water and mud. Everything not specially protected will be soaked. Cameras should be held over the head or thrown to someone on the other side before crossing. Small pocket items such as matches and identification papers and film can be kept dry with GI contraceptives. Items can be put in the rubbers, tying the necks closed."

In a section entitled "Some Tips on Official Information," Mal painted a portrait of a local landscape rife with duplicity and misrepresentation. "No government is above distorting or concealing information to serve its own ends, and in Vietnam the situation is particularly trying to newsmen. Most official information not only from the Saigon government and its agencies but foreign sources must be mistrusted. Figures on casualties and reports of military engagements are especially subject to distortion. In covering a military engagement you must make every effort to count the bodies yourself before accepting any tabulation of results. In any case, cross-check American and Vietnamese tabulations of casualties; there are often wide discrepancies. Beware of claims of military victories; this is not the kind of war from which real victories turn up often on either side. Saigon and Hanoi are equally extravagant in their claims.

"Beware the similarity of American official reports of such things; Americans have occasionally had to make their reports on nothing more than the Vietnamese claims although this has been reduced as American advisers are reporting more effectively. Beware in particular of any information at all you get from certain officials who can be counted on to tell bald-faced 180-degree whoppers nearly every time; a list of these officials and their relative credibility indices is available at the AP office. Unfortunately, some of them are in high positions. Remember in general that any information given out by the Saigon government has been well filtered by the propaganda apparatus and would not be given out at all if it were not intended to have some propaganda effect.

"Rely basically on your own private sources and the same naturally goes for anything broadcast out of Hanoi. Even in the field beware of impressions you get from things shown you by officials. If you ask to see a strategic hamlet and are taken to one by officials they obviously will show you only the best they have to offer. You have no one but yourself to blame if it is not typical of strategic hamlets in general. After cultivating an instinctive suspicion of all official information, don't become so suspicious you automatically reject all statements and claims. Check each one; sometimes the truth will pleasantly surprise you."

Browne suggested I get out on my own to report the news, and his memo gave me some guidance on available opportunities. "Embassy sources in general are very useful; they can be tapped in office interviews, at luncheon dates or at cocktail parties. A resident correspondent in Saigon is invited to three to five cocktail parties a week, sometimes more. It is wise to attend as many as possible because even though the faces and subjects of conversation don't change much, people you can't get to interview in any other way you can nail down at receptions.

"Here are some subjective judgments of the news value of the various embassies in Saigon: American, variable, the higher the official the more vague he is likely to be; British, generally closed-mouthed but extremely well informed and excellent sources; French, except for the ambassador, who won't talk at all, rather poorly informed and deeply suspicious of the press; German, very good company, excellent press dinners but worthless for any other kind of news; Japanese, generally well informed and anxious to swap information with correspondents; Indonesian, fairly well informed, extremely talkative but apt to be inaccurate; Philippines, poorly informed, mainly concerned with boosting relations with the Vietnamese government; Polish, good parties, little information."

I finished my reading and inspected the decorations of the small AP office. What I had taken to be a twig hanging on the wall was a blackened human hand found at the scene of a Vietcong ambush and brought back by the part-time AP photographer Le Minh. A bamboo water container was stained dark red. Bill Ha Van Tran explained that it was human blood. Mal was still tapping on his typewriter.

AP photographer Horst Faas had arrived the same day I did, flying in from Bangkok on his first visit to Vietnam to iron out the kinks in the wirephoto operation. Faas was a German, a year older than I, and he had earned a reputation for aggressive coverage in the Congo and Algeria. I had worked with him briefly in Laos. He was single-minded and ruthlessly competitive. When I had praised one of his African pictures, he had responded matter-of-factly in his strong accent: "Great photographers are not born, they just get up earlier in the morning."

In those years the visual images that seared people's minds were the black-and-white photos that ran on the front pages of newspapers and in *Life* and *Look* magazines, and the AP competed as furiously in news photography as it did in the printed word. With more servicemen arriving in South Vietnam in 1962, there was growing international interest in the story and the AP wanted its Saigon photo operation to match the news side. The company had recently pioneered a wirephoto system that permitted the immediate transmission of black-and-white pictures from any place that had an international phone line.

Horst represented technical innovation. Most American photographers were just graduating from the large, unwieldy Speed Graphic camera of Korean War vintage to the smaller, equally clumsy Rolleiflex. Horst used the 35mm Leica series, small finely machined cameras that he hung around his neck like Hawaiian leis. Over breakfast our first morning in town Horst told me that New York was complaining that the photo output from Saigon in recent months lacked variety; he had been directed to sharpen it up. By day's end Horst had discovered that our enterprising Vietnamese stringer photographer Le Minh was reusing film he had exposed on earlier military operations, simply clipping different negatives from material already sent. Horst found him out when he noticed that the same American military adviser appeared in half a dozen supposedly different military actions.

Horst announced that he would set up shop himself in Saigon to guarantee the purity of the photo product. Unfortunately for all of us the only available space with a water supply was the tiny office toilet, which Horst proceeded to turn into a permanent darkroom cluttered with the paraphernalia of the trade—the containers of solvents and solutions, the metal film clips hanging from clothes lines, the dryer and the guillotine for trimming the prints. Photo processing took priority over human needs. Bill Ha Van Tran muttered that Faas was a bully, but this view was not shared by the other Vietnamese staffer, Pham Van Huan, our diminutive office boy, whom Faas designated to darkroom duties. Huan was a Vietnamese Catholic with a large family and a small salary and he was eager for the additional source of income.

After talking to Conrad Fink, an AP correspondent temporarily visiting from the Tokyo bureau who came into the office caked with mud and full of tales of combat in the Mekong Delta, Faas was impatient to get into the field to cover the war. Horst matched Fink's tales of combat with some of his own. Several months earlier, Katangese soldiers in the Congo had forced him to eat his plastic United Nations press credentials. He said he had added a small bottle of Tabasco sauce to his backpack in case he was ever forced to do so again.

When our government credentials came through a few days later, Mal suggested we visit the Central Highlands region, where the CIA was recruiting mountain tribesmen for local militia forces. We rode an Air Vietnam C-47 transport to the provincial capital of Ban Me Thuot, a distant, dusty rural community with rutted roads and grubby, indifferent people. We checked into a small two-story wooden hotel with the bathroom at the end of the hall and warm tea in porcelain pots in each room. Horst was joyous at the simplicity of it all. He said it reminded him of the Congo.

We headed down the main street toward the American military advisory compound located in the large teak hunting lodge of the former emperor of Vietnam, Bao Dai. But before we arrived we were stopped by Dennis Warner, a well-known Australian correspondent, who told us that the advisers were celebrating the Fourth of July and non-Americans weren't invited. We settled into a sleazy bar that served warm 33 brand beer and Horst told his Congo stories and I threw in a few of my own from Indonesia. Later that evening Horst, slightly tanked, began talking about his early career with the AP as a sports photographer in Germany, where he was frequently required to drive long distances at dangerous speeds to complete his assignments. I asked him what it was like growing up in Germany in World War Two and he started talking about serving in the Hitler Youth movement.

Horst noticed my reaction and explained, "Heh, I was only nine years old."

.   .   .

As a regional photographer Horst was free to travel where he pleased, but I was bound by the daily news grind, required to write a story or two each day. As he explored the head-high elephant grass valleys of the central coast with the Vietnamese marines, I was poring over government handouts and interviewing economists in Saigon. When Horst returned suntanned from the Mekong Delta with mud stains up to his shoulders and tales of derring-do with gung-ho American advisers, I could only offer stories of minor terrorist attacks on city markets and an evening spent in a strategic hamlet on the outskirts of the capital with young Vietnamese militiamen who were more scared of the dark than I was. The daily routine forced me to understand the dominant forces at work in the country, and at the time it was not the Vietcong waging war in the countryside but the Ngo Dinh Diem government.

President Diem was a small, plump man who seldom laughed. He had come to power in 1954 and had defied the oddsmakers' predictions that he would last only six months in office. I attended the celebrations of his presidential anniversary on July 7, walking to the Gia Long Palace along Saigon streets flying red and yellow bunting and painted patriotic slogans. Well-nourished citizens were strolling the boulevards, buying trinkets from sidewalk vendors and stopping for snacks at one of the many downtown ice cream parlors. A group of foreign tourists staying at the Caravelle Hotel were amazed to find a peaceful, prosperous and beautiful city where they had expected war-torn shambles. There were American soldiers in uniform but none were carrying their weapons. They were under orders to keep them wrapped up and out of sight while they were in the capital.

I was allowed to mix for a while with the foreign diplomats and various professional and sports groups who had been invited to the palace to pay their respects to the president. Diem, in a neat dark suit pulled tight around his middle, was smiling quietly as he accepted the greetings of the crowd. Every year since 1954 there had been and still were persistent rumors of another coup attempt against him. Yet, he had always managed to keep the lid on the cauldron, surviving at least three attempts on his life, four armed insurrections and a series of determined plots against his government both from within Vietnam and from outside.

Hidden behind the ceremonial facade was the dictator's iron fist that could order up mass arrests of political opponents and inflict drumhead military justice. His supporters argued that without this control Diem would have been long dead and the country in ruins, but his detractors saw little difference between his reign of terror and the communists'. In some quarters the sixty-one-year-old Diem was regarded as a man of the highest principles, one of the reasons he had been "chosen" by the United States to lead the anticommunist south. But he was dreamy and detached from the practical affairs of government, willing to leave that side of things to his brothers whom he had appointed to positions of power. His younger brother Ngo Dinh Nhu was his closest adviser.

Because Diem was a bachelor, Nhu's attractive, strong-willed and outspoken wife, Madame Nhu, was the official hostess and unofficial first lady of South Vietnam. She was the subject of endless gossip; it was rumored she liked pushing her brother-in-law around. The Saigonese had a more informal title for her, the Dragon Lady. Madame Nhu knew and didn't care, working hard as deputy to the National Assembly, head of the nationwide paramilitary Women's Solidarity Movement, a leading spokeswoman for women's rights in South Vietnam and a biting critic of the United States. I watched her parading one windy day with members of her women's solidarity brigade, the breeze tugging at her tight-fitting dark blue ao-dai and tapered satin trousers but making no mark on her lacquered curls.

Madame Nhu had banned dancing in the capital's nightclubs by having the National Assembly pass an austerity law. "If the Americans want to dance they can go to Hong Kong," she declared, threatening to arrest even those who gamboled in their own homes. The storm in a teacup made for some lively AP copy but I was never much of a dancer, anyway. At midnight, curfew time, some clubs just locked the doors and let everyone inside dance till dawn.

One evening, Horst and I visited the Papillon Bar on the Catinat and got so carried away by the revels that we allowed ourselves to be locked inside with nine bargirls and a barman all eager to do business. Horst got into the spirit, consuming large quantities of Scotch and dancing on the bar. I stuck to 33 beer, a local potion that many believed was laced with formaldehyde, a preservative with the side effect of diminishing the sex drive.

Later, we remembered that we were scheduled to fly with a pilot friend to Soc Trang in the Mekong Delta for the day. At dawn we dragged ourselves to the airport. At Soc Trang we learned that a T-

28 fighter-bomber had crashed into the Mekong River a few miles away, and we boarded a helicopter to look for the lost plane. I encouraged Horst to join the search party plowing through the thick mangrove swamps below, while I returned to the air base to file a story over the telephone and then promptly fell asleep inside a pup tent for the rest of the day. Horst found me that evening rested and dining in the officers club, while he was mud-drenched and ill and furious at being outmaneuvered.

First Combat

I ROSE AT DAWN on August 29, 1962, to cover my first combat operation, my T-shirt drenched with sweat from the humidity as I crawled from the mosquito net draped over my army cot. I splashed water on my face from a canvas storage bag hanging from the tent pole and I lined up at the marine chow line. I was eating with "Rathbun's Ridge Runners," the U.S. Marine Corps's 163rd Helicopter Squadron, recently assigned to Soc Trang, a small provincial capital in the Mekong Delta. Colonel Robert L. Rathbun, a veteran fighter pilot of World War Two and Korea, had offered me a tent for the night.

Across the airstrip a score of H-34 helicopters were parked in a row, the designation "Marine" emblazoned in white paint across their tail sections. Their crews were sitting beside their crafts in spotted camouflage uniforms and soft khaki utility caps. I watched straggly lines of Vietnamese soldiers from the Twenty-first Infantry Division assemble alongside the aircraft, most of them wearing metal helmets and light cotton khaki uniforms. They were armed with an assortment of Thompson submachine guns, Garand M1s and grease guns and a miscellany of older weapons I could not identify. They were chattering to one another in apparent unconcern, though they knew they would soon be flown into combat.

The soldiers grinned at me as I approached and I felt out of place. I was wearing an Australian bush hat, the brim tacked up at the side in World War Two style, dun-colored trousers I had purchased in Saigon, a short-sleeved khaki shirt and a new pair of leather combat boots. My pack contained the items Browne had mandated in his booklet, with the exception of the pistol, which I doubted I could ever use, no matter how terminal the situation.

To pass the time I read "Some Pointers of Guerrilla Warfare" from Browne's booklet. "At times, you will find yourself in combat situations, and you should react to them like a soldier, by doing everything you can to keep yourself alive and unwounded. Try to keep in good physical condition so you can march or run for a reasonable distance; you might have to save your life doing this at some point. You should know how to swim; canals and ditches often are above your head. If you hear a shot and think it's not from your own side don't get up and look around to see where it came from; the second shot might get you. Lie prone under fire and move only on your belly; look for cover and move toward it. When moving with troops do not stay close to the head of a column or the point man in a formation; professional soldiers are paid to do this. Do not stand or march next to a radio man or an aid man because they are the prime targets of the enemy. Stick close to the commander, who is generally in the safest position available; you'll learn more from him than most of the others, anyway.

"The whole idea of covering an operation is to get the news and pictures back, not to play soldier yourself. When moving through enemy territory, and a good part of Vietnam is enemy territory, watch your feet; spikes, mines, concealed pits and booby traps are everywhere. When possible step in exactly the same place as the soldier ahead of you; if he wasn't blown up you probably won't be. If you should get stuck under a mortar barrage or accidental air strike on your own side, the best place to be is underground. Holes are better than nothing; most Vietnamese huts have root cellars inside them that offer fairly good cover. If you are traveling in an M113 armored amphibious personnel carrier do not stick your head out of the hatch when the vehicle is under fire; the gunner has to because it's his job.

"Do not pick up Vietcong flags or other souvenirs from haystacks, tree branches or poles; they are often booby-trapped with grenades. Never be the first to walk into a hut. Beware of water buffalo; when they get excited they stampede, charge and kill. Vietnamese forces suffer a number of casualties from water buffalo. Don't be misled by seeing children playing on their backs; children and buffalo are friends."

I was delighted with Browne's instructions. There was nothing about being brave, just save your ass and get the story back. I watched the rotor blades begin to whirl and Vietnamese troopers leap aboard. My turn was coming. I was joined by a Catholic chaplain. He wore a steel helmet with a white cross painted on the front, a khaki uniform with a white cross stitched in cotton into his collar and he carried a 12 gauge shotgun. "Don't think I'm going to use this unless I absolutely have to," he said. Arms were technically illegal for American advisers in Vietnam at that time and questionable, I thought, for men of God at any time. "Sometimes the VC don't shoot at us because they know we are under orders only to return fire and not initiate it; I'm just helping the Lord watch over us."

The rotor blades kicked up the dust of the sandy airstrip into a stinging, suffocating blast and I hauled myself into the cargo hatch, where the Vietnamese troopers hunched over their weapons. I would not be unloading with them at the landing zone, but proceeding to the command headquarters deeper in the swamps at Ca Mau district. The chaplain pushed himself into position beside a porthole and shoved the barrel of his shotgun through it, peering over the sights professionally. I hung on for dear life as the helicopter pitched and corkscrewed its way to join the other dozen craft in a loose formation about a thousand feet above the ground. The hammering, jarring roar of the Sikorsky H-34 made thinking impossible. Mal had neglected to mention earplugs in his must-have list. I could barely see through the open door, where three Vietnamese soldiers were sitting casually with legs dangling into the slipstream; I could discern that the flooded paddyfields below were yielding to the thick patches of green mangrove shrubs that marked the upper reaches of the swamps of the peninsula.

We dropped to a small patch of dry land in a combat descent that shook up my entrails and pumped blood furiously into my throbbing heart. Three craft were on the ground unloading soldiers as others circled waiting their turn. Our ship was hovering a few feet above ground. The soldiers spilled out from the door into the blowing grass, some landing on their feet and others tumbling on their faces and butts. Then we were airborne again and speeding over the mangroves and stunted trees, shuddering and straining to gain elevation. We passed over another patch of open ground bordered by a narrow canal. I gasped. Two hundred feet below were groups of black-shirted, bare-legged men carrying weapons, running for their lives, ducking under bushes or jumping into the canal waters. We had surprised a platoon or so of Vietcong and they had panicked. I glanced over at the chaplain and he was still aiming through the porthole along the barrel of his shotgun, but he didn't fire and we were soon out of range and nearing my destination, Ca Mau, the embattled center of An Xuyen Province, a small village surrounded by sandbagged walls, barbed wire and tall watchtowers.

Inside the command post I was greeted by Colonel Pham Van Dong, the chief of staff of the Vietnamese Army's Third Corps region. The amiable colonel was our sole contact in Saigon with the Vietnamese Army high command, an organization that only grudgingly dealt with the press. Two or three times each week over cups of green tea he would receive us in his Saigon office to give limited background updates on the war and offer a few statistics. This current operation was already two weeks old, the biggest ever launched in his command area, and he had taken personal field responsibility and invited us down. Browne had been there several days earlier. The operation was named Big Pacification. As many as four thousand Vietnamese troops were involved, according to Colonel Dong.

It was, at this point, a rare opportunity to see actual combat, and several other press people had made the trek. One of them was Michel Renard, a tall Belgian freelance photographer with a truculent manner who hung out in the AP bureau. He was wearing a striped camouflage uniform spotted with mud, had a large sheath knife hanging from his belt, and was carrying a fistful of film canisters that he was taking back to Saigon that afternoon. Renard got along with the Vietnamese soldiers because he spoke French and jokingly bossed them around like a colonial military officer.

Renard was a fountainhead of incidental intelligence about the war and entertained us with stories of his recent adventures, including a military operation a few days earlier with a company of Vietnamese Ranger troops. The objective was a waterlogged, thatched-roof village in the mangrove swamps, presumed to be a Vietcong settlement. As the soldiers waded through the swamps there was rifle fire and they called in air strikes to help them, blowing the village apart. Renard said he saw a young girl crying hysterically in the wreckage with her hands pinned to her ears. She ran toward a dike at the edge of the village shouting "cha cha," the word for father, and a man had risen out of the tall swamp grass with a rifle pointing toward the soldiers in one arm and reaching out to his daughter with the other. A burst of gunfire knocked him down. "I've got it all on film; the AP will pay dearly for this," Renard exclaimed.

Peter Kalischer of CBS was also at Ca Mau, pushing Colonel Dong impatiently to provide transportation for us to travel toward the front lines. His cameraman was nursing a large, heavy Oricon film camera with a harness attachment that would make the equipment easier to carry in the field.

Eventually Colonel Dong found us a ride with the U.S. Army's Fifty-seventh Light Helicopter Company, which was moving a company of soldiers into action. The aircraft, H36s, were already landing on the small dirt airstrip. The largest helicopters then in the military inventory, the ungainly tandem-rotor aircraft were coming in at fast speeds, rotating their noses in the air at the last possible moment and thumping to the ground in a thunder of roaring rotor blades.

I scrambled on board after a dozen Vietnamese troopers, squeezing through the narrow side door as best I could and helping the cameraman and his heavy load aboard. The helicopter bucked like a steer as it positioned for takeoff, tilting forward as it gained speed and clambering over the nearby treeline and into the sky. Within minutes we were descending. This time I would jump out with the troops to see the war for myself.

The Vietnamese troopers were out first, leaping several feet to the grass below and bracing against the blast of the rotor blades as they moved off to the edge of the clearing. Then the CBS team was on their way and it was my turn. I felt the mud oozing up my legs as I hit the ground. Kalischer shouted, "This way" as he headed after the troops, but his cameraman, with his heavy equipment, stepped into a water hole and sank up to his armpits. Two soldiers came to his rescue. I was glad to be in print as I left my TV colleagues behind and joined the command group.

There was no escape from the thick, slimy swamp. The knee-deep mud beyond the clearing soon became waist-deep as we swam through the mangroves on the way to our first objective, a village a mile ahead. When we entered dense bamboo groves the going got even worse, and the unit was given a rest stop every hundred yards. The soldiers just flopped down in the water, gasping for relief in the few minutes allotted them. I was past exhaustion.

By late afternoon we were on the fringes of the village, walking finally, through cultivated gardens and then over deep defensive trenches lined with sharpened bamboo poles. There was no opposition as the troops entered but there were surprises: several white cloth banners with slogans painted in red in Vietnamese were stretched across the thatched-roofed houses, attacking the government and the American military assistance effort. Inside there were communist propaganda leaflets and pictures of the wispy-bearded communist leader, Ho Chi Minh, on the walls, the frames garlanded with flowers. The only inhabitant discovered in the place was an old man hiding in a hole who was allowed to go free. The community was a graphic illustration of the extent of the Vietcong insurgency.

The operational instructions were to destroy all fortified hamlets and the soldiers went about their task with enthusiasm, wielding machetes and matches expertly. By late afternoon we left the blaze behind us and were seeking a bivouac for the night. The unit commander decided to camp on dry land by a narrow river, and we had barely settled in early evening when I came under gunfire for the first time in my life. A sniper opened up on the command group and the bullets thwacked into the trees around us. The response was deafening; the whole unit returned fire. When the sniper persisted the commander called in a fighter plane to teach him a lesson: two T-28 aircraft bombed, strafed and napalmed the riverbank for nearly a whole hour, searing our faces and leaving the landscape blackened and smoking. Nothing could live through that I thought. At 4:30 A.M. after a wet, restless night wrapped up in a plastic ground sheet, I was awakened by the sniper as he resumed his fire into our camp. The Vietnamese soldiers were too tired to return it.

At dawn we were on our way again. There were no signs of the guerrillas, but armies of half-inch red ants were in the trees and shrubs of our route; they fell on us, biting necks and chests and crawling into our clothing. The column was held up frequently as soldiers called to their buddies to help pick off the attackers. By late afternoon I had had enough. A marine supply helicopter came in with batteries for the unit's radio equipment and I hitched a ride out, exhausted, mud-covered and hungry.

I learned a lot from my first direct encounter with the Vietnam War. I found Mal's booklet invaluable. I found, too, that despite my odd garb and my inexperience, the Vietnamese soldiers in the field, and the American advisers with them, were quick to friendship, and always helpful. I found that no briefing back at headquarters could compensate for the drama of actually being in the field of struggle. I discovered that I was neither repelled nor excited by the limited action I had seen; I felt detached from it all, observing. The best lesson of all was that, unlike the soldiers, I could leave anytime I wished.

Ap Bac

WHEN I ARRIVED IN VIETNAM in 1962 America was spending more than a million dollars a day trying to win its only shooting war. The atmosphere was upbeat. "Win the war by '64" was the unofficial slogan. The military strategists I talked with in Saigon were convinced that their experimental, expensive "counterinsurgency" approach would reverse the tide of the "peoples' war."

The U.S. commitment was also visible in the stars—the stars on the shoulders of a dozen experienced generals who by year's end were on duty in Saigon, heading sophisticated commands. The gung ho Brigadier General Joseph W. Stilwell headed the U.S. Army Support Group, which included a new generation of combat helicopters. Stilwell was the son of the famous General "Vinegar Joe" Stilwell of World War Two renown, and he liked taking us along when he rode as a gunner on his choppers, hosing down Vietcong guerrillas with his .50 caliber machine gun.

Other U.S. generals ran an army concept team, advised the Vietnamese Air Force, and operated a policy-planning command. There was one general per one thousand American advisers in Vietnam at that time. The officer in charge of this U.S. Military Assistance Command, known in military jargon as COMUSMACV, was a four-star general, Paul D. Harkins, a sharp-featured, blue-eyed West Point graduate. He had served with General George S. Patton, Jr., during World War Two and had been chief of staff of the Eighth Army during the Korean War. Harkins looked the part of the commanding officer, always impeccably uniformed and often puffing on a large cigar.

The consensus of the American high command was that their efforts were paying off in Vietnam, but that winning would take longer than anticipated. The reporters generally concurred in that view and I heard none voice doubts that the war was worth fighting. Mal Browne believed it was being won, and his AP news analyses reflected that view, but he had no illusions that the road would be easy and predicted that it would be a prolonged, grim campaign that would need some course corrections. Though the media and officialdom in 1962 essentially agreed on the wisdom and the course of the war, we fought like cats in a sack over the news coverage. The problem was that the Kennedy administration was going to war in South Vietnam without declaring it, trying not to tell anybody, and endeavoring to conceal the rapid buildup of men and machines and the increasingly heavy burden they were bearing for getting the job done.

I found to my surprise that these sensitive tactical undertakings were details the Saigon press corps saw no reason to conceal. In fact, Mal insisted it was our duty to reveal them, and that secrecy stamps did not apply because if we could watch arriving arms shipments and troop deployments then so could the enemy. Supporting the official American policy of concealment was the politically repressive Vietnamese regime that was distrustful of all comers, and all too willing to bully and intimidate the foreign press. Any reports that we filed questioning the claims of war progress were taken personally by the Diem regime. Additionally, the authorities wanted to stifle our coverage of the cultural conflicts between the headstrong American soldiers and the conservative local populations. We were expected to present a picture of sweetness and light in a place where hostility was swelling as the American military presence and the resultant social dislocation rapidly increased.

I took my reporting cues from Mal Browne, who would not be bullied. He was more than a match for the officials who attempted to orchestrate our professional lives. From his first week in Vietnam in 1961 Mal had raised the hackles of the authorities. From the start he noticed that American involvement was far greater than he had suspected, and with a little digging he discovered that American pilots were flying combat missions against the Vietcong in Skyraider bombers provided to the South Vietnamese as training planes. Mal refused to conspire in the secrecy demanded by the American Embassy and the Saigon government. He passed his stubbornness along to me.

The AP was not the only news organization to critically scrutinize the developing war. During a six-month tour of duty, Pulitzer Prize winner Homer Bigart had been roiling the waters of doubt over the American effort with penetrating, bitter reports and analyses for the *New York Times*. Thirty years of foreign reporting made him the foremost war correspondent of his generation. Soon after I arrived in Saigon, Bigart ended his tour. At his farewell party I first met François Sully, a debonair, amiable Frenchman who had been in Vietnam for the past seventeen years and was far more knowledgeable about what was going on than most other correspondents. Sully was the *Newsweek* correspondent, and in his frank accounts he made it clear that he thought the increasing American commitment was beginning to mirror the failed effort of the French forces a decade earlier.

The authorities could not understand why we didn't champion the war effort as reporters had done in World War Two and Korea. They first lost patience with Sully and refused to renew his visa. Most of the Saigon press corps cabled an appeal to President Kennedy, but to no avail. Sully was charged with "systematic hostility" in his reporting and he departed September 9 for Hong Kong. We went to the airport to see him off, and wondered who would be the next forced to leave. It turned out to be Jim Robinson, an experienced NBC correspondent, envied for his sartorial elegance. He had designed the TV suit, a trim matching tunic and trousers outfit that became de rigueur for all television correspondents for the remainder of the war. It enriched an obscure Saigon tailor we called the honorable Mr. Minh. Robinson owned the suit in ten different colors and cloths. His crime was not sartorial overkill but a casual remark that President Diem gave boring interviews. Made in the presence of officials, it was a slight that was not forgiven. Robinson's ouster on November 1 convinced us that the American Embassy was indifferent to press freedom and unwilling to call the regime on its increasing paranoia. We labored on with an increasing sense of isolation, dismayed by a blanket of restrictions on news coverage that was aimed at freezing us out of critical war areas in the countryside.

We soon learned that the campaign to blunt our coverage was aided and abetted by government agencies in Washington. The U.S. Embassy was willingly acquiescing to their directives. Proof of these fears came in a September 19 memo from the AP Washington bureau informing us that the State Department, the Pentagon and the Vietnamese Embassy were highly critical of the Western press performance in Vietnam. The AP management assured us they were not buying this entirely, but they were puzzled that the official briefings in Washington, which seemed frank to them, were "about 180 degrees off" our assessments. The memo writer was told privately that the deputy Secretary of State Averell Harriman had complained to the editors of the *New York Times* about the coverage, and was contemplating complaining to AP and UPI.

Browne's response to the memo acknowledged our awareness of an antipress feeling, and went on to say that, "While the official view of the war differed substantially from ours, we had not reported that the war was lost or hopeless." Ironically, Mal praised the strategic hamlet program, which in many areas "seems to be working effectively." It fell to me to torpedo the optimism over even that facet of the American effort.

By late 1962 that sociomilitary experiment had become an important tool to break communist control of the countryside by closing off the village populations from the Vietcong. A similar program had been introduced successfully against communist insurgents in Malaysia in the 1950s. Millions of dollars of American aid were being spent on the strategic hamlets in Vietnam, and by that autumn more than three thousand had been constructed, sheltering four million people. More than a quarter of the entire population was now living in rural settlements behind deep moats and earthworks studded with sharpened bamboo stakes and foot traps to keep strangers outside. The gates of the hamlets swung shut between sunset and dawn, the time when the VC were most active.

The pilot site was located north of Saigon in the rubber plantation area near Ben Cat at the edge of one of the most insecure areas in the country, War Zone D, named in the French war; it was a forbidding landscape of scrub and jungle that extended back to the craggy hills of the Cambodian border and the legendary southern supply route for the communists, the Ho Chi Minh trail. The project had been given the name Operation Sunrise when it was launched in March 1962, and had become a mecca for visiting congressmen and journalists, proof that American aid money was being spent wisely and well. When I visited in November, the place was falling apart.

With an official from the Vietnamese Information Ministry, I drove north up Route 13 past the remains of ambushed convoys and battle-scarred villages to the main hamlet at Ben Tuong. It was an approved trip to what the government still claimed was a showplace of the war's progress. The mud walls of the hamlet were studded with so many sharp bamboo spears that they looked like stubble on a vast unshaven chin. We drove inside through tall, barbed-wire festooned wooden gates to a dusty courtyard surrounded by thatched-roofed homes and a more permanent iron roofed government office. There was an air of caution among the Vietnamese regular soldiers who lounged around inside. All were armed and I noticed that their American advisers also had their weapons near at hand even as they ordered beers and cokes at the shanty shops built inside the entrance.

Only four of the planned fourteen hamlets had been built in "Operation Sunrise." The others were on hold—it was difficult to gather enough people to live in them. A total of three thousand farmers and their families had been uprooted from their home villages to populate the few established hamlets, many against their will. There were many more women than men, a telling statistic. The absent men were presumed to be members of the Vietcong, but none had been persuaded to give up in the months since they had been separated from their families. My official guide pointed to the stability of the population as a favorable factor and argued that the American-financed program of free housing, food support and health care was successfully persuading the population to remain under government care. Later, an American adviser showed me a letter recently found on a woman heading out to the rice fields; it was apparently intended for her husband. One sentence read, "Don't worry about me, my darling, we are well taken care of. Go ahead with your work."

I wrote a long article to the effect that the Operation Sunrise hamlets were becoming more trouble than they were worth: each required a Vietnamese regular army company for security because the authorities were unwilling to arm the inhabitants for their own defense; it was feared such weapons would be used against them. I wrote that the experimental hamlets had in fact become expensive internment camps. The decision was eventually made to concentrate population control on more secure areas. The special program was gradually phased out. But my bellwether story did not bring me any plaudits from the authorities who saw it as just another carping criticism from the press.

The attempts by government to restrict the news flow in Vietnam by intimidation from above were doomed to failure. The Achilles' heel of the policy was that the Americans in the field did not look upon the press as a fifth column of spies. The soldiers I met in those first months were zealous and self-assured. They believed in their mission and saw little reason to conceal what they were doing. Their idealism did not surprise me; I had come to expect it from Americans. My childhood was lived through the drama and victory of World War Two in which the United States played such a dominant role. I shared their dream of a world made safer for all of us, and this affinity helped me get along with the American soldiers and win their confidence even though I was from another country. For all the quarrels reporters had over the years with officials in Saigon and Washington, we rarely clashed with servicemen in the field, and what was true for the beginnings of the war was still true at its end.

For the American servicemen in Vietnam, the early years were times of optimism and adventure. Their enthusiasm was catching, and it often pervaded our reporting as we accompanied them into battle and shared their experiences. We particularly glamorized the helicopter crews; the chopper was the one reliable way to get quickly in and out of the war, and it was a symbol of how this conflict differed from those that preceded it.

I quickly made it a point to befriend the officers and men of an experimental helicopter unit assigned to Saigon in September 1962, the Utility Tactical Transport Company, a typically dull bureaucratic name for the hottest innovation in warfare since the jeep. They flew the Bell Company's new turbine-powered UH-1A Huey helicopter, a smaller, more maneuverable aircraft than the noisy behemoths that were lumbering through the Vietnamese skies loaded with combat troops. With the arrival of the Hueys there evolved the concept of air mobility that was to dominate the future course of the war. The choppers were initially armed with two .30 caliber machine guns and sixteen 2.75-inch rockets and they accompanied the troop carriers into battle, spraying the landing zones with heavy fire before the troops unloaded, and covering their evacuations. We figured that in this helicopter war the best vantage point was from a helicopter.

The energetic young unit commander was Major Ivan Slavich of San Francisco, California, who from the beginning was friendly and had no problem with our presence. He was immensely proud of the innovations his unit was introducing in military tactics. Slavich's outfit was experimental, and it fell between the cracks in the carefully controlled official information order of the time. The UTT reported to the Army Concept Team in Vietnam headed by a general whose concern was evaluating tactics and not news coverage. The armed Hueys were the support for the three U.S. Army transport helicopter companies flying the Vietnamese into battle; they were in on nearly every major military action of the war and there was usually room for us on the choppers.

I loved riding them, seatbelt fastened and the wind blowing at my hair as the young gunners leaned out the open sides of the craft with their eyes on the ground below and their fingers on the trigger. Private First Class John C. Dickerson nicknamed his chopper "the hot box" because of the five hits it had endured from Vietcong ground fire. He told me, "Your stomach turns over a little when you see them shooting at you. Sometimes it's close enough you can feel the burn of the passing bullet. It's not too pleasant but you can shoot back." The escort ships would skim along only a hundred feet or so from the ground as they ranged over the flat, green battlefield of the Mekong River Delta. Dickerson had volunteered for Vietnam and was offering to extend for a second tour to finish out what he called "my time in hell" before going home for good; he was wounded and went home earlier than he had intended. Because they were based in Saigon, the UTT crews could visit the city, and we sometimes dined with the officers and men and went barhopping with them, further cementing our relationships. Military men socializing with the press. It was an army information officer's worst nightmare, but they could do nothing to stop it. The UTT and its officers and men were our passport into the burgeoning conflict and they were a reliable guide to the fortunes of the combatants.

We were also captivated by the U.S. Army's Special Forces, the "Green Berets." I spent several days with Detachment A-113, one of the first Special Forces Units in the war zone, assigned to the Ban Me Thuot area of the Central Highlands plateau. This was a place of rolling, forested hills and swift streams, and was once one of the premiere game hunting locations in Asia, but now the Vietcong were navigating the jungled leopard lairs and the bear trails, traveling freely among the Rhade tribal population. The Green Berets were assigned to turn the tide in such regions, to stop the Vietcong in their tracks. They were secretive and privileged, worked under the orders of the CIA and were generally independent of all military and civilian authorities in their area of operations.

Detachment A-113 had arrived in Ban Me Thuot in 1962 in an unmarked C-46 transport flown by Taiwanese pilots to set up a village defense program for the Rhade, the largest and the most advanced and intelligent mountain tribe. When the veil of secrecy was lifted, I was invited in to witness the program's success; in a whirlwind of bold plans and initiatives the eight-man team had organized the inhabitants of eighty tribal villages and hamlets. They supervised the building of bamboo fortifications and underground bunkers at each location and provided basic military training to young tribesmen, replacing their crossbows and spears with 4,500 rifles. I was shown around by the tanned, rangy team leader Captain Ron Shackleton.

We first cracked a can of warm beer because the Americans preferred to live like their hosts, primatively, and disavowed refrigeration and other modern technology. Then we met the locals, the tribal elders with their wispy white beards, puffing tobacco-filled bamboo pipes, young smiling militiamen proudly toting their new weapons, and the shy giggling women of the village dressed in dusty black and red traditional garments. I didn't meet with the CIA handler who discreetly stayed out of sight in a hut whenever I walked by.

The CIA had chosen the Rhade tribe as the subject of their counterinsurgency experiment not only because of their strategic location on the high Annamese plateau bordering Laos and Cambodia, but because they were basically a neglected people, ill-served by the Vietnamese, who treated them as savages. The Rhade and the other hill tribes responded with a baleful enmity for all Vietnamese, whatever their political persuasion, following the wind that blew fairest. The Americans blew fairest of all; they brought no historic prejudices, only resources and unbridled enthusiasm.

I watched Shackleton's efficient team at work: the medic, Sergeant Manfried Baier, dispensing simple but effective treatments to a people previously denied the basics of health care; the weapons men, Al Clark and John Lindewald, patiently running through the practice sessions for automatic weapons with recruits whose fingers were so calloused from pulling the strings of crossbows that they could barely get them on the triggers. The Americans brought other specialist skills; two of the team spoke Vietnamese and another French, enough to communicate adequately with the locals. When I returned to Saigon I wrote a long, positive story quoting senior American military authorities as saying that the Green Beret program was "the most significant yet devised" to quash the Vietcong movement at the grassroots level, which was true enough as far as it went. I also wrote a story about how the first CIA operatives in the Central Highlands arrived the previous year posing as zoologists, and walked around Ban Me Thuot swinging butterfly nets. The information came from Captain Shackleton and his spirited team, and I later wondered if I had been fed a whopper to embarrass their CIA handler.

The Green Berets were the pride of the Kennedy administration. The president himself supported special funding for the paramilitary operations and unconventional tactics the teams perfected. The regular army officials forced to follow a conventional life-style, resenting the glamour of the Special Forces, sometimes sarcastically called the beret-wearing warriors "Jacqueline Kennedy's Own Rifles," a takeoff of the British Army unit designations that included "The Queen's Own Rifles."

The ranks of Saigon's resident press corps swelled in late summer with the arrival of the *New York Times* correspondent David Halberstam. His reputation preceded him. Horst Faas had worked with him in the Congo and had arranged to share a house with him. The normally phlegmatic Horst described Halberstam to me in near-mythic terms as a generous, gregarious, competitive and professional newsman. When they met, the tall Halberstam wrapped Horst in a bear hug and shouted in a loud, fake German accent, "Horst Kaspar Adolf Faas of the Nazis." Horst smiled in approval. David used the AP bureau as his office, and we made a few reporting trips together into the countryside, visiting Nha Trang and Da Nang and the Mekong Delta. His reporting was prodigious, perceptive and detailed, and he and Mal became friendly rivals. Halberstam's dismissal of cant revealed a toughness that I admired.

Halberstam arrived at a time when the press corps was approaching a particularly difficult juncture; it would not be too long before we were on the hot seat as never before because of our reporting. The name that triggered it all was Ap Bac, a trivial place beyond government lines in the no-man's-land that merged the Mekong Delta with the swamps and rice fields south of the Saigon capital district. The cluster of thatched-roof homes and banana trees and pig pens was typical of the Vietcong hamlets that dotted the countryside, a desperate place subject to frequent government bombings and strafings and random artillery firings because it remained just outside the so-called pacified areas.

On the morning of January 3, 1963, the South Vietnamese Seventh Division launched several battalions of infantry and airborne troops against Ap Bac in a military operation aimed at capturing a portable Vietcong radio station operating in the vicinity. The operation went terribly wrong; we first heard about it early that afternoon when our sources at an American Army Aviation company based at Tan Son Nhut Airport called to say that eight helicopters had been hit and at least four crewmen were wounded. The news got worse. By late afternoon Browne was writing that Ap Bac represented the costliest defeat up to that time for the American support effort in South Vietnam. Halberstam and I hurried out to the airport to talk with returning helicopter pilots. Fourteen of the fifteen helicopters participating in the operation had been hit by a devastating wall of ground fire; five ships were lost on the battlefield. Three Americans were dead, two of them helicopter crewmen and the third an army captain advising the ground troops. Vietnamese troop losses may have numbered as many as a hundred.

The full dimensions of the disaster became clearer the next day when Halberstam and I, learning that our competitors Neil Sheehan of UPI and Nick Turner of Reuters had driven to the action scene, prevailed upon Steve Stibbens of the *Stars and Stripes* newspaper to take us to the front. We persuaded Steve to change into his U.S. Marine uniform because Vietnamese authorities had been preventing newsmen from driving in through the northern Mekong Delta. We headed south through Cholon. The road was jammed with long lines of cars and buses undergoing security checks at heavily guarded bridges and villages.

Beyond the provincial capital of Tan An we turned right into a country lane and bumped across a mile of dirt road to the village of Tan Hiep and discovered a scene of near chaos: jeeps and trucks and helicopters competed for space on the small runway, and soldiers milled around waiting for orders to go somewhere. The senior American adviser to the Fourth Corps region, Colonel Daniel Boone Porter, gave us the first inkling of the dimensions of the loss. For the first time in the war, he explained, the Vietcong had stood their ground and fought back rather than hitting and melting away into the countryside. The Vietcong unit, the 514th battalion, battle-hardened but numerically inferior to the attacking force, had offered exactly the kind of confrontation many American advisers had told me they were hoping for. They could hardly wait for the opportunity to bring their superior firepower to the battlefield. But it was the South Vietnamese force that had backed off.

Dave and I hitched a ride on a helicopter that was surveying the battlefield. Down below we could see dead bodies in the mud and fields, and the tracks of Vietnamese armored personnel carriers that had approached the hamlet to reinforce embattled units and been turned back. The Vietcong had escaped easily, leaving sixty-five government soldiers dead, a helicopter massacre and the taste of defeat for the American military advisers.

On our return to Tan Hiep airstrip we noticed a Vietnamese honor guard drawn up for senior commanders, including General Harkins. We asked the general what was happening and he commented with a straight face, "We've got them in a trap and we're going to spring it in half an hour," but he was gone before we could pursue the questioning. We sought out Lieutenant Colonel John Paul Vann, the peppery senior adviser to the Seventh Division. Vann was a no-nonsense officer. He drew us aside and contradicted General Harkins's assertions, launching into a fierce attack on the performance of the Vietnamese soldiers, declaring it was "a damn shame" that such a debacle could happen after all the efforts made by the United States to equip and advise them.

Sheehan later staggered out of a helicopter mud-covered and shaken, saying that he had been fired upon by friendly artillery while visiting the battlefield. The Vietnamese were so hopeless that Vann assembled his sixty-man American advisory staff including cooks and office clerks, and sent them off to waylay some of the Vietcong. Most of the VC got away.

The Ap Bac story was the biggest I had covered in my six months in Vietnam. It exposed the glaring weaknesses that were to haunt American military planners seeking to shape their ally into a fighting force; and it highlighted the cleverness of the Vietcong, a generally maligned guerrilla organization. The battle convinced the Saigon press corps that either the authorities were unaware of the full dimensions of the insurgency, or these dimensions were being concealed from us. This discrepancy, which later became known as the credibility gap, grew wider.

Death by Fire

THE BATTLE OF AP BAC sent a clear signal that American officers might have to take command if South Vietnam was to survive, but it was also the moment when the news coverage of the war came of age. The eruption of headlines and editorial comment was brought to page one, where it would remain for more than a decade. We were revealing policy decisions that Washington preferred to keep concealed, about vastly increased military assistance and expanded rules of engagement that required American soldiers to use their weapons, decisions that were pushing the United States deeper into the conflict. It was a constant tug-of-war. The authorities wanted to fight the war in secret and we wouldn't let them. John Paul Vann was reprimanded for his outspokenness to reporters and eventually he quit the military service.

American officials were also furious that the press corps was targeting the misdeeds of the Ngo Dinh Diem regime. In a speech in mid-February, Ambassador Frederick Nolting rebuked us and called for an end "to idle criticism, from snide remarks and unnecessary comments and from spreading allegations and rumors which either originate from communist sources or play directly into communist hands." The Saigon government was openly suspicious of our activities and, ironically, believed that American officials were telling us too much. Our relations with the United States Embassy were bad and we found our best sources outside the capital in the provincial towns and districts where the war was being fought.

The continuing imbroglio helped the community of correspondents come together and prepare for all that was to follow. My own profile as a reporter was rising and Don Huth advised me that Wes Gallagher had approved a recommendation that I be given AP staff status, including a paid home leave every three years and a one-month annual vacation. I was more secure than I had ever been in my life. Mal Browne was the ship's captain and I was first engineer mate. Horst Faas remained the implacably capable technocrat with his arms full of cameras and gadgetry and his lens focused on the war. I relished working beside Mal and Horst and David Halberstam. But David was spending more time across town with Neil Sheehan of UPI. It was not too long before he packed up his typewriter and moved out of our office.

In the midst of all this, we were all trying to get our emotional lives in order. Mal's wife and family had not joined him in Saigon, and he indicated that the marriage was over. He had started dating an attractive Vietnamese woman named Le Lieu who worked at the Government Information Office, whom he would later marry. Neil Sheehan and David Halberstam had established liaisons with local women. Horst was joined by his German fiancée, Ursula. I met Nina Nguyen, a slim, vivacious Vietnamese girl, at a lunch hosted by François Sully to introduce us "to some respectable girls for a change." I raced to escort Nina to a chair, just beating out my New Zealand colleague, Nicholas Turner of Reuters. Nina had recently returned from the United States, where she had graduated as a medical librarian from the University of North Carolina. Her family had fled the communists in the north in 1954, and her father was the chief administrative officer of the South Vietnamese National Assembly. I was totally entranced.

We were, it seemed, settling down none too soon. In the winter of 1963 an unexpected national emergency overshadowed the war and pitted the press corps in new conflict with the Vietnamese and United States governments. The controversy threw another international spotlight on Vietnam and reshaped the entire American effort in a way that was still controversial thirty years later.

The crisis began in one of my favorite cities, at Hue, the former capital of Annam that straddled the Perfume River in central Vietnam. I had been there many times to enjoy the beauty of the old Imperial City, surrounded by a wide moat and high, thick brick walls con-

99

structed two hundred years earlier by a French engineer for a nervous emperor. The palace and its environs were particularly charming and were said to be an accurate miniature copy of the Forbidden City in Beijing. The grandiose tombs of Vietnam's greatest kings were modeled after their Chinese counterparts and were gentle arbors of masonry and vegetation. The Perfume River, which flowed sluggishly from the distant low hills through Hue, was a floating city in itself, with houseboats for rent and sampans selling all you could eat and drink and romance.

Hue was also the family home of the Ngo clan, where President Diem's brother Ngo Dinh Can ruled with an iron hand. Another brother, Ngo Dinh Thuc, was the Catholic archbishop. Diem was a Catholic president in a country that was 80 percent Buddhist or Confucian. Distrust and dissension had grown when Catholic refugees had moved south in the mid-1950s after French forces lost the war against Ho Chi Minh, and resentment grew as Catholics seemed to prosper more than Buddhists. There were charges they received disproportionately more education scholarships, army promotions and land grants from a government run by their own kind.

The religious situation was of little interest to American officials who were arming the Diem regime to fight the communists, and counting on the whole population to support the struggle. Neither were we in the press much interested in the religion, perhaps because we assumed that Buddhism was less an organized and institutional orthodoxy and more a state of mind. My casual association with monks in Thailand and Laos had been amiable, but I had the impression that the order attracted a motley selection of adherents. A monk once told me that he was certain that his begging each morning would bring him enough food "because the people know that a hungry man knows no laws" and that it was preferable to cater to their needs than ignore them. In Vietnam I had seen pagodas in most villages I visited and occasionally went inside to marvel at the decorative altars and to smell the pungent incense that curled through the air, but I made little effort to find out more.

We soon learned that Buddhism was fully engaged in the politics of Vietnam, with youth organizations, schools, nurseries and orphanages quietly in operation all over the country, and that its leaders had a grudge against the Diem regime and were waiting for an opportunity to exploit it.

At the Tu Dam Pagoda, the center of the Buddhist religion, the elaborate celebrations of the Buddha's birthday were held on May 8.

The government had ordered all religious flags to be taken down, preventing them from flying their traditional five-colored banners at the Buddha's birthday. They were further antagonized because Roman Catholic banners continued to fly in various Vietnamese catholic communities. Angry crowds gathered to hear leading monks deliver critical speeches; not since the start of the Diem administration nearly a decade earlier had anything like that been heard in public. Thousands of followers led by silent yellow robed monks and nuns marched from the pagoda along Hue's main boulevard and demanded entrance to the radio station to broadcast their complaints. The local security officer, a soldier named Major Dang Sy, lost his nerve and ordered his soldiers to stop the demonstrators. There were two explosive blasts from hand grenades thrown by the troops. In the resulting melee, armored cars crushed fleeing demonstrators; eleven people died, including several children, and scores were injured.

We were far from the scene at our bureau in Saigon and at first reported the government line—that the incident had been fomented by communist agitators and that a terrorist grenade blast had torn the victims to pieces. Within a few days the true story of government complicity emerged from eyewitnesses who came to our bureau with details. The Diem government had never leveled with the foreign press in the past and was unwilling to do so at this time. The whole incident would have been forgotten if the Buddhists had not come to us directly. We were, they realized, the crucial link to world opinion, and we portrayed the crisis as a human rights issue. When our reports were broadcast back in Vietnamese from international radio stations the protests grew louder. The Diem government was incapable of accepting responsibility for the bloodshed and punishing the perpetrators and compensating the victims. Overnight the Buddhist flag became a rallying point for social protest by every faction opposing the regime. Men and women who had not attended pagoda services in years began to chant long-forgotten prayers and demonstrated in the streets, defying the armed soldiers and the police, who often arrested them and threw them into trucks.

Buddhist officials were now routinely calling the Saigon press corps with news tips, and on June 11 we were advised that another demonstration would be held in Saigon. Such events were starting to become commonplace and only Malcolm Browne and Bill Havantran, the AP's Vietnamese office manager, attended the morning event. As usual, police cars cleared the streets ahead of the silently marching monks as they left a small pagoda and headed up Phan Dinh Phuong

Street. A gray sedan in front of the procession stopped abruptly in front of the Cambodian diplomatic headquarters. Three monks stepped out and the several hundred marchers formed a circle in the middle of the intersection. Then an elderly monk, Thich Quang Duc, seated himself on a cushion and folded his legs as his two companions poured gasoline over his shaved head and yellow robes. He lit a match in his lap and then folded his hands in the lotus position as flames enveloped him. Browne clicked pictures methodically as another monk shouted to the crowd in Vietnamese and English, "This is the Buddhist flag. He died for this flag. Thich Quang Duc burned for this flag." The photograph of the aged monk enveloped in smoke and flames shocked the world.

The Buddhists stepped up their publicity efforts. At the Xa Loi Pagoda in Saigon, students and Buddhist youths helped the monks crank the mimeograph machines on which they produced tracts and policy statements and leaflets to distribute to the press corps and throughout the country. We were usually briefed at the pagoda by a slim, dapper monk named Thich Duc Nghiep, who spoke fluent English and served delicate Chinese tea in tiny cups in his upstairs office as he fed us snacks of philosophy and propaganda. Buddhist leaders were telling us that we were their only hope of getting their message to the outside world, and as a result the locals did all they could to help us.

Horst was invited into a Vietnamese home at the height of one riot and guided to an upstairs balcony where he had a fine vantage point to photograph the swaying battle. He didn't stay long. The crowd below was ruining most of his shots by cheering wildly every time he clicked the shutter. I stopped in a store after a Sunday evening riot to purchase some groceries. The questions tumbled out, "Were you there? Will you send reports abroad? Were there photographers there?" The shopkeeper patted me on the back, and his workers gathered around me and cheered.

The Diem regime denounced our reporting, and of course the government-controlled newspapers echoed that view: I was physically assaulted outside the Chantareansay Pagoda in the northern suburbs on July 7. We were covering a surging group of demonstrators when I was set upon in an alley by two plainclothes policemen who punched my face and shoved me to the ground. They would have done more if Halberstam had not come to my defense, swinging at the attackers, scattering them. I was stunned by the attack and my camera was smashed, but Browne had climbed up a power pole and clicked off a picture of me and my bloody face that was widely published. When the American Embassy refused to make a protest, a committee of colleagues sent a message of protest to President Kennedy.

The police were not finished with us. On Monday, Mal and I were ordered to the main Saigon police station and charged with assault and battery by the two plainclothes policemen involved in the melee at the pagoda. After a four-hour interrogation we turned the tables and demanded to file our own charges against our attackers, and to ask for compensation for my damaged camera.

The violent street confrontations paralyzed the capital, threatened to harm the war effort and made headlines around the world. President Kennedy replaced Ambassador Nolting with Henry Cabot Lodge, Jr. Nolting was on vacation with his family in Greece and when he returned he had a last meeting with President Diem. Diem asked Nolting if Lodge's appointment meant that American policy was changing, and the departing ambassador assured him not to worry, a view he later confirmed with the U.S. State Department. Officials advised him from the highest authority, which was shorthand for the president, to assure Diem there was no change in American policy. Ngo Dinh Diem had survived nearly a decade of political and military crises, but in fact American policy was now changing, spurred along by the Buddhist crisis and our reporting of it.

The Pagoda Raids

By MID-AUGUST the Buddhist crisis was like a Barnum & Bailey circus with bizarre exhibits, a cast of thousands, eager sightseers and souvenir stands. Tourists mingled with the Buddhist faithful at the open-sided pavilion at the Xa Loi Pagoda, stepped carefully around the several hundred worshippers, mostly women in colorful silk ao-dai dresses who were kneeling before an altar where the charred heart of the immolated monk, Thich Quang Duc, was being kept in a glass jar. In the courtyard around the building monks were handing out mimeographed copies of the latest edition of the Buddhist "newspaper," which was currently featuring a story that Madame Nhu's father, the ambassador to Washington, had verbally slapped her wrists for speaking disrespectfully of Buddhists. A stall in the shady corner of the courtyard was open for business with a monk at the counter offering religious articles, books and pictures of the monk's fiery public suicide for modest prices; but the display was not sufficiently enticing for one middle-aged American woman tourist in a bright print dress whom I saw glance at the wares in the shop and walk on. In the cloisters of one building, brown-robed monks went about their daily chores amid a din of gongs and drums and a mixed smell of incense and sewage. On the street outside the pagoda walls, which had been topped the week before with barbed wire, news reporters arrived and nodded to security police, familiar with one another now after frequent scuffles at demonstrations. A hawker was selling cigarette lighters with lacquered flags emblazoned on both sides, on one the five-colored patchwork Buddhist flag, on the other side the national flag. The salesman explained, "It's hard to tell who's going to win this thing but with the flags of each side on the lighters we can't lose."

Ambassador Nolting's indifference to the Buddhists was based on his belief that the movement was political and not religious, "misinterpreted in our own country and in other countries, Europe and Canada and other places, as a genuine revolt on religious grounds against an oppressive Roman Catholic regime, it was called." Nolting thought they were trying to undermine the Saigon regime, a situation that he believed hurt American interests. He encouraged Diem at his final meeting to "treat this matter gently and reach a political compromise and exacted a promise that the Vietnamese would not order violent action against the Buddhists." Nolting "never had reason to doubt his [Diem's] word, he was always honest with me and I tried to be completely honest with him." Present at the departing ambassador's airport farewell party was the president's enigmatic younger brother Ngo Dinh Nhu, a man Nolting had assiduously attempted to cultivate, spending hours with him in philosophical discussions.

Diem didn't attend the farewell party at the airport; his brother was there in his stead. I watched Nhu, mild-mannered as he chatted to the ambassador. But his sunken cheeks, prominent cheekbones and deeply furrowed brow suggested a moody personality, and in fact Nhu was a loner, with few intimates, with even less crowd appeal than his brother, the remote president. Nhu held no elective post in the regime but he headed the secret police organizations and ran the revolutionary labor party, a nationwide network of informers. He also controlled the one million strong military-type organization called the Republican Youth Movement and directed the important strategic hamlet program. But by far the most important job Nhu held was that of political adviser to his brother the president, a man he dominated intellectually and physically according to Saigon gossip. Little did Nolting know that the philosophical soulmate who bade him such an affectionate farewell at Saigon airport on August 15 was secretly planning to use the time of the vacuum between American ambassadors to launch a series of vicious, unprecedented attacks on the holiest places of worship.

When I returned to our office from the airport, Mal wanted me to fly to Nha Trang to cover the aftermath of the immolation of the first Buddhist nun. I was happy to be heading to the coastal resort famous for its white beaches, lobsters and tiny bikinis. But a demonstration was in progress in Nha Trang as our plane arrived, and tanks and troops were on the streets trying to enforce a curfew. I learned that the authorities seized the nun's body and had given it a pauper's funeral.

I retreated to François's Hotel and Restaurant on the beach, a landmark since the French era, to reexamine my options. Early Sunday morning I hired a cyclo and pedaled up the coast road to Ninh Hoa. I was prevented from entering the village by soldiers who turned me around and sent me back to Nha Trang. I tried to visit the blockaded Hoi Pagoda, where the monks were demanding the return of the nun's body, but again soldiers kept me away. Angry onlookers glared at the military men, disregarding the smell of tear gas that hung in the air. Over the phone Mal told me that Hue, Da Nang and Saigon were erupting in demonstrations after yet another immolation, this time by a monk in Hue. I said a government official had informed me confidently, "We are capable of handling any further demonstrations," but Mal said, "Don't you believe it. The whole place is going sky high."

He was right; it blew up Monday night, August 21. Earlier that day the monks at Xa Loi expressed concern that Ambassador Lodge's three-day delay in arriving in Saigon could bode ill for their movement. Thich Duc Nghiep told Mal he was afraid that the government would try to play a terrible trick on them: a false assassination attempt on Lodge for which the Buddhists would be blamed, for example, or a phony coup d'etat. Mal watched young monks hauling benches across the floor evidently as barricades. But the Xa Loi Pagoda remained visually cheerful, the blue neon swastika, the Buddhist emblem, glowing from the pinnacle of its central building with colored lights strung around the stone archway into the courtyard.

At about eleven o'clock that night, Duc Nghiep phoned Browne at his apartment, telling him that he had just received news that the police had orders to mass around Xa Loi. At about twenty minutes past midnight he called again. "The police have come. They're at the gate. Tell the American Embassy quickly." Then the line went dead and when Mal arrived at the scene several minutes later he found that several hundred American-trained Special Forces troops, police and uniformed palace guards had blasted their way through Xa Loi's iron gates with explosives. News reporters were chased from the immediate area at pistol point as monks and nuns were dragged into the courtyard and driven off in trucks, and by 1:30 A.M. the whole pagoda, including most of Vietnam's top Buddhist priests, was entirely empty. Only two escaped, monks who scaled the concrete wall of the neighboring U.S. aid mission.

Similar scenes were taking place everywhere in South Vietnam; all key pagodas were hit, the monks and nuns arrested and beaten, their bedding, furniture and doorways smashed and ripped with bayonets. It happened at Nha Trang, too, but since I was prevented from going anywhere near the main pagoda, I flew back to Saigon. By now more than one thousand monks and nuns had been arrested, martial law had been declared across the country and troops had taken over the telecommunications center and all other key installations. There would be tough curfews, rigid press censorship and other restrictions. I was able to contribute a story to our coverage, expressing the anger of American servicemen who had seen the violence or were near at hand when it occurred. A U.S. Army captain told me in Nha Trang, "In one night Diem lost all the goodwill that we had helped build up here in the past eighteen months." Another U.S. officer who said he had just returned from a grueling forty-four-day patrol in the Central Highlands complained to me at François's Restaurant, "We are trying our utmost to win people to the Saigon government in the mountains but we are losing them in the cities."

For the reporters there was anxiety that we would be the next targets. For three months the Buddhists had been a front page story. Official Saigon hated us. Mal and I discussed checking out of our apartments and into the Caravelle Hotel for safety. Some correspondents moved into the homes of American diplomats for a few days. One day the Australian correspondent Dennis Warner came to me and whispered, "Peter, you're the top of the hit list now because of your Nha Trang trip."

There was a near news blackout; the rigid censorship had cut us off from the rest of the world and we were in an hourly race with our competition to find ways to slip our reports to the outside world. The embassy had promised us some cooperation in sending news dispatches but had only allowed UPI the privilege, leaving the AP far behind. Mal raged at the chargé d'affaires, William Trueheart, who claimed the stories were being held up in Washington. There was no Mekong River for me to swim across this time.

The New Ambassador

HENRY CABOT LODGE arrived on the scene with an outstretched hand. We clutched at it eagerly. The conventional wisdom among the journalists was that Nolting's "sink or swim with Ngo Dinh Diem" policy was being replaced by a more demanding attitude toward human rights and political freedoms, military competence and accountability.

If anyone could shake things up in the embassy, my American colleagues argued, it would be Lodge. Halberstam and Sheehan, both well versed in New England patrician lore, joked in our escorted bus heading through the curfew-silent streets to the airport to cover his arrival that Lodge's appointment was a challenge to the Vietnamese authorities that "our old Mandarin can lick your old Mandarin."

Lodge had radioed from the plane that he would have no statement to make. But the tall figure who emerged from the air force DC-6 and climbed briskly down the steps didn't disappoint us when he saw the television lights and three dozen eager upturned faces. He had some warm words about American democracy and the essential role of the press, and harked back to his days with the *New York Herald Tribune* when he had made his first trip to Vietnam as a youthful reporter. He promised to help us do our jobs, and with a tip of his hat was off into the dark night with his wife, Emily.

There was no news in Lodge's statement, but some solace: his assurance of support suggested that our isolation was ending. As a gesture, he allowed four newsmen to accompany him on the flight from Tachikawa air force base, one of them Robert Eunson, the AP's chief executive in Asia. Eunson took me aside and said, "The ambassador's on our side," then introduced me to one of Lodge's aides, Major John Michael "Mike" Dunn, who nodded his head in confirmation.

A few days later Lodge invited Mal Browne to a private lunch and told him that he had seen Mal's picture of the immolation of Thich

Quang Duc on President Kennedy's desk. He later elaborated to me, "I remember going into the Oval Office and there was the picture of this old man sitting cross-legged burning himself alive, and President Kennedy said, 'Look at that, look at what things have come to in Vietnam. I have confidence in you, I want you to go out there and see if we can't get the government to behave better.' "

If at the time we were exaggerating Lodge's commitment to our journalistic rights, there was no argument that he was comfortable with the press, and that he had clearly arrived in Saigon with President Kennedy's directive to shake up the Saigon regime. Unlike our numerous critics, he did not appeal to us for restraint; instead he seemed to encourage our analysis, seeing it as another weapon to force change.

Lodge was quickly and conspicuously visible in Saigon. On his first morning he drove along the city's embattled streets through intersections where armed soldiers stood with bayonets bared, and past city parks where tanks and armored cars waited ready for action. On some street corners anxious residents gathered in hushed knots exchanging the latest rumors and wondering what would happen next. Along one thoroughfare near the compound of Saigon University, more than two thousand bicycles and scooters and motorcycles were piled up on the sidewalks under the tamarind trees, mute witness to the arrests of many hundreds of students, and their continued incarceration.

The ambassador visited two Buddhist monks who had been granted asylum at the U.S. Military Assistance and Advisory headquarters on Pasteur Street. By his first weekend he had presented his credentials to President Diem and met with Ngo Dinh Nhu, privately telling reporters afterward that he was not impressed with either of them and would continue to apply pressure for reforms. Lodge endeared himself to us by wandering around the city with his wife and an aide or two.

The ambassador defied his security guards by inviting fifteen of us on one unorthodox sightseeing jaunt, strolling along the Rue Catinat toward the Presidential Palace, and at six feet three inches tall towering over most of us and looking relaxed with his shirt open at the collar. Just hours earlier a huge government demonstration had been held in the vicinity. Thousands had shouted support for the regime, and those troops standing guard at the intersections who recognized Lodge stared with their mouths open. Newsboys tried to sell him copies of the local English language paper, the *Saigon Post,* which featured a blistering attack on the U.S. State Department. Lodge smiled at the newsboys and said, "No thanks, I've got it." He stopped two nineteen-year-old American GIs walking along the Catinat and asked them how they were and wished them good luck. A Vietnamese civil servant leaned out a window and yelled to a newsman, "What the hell is going on here?" When told, he answered, "It's a revolution; this is the first American ambassador who has ever walked this way along the Catinat."

Lodge fired the first warning shots at the Diem regime but its defenses were strong and the sallies were ignored. When the ambassador made a formal protest over the censorship of the press, the authorities simply tightened the controls.

Our days and nights were filled with the challenge not only of gathering the news but getting it out. The first hurdle was the censor's office in a government building near the central market, where we were required to take all our news copy and photos to military censors and later civilian officials for clearance. They would quibble over the smallest points.

On August 27, the censor mutilated one of my dispatches, allowing me to write that we had entered the seventh day of martial law, but crossing out with a thick red crayon the next sentence, which stated, "Troop concentrations in some key downtown areas are still heavy, particularly the plaza in front of City Hall." I was allowed to state that barbed wire barricades were lifted early Tuesday from the uptown area, but the censor crossed out the rest of the sentence, which read, ". . . where Saigon University's faculties of law, medicine and pharmacy are situated. Many students were arrested by police there Sunday as they converged for a demonstration." I was permitted to say that civilian censors had taken over the job of processing news copy, but I was forbidden to report that many people arrested earlier in the week had been freed. The censor stamped and signed his approval, and then a final opinion was necessary from the military governor's office, where another stamp was applied to each page. Often up to 90 percent of our dispatches were cut and sometimes whole reports were struck. They even cut out descriptions of President Diem as a Roman Catholic.

Transmitting photos was just as difficult. Censors allowed pictures of Ambassador Lodge presenting his credentials to President Diem, but they were later rejected by the military governor's office and were not sent. Television and radio reporters lost direct contact with their home offices when all international phone lines were cut. Even the

U.S. Military Assistance Command's official organ, the *Observer,* required approval. Peter Kalischer declared that the censorship was worse than the Kremlin's.

We fought back as best we could, sending carbon copies of our stories and extra prints of photos by hand carriers, usually Westerners flying out of Saigon on late-afternoon flights to Bangkok, Hong Kong and Manila, where we hoped they would deliver the material to our bureaus. We bribed the amateur couriers with a fee of fifty or one hundred dollars, and labeled the packages "Bundles for Bassett" in honor of our foreign editor, Ben Bassett. They usually got delivered, though some packages didn't make it. It was like throwing a sealed bottle into the South China Sea and hoping for the best. Sometimes, we pulled some pretty good fast ones. Mal scored a news beat by replacing an innocent caption on an approved photo of a street scene with the dramatic news that Foreign Minister Vu Van Mau had shaved his head and resigned his job in protest over the pagoda raids. The photo and the trick caption were wired out of the country and our New York headquarters was so ecstatic over our enterprise that they wrote a story about it for our hundreds of subscribers, including the Voice of America, which broadcast it back to Saigon. We were sure that the authorities were aware that contraband news and photos were getting through the airport but didn't come to stop us. Perhaps they wanted to avoid disorderly confrontations.

There were those in the mainstream American media who did not like what we were doing and complained that our reporting was wrecking a critically important American policy. They blamed our "insensitivity" on our inexperience. Joseph Alsop, the immensely influential columnist, began calling us "young crusaders" and complaining, "It is easy enough to paint a dark, indignant picture without departing from the facts if you ignore the majority of Americans who admire the Vietnamese as fighters and seek out the one U.S. officer in ten who inevitably thinks that all foreigners fight badly." A star reporter from the Korean War and World War Two, Marguerite Higgins, was in Saigon often. She accused us of being unpatriotic, aiming her sharpest barbs at Halberstam, who returned them enthusiastically. The word went around town that she had told acquaintants in Saigon, "Reporters here would like to see us lose the war to prove they're right." *Time* magazine suggested we were excitable youths overwhelmed by the story and dead wrong in how we were reporting it. Charles Mohr, *Time*'s Southeast Asia bureau chief, quit in anger along with the *Time* stringer in Saigon, Merton Perry.

A few weeks later, *Time* revised its assessment, beginning a story, "Someday there will be novels about that hardy band of U.S. correspondents covering the war in Vietnam in 1963. Presumably, being fiction, they will make everything clear and have everything come out right. But today telling the truth about the Saigon press corps is a difficult job." The article went on to say, "Personally, the correspondents are serious, somewhat on the young side, ambitious, convivial, in love with their work. So in love in fact that they talk about little else. They have a strong sense of mission." We also had our supporters, often editors from American newspapers who came out to see for themselves what all the fuss was about and checked in with our Saigon bureau, joining us in our reporting and social sorties.

Our troubles with the AP head office had been resolved when the battle of Ap Bac confirmed our assessments of the war effort and undermined Washington's official optimistic pronouncements. The Buddhist crisis had pushed the story onto page one in every newspaper in America, the place the AP yearned to be. Now we had total support from our executives back home. Each day now the Saigon press was attacking us as communist stooges trying to destroy the country, and cartoons depicting foreign correspondents as dangerous political enemies appeared frequently, reflecting the paranoia and the vindictiveness of the regime.

The critics examined us and noted our youth and our small numbers, the massive size of the story and the similarity of our reporting and assumed that we were in collusion. But as the story gained in prominence and a permanent place on page one, the laws of commercial journalism began falling into place and editors back home began evaluating the performances of AP and UPI and the *New York Times*. We all yearned to be first to report the latest development or to write the most perceptive analysis, and were quickly reminded by our competitive foreign desks to pep up if we were too slow.

The most influential correspondents were Mal Browne and Dave Halberstam, both willing to write bold, controversial analyses and both indefatigable. The AP bureau was always well staffed, with Roy Essoyan often in from Tokyo along with Ed White, to help us out; and of course there was the unflagging Horst, who preferred the photo possibilities of the war in the paddyfields of the Mekong Delta and in the Central Highlands to the chaos in Saigon's boulevards.

Sharing their thoughts with us were Beverley Deepe, the only woman reporter living in Saigon at the time, stringing for the *New York Herald Tribune*, François Nivolon of *Le Figaro*, who lived in an apartment in our building, and freelance photographer Michel Renard. At any one time we could assemble soulmates to help us cover the tangle of events in the city. Halberstam was at the core of a group that included Neil Sheehan and Ray Herndon of UPI, Nick Turner of Reuters and Mert Perry, along with the usual numbers of visiting news people.

Two robust groups of competing, ambitious reporters does not make for collusion. We competed day to day and tended to be secretive. We guarded our special sources and insights. Browne's coverage of the immolation of Thich Quang Duc had been a world news and photo scoop; UPI got the better of us with the first reports of the pagoda raids. Halberstam was scoring with his perceptive military analyses.

In the aftermath of the pagoda raids we noticed that UPI, the *New York Times* and Reuters were playing up the potential for a power struggle in the regime. Mal downplayed it.

Official American policy began coalescing around Lodge. His aides leaked us information that when he had met President Diem he disliked Diem's aloof manner and his obscure conversational gambits that avoided realistic discussion of the most pressing issues. The distaste was mutual; Madame Nhu had described Lodge as a "proconsul." President Kennedy told Walter Cronkite, in an interview for CBS, that the Diem regime "has gotten out of touch with its people"; the Voice of America quoted Washington officials as threatening a reduction of the $1.5 million a day aid package unless the ruling family thinned its ranks. Those were all signals of America's desire to see Ngo Dinh Nhu and his wife depart from government.

As Lodge's signals became more blunt our daily reporting hammered the indictment. The protests of the Buddhists were being taken up by the children of the urban middle class; students began barricading themselves in their classrooms in cities across the country. Driving up Doan Thi Diem Street one midmorning I noticed several hundred bicycles thrown under the trees alongside the road and soon learned they belonged to the entire student body of the nearby Marie Curie private girls academy. The girls had been rounded up on their way to school by soldiers and driven off in trucks because of student protests against the regime. Neighbors who witnessed the scene asserted that the vehicles bore the Stars and Stripes and handclasp emblem of U.S. aid to South Vietnam; the letters "US" were stenciled in black paint on the cartridge belts of the troops. By late afternoon desperate parents were searching for their daughters' bicycles and swapping terrifying stories of alleged torture and other atrocities. Among the tight-faced adults at the tearful scene were high-ranking uniformed military men and well-dressed midlevel government officials and I wondered at the stupidity of this crude attempt at intimidation by the regime.

At our New York foreign desk's request I filed this somewhat emotional analysis of the student revolt on September 14. An edited version ran on the AP national wire the next day:

"The satchel-swinging schoolboy has made his unlikely emergence in South Vietnam as the newest symbol of resistance to the authoritarian regime of President Ngo Dinh Diem. Never before has he been much of a force in his nation's destiny. But in the eyes of the Vietnamese population he is now daily winning his spurs in scuffles with troops and combat police. Saigon mothers have come to expect that when he sets off for school in the morning he may not return home for days. So far Saigon authorities have arrested nearly three thousand of his high school and university classmates and flung them into prisons and concentration camps. Over one thousand are still detained. In recent nights, secret police and troops have raided his home under the cover of martial law, dragging him and his sisters off for interrogation. Yet his 'gloriously stupid' protest, as one foreign observer put it, continues; he is still plotting more trouble at more schools. He himself may answer when asked why he defies martial law and throws inkwells and chairs at bayonet-toting troops: 'We are Buddhists and they (the Diem regime) are trying to crush us.' "

I concluded my report by suggesting that the student revolt was a direct result of parental disapproval of the Diem regime, and quoted an unnamed Western observer as seeing the protest as a challenge to communism, which up to that time was regarded as the strongest unifying force in Vietnam. "This is the first true manifestation of public feeling in free Vietnam since Diem took over," I quoted the observer as saying. There were no locators in my story or names because such information could have led to further repression.

Roy Essoyan weighed in with a trenchant, direct analysis of the explosive political situation, quoting one of the fourteen thousand American servicemen in Vietnam as saying, "How long are we going to let them shove us around?" Another adviser was quoted complaining, "When I came out here three months ago my wife thought I was going to be a hero but now she writes me and asks if I am helping President Diem's soldiers to arrest schoolboys." Essoyan added,

"Many Americans here—servicemen, generals, embassy secretaries and diplomats—are beginning to feel the tail has been wagging the dog too long, and that it's got to stop. The big question is how."

If we could believe reports that were leaking from sources inside the American Embassy, Lodge had decided that change could only come with the overthrow, at the appropriate time, of the Diem regime. This view was never officially placed on the record but appeared to be inserted into the rumor mill intentionally. Lodge later told me, "When I first got there there were these rumors about a coup and how I had been sent out from Washington to press the button and bring about the coup. Well, I discovered that there wasn't any button, there was nothing to press, that this was a sort of romance. The Vietnamese generals were unwilling to take us into their confidence because they thought Americans talk too much, that it was impossible for an American to keep a secret. So the whole so-called coup evaporated."

Relations worsened between the U.S. Embassy on Ham Nghi Street and the Presidential Palace opposite our bureau on Rue Pasteur. A coup watch began as we listened for signs of revolt. The ruling family used the pages of the English language *Times of Vietnam* newspaper, run by an American confidant of the Ngo family, Anne Gregory. Under a five-column headline on page one the newspaper editorialized that the visit to Saigon of Defense Secretary Robert McNamara on September 24 was planned to pave the way for the destruction of the regime. Under similar-sized black headlines the next day Mrs. Gregory asserted that the CIA had already launched two failed coup attempts and was working on a third. What had really happened was that on August 24 the State Department had messaged Ambassador Lodge to express to the Vietnamese generals America's concern over the situation, a cable interpreted as a green light for a coup d'etat.

Madame Nhu, who was traveling abroad, said at a press conference in Rome that young American army officers stationed in South Vietnam were "engaging in irresponsible behavior and acting like little soldiers of fortune." We passed the telexed reports of these remarks on to the American Embassy, shaking Lodge out of his public silence. He dictated a response that was quickly phoned to us by his press aide. "It is a shocking statement. These junior officers are risking their lives every day. Some of them have been killed side by side with their Vietnamese comrades. It is incomprehensible to me how anyone can speak so cruelly. These men should be thanked not insulted."

The war of words was accompanied by a war of nerves. Mal told me one afternoon that he had learned that Lodge sat at his desk with a loaded pistol beside him because of the stream of assassination threats relayed to the embassy, threats that could come only from the very same government security apparatus obligated to protect Lodge and the foreign community.

By late autumn, there were some in the American mission who were arguing that President Diem was responding positively to the American demand for policy change, that he was reconciling himself to removing his brother and sister-in-law, and that he was prepared to conciliate with the Buddhists. Officers on General Harkins's staff were arguing that the almost forgotten military situation was not worsening and that some needed administrative reforms were being made. To press for what would amount to Diem's surrender, the United States began suspending some aid to Vietnam. The Kennedy administration also announced a bold move that was aimed at confounding critics at home and abroad, declaring in early October that American advisers could be safely phased out of Vietnam by 1965, and that the first one thousand would be home for Christmas. In an analysis written for the AP that day I wrote:

"The Kennedy administration appears to have taken a calculated risk in forecasting that the major part of the U.S. military task in South Vietnam can be completed by 1965. A high American source admitted Friday that the optimistic report given to Kennedy by Defense Secretary Robert McNamara 'took in a lot of imponderables' relating to the Vietnam armed forces' ability to hold guerrilla territory that they are now contesting, and also the professional standards of the army itself."

In later years a conspiracy theory would take shape around Kennedy's decision to start withdrawing the troops in 1963, a theory that suggested he was assassinated the following month by extreme conservative elements who believed such a policy would deliver South Vietnam to the communists. Had Kennedy's policy been implemented there is no doubt in my mind that the communists would have been in a commanding position to settle the war on their terms, but I don't believe for a moment that the American president planned to move ahead unless other elements fell into place that would guarantee the peace. In my story, I quoted a highly placed source as saying that the Kennedy administration's interpretation of a completed military task in South Vietnam was what it took to reduce counterinsurgency to proportions that could be handled by the Vietnamese Army itself, that is, a guerrilla movement with its back broken and unable to

115

organize the kind of attacks that had taken place earlier in the year.

I concluded, "The general impression in Saigon is that McNamara and Taylor ordered military leaders to come up with an estimation when the United States could profitably pull out. A highly placed source told me, 'McNamara wanted to know if we could win, if we could win with Diem, and if we could pull out.' This new policy statement sort of takes all three of those factors into mind." Looking back, it seems to me that Kennedy was exercising his political options, signaling the recalcitrant Ngo Dinh Diem that the United States was not necessarily in the war to the end, and showing increasingly strident domestic critics of the Saigon government that he was flexible in Southeast Asia.

On October 5, a Vietnamese woman called several correspondents, promising that "something will happen at the Central Market today." Roy Essoyan and I walked to the market searching for the mobile "antisuicide" squads that still roamed the streets in jeeps loaded with fire extinguishers and armed soldiers. Our small cameras were tucked away in our pockets. *Washington Post* reporter John Sharkey was already at the traffic island trying unsuccessfully to look inconspicuous. David Halberstam arrived along with Grant Wolfkill of NBC, who was carrying a sturdy Bolex camera behind his back. The quorum of resident reporters was enough to worry the security police, and I noticed several familiar faces watching us from the far side of Le Loi Boulevard. As traffic thinned after the noontime rush, we figured we'd been given a bum steer and discussed going to lunch down the street.

I hardly noticed the small blue Saigon taxi slide around the traffic circle and come to a stop ten feet in front of me. The door flew open and a young man emerged quickly, clasping something to his body. "By God, an immolation," I heard Essoyan shout, but I doubted it. This man had his head shaved, but was dressed in brown cotton religious robes, not the yellow ceremonial cloth of the ritual suicide.

As the taxi sped off, the man pulled a small jerry can from his bag and squatted down on his haunches in the lotus position. His eyes gazing off into the middle distance, he emptied the can into his lap, drew a small cardboard box from his left sleeve and lit a match. The tiny yellow flame flickered as he touched it to his garment. He returned his hands to his knees, making no sound at all, even when the red flames burst around him. As the blaze leapt up to his face, I had to back away from the searing heat. I saw him wince and grit his teeth, but that was his only expression.

But I was remembering Madame Nhu's mocking description of these

Buddhist immolations as "barbecues." I clicked my camera a few times and tried to make notes but my hands were shaking with terror.

Essoyan was ashen-faced next to me. A low moan rose from the gathering crowd. I heard a woman laugh hysterically; a baby held in the arms of another woman cried and cried but the mother's eyes were rooted to the burning monk. A young man in the crowd pushed at Essoyan and me and said, "You take pictures, you write story. You must tell Mr. Kennedy what is going on in this country." A woman grabbed me by the shirt, and with tears streaming down her face she tried to say something but the words would not come. She kept pointing to the monk and pulling at my shirt as the flames crackled around his body. A policeman grabbed the conical straw hat off a Vietnamese woman vendor's head and made his way through the crowd and tried to blow the flames out but his efforts only fanned the fire and it roared higher. The policeman staggered back clutching his stomach; the murmur of the crowd rose to a muted growl punctuated by wails and cries. Finally, a man in military uniform threw a thick straw mat over the prostrate form and firemen turned extinguishers on the flames. A Vietnamese paramedic unit bundled his body in a sack and threw it into a waiting ambulance and drove off. All that remained was a charred circle on the sidewalk covered with foamy fire extinguisher liquid.

The antisuicide squads had missed their chance but the security police jumped the photographers less than a minute after the monk lit his match. I put my camera in my pocket, hoping to sneak away with the few frames I had taken. The goons were concentrating on Grant Wolfkill, trying to grab his camera, but he was tall and held it up over his shoulder, far above the heads of the small Vietnamese security men. Wolfkill was a veteran and had been shot down in a helicopter over Laos in 1961 and held for fifteen months by the Pathet Lao, six of those months in wooden stocks: he was not going to surrender his prize easily.

I saw Halberstam and Sharkey rush to his assistance and there was shouting and flailing arms, and I moved toward them until I felt the hands of a security man patting down my body. I knew I had to save the photographs. I pulled away from my assailant and dodged through the crowd, slipping across to the market as soldiers and tanks began arriving. On Le Thanh Ton Street I picked up speed and ran behind the Gia Long Palace to our office.

Horst sent his log notes to photo headquarters in New York that evening, explaining what happened next: "I walked into the office and

Arnett gasped, 'There's been another burning,' and handed me two cameras. The Minolta that Essoyan used had jammed before he could take a shot. The Leica Arnett used had condensed water inside from a previous military operation and all five negatives were fogged. With heavy heart I worked over Arnett's negatives, developing them shorter than usual and printing them on extra hard paper. They looked eventually like prints from an 8mm movie camera but they were usable. As Essoyan rushed in to write new leads to the story, Arnett rushed out and found a hand carrier heading for a plane to Hong Kong. Within eighty minutes of the burning the pigeon was on his way. The Saigon government blocked our picture transmission from the post office but the pigeon got through. And Arnett did manage to dictate three takes of the story to Paris by telephone."

Essoyan had more to tell. A dozen plainclothes security police had pressed their assault against our colleagues, trying to grab Wolfkill's movie camera, the only one at the suicide scene. As he had come to my assistance in an alley months earlier, Halberstam rushed in to assist Wolfkill, plowing through the goons. The cameraman was knocked against a parked car but he was able to pass the camera on to John Sharkey, who then had to contend with a security man jumping on his brawny shoulders. Sharkey passed it on to Halberstam, who tried to make an end run to a nearby hotel, but was knocked down and the camera skittered across the sidewalk. Wolfkill planted a protective foot on the equipment but a plainclothesman kicked it from under him and it flew off the curb into the arms of another policeman, who tucked it under his arm and ran off.

The goons were just beginning to fight. As Sharkey was bending down to help pull Halberstam up from the sidewalk, a policeman smashed a wooden stool on his head, inflicting a wound that took six stitches to close. Wolfkill was clubbed in the back with a pistol butt and looked up to see a policeman waving a gun in his face. It was not the violence he later remembered but the frustration of missing the scoop, "The heartbreaker of having such a sensational event on film and then having it stolen from you."

Ambassador Lodge made a formal protest. The immolation of the young man brought another confrontation between the American government and the Diem regime, but worse, it revived the specter of more fiery suicides and more protest demonstrations, something the authorities assumed they had put to rest with the pagoda raids six weeks earlier.

Our journalistic efforts did not impress all our subscribers. An editorial in the *New York Herald Tribune* complained that the Saigon press corps had its priorities askew, that we should have saved the monk's life rather than let him die.

My response was that perhaps I could have prevented the immolation by rushing at the monk and kicking the gasoline away if I'd had my wits about me. As a human being I wanted to; as a reporter I couldn't. If I had stopped him, the secret police who were watching from a distance would have arrested him immediately and carried him off to God knows where, and this was at a time when we believed that opposition monks were secretly being killed. If I had attempted to prevent them doing this I would have propelled myself directly into Vietnamese politics; my role as a reporter would have been destroyed along with my credibility.

In his comprehensive analysis of relations between the press and the military during the Vietnam War, army historian William M. Hammond quotes my response but takes issue with my reasoning, stating that by releasing what I had seen to the world I had intervened in South Vietnamese politics as surely as if I had lit the monk's match. I don't think it is fair to blame the messenger for the content of what he carries. The Greeks used to kill the bearers of bad tidings.

The Coup

CROWDS GATHERED for five days at street corners throughout Saigon, their heads craned to the sky waiting for a Buddhist miracle that had been predicted by a soothsayer, an act of the creator that would shake the sun out of position. "Even the heavens are protesting the miserable fate of Vietnamese Buddhists," one of the sun watchers said. "I have heard that the sun has begun turning in small circles in the sky as a sign from heaven." Soldiers with orders to prevent public assembly were breaking up groups of skywatchers wherever they found them but the security men themselves were noticed squinting into the sun, swept up in the dark mysteries and holy miracles that were casting long shadows over superstitious Vietnam.

If the Ngo family read anything into the celestial portents they did not reveal it. They were more concerned with the down-to-earth machinations of their armed forces, which had been shaken by the Buddhist rebellion and the viciousness of its repression.

There had been obvious enough signals of encouragement from the U.S. government for a forced change of regimes, enough writing on the wall for ambitious generals to read; a series of critical pronouncements on the Voice of America, a threat to cut back the aid program, a stubborn "proconsul" of an ambassador who had cut contact with the government down to the bare minimum. We could only guess at the behind-the-scenes conspiracies and at the level at which they were being conceived. And the regime was paranoid.

On October 30, Miss Ly Thi Lien was cycling past the Caravelle Hotel in downtown Saigon wearing her white ao-dai dress when a *Newsweek* photographer called her over to pose with Ambassador Henry Cabot Lodge. The high school student was on her way home to a Catholic orphanage where she lived with her mother, but she agreed to the request, pleasing the amiable ambassador, who chatted with her briefly. A half a block away a plainclothes policeman arrested her and led her off, presumably to find out what she had talked about with the ambassador. Indignant American Embassy officials began an immediate investigation through the Foreign Ministry and the teenaged girl was released later the next day and allowed to go home.

Western reporters, who were often the first to know of impending public suicides or demonstrations, were under heavy surveillance. Mal noticed that the office and his apartment were continually watched by plainclothesmen. Fearing an "official burglary," Mal sent a case of private files over to the U.S. Embassy for safekeeping. We knew the office telephones were tapped and every call coming in was accompanied by a telltale ping in the line that meant someone was monitoring. Some people who telephoned the office were arrested, and for a while we answered, "Associated Press, this line is being monitored by public officials. Go ahead please." Five chauffeurs who worked for foreign correspondents were arrested and interrogated about their activities, and desk clerks at the Caravelle and Majestic hotels, where many visiting correspondents stayed, were instructed to furnish reporters only with cars with government drivers.

The authorities were watching the wrong people. We were the last to know about what was really going down. Keyes Beech of the *Chicago Daily News* was so convinced that all coup ideas had perished that he wrote a story that appeared in newspapers of October 30 headlined, "Why the U.S. Didn't Oust Diem." He wrote, "The fact must be faced. Americans can produce more autos, more bathtubs, more telephones, more wheat and more corn—along with the silos to store it in—than any other people in the world. But Americans aren't any good at overthrowing governments, and the latest government we haven't bounced is the family concern in South Vietnam."

But by next day, Friday, November 1, the air was electric with rumors and tension. The city was empty and silent for the traditional noon siesta when Henry Cabot Lodge called on Ngo Dinh Diem for a farewell visit before his departure for consultations in Washington two days later. When Lodge was saying goodbye to Diem I was in Laos, on a three-week assignment in my old stamping ground of Vientiane, about to take off on a return flight back to Saigon. I had been watching the news with interest but I had no inkling that a coup d'etat was near. Years later, Lodge recalled Diem telling him, "Every time an American ambassador goes away somebody starts a coup." Lodge added, "Diem said I know there is going to be a coup but I don't know who's going to do it or where he's going to do it at, and the coup planners are much cleverer this time than they've ever been before because there are a number of them and I can't find out which is the real one." Lodge recalled seeing Admiral Harry D. Felt off at the airport and returning to his villa with Harkins, "And we were sitting having lunch when there was this tremendous automatic fire, it sounded as though it were right in the next room, and the planes flew overhead, and that was the beginning of the overthrow."

An hour earlier Mal had been alerted to unusually heavy military activity around the central police station. Then a source we employed in the American Embassy security detail called with the news that a coup was in progress, and that the naval headquarters on the riverfront was already under siege and surrounded by rebel troops. Mal jumped into the office jeep and raced over to the navy compound ten minutes away. He was half a block beyond a security post before he heard a guard yelling and had to turn back. It was not until the bombers roared over at about 3 P.M. that the certainty of battle became apparent; the combined sounds of the bombing and strafing of the Presidential Palace across the street and the heavy anti-aircraft return fire was shattering and frightening. A loyalist guard may have saved Mal's life by yanking him through a hole in a wall out of reach of the burst of an incoming shell.

My Air Vietnam passenger jet touched down at Phnom Penh and was flying into Vietnamese airspace around three o'clock when it veered sharply and began returning to Phnom Penh. I banged on the pilot's cabin door and my fears were confirmed by the captain, who

121

was talking with an air traffic controller; a coup d'etat was in progress; bombers were in the air over Saigon, blasting the Presidential Palace. I would miss the biggest story of my life because Tan Son Nhut Airport was closed to all traffic.

I begged the pilot to reconsider. I raised terrible possibilities about the fate of his and his crew's families in the embattled city; I argued that the aircraft had a right to land on its own soil. Miraculously the captain agreed. As he wheeled the aircraft around in the sky he told the Saigon traffic controller he was coming in anyway and would stay low and make a direct approach. Twenty minutes later we touched down at the tense airport ringed by tanks and armored cars.

The ground crews had fled. Smoke was rising over downtown Saigon three miles away and the muffled crack of artillery and small arms fire echoed through the airport terminal. The taxi stands were abandoned and I waited impatiently for transportation. An airline bus took me as far as the new Presidential Palace before the driver lost his nerve and dumped me off. I dodged down Rue Pasteur toward our office from one tamarind tree to the other. Gunfire roared and ricocheted around me. I could see soldiers firing from upper-story windows at the Gia Long Palace. Our three-story office and apartment building had been turned into a fort with soldiers firing their weapons at the palace across the street, protecting themselves behind makeshift sandbagged emplacements in the parking lot and the first-floor balcony outside my apartment door.

I burst into the office. Ed White was sitting at a typewriter, quietly tapping away. He looked up at me and said, "The others are at the Caravelle and I'm holding the fort, which is something I've said plenty of times in the past but for once it is true." Ed looked relaxed puffing on his pipe. He said normal communications had been completely cut off when the coup began but that we had managed to send several dispatches through the American and Korean embassies and he said we were more comfortable with the story than we had a right to be. I suggested he leave the office before darkness fell.

During a lull in the shooting I made my way to the Caravelle. Mal and Roy Essoyan were surveying the city landscape from the upper floors, pointing out to me the continuing major battle centers at the Gia Long Palace and the Palace Guard barracks—ablaze after its ammunition storage depot had been hit. With only a few shots fired, the national and municipal police headquarters and the Defense Ministry had been seized in the first few minutes of the insurrection along with the radio station and the telecommunications center. The naval headquarters on the riverfront was taken after a series of bombing attacks by six fighter-bombers. The rumors and the speculation of months past were coming true before my eyes and I watched it all, with a glass of Johnnie Walker Red Label Scotch in one hand and a cigarette in the other.

I walked down to the Catinat and two American soldiers stopped me and asked me the way to the nearest open bar. Children were dashing around the sidewalks laughing and collecting spent cartridges in the dusk, and a mother played with her young son on the grassy traffic circle in plain view of a tank. Two American drunks sauntered past the National Assembly building; one of them complained loudly, "Tell them to knock that off, they're scaring everybody." I walked over to the Rex Hotel, an American military billet whose rooftop officers mess overlooked the palace; the place was crowded with soldiers warned off the streets. They were whiling away the time rolling dice or playing the slot machines.

Mal suggested I stake out the U.S. military mission overnight and I made my way carefully back up Pasteur Street. There was plenty of coffee and cookies on the table, enough for a full night's vigil. A U.S. intelligence officer offered to brief us in the evening about what he was learning—a rare display of generosity toward the media.

Radio traffic revealed that the coup was being led by two popular officers, Generals Tran Van Don and Duong Van Minh, and was backed by practically every senior commander in the armed forces. The apparent clockwork precision of the operation led our briefing officer to comment, "It shows that the Vietnamese can run a pretty good war if political considerations are removed," and I got the feeling that he was already recasting in his mind the dramatis personae, setting the stage for the new players in the show.

By midnight the Palace Guard barracks fell after a pitched tank battle that blew out the center of the rambling, six-story structure. That left the Gia Long Palace as the last symbol of the Diem regime. Tanks began moving as quietly as their clanking treads permitted, slipping across main boulevards from the west and from the riverfront, taking up positions outside the palace walls. At 4 A.M. the attack began. The blast of cannon, machine guns and rapid-fire pieces blended into a continuous roar. The dark shapes in the street spat clouds of green, yellow and blue fire and great lobs of red flame marked the exploding shells. Buildings near the palace became infernos. Soldiers darted from door to door to get closer. The defenders held out bravely for more than two hours. At 6:37 A.M. a white flag was finally hoisted from the palace and a cheer broke out from the street outside as rebel marines poured in through gaping holes in the wall surrounding the compound and claimed their prize.

I returned to my apartment to find the bodies of two dead soldiers on the balcony, their blood staining the tiles. Big chunks of concrete were torn out of the building walls but our apartments and office were not damaged. We learned that Diem and his brother Nhu had somehow escaped and fled to the suburbs. But by that afternoon word came that they had given up and then died.

We all regrouped at the Caravelle Hotel for breakfast, grimy, exhausted but elated that it was all over and that we were alive. Horst had arrived back from a Mekong Delta operation in time to enter the palace with the victorious marines, and we were soon out on the streets again, watching delirious crowds ransacking Ngo family businesses and tearing down statues. That night the generals who had plotted Diem's overthrow traveled the nightclub circuit, partying with the citizenry and toasting a new era. I joined Generals Don and Minh at the La Cigale.

·   ·   ·

We pieced together the inside details of the coup as best we could. We were told that Lodge talked with Diem. The Vietnamese leader had telephoned him from the palace in the afternoon to inform him that the coup had started. He asked the ambassador what he intended to do. Lodge said, "I told him the obvious truth, that I had no instructions and that it was four o'clock in the morning in Washington, and I had no opportunity to get instructions. 'Oh, well,' Diem said, 'you must know what the policy is,' and I responded that I did not know what the policy was for every circumstance, adding that I was worried about his safety and that I had made arrangements for him to get safely out of the country. I also told him, 'I have made arrangements that would authorize you becoming titular head of state and you can stay here in a position of honor and you'll be relatively safe.' 'Well,' Diem said, 'I don't want to do that, I want to restore order and I'm going back now to restore order,' and with that he hung up."

The American ambassador was lying to Diem and the Vietnamese leader had guessed it. Lodge told me that he had not known the exact timing of the coup. "I wasn't brought into the picture in a complete way until the night before," he said. General Harkins was mostly in the dark and, when he was made aware of it, he had informed Lodge of his deep opposition, but by then nothing could stop it.

General Tran Van Don told me that in the late autumn he had personally asked Lodge for the support of the United States in overthrowing Diem, and the coup plotters had used a veteran CIA agent Lucien Conein as the go-between. Conein was a familiar figure in Saigon, a stocky talkative man, a frequent habitué of the Continental Hotel bar and other watering places. Conein later said he was with the coup plotters when they implemented their scheme, carried a special radio that kept him on a special net directly to the American Embassy, and had been given a direct telephone line to the embassy.

It was Conein who had tried to arrange for an aircraft to fly Diem and his brother out of the country. The plane was never needed. On the orders of one of the rebels, Diem and his brother were murdered in an armored car after surrendering from a hideout in Cholon. Initially, we had had only scattered initial reports of the murders and were desperate to confirm them. Our suspicions were verified when a Vietnamese Army major came to our "temporary bureau" at the Caravelle Hotel with pictures of the remains of the brothers inside a military vehicle. He offered to sell us the pictures for two thousand dollars, and while Essoyan was on the phone to our New York headquarters haggling over the price, the officer disappeared. He sold the photos to UPI.

The bloody conclusion of the coup did not please President Kennedy. General Maxwell Taylor told me in a later interview that he was in a White House meeting with the president when "the cable came in, as I recall, brought in to him from outside by one of his aides and put in front of him and he read it. And there was a great silence around the table and the president was obviously shaken by this and sprang to his feet and walked out of the room saying nothing to anybody, and stayed out of the room for some minutes and eventually came and took his chair, collected, and then discussing as we all did the consequences and the causes and what would we do about it."

The fears of Diem's critics were confirmed when the prisons were opened and thousands of political detainees emerged with tales of torture and abuse. One of these was Hoang Thi Dong, a twenty-nine-year-old Buddhist woman who held a clerical job at the British Embassy, and who was arrested at 5 A.M. on the morning of the coup by security police. In a quiet voice she told how they had driven her blindfolded in a jeep to a house where several other women were being detained, how she was led into an office about an hour later, her blindfold removed, and was informed by a man at the desk that they learned she had been taking Buddhist documents to the British Embassy, giving them to foreign correspondents and also to the United Nations office and the U.S. Information Service.

After denying that she knew the whereabouts of a prominent fugitive Buddhist monk, Miss Dong said two more men came into the room, and she described what happened next in a quavering voice. "They made me sit on a bench and stripped me. They made me lie down and one tied my hands behind the bench while the other tied my feet and hips down. They put a cloth over my nose and mouth, and poured water over the cloth from a filthy can I had noticed on the floor when I walked in. One of the men stuck his fists into my sides and another slapped my cheeks and I screamed when they released the cloth for a moment. One jumped up and down on me to force the water out of my mouth and the other beat my legs with a club and I became unconscious. When I came to they made me get up and clean the room and get dressed and told me I would be tortured again in the afternoon because they said they had decided that I was a communist agent and should be punished."

Dong said a young girl was taken to the room after her, and she heard her screaming, but she also heard the sound of aircraft in the sky and jeeps and motorcycles were roaring in the vicinity and someone shouted that the air force was making a revolution.

"We waited all through the night and through Saturday and saw military trucks pass by and officials burning papers and we prayed that the government side would lose because if they didn't then we would surely die." She said the torturers finally released them and apologized for their behavior.

Another student told Mal bitterly, "Americans must share some responsibility for these things. You must have known about them for a long time, but you closed your eyes and went on training and equipping the police. I have heard American newsmen saw Nazi concentration camps in Germany and wrote nice reports about the flowers they saw planted outside."

The new era dawning in Saigon seemed to have an element of hope. The air in the city was taking on a strange new quality, an intangible sort of feeling made up of many little things, the most important of which was probably the relative absence of fear. People weren't looking over their shoulders, they didn't stop in midsentence to wonder if they were being overheard. People were not scared to talk with Americans anymore. Buddhist monks in brown robes strolled the streets and Westerners didn't shun them for fear they might be walking Molotov cocktails. Students, professors and politicians told us that another element of fear was gone, the fear of the midnight knock on the door that filled the Saigon jails to overflowing with opponents of the regime.

No one dared believe that all this freedom would be more than a temporary relief. There was still real war in the countryside. But a scholarly old Vietnamese newspaper editor told us, "You must be able to see our glee. We are all so very happy." The main streets of the city seemed bare without the barbed wire barricades that had protected Diem and his government.

The future was thrown into question by the assassination of President Kennedy. It stunned the Americans in Vietnam, as it did the world. When I heard the news I ran to the U.S. information office to find out more and I met a tearful Bob Burns, who had been reassigned from Laos to Saigon, and offered my condolences. "Damn it, that's not enough, you don't understand what this means to us," he responded, brushing me aside. I wrote a story that evening saying, "America's sixteen thousand military advisers in South Vietnam reacted with stunned disbelief when the news was flashed through the country." I quoted General Harkins that Kennedy's "bold decision to come to the aid of Vietnam in its fight against the communist Vietcong was one of the highlights of his tragically abbreviated but illustrious term as chief of state."

The next day I flew by helicopter to War Zone D and joined a Vietnamese Ranger battalion on operations in the deep jungle. The American adviser, Captain David Thorenson, knew only that the president was dead, information that was radioed to him the previous afternoon from an L-19 spotter plane that came briefly overhead. I gave him details of the assassination and he responded bitterly, "What do the people of Dallas have to say about this?" The Vietnamese soldiers began asking him "how could this happen in the United States," a question that was also on my mind. "I don't know what to tell them," Thorenson replied. The depth of political disillusionment in Vietnam was evident by its people being more concerned by the death of the American president than their own.

David Halberstam ended his Vietnam assignment on December 9, and we all gathered at the airport for a boisterous farewell. David crunched us in his huge arms and said his only regret was leaving before General Harkins, whom he detested. It was a victory party. Dave was perceived at home as the star of the resident press corps because of the commanding influence of the *New York Times*. His prominence was not begrudged in Saigon. I had found reason to admire his physical strength when he came to my aid in the alley at the Chantersaray Pagoda in July. I also had much reason to respect the intellectual courage he displayed in his challenging analyses of the war. As he was walking to the plane he turned to me and said, "I'm sorry we did not work more together, Peter." Remembering our earlier trips into the countryside, I laughed and told him that I had learned from him anyway. That year, Halberstam and Mal Browne shared the Pulitzer Prize for reporting from Saigon.

I had decided to stay on in Vietnam indefinitely with Mal and Horst after our eighteen-month baptism by fire. Earlier in the year I had feared expulsion because of my reporting; it would have been the third successive country I had been ejected from in three years. But now that danger was over. The new government in power was more aware of our needs, or at least less impatient with our demands. The three of us were a tight little team, in love with the beautiful, sprawling sweltering city of Saigon, where there was more news per square foot than any place I had ever been. Browne was convinced that Saigon came close to the perfect setting for the old-time movies with foreign correspondents wearing trench coats playing the leading roles. I reminded him that Saigon was much too hot for trench coats, and that the uniform was khaki trousers and sports shirts. My courtship of Nina had turned into an enduring relationship.

By now our office was packed with five large desks, with one wall dominated by filing cabinets and the others by enormous wall-to-ceiling sector maps of Vietnam with plastic overlays on which we kept track of important military actions. Our one telephone was held together with adhesive tape because of its many cracks; new telephones were almost impossible to get. Mal and I managed to have phone extensions to each of our apartments above the office, and almost every day we would be woken by ringing, often around 5 A.M. The calls invariably meant trouble; a bomb in some part of town, a coup attempt or even a military operation kicking off. We could join if we hurried.

Mal had a pair of boots made by a local leather store with steel plates in the soles, which he ordered after stepping on a Vietcong booby trap in the delta and a barbed spike went through his boot and well into his foot, causing a painful injury. He touted his superior boots to all his friends and the store flourished until he learned a year or so later that his boot was a phony, that no metal strip had been inserted in it at all.

Covering the war was always arduous, sometimes exciting and often the only way to get news at all—information from the battlefront traveled slowly to Saigon and was usually fragmentary. American authorities became a little more helpful in getting us helicopter rides to the battles. Sometimes we hired blue and white metropolitan taxis to transport us to actions nearer to Saigon, and Mal purchased an office Land Rover, which he painted bright red like the color of the socks he always favored. Sometimes when we heard of distant battles on the Radio Catinat grapevine, Horst and I would jump into my white Karmann Ghia and drive into the countryside, looking for flying helicopters, which we would follow until we heard gunfire and passed dead and wounded soldiers and civilians on the roads.

We were young and headstrong and ambitious and worked seven days a week, with one of us in the battlefield at any time, the others in Saigon to cover the political story. Communications were unsophisticated; no teletype machines were permitted in our office because private organizations were not allowed to operate their own equipment. Incoming messages were brought to us each day by government messengers and at night they banged on our apartment doors.

Browne and I lived simply in single-bedroom apartments, and we both hired old Chinese women servants to do the laundry, marketing, cooking and cleaning for about thirty dollars a month, top wages at that time in Saigon. I did no cooking but ate every meal out in Saigon's multitude of French, Vietnamese and Chinese restaurants.

I would be thirty years old in 1964 and I began thinking it was time for me to settle down and raise children as my parents had done and many of my friends were contemplating. Nina was a fine person and I loved her, but the prospect of abandoning my freewheeling bachelorhood was frightening; when I asked her to marry me I stumbled so badly over the proposal that she was convinced that I was trying to tell her our romance was over and she burst into tears until I reassured her that I meant the opposite.

Marriage

BY LATE 1964 the Johnson administration was preparing the American public for escalation, responding to Vietcong attacks on American installations and ships with retaliatory air strikes against North Vietnam, and assuring the Saigon government of the fullest necessary support to survive. The pressure on us for news coverage increased.

Mal, Horst and I had by now melded into a team. We saw ourselves as an infantry squad that had been fighting in the same theater for years. We knew our strengths and weaknesses.

In the midst of all the action I had gotten married, slipping off for the ceremony to Hong Kong, seeking the assuring predictability of British authority, and avoiding the unfathomable tangle of Vietnamese bureaucracy. Many Westerners talk of having a special fondness for the Vietnamese people. After initially being put off by the grittiness of the country and its people's aggressive ways, I was just the latest to fall under the spell, entranced by Nina's sharp wit and glowing mien. I knew that she would be a caring and affectionate wife and mother. Her genteel family adopted me and seemed willing to forgive my rough-hewn ways. It was through their eyes that I was beginning to comprehend the deep-seated social and political schisms that were cracking the surface of Vietnam and that went deep into its core.

Nina's misfortune was to be born in a country on the verge of revolution, in a family whose privileged place was being swept away. As a child she had lived in Tuyen Quang, where her father was an administrative officer for the French government and her mother was the supervisor of the provincial hospital's maternity ward. When the Japanese occupiers ousted the French and gave the Vietnamese their independence, Nina's father took his family to his home city of Vinh Yen, and ran for a seat in the new nation's representative assembly, winning as an independent. His political career was short lived. The

130

French regained possession of their former colony in 1946, and war broke out.

Nina's father sided with the resistance forces. Ho Chi Minh had not yet revealed his true hand, and the independence movement seemed broad-based and moderate. The family had to flee from their ancestral home in 1947 when Senegalese soldiers spearheaded a French attack on the city. The resistance demanded that they torch their home and the valuable possessions it contained. They watched it burn as they fled through the paddyfields, each carrying a small handbag of personal items.

Her father was distrusted by the communists because of his privileged birth. Her oldest brother had been killed in the war. Her oldest sister had enrolled in a military medical school run by the communists and the family lost track of her for years.

The family lost faith in the independence movement. Nina and her sister Miriam escaped to French-controlled Hanoi, where they were joined in 1954 by the parents and other siblings. In 1955, soon after the country was divided, they fled to Saigon in an American evacuation airlift. Her older sister chose to stay behind, and her two surviving brothers missed the opportunity to leave and were stuck. For the first few years it was permitted to exchange postcards with those they left behind, but even that limited communication between the two countries was ended.

·   ·   ·

Two of Nina's sisters came with us to Hong Kong for the wedding. We stayed in Michel Renard's apartment overlooking Causeway Bay, and my pal from Sydney and Bangkok, John Cantwell, was best man. Danger flags were flying around the harbor because Typhoon Tilda was in the area. We took a taxi to City Hall. The marriage ceremony was very brief. The registrar led us to a table, told us to sign two papers, and I thought that was it. Nina looked over at me, disappointed. She said, "It's like cashing a check." But then the registrar brought us to a large, ornate room and asked Nina and me to sit side by side at a large table, with the witnesses opposite. He had us repeat the oath and then pointed out the grave solemnity of the marriage contract, asked me to place a ring on Nina's finger, and we were man and wife. We celebrated that night with a wedding dinner in the posh Jade Room in the Hong Kong Hilton.

Live from the Battlefield

* * *

Nina was understanding about my job. We lived in my small apartment over the AP office next door to Mal Browne and his wife, Le Lieu. Nina was soon pregnant. The AP family was growing too: John Wheeler and Ed White arrived for permanent assignments.

* * *

The new AP president, Wes Gallagher, visited Saigon for the first time in 1964, to see the front lines for himself, and he had some blunt advice for me. "Get along with the generals and the top sergeants, and be polite and you'll do fine. And no matter what you write about them, it's your personal demeanor they will remember and judge you on, not your stories." His advice was well intended but out of date, from a time when military censors simply carved away the controversial parts of news stories.

A few days after Gallagher arrived, he was confronted with the increasing ugliness of the war and its controversy, and it tested his tolerance. Horst Faas walked into the bureau after four days in the field with several rolls of the most gruesome film since Mal Browne had photographed Thich Quang Duc a year earlier.

Faas had talked his way aboard an armored cavalry operation launched by the South Vietnamese Seventh Infantry Division on the Plain of Reeds, an unnavigable swamp most of the year. But now at the height of the dry season its hardened mud was ideal for swift military raids. The targets were a string of desolate hamlets and villages of thatched-roofed houses and withering fruit trees straddling the poorly defined Cambodian border in the northern Mekong Delta. The Saigon government had never attempted to impose permanent control in this area, and it was known to be dominated by the communists, thus fair game for the military planners. Horst rode aboard an armored personnel carrier for two uneventful days but on the third the unit encountered a Vietcong guerrilla force. They traded heavy weapons fire from the underbrush for an hour and then the guerrillas retreated through a village toward the border. An American military adviser in Horst's vehicle called in air strikes to block the getaway, and within minutes bombs and napalm were falling on the houses. The armor line moved forward as the aircraft roared away and the soldiers pursued the Vietcong through the smoke and fire of burning houses.

Horst stayed behind. It was the first time he'd been in a village immediately after an air strike, and he was shocked by the carnage that lay before him. When he came into the bureau that night he told me it was the worst he had seen in three wars, and as the prints rolled off his processed film I saw what he meant. In one, a farmer clasped his two year old son in his arms; the child's clothes had been burned from his body by napalm and his scorched skin hung off him in sheets. In another picture, a peasant held the body of his wounded child up to soldiers who were peering indifferently from the top of an armored personnel carrier.

Gallagher came in later after an interview with Lodge. Every picture editor in America, Gallagher said, would want to know how such a thing could happen when American servicemen were involved. The incident required balance, he said, to avoid the wrath of government officials in Washington who might accuse us of bias. That meant we must point out that the Vietcong was responsible for similarly disturbing actions.

At his request I wrote a story for the pictures, pointing out that with both sides building up their arsenals the war had entered a new phase of violence and brutality. I quoted an observer as saying, "The hate is building up on both sides. There are many more scores to settle now," and I suggested that civilians were at greater risk because of the use by government forces of napalm and white phosphorous projectiles. "The moral dilemma we face here is what we faced in Korea and every other war we fought in," I quoted an American adviser who had talked with Horst in the field. "We don't want to see civilians killed and yet they are killed because that is a horrible by-product of war."

In January several hundred Vietcong had entered the Ben Cau complex in Tay Ninh and the province chief had ordered artillery barrages to raze the village, killing many of the enemy but also scores of innocent civilians. I pointed out the Vietcong slaughter four days earlier at the Nhi Binh outpost twenty miles south of Saigon where dependents of South Vietnamese soldiers—women and children— were bayoneted to death. I noted the burning of Cao Dai village in Phu My in September because the population refused to disown the government, and the beheading of farmers in Kien Hoa province for refusing to pay Vietcong taxes.

Gallagher was satisfied that with our catalogue of battlefield atrocities we had brought perspective to the horror. Both sides were implicated. If it were true that a picture was worth a thousand words, I thought, I doubted that our careful explanation would diminish the impact of Horst's photos.

Now reporters routinely began carrying cameras and the war was discovered by freelance photographers, who risked their lives for the fifteen dollars a photo that Horst paid them. Sometimes words couldn't convey what a photo could. Mal Browne snapped a Vietnamese militiaman trying to strangle a wounded farmer by stamping on a stake across his throat. A stringer brought in a picture of a Vietcong prisoner being dragged to his death on a rope tied behind an armored personal carrier that went careening through the swamps. Another stringer sold us a photo of a Vietnamese marine carrying the bloodied severed heads of three Vietcong guerrillas.

In October 1964, freelance photographer Jim Pickerell accompanied a Vietnamese Ranger battalion near the Cambodian border that picked up three civilians who were suspected of an ambush the previous week. The hands of all the prisoners were tied behind their backs and the soldiers began applying the water torture to make them talk, forcing them to their knees, pouring water on cloth laid over their faces. The effect is like drowning, and carried to the extreme it causes death by suffocation. Jim photographed a variation on the ugly theme: one of the prisoners was plunged head first into a large water jar, where he was held for some minutes before being pulled out nearly drowned.

It fell to Mal to try to interpret this brutality, writing in an explanatory story, "Terror and counterterror, persistent themes of Vietnamese political and military history for many centuries, continue to play a dominant role in the increasingly bloody war raging here." He described the torture and concluded that the victims, all of whom lived, "were lucky. The chances of surviving field interrogation often are extremely poor. Death can come for prisoners under the tracks of armored vehicles, by decapitation or by bleeding to death after both hands have been chopped off, or by a bullet through the head. It is all part of the war in South Vietnam."

Someone remarked at the time that the Geneva Conventions were never translated into Vietnamese and that is why no one observed them. It was a joke. In fact, everyone gave lip service to the international laws of war and blamed the other side for violating them. Our news coverage tended to throw the spotlight on the government side because we had no opportunity to cover the secretive Vietcong. We saw only their reflection: the dead bodies or the prisoners on the battlefield or in the wreckage of the communities they attacked.

American reporters did not seek to become instruments of international hostility, yet were being drawn into that predicament. We could establish no compelling basis for ignoring the reality of the battlefield and closing our eyes to the fact that American policy was failing.

By mid-December, in a spectacular new offensive, the communists were launching two battalion-sized attacks each day against fortified villages and infantry units with marked success. In just one week, I covered the bloody aftermath of three such attacks south of Saigon. The climax came at year's end at the Catholic refugee village of Binh Gia forty miles east of Saigon. Horst was first at the scene, alongside Vietnamese marines who liberated the town after it had been held for three days by the Vietcong. It took me a day to get there. Photographer Henri Huet and I tried to hitch a ride on a helicopter but we failed and instead headed off in my white Karmann Ghia. We zipped around military vehicles and horse carts and people on foot until we saw the first wounded soldiers being treated on the highway.

The first stage of the battle was over and the scene reminded me of Ap Bac two years earlier, when a Vietcong battalion had decided to stand and fight and win the day. At Binh Gia a South Vietnamese battalion had taken on a communist regiment and had been routed. We watched several thousand troops being brought in to join the fight. We were told that a marine battalion with its U.S. advisers had gone in to one of the nearby French rubber plantations searching for the wreckage of a helicopter that had gone down in flames with four Americans aboard. During the night we heard the roar of battle half a mile away as the marines engaged the Vietcong. Next morning Huet and I walked to the plantation and into a scene of desolation. I wrote:

"Binh Gia, South Vietnam, January 2. The young U.S. Marine lieutenant first saw the Vietcong through his binoculars about a thousand yards away: there were hordes of them. Dressed in khaki uniforms, field gear and steel helmets, the Vietcong moved slowly closer, dodging through the rubber plantation from tree to tree, through air strikes sliced down on them by the Vietnamese Air Force, and murderous armed helicopter machine gun fire.

" 'These aren't guerrillas, they are regular troops,' the marine yelled over his radio to his command post flying above the rubber trees in a helicopter. 'Bring in more air,' he shouted. That was the last that Lieutenant Colonel John B. Wadsworth, the senior special zone adviser, heard from the marines over that radio; it had been shot from the back of the adviser toting it. 'All we knew was that there was a hell of a battle down there,' Wadsworth said later. 'Now we know how bad it was.' "

His remark proved true on Saturday. The floor of the cool, silent rubber plantation was scattered with dead marines. Rows of marine bodies were lying in the blistering sun beside a helicopter pad, banana leaves thrown loosely over them. Other marines kept trundling bodies out of the plantation on primitive litters. Newsmen stumbled over a wounded ranger hiding in the brush with bullets in his legs. He had been there since a ranger battalion was destroyed the previous Tuesday. Three U.S. Marine lieutenants were sprawled listlessly beside a field radio, one of them rasping into the speaker, "How many you say? How many? Okay, sixty-seven." Turning to a newsman he commented, "That's how many we have now, dead that is. We got the bodies of the four Americans too."

It was the search for these four Americans, shot down in flames over the rubber trees in a helicopter Wednesday night, that led to the Fourth Marine Battalion's trek into the plantation, and disaster. "We just had to get those Americans out," a U.S. officer commented at Binh Gia. The price was high—about 250 marines were casualties, about half the battalion. Some U.S. officers say that the marines were asking for trouble by waiting fourteen hours before they headed in to search for the wreck.

Colonel Wadsworth said, "Our marine advisers told them they might be walking into a Vietcong trap laid with that helicopter wreck and the bodies. We went in with our eyes open."

Not open enough.

The battle of Binh Gia marked the end of a bad year for Vietnam, and the bloody opening of a worse time, a decade of struggle that would put Americans in the gunsights of the Vietcong and plunge the United States into turmoil. To us reporters the military skills of the communist troops and their bravery were clearly formidable. However, we were usually dissuaded from describing their combat skills.

A message to the Saigon bureau from AP foreign editor Ben Bassett spelled out the rules. Bassett wrote, "We are approaching the stage if we have not already reached it where our copy is going to be subjected to searching study by officials for any lines indicating pessimism or what might be considered an editorial tone. This need not forestall our telling the story accurately as we observe it, continuing your superb job, but we do want to give our copy a good second reading to make sure of our footing. I hesitate to single out an example because the subject affects us all, but I call your attention to the last paragraph of [John Wheeler's] Saigon story dated August 6 saying, 'Well trained and fervently dedicated to his cause, the Vietcong gives every indication of continued success with methods that have so far not been seriously challenged.' I don't doubt that this in its components and within the stated context is true, but we can avoid superfluous tributes to one side or the other and especially avoid forecasts we cannot fully support and back quotably. While continuing to tell the story as we see it, we can also be sure that we cover anything that might be considered positive or optimistic from the U.S. point of view. In other words, let's not be circumscribed in telling the story but make sure we are telling it fully."

In a covering note to our bureau chief, Bassett wrote, "I am sure you understand what I'm talking about. It's a matter of impressing the whole staff with the philosophy entailed. It is a time for cool heads and reflection on how our copy may look if it is challenged. I sent you earlier in the week a printer copy of a Wheeler story, showing how some of the phraseology had been changed here without diluting the essential points of a fine story. None of this, I'm sure you realize, bespeaks any lack of confidence in you or in your staff. I know that some of the copy that comes out of Saigon at odd hours must be filed without too much desk attention. We will try to do our part at this end."

Getting Along

WHEN AMERICA BEGAN to wage war seriously in Vietnam I tried to adopt Gallagher's advice to get along with the generals. I respected the power represented by the silver stars, as only a former private would. My first experience with an American officer of senior rank had not been a fortunate one, however; General Paul D. Harkins, who had been chief of the U.S. military command in Diem's era, had treated the Saigon press corps as dangerous imbeciles to be ignored as much as possible. On the few occasions I encountered him I thought that he lied to me outright. When Ngo Dinh Diem was overthrown, we had all assumed that Harkins's days were numbered. When he retired in June of 1964 we were eager to start a clean sheet with his successor, General William Westmoreland. I was at Saigon's Tan Son Nhut Airport with the attending press corps when the lean, graying fifty-year-old officer arrived, with a reputation as a hands-on commander.

The AP thought it had an in with Westmoreland because Wes Gallagher had once rescued Captain Westmoreland when his jeep had crashed into a roadside ditch during the North African campaign in World War Two. Gallagher had kept in touch with Westmoreland as they rose in their respective careers, and they were friends. We received no real favors from the commander, but Westy allowed the AP's Roy Essoyan to travel with him on a nine-hour inspection trip around the war zone and spoke with him about the urgency of uniting the government and the people behind the military effort. Essoyan wrote a flattering profile of Westmoreland, as did many of my colleagues. But I never got close enough to him to write one, and as the war proceeded I sensed the American high command didn't like me at all. I knew I had failed to execute Gallagher's orders when he informed Robert Tuckman, a subsequent AP Saigon bureau chief, "It's your job to get along with the generals, and let Arnett and the others get out and do the reporting."

The military authorities wanted us to paint an image of Vietnam as a valued, threatened ally. But that did not square with what we were seeing: a corrupt, irresolute leadership and a country sinking into its own effluent. In earlier American wars there was a sense of national purpose and a censorship that maintained a climate of workable cordiality between the military and the media; in Vietnam there was neither national purpose nor censorship. The authorities were unable to generate the first and unwilling to impose the other.

So, despite Westmoreland's earnest attempts to approach the press and our honest endeavors to accommodate him, it was hard to stay on good terms. The rush of events demanded coverage and analysis, and we were obligated to question whether South Vietnam could be saved by its own people and to challenge the assumption that a political solution was unthinkable and unnecessary. The war was upstaged by political crises during all of 1964 as military officers fought over the spoils of the ruined Diem regime, launching inept coups d'etat and farcical power plays. The cumulative effect of the Vietnamese military leadership's machinations was discontent and disorder. The jubilation over the fall of the House of Diem was replaced by the unraveling of national unity.

We plunged into the fray with our notebooks and cameras, negotiating hazardous streets and watching Catholics battling Buddhists, and students battling each other, and the police and army battling all of them. In a log note to New York on August 31, Mal wrote, "By the end of last week the Saigon AP staff looked more like street rioters than newsmen. The entire group was unshaved, filthy, hungry and near complete exhaustion. Clothing was muddy and soaking, and every staffer had a dozen scrapes and bruises. There had been many close calls for all of us, ducking along walls to evade flying bullets and rocks, and running at top speed to escape pursuing mobs along back alleys and side streets."

Browne wrote that Horst was standing next to a German television cameraman, Gens Uwe Scheffler, with a mob of Catholic demonstrators outside General Staff headquarters when troops opened fire, felling Scheffler with a bullet through the leg. Faas dragged him eighty yards behind military lines for safety and when he returned to his rented car later in the day he found the bloody body of one of the demonstrators in the rear seat, which he unloaded at a nearby gas station before driving off. In one outlandish crisis, Saigon's security forces pulled back into their barracks during a political standoff and mobs of grubby urchins took over the streets, blocking main thoroughfares with makeshift barricades for several days and defending their turf with nail-studded sticks and sharpened bamboo stakes.

At night, Saigon closed down and river rats took over the streets, pouring out of the sewers by the thousands and scavenging for garbage. In the early mornings as I walked home I kept my distance as best I could from the hissing, scurrying packs of them glistening dark in the streetlights as they foraged for food. The unusual calm similarly emboldened Saigon's large, tropical cockroaches to leave their secret cracks and crevices to savor the cool evening air, swarming over hallway walls and stairwells and cracking under our shoes like popcorn. One night I approached the Eden Arcade thinking the streetlights were out because the open-work steel gates seemed so dark, only to find when I pulled on the handle that I grasped a handful of squirming cockroaches. The whole edifice was curtained with them.

It was a callous, dangerous time and our coverage reflected it, raising questions about America's Asian ally and cooling off the Johnson administration's public enthusiasm for enlarging the conflict. So much so that in his presidential election campaign against the Republican candidate Barry Goldwater, the president promised that there would be no wider war, and that American boys should not be required to serve in a faraway conflict that Asian boys should be fighting. I watched the news accounts of Johnson's assertions click off the AP teleprinter in our office and I had no reason to disbelieve him; his caution was reflected in official comments made by the American high command in Saigon and by Westmoreland himself.

But what President Johnson and his aides and the Joint Chiefs of Staff plotted in the secrecy of the White House would ultimately be revealed in Vietnam, sooner or later. As Johnson geared up for substantial hostilities, he also endeavored to line up America's news organizations, coaxing editors and news executives to color their product to his hue, trying with an arm squeeze to achieve a censorship that other presidents enforced with executive orders. Gallagher challenged the whole notion by offering to accept censorship if that would prompt the military to release adequate information about air strikes being launched against North Vietnam from the Da Nang air base, but his suggestion was shelved, so we stood at the end of the airfield and watched the bombers taking off and counted them on their return to see if any had been shot down.

Secretary of State Dean Rusk later argued that he was unwilling to create what he called "a national hysteria" by implementing censorship and the probable state of emergency that would have to come with it. Officials on the ground in Vietnam agreed that realistic control was impossible because of the necessary involvement of Vietnamese officials in the process, and that the large numbers of reporters from many countries would be difficult to oversee. Westmoreland later wrote in his memoirs that he considered, but rejected, some form of censorship on news coverage on the grounds that it would be unenforceable. He opted instead for more openness in the belief that "greater benefits might be derived from a policy of maximum candor." The situation was ripe for dispute and misunderstanding and resentment, creating a climate of discord that would permanently tarnish our relations with the military and designate the press a handy whipping boy for the disasters that were to come.

The American officials on the scene in Saigon were so sensitive to provocative news stories that Westmoreland's policy often degenerated into what *Los Angeles Times* reporter Jack Foisie described as "maximum candor with minimum implementation."

In March 1965, I began to research the use of nonlethal destabilizing gases on Vietnamese military operations. I had picked up rumors the previous month from an American civilian aid adviser in Binh Long Province, and I filed it away for later reference. I also saw that exotic gadgetry was being introduced into the Vietnam war, from lie detectors for use on Vietcong prisoners to "people sniffers" that allowed heli-copters to pick up urine smells and thus track the movements of Vietcong units in the deep jungles. On my travels along the bumpy roads outside Saigon, visiting with civilian advisers and military units, I began piecing together a story about chemical agents, learning that they were being used in the Second Corps region of the highlands, and in the Third Corps region around Saigon. One type of gas caused extreme nausea and vomiting, another completely loosened the bow-els, a third caused temporary blindness. The most prevalent was CS, a more potent form of tear gas.

My dossier was fattening and I decided to visit the information liaison officer, Captain Richard Bryan, at his Third Corps office in Bien Hoa. We lunched often in Saigon and I thought we got along well, but he declined comment on my material, and grew agitated when I pressed him. He promised to take the question to his superior, the senior adviser to the Third Corps, Colonel Jasper Wilson. The authorities never responded and I figured that the whole operation was under wraps. Still, I had learned about it and presumed the Viet-cong had, too, and saw no reason for the news blackout. The gas story burned in my notebooks but it failed the supreme test: I hadn't seen it happen, nor had anyone else in the AP, and until we did, it did not exist.

·   ·   ·

Horst made the breakthrough. On March 20, an American adviser had come by his house to invite him on a Vietnamese infantry op-eration in Hau Nghia Province the next morning. The operation, he revealed, would have a new wrinkle: the soldiers would be experi-menting with chemical agents. I waited impatiently in our office. Horst reappeared in the early evening, triumph on his sweaty face as he banged several rolls of film on the table. About half of the soldiers in the Vietnamese battalion had been equipped with rubber gas masks and gas canisters, under orders to explode them if they were pinned down by attacking Vietcong forces. The chemical agents were not used that day but the officers had talked freely about them. They mentioned that U.S. helicopters and fighter-bombers had been equipped with special large containers to hold the gas in powder form, and hoses to spray it out over the battlefields. It could be particularly effective for rescuing prisoners, when the objective was to knock out the enemy quickly, get in and get out.

We decided to go with the details immediately, without seeking further comment from the military authorities since they had been indifferent to my earlier request. I typed a story lead and showed it to Horst: "The United States is experimenting with gas warfare against the Vietcong, highly reliable sources said today. Both American and Vietnamese forces have used gas against the communist guerrillas, the sources reported. Some experiments have been successful, others have failed and they are expected to continue. Various non-lethal-type gases have been used against the guerrillas in the Second and Third Corps regions of Vietnam."

Horst nodded as I typed on, detailing the varieties of chemical agents used, and pointing out that they attacked through the eyes and nose and created intense burning in the throat and lungs, stopping anyone in their tracks. I wrote that Faas had been in the field with the Vietnamese on one of the special experimental operations. I quoted a Vietnamese officer as saying, "It is a humane way of clearing out an enemy area where women and children are being held," particularly when they were discovered in the tunnels the Vietcong favored as hiding places.

I included a contrary view from Horst's adviser friend, that the use of such a weapon was only in the experimental stage and had not been proven to work, and that "even though the stuff used here is nonlethal and has no lasting effects, the idea of it all brings back memories of World War One and mustard gas."

The story had more impact than anything I had written. It was my first certifiable scoop. There was a debate from the Soviet Union to Tokyo. The issue was argued in the British Parliament, protests were held in Scandinavia, new misgivings were expressed by the critics of the war in the United States.

The U.S. Military Assistance Command in Saigon was stuck. Our competitors were banging on the doors of the information offices, demanding material for stories to match what we had reported. Washington officials downplayed the significance of the experiment, even as they admitted that the material had been used on three separate occasions.

I argued that if the U.S. command had responded to my queries for an explanation weeks earlier I would have included their viewpoint in the story.

The U.S. government decided to withdraw Westmoreland's authority to use chemical agents for many months, until the controversy cooled down and by which time other weapons such as napalm had become more controversial.

Westmoreland would later write that the dispute over the use of nonlethal gas was one "of the more inane controversies of the Vietnam War," and he called such chemical agents "one of the most humane weapons at my disposal."

My story did not win me any friends in the expanding U.S. military and diplomatic establishment. Americans were taking over the widening war and anxiously trying to soften the image they were creating. In earlier wars, I was told, reporters were encouraged to emphasize the positive when writing about the soldiers so the families at home would not worry. Mothers with sons in Vietnam, early in 1965, picked up their local newspaper on March 4 and read AP reporter George McArthur's story on their loved ones' adventures in Saigon, where an American soldier stopping to joke with a young Vietnamese boy "might be bowled over by six or eight kids, tripped, thrown to the ground and robbed of his watch, billfold and sometimes even his boots, all in the space of seconds before the kids flee." Pickpockets were also active; the police chief complained, "Your soldiers' uniforms are partly at fault, the pockets are too shallow and have no buttons and sometimes you even see a soldier's billfold already sticking out." The soldier was also an easy prey for "a veritable horde of female pickpockets who are also prostitutes, and two or three of them will engage the happy soldier in amorous horseplay in bars or dark streets and when it's over he's a poorer man."

A grizzled U.S. Army engineer complained to me in Bien Hoa that "I was better equipped in World War Two than I am here," and he held up some rusty cartridge magazines that had been issued the previous day he was afraid to use. He said that back home before embarking for the war he was issued a World War One pistol belt and an old cargo pack, "And this was after I had read that the Defense Department says the Americans in Vietnam are the best equipped fighting men ever to go overseas. They still have to show me that." A U.S. Marine adviser complained he was issued iodine tablets to purify water for drinking "but when I tried to use them out in the jungle I found they had deteriorated into powder." I found an army lieutenant who said, "I know that if I went to U.S. military headquarters and made a scene I would get issued with a poncho liner and the other items I am lacking, but then I would remain a first lieutenant all my life."

Our relations with the military command were already strained when I wrote the story. I alerted our Washington bureau to call the Pentagon, but I decided not to wait for official comment.

Westmoreland was furious. One of his aides phoned Mal to complain that the story was sensationalized, not representative of the facts; but we stood by it. Mal warned me I was in the high command's doghouse and could expect little future cooperation from them, and I was beginning to be somewhat distressed by the fierce reaction my stories were arousing. I was sensing another climactic confrontation on my horizon, a gathering storm that threatened to swamp my budding career. Yet I felt firmly grounded in the Vietnam story, personally and professionally. My three years had been a journalistic finishing school under the tutelage of the Associated Press and Mal Browne and Dave Halberstam that had helped prepare me for the challenges ahead. At age thirty I still had that swagger of youth that helped me overcome my fears on the battlefield and allowed me to bond with those fighting the war, the newly arrived marine units and the American advisers who had long been going into action with the Vietnamese military.

I figured I would never be invited to travel on General Westmoreland's helicopter, but there were plenty of other ways to get around Vietnam. On the days when the war slowed down and I didn't have to hitch rides to battle sites on U.S. Air Force transport planes or Army helicopters, I would gas up my sporty white Karmann Ghia for excursions in the countryside. With the increase in the Vietnam AP staff, I had gained some independence and could visit spots I was interested in.

Sometimes I drove very fast over the new American Friendship Highway to the crossroads city of Bien Hoa, knowing that traffic patrols were a casualty of the war. I saw the clear signs of a budding entrepreneurial response to the American military buildup: the rural population set up roadside soft drink stands to attract passing soldiers and peddle Coca-Cola and Fanta in worn bottles cooled by dusty slabs of ice. There were other services; American military trucks rumbling by with building materials for new bases were not infrequently tempted to pull into hastily built shelters offering both car wash and massage services, where cheerful youths worked over the cumbersome vehicles with buckets of soap and water out front, while their sisters were similarly scrubbing off the lust and loneliness of the grateful drivers out back.

Beyond Long Binh were Route 15's first Vietnamese guard towers and protective road blocks where the soldiers puzzled over my car and then waved me through, sure that I offered no discernible security risk, and if they did pull me over I would brandish my press card and exclaim arrogantly, "Bao chi, bao chi"—journalist. Then came the rubber plantations of Long Thanh straddling the highway in sinister orderliness, their corridors of trees stretched off into the distance, convenient pathways for Vietcong guerrillas who sometimes swooped down on the road, their guns blazing in bloody ambush. I rarely drove alone at night. It was commonly said that the night belonged to the Vietcong because the South Vietnamese rarely ventured into it.

When Washington announced on March 7, 1965, that three thousand U.S. marines would be landing at Da Nang the next morning, I was worried. Some American military advisers were in the habit of saying that when they were frustrated with their Vietnamese allies, all that was needed to clean up Vietnam was to land a U.S. Marine battalion at the Ca Mau Peninsula and walk it all the way to the 17th parallel, the 1954 demarcation line between north and south. That may have worked when the Vietcong guerrillas fought in twos and threes, but now they were organized, and massing in units as large as marine battalions.

My reporter's impulse took over and I put aside my concerns. The arrival of the first American combat troops was a breathtaking prospect for us all. I joined the scores of reporters going north to Da Nang to cover the marines. The American military men I had known in Vietnam up to that time had impressed me with their experience and maturity; they were all career officers and enlisted men specially selected for the delicate task of working with the Vietnamese.

The "shavetail" marines in Da Nang with their crew cut hair and bravado were much younger. They, like street brawlers, had come to fight. The first marine patrol I accompanied in April was confident and high-spirited, and for a while some in the population thought the French army was back. "Vive les Français," shouted an elderly Vietnamese man dressed in a black silk coat and white trousers as the platoon of marines trudged down a clay road skirting the hills above An Suk. The shout seemed to echo around the rows of blackened concrete bunkers along the hill crests, crumbling memorials to France's unsuccessful attempt to remain in Indochina a decade earlier.

"What's the old guy want? Candy?" asked a young marine loaded down with heavy military gear in the blazing sun. "Sounds like he thinks we're Frenchies. What a laugh," said another. "They lost didn't they, well we won't."

They were from the Second Battalion, Third Marine Regiment, and were swinging along pretty well. Word had just reached them of President Johnson's new tax exemptions for military men serving in Vietnam. "I just hope I live to spend what I save," commented a lance corporal. The soldiers had been out once before, on patrol outside the Da Nang air base perimeter, and today they were spoiling for a fight. "I know I'll get hurt one way or another before I get out of Vietnam. Why not today?" one commented. Another replied, "Why can't I get shot, man, I wonder what it's like?"

The temperature soared to over a hundred degrees before noon. "We've got a great bunch of kids with us," said the company commander, Captain Peter Yardlowsky, a fatherly-looking but tough soldier. Told that the 81mm mortar men, heaving the heavy tubes and ammunition, had consumed nearly all their water before noon, he said, "That's just too bad. They had two canteens to last them the day. That's all they get."

The mortarmen filled up from their buddies' canteens anyway. The heat grew worse; the second platoon was lagging and the captain was worried. He was out of radio communication because they were too far off but the platoon eventually came up the road, mud-splattered and sweating, and casually mentioned they had clashed with their first Vietcong guerrillas in a thirty-minute firefight and had taken one wounded.

"I knew they must have tangled with something; that platoon leader's too good a man to lag," said the captain with satisfaction. Told he would get a Purple Heart, the wounded marine muttered, "Better than one of those posthumous ones."

In the meantime a fireteam had seen some excitement, jumping a Vietnamese man clad in black and carrying a rifle and a bandolier of ammunition, just like the Vietcong. "Man, we jumped him real quick," said Corporal Nieto, but they had to let him go because he was a Vietnamese Popular Forces militiaman and fully entitled to the clothes and the gun.

"Problem around here," said Captain Yardlowsky, "is who the hell is who?" Hundreds of thousands of other Americans would soon be asking the same question, and having far more dramatic walks in the sun than Second Battalion, Third Marines.

Song Be

INTEREST IN THE AMERICANS became so insistent that our coverage of the Vietnamese military effort lessened. Hometown newspapers were more interested in stories about soldiers from their neighborhoods. Newspaper editors played up the local angles, more enthusiastic about our war reporting now that American boys were directly involved.

John Wheeler, Ron Deutsch, Ed White, George Esper, Bob Poos, Hugh Mulligan and I kept the AP wires humming with "hometowners," aware that whatever we wrote about those men and women would be published at least in their hometown newspapers and clipped by relatives and sent right back to Vietnam for them to read.

I understood the emphasis on the Americans but regretted it. I had made many friends among the officer corps in the Vietnamese Marine and paratrooper units. They had always fed and enlightened me and got me home unharmed. The American officers who advised these units were around my age or a little older, and I liked being with them and talking about the war. I still tried to find opportunities when I could.

Covering American combat units required planning. I had been used to heading off to wherever I wanted to go. My meanderings across Vietnam anchored me, I felt, to the place and people. There was a presumption that all the Vietnamese who were not out in the jungles with the Vietcong were on our side. We saw them every day, and they all seemed friendly enough, straining under wide-brimmed conical straw hats to pilot their cumbersome ox-drawn plows through the rice fields, cycling briskly through town to school and store and office, sorting through exotic papayas, mangoes, pomelos and custard apples at the markets, and serving as amahs for our children and maids for our households. There were many Vietnamese who bore grudges against the communists, reinforced by years of conflict, and who feared their victory—my father-in-law for example.

Not all Vietnamese did. When I was down at the southern Mekong Delta town of Soc Trang early in 1965 they were still talking about the thirty-four-year-old laundrymaid from the neighboring community who for six months had washed the sweat-soiled clothes of the American helicopter pilots based there, and cleaned up their always untidy barracks, and became an integral part of the social order until she arrived one day with her waist bulging suspiciously. As American military police watched, the Vietnamese gate security detail ripped off the laundrymaid's dress and pulled a string of plastic explosives out from under her petticoat. Then they took her off to a nearby military post for questioning. An hour later they drove the weeping woman to the end of the small airstrip where two soldiers led her out into the paddyfields and shot her dead, leaving her body where it fell. The American chopper pilots were less upset by the harsh battlefield justice than about the loyalty of the seventy other local women employed at the base, many of them held with the same casual esteem as the laundrymaid whose corpse was rotting in the green rice shoots off the end of the runway. The story was not a unique one: you could hear similar tales around many of the mushrooming American bases. Duplicity and brutality were becoming cohorts, riding through Vietnam with America's more noble impulses.

I still had some opportunities to cover the Vietnamese side of the war, usually when disaster struck. I made my way north to Phuoc Long Province with Horst one morning in May 1965 after we learned that the town of Song Be had been overrun by the Vietcong. We hitched a ride on a Vietnamese Air Force Caribou transport plane to Ben Cat and traveled the rest of the way in helicopters ferrying in Vietnamese soldiers ordered to retake the town. We arrived at the muddy dirt airstrip early afternoon and cautiously walked the three miles into Song Be with a battalion of Vietnamese rangers.

We all feared an ambush. It was so quiet that I could hear the tall stalks of the bamboo trees bumping and clicking in the breeze. Then we rounded a curve in the road and saw the town, clouded in black smoke, stretching along a river in the shallow valley ahead of us. Shooting broke out, not at us, but raking across the black tiled roofs of the government compound in the center of town.

We bobbed and weaved our way into Song Be and tried to keep up with our ranger escorts, who rushed ahead and entered what was left of a district headquarters that had been flattened by dynamite. The debris partially covered the broken bodies of fifteen of the defenders. I heard the roar of jets, and Horst said knowingly, "B-57s," and aimed his Leica as a pair of the sleek black bombers appeared from behind Song Be Mountain. The planes zoomed down toward a target in the rubber plantations to the west, unloading their bombs and blasting with their 20mm wing guns before careening off. They were followed by three helicopters that scrubbed the landscape with fiery detergent.

A Vietnamese Ranger officer told us that one hundred South Vietnamese soldiers had already been killed and wounded. The Vietcong attack had begun at dawn and rolled across much of Song Be during the day, with the enemy now thought to be regrouping outside town for a second assault. The officer offered to get us out of town. Horst and I agreed the situation was dangerous, but we also felt that the story required one of us to stay behind.

I volunteered and Horst headed back by jeep to the airstrip for a flight out. The vehicle returned with *Stars and Stripes* newspaper photographer Sergeant Al Chang, chomping, as usual, on a fat cigar. When I briefed him on the security risks, he suggested we spend the night at the American military advisory compound, where we presumed there would be adequate safety and with luck some cold beer. There was neither; the barbed wire defenses of the rambling complex had been breached in the early-morning hours by a Vietcong suicide team that killed five of the thirty American advisers, wounded others and blew up the recreation rooms and the mess hall. I later wrote:

"Song Be, Vietnam, May 13. They found the sergeant dead at dawn Tuesday, spreadeagled against a bloodied pantry door in the U.S. advisory group's mess hall. His upraised right hand clutched a penknife. He was Sergeant Horace E. Young of Fayetteville, North Carolina, one of five Americans killed in the Vietcong attack on the provincial town of Song Be seventy-four miles north of Saigon. The camp medic, Sergeant William D. Benning, of Cincinnati, Ohio, died while trying to save a dozen wounded men from both their wounds and the Vietcong. A red suicide squad crept up on Benning while he worked in the mess hall and lobbed grenades. Benning died instantly, and so did two other Americans near him who cannot yet be publicly identified because their next of kin have not been notified. The fifth to die was Sergeant Johnnie K. Culbreath of Callison, South Carolina. Hearing the grenades exploding, Culbreath leaped from his foxhole near the western edge of the American camp. 'They're going for the wounded,' he shouted and ran toward the mess hall. The guerrillas inside shot through the door and killed him."

Major Mitchell Sakey showed us the mess hall where the floor was caked with dried blood and strewn with bits of bandages and clothing. The refrigerator was perforated with bullet holes and leaking its cooling materials onto the floor. An anonymous survivor who had clearly summoned reserves of wit had awarded the refrigerator a makeshift Purple Heart medal, the design drawn in red lipstick on the door. Major Sakey agreed that we could stay the night at his former strongpoint, remarking pointedly that it was vulnerable and exposed, and that there were reports of the Vietcong massing on the slopes below for another attack. "I'll need to press all hands into service, I'll need you two to assist in the defenses tonight," he told us.

I looked at Al Chang, who was nodding resignedly. After Korea he thought he had permanently exchanged a gun for a camera. Major Sakey thrust a weapon at me saying, "Take this carbine and pick up three hundred rounds of ammo at the armory and go protect the mortarman on the western berm." I felt my heart sink and I knew I would do it but I commented, for the record, "I know you're responsible for this place, you're a professional soldier. What about the Geneva Conventions prohibiting civilians doing this sort of thing?" He just looked at me. "You want to believe the VC are going to respect your civilian status tonight, fella?"

I stuffed my shirt and trouser pockets with ammo clips and stumbled through the darkness with Chang to the mortar pit where he had been told to assist the gunner. As my eyes became accustomed to the dimness I noted that the sandbagged revetments around my position had been blasted away in the earlier attack and I looked down the slope through the tangled remains of once protective barbed wire defenses to the scrub and brush of a gully below. In my three years in Vietnam I had never been so nakedly exposed to personal risk. If ever there was a six-lane expressway opened up for an attacking suicide squad then this was it. I whispered to Al an urgent question about tactics: just what the hell would I do when the bad guys came storming up the slope? He said something about putting the carbine on full automatic and closing my eyes and pressing the trigger. If I fled my post and hid under a mess hall table, as my heart was telling me to do, I would be so humiliated by morning that I would never have the courage to show my face in a war zone again.

I watched gunfire bursting like meteor showers as old C-47 transports dressed up with new miniguns and infrared sensors roared across the sky. These Puff, the Magic Dragon planes fired at targets in the inky landscape in front of me. Enemy gunfire answered into the air. Al's mortarman fired many shells at shadows in the jungle beyond us, the rounds screaming over my head as I lay prostrate in the dirt, rifle at my shoulder. The expected ground assault never came. By morning, my body cold and stiff, I had found out something about myself, that I could still function despite fear, and that I was willing to take any kind of risk for a good story.

Schwarzkopf

AS THOUSANDS MORE American troops arrived, their fate overshadowed all else in Vietnam. President Johnson had Westmoreland teeter on the brink of war for months as the military buildup continued and American troops were kept out of actions like Song Be. However, it was becoming clear that Westmoreland would soon be allowed to commit his soldiers to battle.

We plotted ways to outmaneuver our rival wire service, UPI, whose reporting team of Ray Herndon and Mike Malloy had been reinforced by a benchful of daredevil recruits from home.

We speculated that a remote strongpoint near the Cambodian border named Duc Co might be the tinderbox for a wider conflict. It was located on a primary infiltration route for communist troops and supplies, through tracts of jungle where few people lived. It had been under siege for two months and its defenders were in despair. I volunteered to take a look. I rode a Vietnamese supply convoy up Route 19 to Pleiku and jumped into the cab of a large ammunition truck, with only the driver for company. As the truck struggled up a slope in the foothills, the driver put on his steel helmet and pointed to a curve ahead where the steep winding road disappeared into heavy brush and hills. He hitched up his trouser leg to reveal an ugly scar and in halting French explained that he had been ambushed several years earlier at that same spot and was worried about it happening again. I was hardly reassured by the appearance of several armed men at the roadside, some dressed in black shirts and pants and wearing cowboy hats, others in red sweaters, who banged on our truck and the other vehicles and waved to us in a friendly-enough manner to suggest they were on our side. According to the driver, they were scouts for a Vietnamese Ranger battalion in the hills. The highway had been closed for years—the Vietcong had methodically destroyed all its bridges. I noted a metal plaque on one large destroyed concrete structure that read "1957–1958 U.S.A." Further ahead, beyond An Khe, there was the forbidding Mang Yang Pass, where in early 1950 the elite French military unit Group Mobile 100 had succumbed to a series of vicious Vietminh ambushes and bold frontal assaults. I had been told that the French dead had been taken up the hills of Mang

151

Yang, and at prior request their bodies were buried standing straight up, facing France.

Our convoy wound slowly up the pass and gained speed as we crested and moved down the other side. There was gunfire in the air from somewhere in the hills but we were not hit. I climbed off at Camp Holloway, where the U.S. Army's Fifty-second Aviation Battalion was located. Barracks sprawled around one end of the old Pleiku airport, the unit's Huey helicopters parked in neat rows along the runway. It was late, but they put me up for the night in the crew chiefs' hootch and invited me to a small shed named the Swamp. Country-western music was playing. The beer was abundant and cold—helicopter pilots could do a lot of people favors in Vietnam and were well rewarded in return. I asked the new commanding officer to get me a ride to Duc Co as soon as possible, but he laughed at me. "That place has been under siege sixty days today and the only people we take there are replacements for the dead. That's the only real estate in government hands between Pleiku and the Cambodian border and it's forty miles away." I thought about it for a while and I said I still wanted to go. He suggested I check with flight opportunities in the morning but to enjoy the beer that night because there would be none at Duc Co. "I hear they ain't even got water there," the colonel said.

Later a Reuters reporter walked in, Dick Myerscoff, a fellow countryman and a colleague from Jakarta days who was on temporary assignment to the war zone and wanted to come along. I had hoped to be exclusive but I didn't have the heart to try to dissuade him, so we were both at flight ops at daybreak with the fog still heavy across the field and the pine forests barely visible in the gray distance. The dispatcher told us they flew emergency missions to pick up the dead and wounded, and tried to send one helicopter to Duc Co each day in quieter times to maintain the belief that the siege could be punctured. Our pilots stated it was one trip too many.

The Fifty-second Aviation had a reputation for daring. One of our pilots wore a wide-brimmed hat and had exotic insignia pinned to his jacket, and he proudly twirled the pointed ends of his waxed mustache as he prepared his aircraft. The other had been in the bar with me the previous night, and he looked hungover. But once in the air they were all business as they maneuvered our clattering machine. Beyond the shallow bowl that was Pleiku city the sky cleared a little and our Huey gained some elevation.

The dark greens of the central plateau stretched to the mountainous horizon, with few roads to scar the beauty, and barely a building in sight, except for the comfortable homes of the tea plantation managers. Then the plateau fell away beneath us, and we descended rapidly toward towering hardwood trees that seemed to wall off our path. I saw a column of smoke in the far distance and noticed one pilot nodding to the other and pointing to Duc Co as we thundered toward it.

The final leg of the trip was a torture of twisting, protesting metal and roaring engines in overdrive. Our pilots chose what they regarded as the safest route to the besieged outpost—over and around and sometimes under the tops of giant gnarled trees that might have been there since the beginning of time. We descended into clearings of dense bamboo forests, then soared over triple-canopy growth, startling the brightly plummaged birds that nested there. I understood that there were anti-aircraft weapons buried somewhere in the forests below. I felt ill and scared, and when I glimpsed the broken, red earth of the airstrip and the barbed wire and sandbagged parapets of Duc Co camp I gasped with relief. I was the first off but it turned out to be safer in the chopper. Shells blasted around us almost immediately.

Myerscoff had his head buried in the dirt beside me and when he lifted his face he said, "I'm outta here, I got my story. The flight in, the shelling. And we broke the siege, didn't we?" The crew chief was throwing off the last of some medical supplies when Dick jumped back on board. I rolled on my back and watched the aircraft roar off into the trees. I was half amused and half angry. I'd been scooped by my old buddy, who would no doubt write a sensational yarn that would make the London dailies, and he would be drinking beer and bragging about his journey in the bar that night while I was looking for water in Duc Co.

The shelling let up when the helicopter left and I guessed that the airstrip was under observation from a Vietcong recoilless rifle location in the forest. I rose to my feet carefully and brushed the mud off my clothes and noticed there were Vietnamese paratroopers with their heads still down in foxholes along the airstrip. I walked briskly past the rusty, tangled barbed wire defenses and entered a creaky wooden gate that a Vietnamese paratrooper had already opened for me. Some shells had landed inside. There were wounded soldiers along a wall, a few getting first-aid treatment on the spot and others being dragged toward some sandbagged structures.

I pulled a camera from my pack and shot a few pictures of one of them who had his right leg wrapped in a compress bandage—his body sagging with effort as he hobbled along with his steel helmet askew on his head. He was leaning on a bulky American in a baggy fatigue uniform and soft khaki cap who towered over those around him and who grunted a brief greeting as he passed me.

The scene was bloody but orderly and I figured they didn't need my help. I followed after the American, passing a protective trench dug deep in the red soil and topped with sandbags, and into the dark recesses of the aid station. The flimsy wooden building was filling up with wounded men but most of their injuries appeared superficial. Two medics were picking metal fragments from legs and arms with forceps and dumping them into buckets. A striking Vietnamese woman was assisting them, her long black hair tied back from her shoulders as she bathed the wounded and applied dressings, smiling encouragingly. I asked her name but she ignored me, and I turned my attention again to the big American, who had just returned with another wounded man and was already on his way out again. I flipped out my notebook and caught up with him outside, introduced myself, and suggested we get out of the open. He led me over to the command bunker where he gave me a reassuring grin and told me he was Norman Schwarzkopf, a U.S. Army major advising the Vietnamese airborne unit now in Duc Co, and that his hometown was East Orange, New Jersey.

The major pushed back his cap, revealing the close-cropped hair of a West Point graduate, and he mopped a sweaty brow and seemed glad to have someone to talk to. His outfit was pinned down at Duc Co, and he was unhappy and worried and he wondered what I was doing there because he had seen few reporters in the months he had been in the countryside. I told him he should choose more comfortable surroundings if he wanted news coverage and he laughed and said that he had forgotten what comfort was. Major Schwarzkopf was frustrated because the Vietnamese airborne strike force he advised had tried to lift the siege but had failed. "We have had a helluva fight all the way," he told me, describing their successful combat assault in helicopters three days earlier near the camp, and an attempt the next day to sweep beyond its perimeter to the north and to the east, only to be ambushed by the Vietcong and driven back with severe casualties to Duc Co in a hail of machine gun fire.

"The truth is we're sitting ducks here," he complained. "The Vietcong can hit us anytime they like," and as if to punctuate his comment the plops of mortar rounds leaving their tubes in the forest were clearly audible, followed by the shouts of "Incoming." The command bunker filled up as American and Vietnamese soldiers came rushing in a few seconds ahead of the whoosh of the explosions. We sat on the dirt floor, gritting our teeth, sweating in the stuffiness of the bunker, and listening to the thunderclaps of the shells landing very close. The radio operator talked calmly to the command center in Pleiku, calling up an air attack to help out, "for the third time today," Schwarzkopf commented to me grimly.

While we waited for the bombers to arrive, I shook hands with the American commander of the camp, Captain Edward Richards. Even in the half light I could see the weariness stretched across his mouth, and his nerves seemed razor sharp. I knew I was getting a taste of what he had endured for sixty days, and I said I understood but he laughed. "No way anyone can understand who hasn't been here. We're scared, but we've learned to live with it. Just slam the door or shout any word loudly and we'll duck or run, that's our first instinct, our survival instinct. But when that first instant of hysteria passes, we'll start thinking, we'll be in control of ourselves."

There were a dozen Americans permanently based at Duc Co, a Special Forces A team stuck out in the middle of nowhere, living in a small, makeshift encampment. The property came with three hundred poorly trained tribesman soldiers and a hundred miles of border to defend. The strategy had been fine a few years earlier when the enemy was Vietcong guerrillas; now North Vietnamese regulars were joining the fight and marching to war right through Duc Co. Richards looked over at Schwarzkopf and said he was glad the Vietnamese airborne had arrived because half of his force of tribesmen had deserted, and the loyalty of those who remained was questionable. Most had stopped fighting and were hanging around the camp, rarely leaving their sandbagged trenches and bunkers because of the shelling.

There was a break so I went outside to look around. There was not a soul in sight. I was joined by Staff Sergeant Henry Allickson, who advised me to move quickly. One recent day five soldiers walking around Duc Co were felled with head wounds by snipers hiding in the nearby forest.

Allickson said he volunteered to lead patrols outside the wire each night to try and keep the enemy off balance, goading some of the reluctant tribesman soldiers into joining him and telling his frightened charges, "I'll shoot the first man that runs away, then I'll race the rest of you back to camp." I had noticed a pungent smell hanging in the air and asked him about it, and the sergeant twisted his nostrils and scowled and said, "Dead bodies rotting out there, probably ours because the VC police up their own casualties."

As if reminded of his own mortality, Allickson pulled a greasy wallet from his pocket and showed me pictures of his wife and five children in the United States whom he missed a lot, and I wondered if his family had any notion of how he spent his days and nights. The sergeant invited me over to his favorite spot, a sandbagged corner of the camp where he spent hours seeking targets for his high-powered rifle. I peeked over the sandbags and saw nothing but thick jungle and expressed doubt that anything human was there. The sergeant grinned at me and pulled back the bolt on his rifle and told me to shoot into the trees. After a moment of hesitation, I did, squeezing the trigger as I aimed at the thick, leafy stem of a wild banana plant. Someone shot back, not with a personal weapon but with a recoilless rifle whose shell rushed harmlessly by our heads. "Holy Christ," I shouted in surprise. Allickson was doubled up with laughter. "Victor Charlie's a mite sensitive today," he said.

In the command bunker that evening the talk was of the lousy food that we had scraped into mess tins from a large cooking pot and were chewing on with difficulty. The Vietnamese cook explained in poor French that it was ragoût de jambon. It was a staple of the Duc Co dinner table, but it tasted like canned ham stew to me. Schwarzkopf commented that his Vietnamese paratroopers ate much better food cooked over an open fire. I offered the group a swig of cognac from a silver hip flask and I felt more welcome than I had all day.

As the bunker filled with cigarette smoke, and everyone half listened for the sounds of danger, the Special Forces men complained more about their predicament. Someone demanded angrily, "Does anyone really care that we are sitting here, risking our lives every minute to hold this tiny bit of real estate?" I tried to explain that Duc Co was a test case for American military resolve and that if the situation truly worsened then U.S. forces would race in to the rescue like the cavalry in *She Wore a Yellow Ribbon.* "Worsened?" someone asked sarcastically. Rumbles of dissent came from around the room. Allickson laughed and said, "They've already sent in the Vietnamese to help," which occasioned another blast. Another sergeant offered a defense of the paratroopers. He held up a page of writing, torn from a notebook. Earlier that day he had been with a patrol outside the camp that had been ambushed, wounding some of his men. As he was crouching under fire tending to the leg wounds of one of them, the young soldier started writing in a notebook and handed him a page, and he read the unsteady scrawl, "In the defense of liberty in danger, always there is you and me. My name is Fam-En." The story shut off any more complaints about the Vietnamese, and the conversation and the company drifted off.

I joined Major Schwarzkopf and his Vietnamese paratrooper officers at daybreak at the eastern berm of the camp. Squinting over the walls, they estimated that the mortar tubes were set up as close as five hundred yards away in the forest, and Schwarzkopf discussed bringing in more attack aircraft to blast the suspected sites. In the post-dawn gloom, Duc Co looked a sorry mess: the roofs ripped from the wooden administration shacks and barracks, and sandbagged defenses torn apart and ragged, their contents spilled onto the ground. I was photographing when the mortars began popping again and we started for the command bunker. The crack of machine gun fire suggested the possibility of a Vietcong ground assault. Sergeant Allickson had said, "They could do it anytime they wanted to, if they wished to give up high casualties," and I was praying that this would not be the time. I monitored the attack from inside the safety of the command bunker, listening to the radio operator channeling information to headquarters in Pleiku. Schwarzkopf was nowhere to be seen, and I presumed he was with his troops in the foxholes helping fend off the ground assault.

At one point I crawled outside to see if I could find him, but I couldn't move. I stared at U.S. Air Force jets screeching low over the trees, dropping bombs that seemed as big as Volkswagen Beetles, hitting just beyond the bunker line. I heard metal splinters slamming into the walls of the command bunker next to me. I could see Captain Richards near the eastern berm pushing his soldiers to firing holes. They were leaning into the wall and pulling their carbine triggers quickly and reloading fresh magazines. They seemed to have gotten the message that this could be a fight to the finish.

Schwarzkopf appeared in the distance, his tall frame bobbing along the bunker line, and he swerved into the command center and grabbed the radio from Hunt, shouting to headquarters, "We are being hit from the west, east and south and a patrol moving north is heavily engaged." He rushed outside again, joining Richards and several American Green Berets who held a brief conference and then barked

157

orders. I got the impression they were going to launch a counterassault. I got out of the way and moved to the aid station, which was filling up with wounded men. I straightened up the clothes of a few of them and tried to make them comfortable as the medics worked on the most seriously injured. One soldier seemed to have lost both his eyes, and a medic told me another had his spinal column severed.

Sometime later, when the sounds of battle had moved a mile or so away, Schwarzkopf came by to check on the wounded. His face was flushed, but he flashed a triumphant grin as he praised his paratroopers who had held the line. As Richards walked in, Schwarzkopf clapped him on the back and said to me with feeling, "I was proud to be an American soldier today. Every one of these Special Forces men gave a totally selfless effort in helping us. Their coolness was astounding."

I had gotten my story and my pictures and I wanted to leave in time to catch the Sunday newspapers, but the scheduled chopper trip had been canceled and I had to wait for the next one the following day. I wandered back to the aid station, where the beautiful Vietnamese nurse was taking a break. Her name was Lien Huong. She was the daughter of a Baptist minister. The Americans were very protective of her, treating her like a kid sister.

Doug Britt, a member of the Special Forces team, told me, "There's no lovers lane around here, but even if there was I wouldn't court her because she's the only single girl in the camp and there are twelve of us, and it would be too cruel on the others, who respect her too much." I wondered if he was kidding me, but I didn't think so. I asked Lien Huong if she had any problem with the men, and she said a Vietnamese camp officer made a pass at her one day but that her American friends had straightened him out. She liked the Americans "because they are so kind to me, they will never hurt me."

One of her patients was getting worse, the soldier with the severed spinal column, and Major Schwarzkopf decided to call in an emergency helicopter. He turned to me and said, "You're on it." By late evening the chopper was overhead and I was obliged by the major to join him and several others on the airstrip with a flashlight to help guide the craft in. It was a dangerous spot with snipers all around. Any one of us could have been killed where we stood. Schwarzkopf told me years later, when he wore general's stars, that the pilot had radioed down asking that the flashlights be shaken so that he could determine exactly where we were. When the instruction had been relayed to me I had responded, "I don't know about you guys but my flashlight's been shaking ever since we got out here."

That evening I sent my first story on the siege, and later I prepared several others on my visit to Duc Co, with Norman Schwarzkopf and Lien Huong and the Special Forces team, and they were widely used. Other AP reporters came later to report on the lifting of the siege, and the departure of Schwarzkopf's Vietnamese airborne outfit to other battles. After a few days' break in Pleiku I wrote a last piece about nurse Lien Huong for newspapers of August 13. It was the most unashamedly sentimental story that I had ever done, a paean to self-sacrifice and virtue and unrequited love.

"Duc Co, South Vietnam. When the night comes and the mortar rounds start slapping this Special Forces camp, a thin wraith of a girl will slip through the exploding shadows like a pale ghost. Lien Huong is searching for the wounded. She will probably be weeping as she crawls from bunker to bunker, sometimes wearing a steel helmet that wobbles unsteadily on her head. Although Lien Huong has watched scores of men die and heard the agonizing cries of the wounded, she has never gotten used to the suffering. Her eyes filled with tears, her blue smock mud-stained, Lien Huong will crawl back to the command bunker, tell the American medics in halting English that a soldier has been seriously hit, and crawl back out again with a box of field dressings. Later when the attack is over and the wounded have been gathered together, she will join the sweating American medics and help them fight for the lives of the dying and comfort the wounded. Lien Huong, just twenty years old last February, volunteered for nursing work at Duc Co twenty months ago. Many nights have brought Vietcong fire upon the camp. She bears up to the rigors of Duc Co with an inner calmness that astounds the hard-bitten American Special Forces men here, who say that Duc Co makes them old overnight. Lien Huong has resisted the ravages of fear, dirt and constant toil. Her waist-length hair has a permanent sheen; her face, which has never known cosmetics because she has always lived in the remote countryside, has a soft and clear complexion. Her eyes are shy, despite the things she has seen. Lien Huong's complete dedication has not blinded her to what she misses in the world. She yearns for a pretty dress but knows that at Duc Co there is no opportunity to wear it. She has never been to Saigon and would like to go there. She misses a young Vietnamese paratrooper sergeant with whom she fell in love while he was based at Duc Co, but she hasn't seen him for three months and may never do so again. Lien Huong has a simple philosophy. 'I want to stay here and help. I like the soldiers and I want to be with them because they need me. I will stay here for as long as the camp holds out. If the Vietcong drives us away I will go to another camp.' "

Ed White suggested I call the story "The Angel of Duc Co." I favored any title with the name Florence Nightingale in it, and we left it up to editors, who used both ideas in their headlines. Readers sent bundles of clothes and cosmetics to the Pentagon to pass on to the needy nurse. When I returned to Saigon, John Wheeler kidded me about my corniness. Horst commented on the story with unconcealed merriment, "Dat's what happens when I leave him alone in the field at night."

The 173rd

THE U.S. ARMY buildup was concentrated near Saigon and they were inundated by reporters and photographers. We drove out to the U.S. Army's 173rd Airborne Brigade camp at Bien Hoa each day, traveling the distance in half an hour or so, bumping across the final stretch of dirt road that wound through an old Vietnamese cemetery with rust-colored headstones. Olive drab ponchos were strung between the graves to shelter soldier sentinels from the searing sun. The camp tent lines were spread out across a small plateau of scrub-covered sand dunes, and by design overlooked the busy Bien Hoa air base in whose defense the brigade had been deployed. The paratroopers were reputed to be among the elite of U.S. military forces, and I was eager to see how they would fare against Vietcong guerrillas.

Their commander was Brigadier General Ellis W. Williamson, whose lean, ramrod stance and crew cut graying hair merited the nickname "Butch" his men used out of his earshot. Williamson had strode off the plane with his troops like General MacArthur wading ashore in Leyte in World War Two. The unit's information sergeant, Don Pratt, had been warned by Westmoreland's chief spokesman, Colonel Ben Legare, to caution restraint: "Get to your general before the press does, and make sure he knows that he is to emphasize the defensive nature of your mission. The 173rd is here to defend air bases and not to fight a war. Make sure he knows that." But Pratt missed Williamson at the airport and the general told the press that he had come to Vietnam to fight World War Three.

I spent my youth in Bluff, New Zealand, until my father sent me to a prestigious boarding school to further my education. But I rebelled against the strict authority and played the double B-flat bass tuba in the school band instead of cricket and rugby. I longed for adventure, to see the world. I still do.

A rainy day in the coastal province of Binh Dinh in Vietnam in February 1967.

My first assignment for the Associated Press was to Indonesia. President Sukarno welcomed me to an official reception in Jakarta in 1961, and I traveled with him around the countryside. But his ministers were not happy about the critical tone of my reporting and expelled me the following year.

Mal Browne, the Saigon bureau chief, wrote a manual for reporters in Vietnam, including a detailed list of what one needed to pack for trips into the field of battle. I bought everything on the streets of Saigon, in the black market.

AP/Wide World Photos

AP/Wide World Photos

The action heated up when American troops began operating in War Zone C in the autumn of 1965, and I began wearing a steel helmet for protection and packed a gas mask. My colleagues, cameraman Vo Huynh of NBC and his soundman brother, Vo Suu, were less worried.

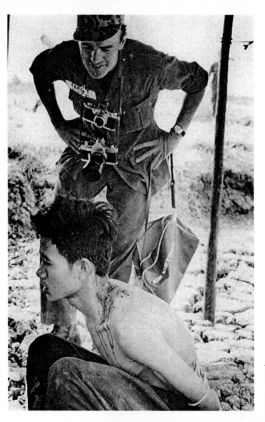

In the early years of the war, the best way to get a story was to go and find one. I drove around the country in my own car and came upon some ugly scenes. In March 1964 I saw militiamen dragging a Vietcong suspect to a hut in Hau Nghia province. My arrival interrupted his beating.

The secret police attacked me during a Buddhist antigovernment demonstration in Saigon on July 7, 1963. *New York Times* reporter David Halberstam dragged me to my feet and confronted my attackers.

I met Nina Nguyen at a reception in 1962 and we were married in Hong Kong. It was difficult to reconcile the dangers of my career with the responsibilities of family life, but I did my best. Nina and I had two children, Andrew and Elsa.

For the traditional Tet celebration, Nina wore an Ao Dai, and we posed with Andrew and Elsa in our Saigon apartment before joining her family for religious festivities.

AP/Wide World Photos

In 1966, I won the Pulitzer. It was the third in a row for the Saigon bureau of the AP. My colleagues Mal Browne and Horst Faas helped me read the congratulatory messages as they came over the wire. Malcolm Browne won his Pulitzer in 1964 for his coverage of the fall of the Diem regime. Horst Faas's 1964 war pictures earned him the prize.

AP/Wide World Photos

AP president Wes Gallagher had backed my controversial Vietnam war reporting despite strong criticism from the Lyndon Johnson White House and the U.S. military high command. He took particular pleasure in my successes.

I dropped to the ground and crawled when sniper fire opened up on us during a search and destroy operation with American troops in the jungles near Rach Kien in January 1967. Several previous operations had failed to dislodge the Vietcong.

AP colleagues in the Saigon bureau in 1971. From left, standing: Hugh Mulligan, Huynh Trinh, Holger Jensen, Richard Blystone, Arnett, Max Nash, Richard Pyle; seated: George Esper, Carl Robinson, Ed White.

It was my AP colleague photographer Eddie Adams (with two cameras) who captured the gruesome moment when the Saigon police chief executed a captured Vietcong soldier during the Tet Offensive. The image won him the Pulitzer Prize. Vo Huynh and Ron Nessen of NBC joined us on the street outside the bureau as we were leaving for another day's coverage.

The North Vietnamese Easter Offensive of 1972 swept through Quang Tri and routed many government units. A military photographer and I saw several soldiers lying wounded on the side of Route 1 north of Hue and helped carry them to a truck for transportation to the hospital.

Wes Gallagher called me in Paris and told me of a chance to go to Hanoi—a trip to the other side—to cover an antiwar delegation that had arranged to bring home three POWs. I sensed immediately the potential for controversy and somehow managed to convince Cora Weiss, the organizer of the group, that I was the best man for the job. We posed at the Beijing airport. From left: Arnett, Minnie Lee Gartley, Cora Weiss, Olga Charles, Richard Falk, Lieutenant Norris Charles, David Dellinger, Lieutenant Mark Gartley, and Major Edward Elias.

In the spring of 1975, Hue and Da Nang fell to the Vietcong. Soon the decision was made to evacuate Saigon. Most of the reporters left on the last helicopters out. Only a few stayed behind. When Saigon fell on April 30, 1975, two North Vietnamese soldiers came into the AP bureau, where Matt Franjola (left), George Esper (second from right), and I were writing stories. They showed us their route into the city and shared soft drinks and stale cookies.

The first war I covered outside Southeast Asia was Cyprus, which the Turkish Army invaded in 1974. I felt at home in the midst of the chaos and crisis. I sheltered from air strikes under a concrete bridge with Greek Cypriot militiamen during a Turkish assault on the capital, Nicosia.

I stood vigil outside the gates of the U.S. Embassy in Teheran, Iran, every morning during my three months' coverage of the hostage crisis in 1979–80, watching the anti-American demonstrators marching past and listening to provocative speeches broadcast over the loudspeakers on top of the gates.

I was sent to Jonestown, Guyana, in 1978 in the aftermath of the mass suicide of more than nine hundred fanatical cult members. Among the bodies was a bloodstained stuffed animal made by the handicraft center at the colony.

Death squads rampaged through El Salvador in the early 1980s, killing those who opposed the military regime. My CNN cameraman, Howie Dorf, photographed skeletons at a killing field in the lava beds at San Salvador Mountain, assisted by soundman Jackie Griffith.

In Nicaragua, I did a standup in the Managua central plaza with cameraman Willis Perry and soundman Tyrone Edwards. CNN wanted to cover all of the world's hot spots, and I welcomed the opportunities to get into the action.

Covering the Israeli siege of Beirut in 1982 was dangerous. Islamic fundamentalist groups were detaining—and later kidnapping—the press. My CNN crew was captured and driven away. My Palestinian driver and I followed in hot pursuit and helped to release them.

Briefly, I was assigned to cover the Reagan White House, but the daily routine of press handouts and Rose Garden gatherings was not for me.

On the streets of Moscow, I covered demonstrations by Jews wanting to leave the Soviet Union and got into many scuffles with the KGB. In December 1987, I was beaten and hauled away by six secret police thugs during a rally in front of the Soviet Foreign Ministry. I was arrested and detained for several hours.

CNN producer Robert Wiener and engineer Nic Robertson cleverly orchestrated the smuggling into Baghdad of satellite communications systems that gave CNN an undeniable edge. They stayed for the opening shots of the war to show me how to use the equipment.

All my news reports from the al-Rashid Hotel in Baghdad were identified as being censored by the Iraqi government.

I was required to work closely with Sadoun al-Jenabi, the senior Iraqi official at the al-Rashid Hotel in charge of the minders who supervised the press. I often argued with him over censorship rules and news coverage, but despite this we had a congenial relationship.

The most controversial story I covered in the early part of the war was the destruction of what the allies claimed was a biological weapons testing center, but which the Iraqis said was a baby milk plant. I visited there several times and examined the wreckage. I found measuring cups packed in milk powder containers.

Baghdad had no electric power from the early days of the bombing, and we worked with limited generator lighting in the hotel. I often gave my phoned reports to Atlanta from the lobby, lit only by flashlights and the television camera.

Jay Ullal, *Stern* magazine

On February 13, 1991, the thick concrete roof of the Amiriya shelter was destroyed as if it were butter. The U.S. government claimed the shelter was used as a military command post; the Iraqis denied it was used for anyone but civilians. The bombing shocked the public; more than three hundred were killed. The press was taken to photograph many of the bodies in the grounds of a Baghdad hospital. I could find no evidence that the Iraqi military had been inside, but the clothes of the victims had been burned off their bodies.

Before I interviewed Saddam Hussein, his security men took me to an empty hotel room and gave me a thorough body search. The Iraqi president turned out to be a cordial though chilling subject. He had a photographer take pictures and had a print sent to me at the hotel soon afterward.

The Boys of Baghdad—Bernard Shaw, John Holliman, and I—meet after the war in Washington, D.C., with CNN president Tom Johnson.

I made my first trip to
Afghanistan in 1982,
to cover the mujahedeen
guerrilla resistance against the
Soviet occupation army.

I returned to Kabul in 1992, the
day after I finished writing my
book. The Soviets had conceded defeat and pulled out,
leaving Afghanistan swarming
with armed militiamen. These
young Shia soldiers had taken
over the road south of the city
and turned a former luxury hotel into a military strongpoint.
They were proud of the variety
of Russian weapons they had
obtained during the war and
vowed they would fight a civil
war to take power.

A persuasive team of promoters handed out invitations to the outfit's combat operations like advance men pushing a road show. Sergeant Pratt talked me into covering what he promised were exclusive stories, but twenty other reporters often turned up. Sometimes, the press outnumbered the soldiers. Still, Pratt, a Southerner, was a candid man, good company and a generous host.

The paratroopers came to Vietnam believing they knew something about jungle warfare: they had trained for it in Okinawa and other Pacific locations. I waited for the first skirmishes, aware that the U.S. marines based in Da Nang were having more difficulty than they had anticipated adjusting to the extreme heat and learning to understand the Vietnamese. In keeping with U.S. government pronouncements, Sergeant Pratt publicly emphasized the brigade's defensive role, but privately he said that it was a bunch of baloney, that the unit would be going into action against the communists as soon as all its heavy weapons had arrived.

Covering ground troops was not a joyride. The going was sometimes so rough—through deep, stinking mud and thick jungle—that everyone had to link hands to avoid getting lost. The vines and underbrush tore at weapons and clothing, and a command would be passed down the line from the point men on back: "Check your grenades, check your grenades." The soldiers had to make sure that a probing vine had not snatched the metal safety pin. "It's like cutting your way through a bowl of spaghetti," someone said. "Wish it was that easy, Tarzan never had it so rough," came the reply.

Even at high noon the sun never filtered through the heavy foliage. There was just a peculiar light akin to twilight. But it never changed and there was no softness about it. Just when you knew you could go no further there might be a sudden sting on the soft flesh of your inner thigh and you knew that a black leech was visiting, crawling up your leg from the ooze slopping at your ankles and feasting and growing bloated on your blood until the next rest break when you could roll down your trousers and burn the intruder to oblivion with a lighted cigarette.

The jungles were predictably menacing, but the populated countryside posed a different kind of problem: people could be more treacherous than tangled vines and slimy mud. This was a war with no front lines and no safe rear, where the loyalty of the Vietnamese you worked with could not be guaranteed. I could see that the anomalies of Vietnam confounded the young soldiers, who had been trained to fight a uniformed enemy in defense of clearly defined goals.

I rode on a patrol of armored personnel carriers and Scorpion self-propelled 90mm guns north of the base camp along Route 1 where Vietnamese intelligence reports suggested that up to one thousand Vietcong guerrillas were assembling to harass the Americans. The paratroopers were wary as they moved off along the highway and were cheered up as they passed through the Catholic refugee community of Ho Nai, where hundreds of local people ran to urge them on. A few miles further up the highway the atmosphere changed: there were crude foxholes and trenches dug along the roadside, and pedestrians and farmers in the fields turned their faces away. A car honked insistently and a small French sedan worked its way impatiently around the armored column, a European man at the wheel, with two smartly dressed female passengers. When the vehicle raced away in front of them the battle-ready paratroopers stared at one another in amazement. The car was apparently from the Trang Bom rubber plantation up ahead.

Just beyond the plantation the highway was scarred with deep ditches that halted the military vehicles. The soldiers plunged into the underbrush and set up their mortars and heavy machine guns, ready for anything, anything that is except the scores of Vietnamese people who suddenly surged around them, some in ragged clothes and unkempt hair and with the strange, wild look of forest dwellers. Others were dragging ox carts loaded with scruffy children. The Vietnamese police officers accompanying the American patrol said they were harmless.

Striking out into the brush, one squad of troopers spotted a black-clad figure in the distance that seemed to fit the description of the Vietcong and they charged in pursuit. They found an old woman cutting bamboo shoots with a sickle. She started shouting hysterically and no one could understand what she was trying to say, but the police confirmed that her ID card was in order and the soldiers let her be. Gongs were banging somewhere in the brush as the troopers moved forward, joined by the armored column that had lumbered off the highway and was crashing through the undergrowth. Later, we came abreast of the Saigon–Hanoi railway line, which hadn't been used in years, and we gratefully followed its railbed back to Trang Bom and rejoined Highway 1 for home. In a day the paratroopers had glimpsed a Vietnam of mystery and contradiction that their military manuals did not anticipate, reinforcing the feeling that they were strangers in an alien land.

The restraints of presidential policy kept the 173rd at a low level of operations for the first month or so, much to the dismay of the commanding general. Williamson was eager, impatient even.

Williamson wanted to generate good press and was sensitive to information that reflected his brigade in what he saw as a poor light. He had a lot to fret about. There were 3,500 troopers under his command and as many as sixty reporters and photographers at any one time poking around. The AP in particular came under his fire because we were there every day, and we covered almost every paratrooper foray beyond the base defense perimeter.

Horst was with an infantry patrol supported with air strikes that supposedly hit Vietcong positions in the hills ahead. He moved in with the scouts to check out the target and saw a column of figures coming toward them. They held their fire. As the people approached, the Americans could see the yellow and brown robes of Buddhist monks and nuns. Some of their clothing was smeared with blood and six people were being carried in slings. When the group made the Buddhist sign of greeting the soldiers moved forward to help. The monks and nuns had been in a pagoda that had been hit mistakenly in the air strike. I wrote a story that said the religious group "had become victims of the confusion that often surrounds war in Vietnam." General Williamson howled.

An Australian infantry battalion moved in beside the paratroopers at Bien Hoa. They were friendly, experienced soldiers who liked socializing with the Americans but were sore about Williamson's prohibition on all beer consumption both on base and in the beer parlors of the town.

I was a beer drinker myself and I expressed sympathy for the men with several tongue-in-cheek stories suggesting that the rough and tough paratroopers weren't mean enough to handle a few beers after returning from the jungle. The general was not amused when the Australian defense minister successfully lobbied the U.S. high command to have the beer ban lifted. To make matters worse, when a women's church group in Texas read my account of the affair, they sent the brigade chaplain five hundred church key beer can openers. The chaplain advertised that anyone attending chapel services the following Sunday would receive a can opener. He broke all attendance records.

In August 1965, when the general committed two of his paratrooper battalions to a five-day sweep operation southeast of Saigon and came up empty-handed, I wrote an assessment of his military tactics. "There appeared to be a chain reaction of mistakes that decreed success virtually impossible even before the operation got fully under way. Many observers feel that the U.S. high command may be embarked on a strategy that brought failure to Vietnamese forces before and could bring failure to U.S. forces now."

Soon afterward, General Williamson decided he'd had enough of my reporting and summoned me to his brigade headquarters. Don Pratt implored me to be nice to the general and to nod dutifully at the forthcoming lecture. "This guy doesn't have a clue as to what you're all about so just jolly him up and it will make all our jobs easier."

I drove out to the brigade base midmorning and walked over to the command. When I passed Pratt he made throat-slitting gestures at me; I flipped him off in return. General Williamson stayed seated as I entered his office and beckoned me to a wooden chair at his table. He had assembled several of his senior staff officers for the session, all of whom I knew pretty well. Williamson leaned back and eyed me. Even though I told myself to be strong, my resolve weakened and for a while I felt like a raw recruit on report for bedwetting. "Why the hell do you and the other correspondents pick on the 173rd and print nothing but stories about the VC's elusiveness? Don't you know that the VC are cowards, they fight only at night and when we catch a bunch of them together they run away. When you say we can't find the VC it makes us look like candyasses, and that we are not." I noticed the staff officers stirring uneasily and I was sure they had heard all this before and much more. The general went on. "Why the hell can't you write positive aspects of the war. The only way to change the tide here is to get Americans to support our actions here in this country. If we want our troops home we have to convince the people and they have to write their congressman about the success we are making here."

I protested that we were doing our best and were reporting events as sympathetically as we could and were appreciative of the hospitality his brigade offered. The general was not impressed. He stood up and barked at me, "That's not enough, we want you on the team." I had heard that before. I tried to explain that the Associated Press was an international news organization with responsibilities beyond the United States and even had subscribers in communist countries, including Tass.

Williamson looked at me incredulously. "Tass? That's a goddamn communist institution." The discussion went downhill after that and as I departed Williamson told the information officer to stay, and read him the riot act for allowing me anywhere on the premises. Pratt came in to the bureau next day and yelled "You blew it" and told me I was no longer welcome with the brigade.

"What the hell, so I'll cover the Big Red One [the U.S. First Infantry Division], and the marines," I replied.

"No way in hell, Williamson may hate your butt but he's headline happy and you make headlines, so I'll put you on combat operations anyway."

Pratt was true to his word. He also kept me apprised of his general's campaign against me. At a meeting in Nha Trang with two government information officials from Washington, Colonel Roger Bankston and Dan Henken, Williamson told them that I had admitted to him that I wrote to please Tass, and that in his opinion I was subversive and should be discredited. Banging the tabletop, he announced that newsmen who were not on the team should be banished, and that reporters who stressed America's mistakes in Vietnam were "obviously incompetent or have subversive tendencies."

The general's soldiers were the people I wrote about, and they enjoyed the attention. My observations on the elusiveness of the Vietcong and the frustrations of the war were the kinds of things they scrawled in their letters home, so they had no quarrel with me. Their goodwill was essential in my continuing ability to cover the actions of the paratroopers, in defiance of General Williamson's instructions, even though it sometimes meant sneaking onto a combat operation like a hobo.

One day Don Pratt drove to our bureau with the information that the First Battalion would be launching a combat assault against a defended or "hot" Vietcong base area north of Saigon, and he wanted to take me along even though press coverage was not authorized—"because I owe you one for getting our beer ration back." A Vietnamese bureau assistant drove me to the helicopter assembly point near the brigade base before dawn, and I crawled through the security fence and joined Pratt and some of his pals from an A Company platoon. With my black market tropical weight green fatigues and my steel helmet, I blended into the crowd. I was the envy of the group because I had purchased the new cleated jungle boots that would give me more traction in the mud than the smooth-soled jump boots the paratroopers were issued. The platoon leader, in on our game, smuggled me onto a troop-carrying helicopter with one of his squads even as senior brigade staff supervised the lift-off.

We flew beyond the Bien Hoa air base and the sprawling community around it, beyond the district towns where breakfast smoke curled from the house chimneys, across the flooded rice fields, over the rubber plantations, and beyond even the dirt roads and the rustic thatched-roofed hamlets of the rural poor. We arrived at an expanse of marsh and jungle known as War Zone D since the colonial war. Our helicopters had conquered the area's legendary inaccessibility and we were soon thundering into a spacious clearing. The paratroopers tumbled off even as the aircraft's skids were making the first, tentative contact with the ground.

I felt Pratt's hand on my shoulder and then we were both jumping through the air. I tensed for the impact only to find myself sinking into a slimy, smelly goo of mud and rotting vegetation. I was buried up to my thighs in the stuff before I could get my balance and haul myself forward in the direction of the soldiers. I pulled myself through tall yellow elephant grass that obscured my view and lacerated my fingers to find Pratt waiting at an ox cart track. He was as filthy as I was. "At least Victor Charlie didn't know we were coming," he said. "Because there's been no contact yet." The way he grinned at me reminded me of the actor Dane Clark from the war movies I watched back home as a child. When I told him so he replied, "Hell no, I'm John Wayne, let's get movin'."

I joined the command group, which was poring over a plastic map overlay marked with thick red and blue grease pencil lines and scribbled coordinates. Radio intercepts at command headquarters had located the presence of a Vietcong communications center on high ground several miles to the west, and the mission was to knock it out and inflict as high a body count on the enemy as was possible. The company commander, Captain Walter Daniel, issued whispered orders to his platoons to move out carefully and to keep their eyes peeled. "This is Charlie country, and don't you forget it, so be careful."

Third platoon led the way with a young point man picking through tangled undergrowth where the visibility was about fifteen feet at best. I heard him complain to his buddies that he was now an old-timer because there were so many new recruits brought in to replace casualties inflicted in battle or felled by tropical illnesses.

The first day we traversed a vine-tangled swamp that the Vietcong had the good sense to avoid. It took us all day to move just two miles. We passed the night uncomfortably in our wet clothes and at dawn started out again. After an hour, the Third Platoon reported it was near the crest of a hill, and then the Vietcong revealed their presence. The jungle erupted with machine gun fire that echoed through the high forest canopy, cutting down the first seven Americans and stopping the rest of us in our tracks. I fell on my face and gripped the dirt as bullets thudded into nearby tree trunks and whined over my head.

Soldiers nearby began opening fire with their M-16 rifles. I looked up and saw Don Pratt and the brigade's chaplain, Frank Vavrin, lying prostrate and it was some minutes before we fully realized what was happening. Several hundred yards ahead Third Company had been ambushed and was fighting for its life; the bullets hitting near us were ricochets. A voice shouted, "Cease firing around here, you're shooting up into your own men," and I crawled over to Captain Daniel's command group. He was crouched over the radio. An urgent voice was saying, "We're hit bad, we're hit bad, and we're cut off and pinned down." Daniel responded earnestly, "No way, you're the Third Platoon, you're never pinned down," but the voice was insistent and it soon reported that the platoon commander had taken a bullet in the head.

Daniel went to see for himself and I dashed after him, half crawling, half sliding down an embankment that sloped to a narrow stream. The jungle floor slanted up from there to the hillside where the crash of dueling automatic weapons was deafening. The captain kept going, brushing aside spiky foliage and skidding in the greasy mud until the bullets seemed to be a hair's breadth away. He fell to the ground and I thought he might be hit until he began crawling to a vantage point where, with his chin in the dirt, he could see into a small clearing. There, the bloodied body of one of his paratroopers was being rolled over and over by a hidden Vietcong machine gunner.

There were two more American bodies at the edge of the clearing and what remained of A Platoon was further up the hill and out of sight but not of sound in the thick brush. Daniel slid back down the hill and crossed the stream to rejoin his radioman. He half demanded, half pleaded with his superiors back at the base for help. "We've taken every other hill we came up against in Vietnam, my company has, but I don't think we can take this one. We'll have to bring the rest of the battalion in."

Captain Daniel moved up the Second Platoon to do their best to break through to the First Platoon survivors, and the thirty or so men scrambled past us with their weapons at the ready, and were soon out of sight down the embankment.

The Second Platoon's rescue attempt made headway, allowing the wounded to be brought back through the lines to the command group. Captain Daniel sent out a few troopers as a thin line of security around us, and the medics began their work. Three of them worked over a seriously wounded paratrooper. "Keep pounding his heart, keep it beating," one medic urged as another applied mouth-to-mouth resuscitation. They stayed with it for an hour as bullets ricocheted around them but the paratrooper died.

Don Pratt, Chaplain Vavrin and I did the best we could to help comfort the other wounded, checking their compress bandages and bathing their heads with wet cloths. There were over thirty wounded lying there by noon, including Sergeant Gerald Mahoney, who had been hit in the knee and the thumb on the first assault. "I'll be nineteen years old on October 17 and I'll have my birthday in the hospital and I don't like that," he said. Chaplain Vavrin patted his head and said to me, "They are terribly brave boys and I'm glad I'm here today," and then crawled over to soothe a delirious soldier wounded in the thigh.

By early afternoon despite the best efforts of all, two of the troopers with serious sucking chest wounds had died, and a sweat-soaked medic in a blood-stained jacket said what everyone was thinking: "We need helicopters to get these people out. Can't we get helicopters?" The problem was that the jungle had a triple canopy, towering two hundred feet over our heads. We would have to blast a clearing out of the trees with dynamite and that took time. By late afternoon the company engineers had carved out a landing zone scattered with broken trees and stumps, and overhead a gap had been left in the canopy that let the first rays of sun into that dark jungle. The landing zone turned out to be too small for the army evacuation helicopters and one that tried to come in slapped its rotor blades against the trees. The smaller air force HH-43s were able to come in and Pratt and I helped load the wounded.

By early evening the battalion commander, Colonel John Tyler, had brought in two companies of reinforcements from behind the Vietcong positions. They searched the crest of the hill, where they found trenches and tunnels and the bodies of eleven of the enemy.

The colonel was not happy to see me. He told Pratt, "The general told us this guy is not welcome around here," but he talked with me anyway. "This is how it has to be in D Zone. There is no other way to rout them out. We have been here before and we'll be back again. If they want to fight like this then we'll fight."

I pointed out to the colonel that eleven paratroopers had been killed, forty wounded, and to continue to fight that way meant establishing a one-to-one kill ratio at best, which did not bode well for the future.

The colonel smiled confidently. "Look, son, we're going to get better at this and the VC worse." In the early evening Pratt and I climbed on the last helicopter out. My trousers were wet—I discovered that we were sitting in two inches of blood, trapped by the lip on the metal floor from the dead and wounded of earlier flights.

I wrote my story late that night. Because we were restricted from detailing specific numbers of dead and wounded, I mentioned that the unit had sustained heavy casualties, reasonable enough, I assumed, because nearly half the company had been hurt. The next day, at the daily military briefing by American and Vietnamese officials in Saigon, which we nicknamed the Five O'Clock Follies, military officials quarreled with my numbers, describing the casualties as light. When I objected, they explained that for a company-sized unit the losses were indeed heavy, but when assessed against a whole battalion they would be considered light and that's how they were looking at it.

I was infuriated at the sleight of hand and there was nothing to prevent it happening in the future.

Supply Column 21

THE JOHNSON ADMINISTRATION grew alarmed at Vietnam news coverage and tried to limit it. The AP was a prime target. My graphic battle reports and stories of riot gas experiments on military operations, and equipment failures and weapons shortages in U.S. Army combat units had so angered Washington that President Johnson ordered the FBI to rake through my life and try to come up with some dirt to silence me. AP headquarters was aware of the generalities, but only much later did we learn the extent of White House unhappiness.

Press secretary Bill Moyers observed in a 1965 memo that the coverage of CBS reporter Morley Safer and me was "irresponsible and prejudiced" and because we were foreign born we did not have "the basic American interests at heart." Moyers promised to "tighten things up" and Johnson scrawled "good" on the memo. Presidential assistant Jack Valenti wrote a memo to Johnson prior to a meeting with Wes Gallagher and other AP executives: "You may want to bring up the problem of Peter Arnett, who has been more damaging to the U.S.

cause than a whole battalion of Vietcong: his stories on defective equipment, antiquated aircraft, use of poison gas."

Wes Gallagher was invited to a White House meeting and he went prepared to counter the president's criticism, carrying a briefcase filled with photos and facts supporting the disputed stories but Johnson made no mention of the war or AP coverage and finally Gallagher decided to raise the issue himself. "Mr. President, I understand you have been critical of some of AP's stories from Vietnam." "Oh, no," Johnson replied as he patted Gallagher on the back. "I think the AP is doing a great job." Gallagher did not challenge him, instead saying, "Well I just wanted you to know, Mr. President, the AP is not against you or for you," to which Johnson responded, "That's not quite the way I like it."

In a memo to Wes Gallagher on August 16, AP personnel chief Keith Fuller explained that everyone in the AP would have to take greater caution in balancing news coverage, which made it "particularly a problem for Peter Arnett because in his role as a non-American who happens also to be one of our most active front-line reporters, it is easy for frustrated officials to vent their ire on him." Fuller said he already had wind of a whispering campaign and would ask my cooperation in a background check. I had no objections to giving the AP all the information it required. Years later retired U.S. Army Colonel Dan Baldwin told me he had spent a month in 1965 flying around the United States with a CIA agent in a government plane interviewing acquaintances of mine who had returned from Saigon, trying to tie me to the Vietcong.

Gallagher's answer to the maze of rules and regulations that the U.S. authorities in Saigon were imposing on the press was to strike back hard, advising us in a letter on June 14, 1965, "I think the best answer at the moment is aggressiveness on all your parts, as you have done in the past, and not be deterred by restrictions." Gallagher's blinking green light beckoned the daredevil in us all and we took him up on his challenge.

On August 18, 1965, Eddie Adams, one of the AP photograhers, informed us that a large U.S. Marine military operation would be launched the next day and that he would be flying to Hue with the marine commander, Major General Lewis Walt. Eddie said there was a ride available on a Da Nang–based U.S. Army helicopter piloted by Captain Irwin Cockett, who was a friend of ours. I rushed home to pack my bag and hitched a ride on a U.S. Air Force C-130 transport plane hauling stacks of body bags to Da Nang. Dawn arrived before we did, and I found Captain Cockett having coffee at the Army Aviation mess hall. He said the operation was actually at the Van Tuong Peninsula south of Da Nang. He cranked up his helicopter and we flew into the rays of the rising sun toward the battle.

Approaching the new airstrip at sand-choked Chu Lai we saw smoke rising from the wooded peninsula to the south. A large military operation was still going on. Cockett put me off near three marine CH-34 transport choppers whose rotor blades were already whirring, and I jumped aboard one filled with drums of gasoline. Then Tim Page, a freelance photographer, who had also been tipped off to travel south, jumped aboard.

We were soon circling high over the peninsula and the crew chief yelled into my ear that the pilot was looking for a place to drop his cargo. We began corkscrewing to the ground in a combat landing and I glimpsed an armored column below us as we came in with a thump. Page and I helped the crew chief roll the gasoline drums to the ground and then noticed a dozen bedraggled marines surging toward us, some wounded and half carried by their buddies. I heard the crew chief yell into his mike, "We're in the wrong fucking place" and the chopper bucked like a deer, then settled down again briefly as the wounded marines scrambled aboard, clinging to the metalwork as it lurched away.

Page and I stayed behind, alone in the clearing, looking beyond the trees to the bulky shapes of several amphibious track vehicles resting in a flooded paddyfield fifty yards away. As we approached them we could see their steel sides splintered and scarred with explosives, and burning hot from the hundred-degree heat of the morning. I peered at the water in horror; staring back at me were the sightless eyes of a dead marine whose face was an inch below the surface. In his right hand a marine K-bar combat knife was still tightly clutched. Page called me to the rear of an armored personnel carrier where another dead soldier lay curled up like a child, and we could see more bodies in the water.

We heard the creak of a steel door opening, and a tousled head peeked out, "Get the hell inside, there's VC everywhere," and he beckoned us to the cavernous interior of the vehicle. "Christ man, we need to secure this goddamn place," Page responded. "If there's anyone else left alive get them out here with their weapons."

The marine pulled himself from the hatch and jumped to the ground and said he was Corporal Frank Guilford of Philadelphia. Page borrowed his rifle and went to the edge of a paddyfield dike and started firing the weapon at something and I told him to cut it out, that it would only attract attention.

When we talked to the surviving marines they told a harrowing tale. Operation Starlite was the biggest American military assault launched up to that time in Vietnam. The unit we had found was Supply Column 21 attached to a Seventh Fleet mother ship anchored a mile out in the bay. Its mission was simple: just get to the beachhead, resupply an infantry company that had landed earlier in the day, and return home.

Supply Column 21 was made up of five amphibious track vehicles each weighing thirty-five tons, and two M-48 tanks as escort. The paths that led to its destruction were paved with confusion. Once they had landed, they were unable to locate the troops and set out to look for them. Out of water the huge Amtracks were unwieldy and flopped from one rice paddy to the other. By 11 A.M., the column had blundered ahead of the advance troops and was in deep trouble.

Concealed Vietcong soldiers rose out of hedgerows and swamps and attacked with rifles and grenades. Lance Corporal Richard Pass said his Amtrack veered aside as explosions erupted around it. The leading tank was hit with an armor-piercing shell. The terraced paddyfields made tactical maneuvering difficult for supply men not trained for it and three of the five Amtracks backed into a deep paddy and bogged down. The other two edged toward the hulking tanks for shelter but one didn't make it and was knocked out by a Vietcong soldier who dropped a grenade down the hatch, killing two Americans inside and wounding others. Mortar fire bounced off the vehicles and a cannon put three holes in one tank. The driver was shot and killed as he squeezed himself through the eighteen-inch-wide escape hatch under his vehicle. A corporal said he saw Vietcong soldiers with ammunition bandoliers, black pajama uniforms and camouflaged steel helmets move right up to an Amtrack thirty yards to his left and kill one of the drivers as he clanged open the doors and attempted to escape. Another marine was plunging through the paddyfield swinging his knife when he went down with the weapon still clutched in his hand.

When a third Amtrack was knocked out the survivors massed in the remaining two, the men taking turn as sharpshooters out peepholes on top of the vehicles. All said they were wounded to some degree. They told of a young corporal who shouted, "Okay men we're marines, let's do the job." He started to climb out of the vehicle but never got his rifle to his shoulder—a bullet hit him between the eyes. By late afternoon after a lieutenant had been killed, marine air strikes nearby helped relieve the pressure but the survivors spent an uneasy night and were thankful when our helicopter came for their wounded in the morning. They were all gone by early afternoon, escorted out by an infantry company, but the destroyed steel vehicles stayed behind, memorials to the first marine battle with the Vietcong.

I flew back to Saigon that afternoon with my unexpected scoop. I wrote all night, and fell into bed at midday after forty-eight hours without sleep. Newspapers in the United States and around the world used the story and pictures. The U.S. Marine Corps did not take kindly to my enterprise because Operation Starlite had been presented as an unqualified success before I had arrived back from the scene. Consequently, my story was flatly denied and Supply Column 21 was said never to have existed. I made an attempt to hand around my pictures at one of the daily Five O'Clock Follies news briefings but discovered that no one believed the marines' version anyway, and assumed I was reporting the truth.

Several months later I received a letter from Corporal Guilford, who said my story had worried his wife but that he was glad I had arrived on the scene and written my account because the American soldiers were not receiving enough credit for their sacrifice in Vietnam. The AP was haunted by the story for months because Marine Commandant General Wallace Greene was telling everyone he knew that the Supply Column 21 incident was a fabrication. Gallagher was only able to shut him up by inviting him to the annual AP board meeting in New York City and insisting he view a slide show of all my pictures. He recanted.

Though it was not his only responsibilty, Vietnam was taking up more and more of Gallagher's time. He was charting our rocky course from ten thousand miles away, aware that as the dangers of the war increased, the young staff he was urging on was walking the ledge between page one and possible death. He also knew that the president of the United States had an AP printer in his private office and frequently consulted it, bawling out his press relations staff when he read stories that displeased him—which was often. Gallagher's own bright future was resting on the shoulders of his journalists. Because he believed in the public's right to know, Gallagher gave us freedom; but he did not believe the public had the right to know everything. Fittingly, it was Horst who tested the limits of his permissiveness.

Horst was a fine companion in the field. Soldiers were comfortable around his affable bulk, and they would relax even as his Leicas were clicking. The troops of the Second Battalion of the 502nd Airborne were no different and took to Horst on the three hot December days he shared their jungle patrol in 1965. These men were among the elite of the U.S. military and were always willing to prove it. The Second Battalion had adopted a sharpened hatchet as their totem. But Horst saw that it was more than a symbol, it was a weapon of ritual. Teams of three or four men would practice tactics together, beheading the air with flicks of their wrists.

As the patrol made its way across jungles north of Saigon, a crude grenade exploded on the trail wounding four of the troopers. Their buddies yelled in anger, and Horst saw two small groups of them throw down their weapons and run into the jungle brandishing their hatchets.

Horst waited and one of them returned carrying the freshly severed head of a human being. They handed it around, holding it at arm's length, posing for Horst, dancing around until the company commander, Captain Thomas Taylor, came up and ordered them to stop. He was the son of the new U.S. ambassador to Vietnam, General Maxwell Taylor. The macabre day was not over. Battalion commander Lieutenant Colonel Hank Emerson came by in his helicopter when he heard the news, and insisted on digging up the head to see it for himself. He had promised a case of whiskey to the first executioner.

Horst was disturbed and angry. The soldiers had been indifferent to his presence and hadn't cared that they were being photographed. While he had not witnessed the beheading, he feared that the victim had been alive.

We decided to throw the ball in New York's lap. I wrote the account of the hatchet teams under Horst's byline and he radioed three pictures. We sent a message asking that Wes Gallagher review the whole package. The next afternoon we received a response, a thank-you for a story well done, and advising us that the pictures were shelved and the description of tracking and slaying the victim omitted from the story. We accepted Gallagher's decision without complaint but we were revolted by the hatchet teams and I made a private initiative to the U.S. high command to discipline the unit. Several weeks later I was told that the hatchets were banned.

Years later Gallagher said he did not remember the incident but that he would have approved of the decision at the time "because it had too heavy a taste." In the present news climate, he said, he would probably have run the entire story but not the photographs. "Taste consciousness has changed, and the Vietnam War brought about a lot of this consciousness that might not otherwise have come out," he said.

Such direct censorship was rare from AP headquarters. When it happened again later in the war I was far less tolerant.

Defying the Odds

GALLAGHER WAS WORRIED that we were imperiling our lives. He wrote Saigon, "I am disturbed about the risk being taken and well aware of the dangers of war, but firsthand reporting on patrol actions is taking an unnecessary risk. The lives and abilities of Peter and Horst are much too valuable to take a chance on the patrol type of reporting. Firsthand reporting is vital on occasion but in nine stories out of ten the information we want would come from survivors of such actions in quotes. I know no exact rules can be laid down but I want Horst and Peter to know that I feel they should pull their horns in a bit and not be pushing the percentages."

Gallagher meant well, I know that, and he had reason to worry. A word of caution now and then was in order. We tended to be cynical of such entreaties. Competition, not caution, ruled. We believed we were the best in the business but sometimes UPI would run away with a story and our foreign desk would go berserk with "rocket" messages demanding we match the opposition's product. When Joe Galloway won front-page newspaper headlines with his reports from the Ia Drang Valley in August 1965, Ben Bassett, the AP foreign editor, barraged us with angry demands to shape up. We got to joking with one another that we never needed to go cover the dangerous stories— unless UPI was there first.

It happened that in the Ia Drang battle, Neil Sheehan, then with the *New York Times,* and I filed the first on-the-scene accounts, with Joe Galloway contributing his series of dramatic battlefield vignettes later in the week. The incident proved to me that in the wire services you had not only to be first with the story, you had to be first every day with it.

Surrounded by death, we were shy about discussing our own dying and brought up the subject only superficially from time to time. Frank McCulloch of *Time* magazine told me his staff had debated the issue: one side insisted the risk each new day was exactly the same, the others asserting that the odds would invariably mount. I was sure that the risk was greater for photographers; in just a few months in 1965 Horst had a series of what he called "unpleasantries." Horst covered the war in a military uniform he had bought on Saigon's black market because he didn't want to stand out from the soldiers and be targeted, and he wore a steel helmet that he picked up off the battlefield; it was heavy and hot but it was a lifesaver. He was under mortar fire three times, was twice with troops mistakenly bombed by American aircraft, was in a helicopter crash and on three occasions was with Vietnamese infantry units that were wiped out by Vietcong attackers shortly after he left. He had been pinned down four times by firefights across the rice paddies.

Horst figured out that on troop helicopter assault missions, riding the first ship was the best way to get the finest pictures because it took ten to twenty seconds for the Vietcong mortarmen to get a bead on the landing zone and that gave him time to dismount and shoot his photographs of the rest of the arriving choppers.

I added a variation. One day I suggested we ride the first helicopter in and dismount with the troops at the landing zone and if there was no immediate fighting we could catch a ride on the last one out. Sometimes it would take three or four helicopter assaults in a morning to find what we called a "hot LZ" and get our story for the day. Horst was happiest when he worked alone with the troops. He told the AP log in April 1965: "I always go on the ground in the area that seems the most promising and stay with the troops until they are through. Often pictures appear only after a couple of days of walking and crawling and much frustration, and patience pays off."

The AP was assembling a formidable team of photographers to join Faas, yet he remained the dominant personality. AP executive Dan De Luce once said of Horst, "Long ago he got on to a secret that the human face is the most exciting copy. I can take any one of his combat photos, give you a close-up of the face—and you won't have to see the rest of the scenery. The face is something by itself; it sells the picture." Horst won the Pulitzer Prize and other major awards for his work in 1965, but the accolades didn't slow him down.

Eddie Adams was his only rival. The skinny former Marine Corps photographer from Pennsylvania was about our age. He had been disappointed that the Korean War had ended before his unit got into any real action, and he had come to Vietnam to cover the newly arriving marines, as gung ho as any of them and eager to prove himself as a war photographer. Eddie was a favorite of the New York office. He was slow to take orders and saw himself as an equal to Horst. I noticed that they got along better when they were at opposite ends of the country. Eddie preferred being in Da Nang with his beloved marines more than anywhere else and he became a close friend of the commanding officer, Major General Lewis Walt. He was soon the favored news personality in the area, sometimes called in to mediate angry disputes between his free-ranging press colleagues and the conservative marine officers running the press camp.

Eddie enjoyed "enhancing" his pictures when he had the chance. When the first marines landed at Da Nang Bay he noticed a line of Vietnamese high school girls in white silk ao-dai dresses waiting shyly up the beach with the city mayor, all of them holding welcoming flower leis. Eddie and Dirck Halstead of UPI conspired to have one girl wade out into the water and place her flowers around the neck of a surprised marine. All the other girls rushed waist deep into the surf, shocking the marine commander. He shouted in indignation at the photographers, "Hey, you've ruined it all, you've ruined it all," as his marines tumbled in the surf with the local lovelies and Eddie and Halstead and the other photographers clicked away enthusiastically. "That's all right," Eddie told the general, "think of the pictures," and the general replied, "That's exactly what I am thinking of." A photo Eddie took of the unsmiling general with a garland of tropical flowers around his neck was widely used in American papers the next morning.

Once when he was photographing me being held at gunpoint by a nervous U.S. military policeman outside a Buddhist pagoda in Saigon, Eddie called out, "Come on, shoot the fucker, it'll make a better picture." Eddie's mind's eye seemed to be aimed not at page one of the *New York Daily News* but the center spread in *Life* magazine.

Eddie was shaken by a close encounter in Hoai Chau, along the central coast near Quang Ngai. The marine company was caught in the open on a hill by Vietcong gunners hidden on a brush-clad promontory a hundred yards away. There were many dead and injured. He brooded about Hoai Chau for days, and when he came down to Saigon he told me he was losing his nerve and wanted to go home before he was killed. I suggested he take some R&R to think about it, but he said that he'd made up his mind and asked me to help him write a letter to Wes Gallagher explaining how he felt and requesting to be transferred back to New York. Gallagher responded that he admired Eddie's honesty and that he could come home anytime he wished, and when he got on a plane in mid-May Horst figured he'd seen the last of him.

Obits

ONLY THE UPI WIRE SERVICE competed with the AP on every story. Newspapers and magazines had far fewer people. The AP Saigon bureau had a substantial staff and we routinely covered the marines in Da Nang. And even though we were way over budget, New York approved staff assignments to An Khe and Pleiku in the Central Highlands, where two divisions of American infantry troops had base camps. The Associated Press was then the largest and most influential wire service in the news business, reaching beyond the United States to five other continents and to millions of readers and radio listeners in their scores of languages.

It was that responsibility that shaped our actions and attitudes and made what was to come tolerable. We defied the odds. But we were unhinged by the deaths of colleagues. We needed to justify their loss—to ourselves, to their grieving families, and to those who believed the risks we were taking were foolhardy. When a soldier died in battle his survivors could take solace that his sacrifice was for the principles of duty, honor and country. A soldier's death would be marked by fitting tribute, a flag-draped coffin wheeled past an airport honor guard for the last ride home, and a military funeral.

There were no flags for the journalists who died in Vietnam and not much glory. We gathered up our own dead and sent them home by air freight. The AP had a roll of honor on the wall of the main lobby of the head office in New York, a metal scroll where the names of the fallen were appended—that was the only tangible recognition. Only the combat soldiers we traveled with, and whose dangers we shared, took our real measure, always curious as to why we chose such dangerous company, and then were generally accepting when they saw that our job was to document their lives at war.

The constant entreaties from our headquarters to avoid serious danger put the responsibility on us when a colleague was killed or wounded. Among ourselves there was a tendency to explain away the circumstance of a fatality as a quirk of fate or a mistake in judgment or just plain stupidity.

We felt awful for the families of our dead colleagues, who struggled not only with their anguish, but with the effort to give meaning to the loss—the White House was trying to make freedom of the press an unpopular cause in America.

Bernard Kolenberg joined us late in September of 1965, and I remember him loping into the Saigon bureau the morning he arrived, plunking down his hefty camera bag and shouting, "It's great to be back." The tall, gangling photographer had spent a week or so in Vietnam during the summer, shooting pictures for the *Albany Times Union,* and now he had volunteered for indefinite duty with the AP.

He persuaded Horst to send him out into the field the very next morning, and then he stretched out on the office settee rather than taking a hotel room and slept for a solid ten hours to recover from his nonstop trip across the Pacific. Bernie was a man with a knack for getting to places, trading on his infectious good humor, which was irresistible to airplane crews and ground staffs.

I saw him three days later at the isolated, besieged valley town of Bong Son along the central coast, chatting with the senior American adviser to the Second Corps region. He had a pair of Nikon cameras slung around his neck and a floppy jungle hat on his head; the numerous pockets of the fishing vest he wore were stuffed with film and he looked in shutterbug heaven. He pointed over my head to the nearby hills. "I was out there this morning, at the Phu Cu Pass.

"I got a shot of a dead marine being carried away in an evacuation helicopter, maybe you can use it," he said, and handed over a film canister. He wanted to stay in Bong Son a few days because, "I like it up here, the Special Forces people are very good to me, I'm flying a lot with the medical helicopters, and I don't have to shave so often," and he laughed, fingering his bristling jowl.

As I departed for Saigon, Kolenberg told me his plans for later in the week; he would return to Qui Nhon and fly with his old buddies, the American A-1E Skyraider pilots, who had been bombing Vietcong positions in the mountains for weeks.

His evacuation picture was as dramatic as he had described and was radioed to New York that night. It was also the first and last picture of his we ever saw. On Saturday Bernie kept his rendezvous with the Skyraiders, riding with his cameras in the back seat of a fighter-bomber that was maneuvering for a better shot at a Vietcong position in the mountains of Binh Dinh Province when it accidentally crashed into another aircraft. Kolenberg was the first AP man to die in the war, and his death stunned us. He had been on duty for just one week while the rest of us had been taking similar risks for years and we were still alive.

Horst was always looking for recruits for what we began calling "Faas's army," a band of photo stringers who would brave the riot-torn streets and battlefields for a few dollars to take pictures for the AP's daily news flow to New York. Horst's credo was that you can never have too many people taking too many pictures. He was particularly impressed by one of these stringers, a CBS soundman named Huynh Cong La, and he courted him and succeeded in hiring him as a full-time staffer, incurring the wrath of the soundman's partner, another Vietnamese, named Ha Thuc Can (who later became famous as Morley Safer's favorite cameraman). Cong La had the slight build typical of many Vietnamese men: it suggested fragility, but disguised a coiled energy. I enjoyed going into the field with him because he had a sense of humor and could gain the confidence of Vietnamese military and civilian officials. He was also a much braver man than I. He would slip off through the jungle with the company point men while I stayed in the comparative safety of the command group and the American advisers. Sometimes he would crawl back to us during a heavy firefight to say, "Too many bullets out there," only to return the way he had come when there was a break in the action. Horst coached him in camera work and analyzed his pictures, strip by strip, with advice on framing and exposures, and he quickly improved his skills.

Cong La's pictures of battle and violence helped us keep a competitive edge over UPI. One day he picked up a battered steel helmet from the battlefield, and drew AP on the front in black ink, and wore it ever after while in action, even though it wobbled on his head. Cong La was leading a charmed life, with four years covering the war for CBS and the AP and not a scratch on his body. But he tasted mortality one May day in the Mekong Delta mud when he was pinned down by sniper fire. He reached over a paddy dike to take a picture and bullets tore into the upper muscle of his camera arm. Before passing out he asked a soldier to photograph him where he lay, and when the film was processed in our office the next day, there was Cong La unconscious in his own blood in the crushed green shoots of paddyfield rice. It might have slowed another man down, but Cong La's greatest concern was that the publicity over his injury would attract the attention of the draft board, which he had avoided for years and which now could put him in some office job. He changed his name to Huynh Thanh My.

CBS offered to triple his one-hundred-dollar-a-week salary to return to them as a cameraman, but Thanh My turned them down. "I don't like TV, too big," he told us, fondly tapping the small 35mm AP cameras he carried. He was hanging around the office taking a breather one October day and proudly showing off pictures of his seven-month-old son when Eddie Adams had to pull out of an assignment with the Vietnamese Forty-fourth Ranger Battalion to do some bureau chores. Thanh My insisted on taking over the story, saying the battalion's officers were pals of his, and then he went to get his steel helmet, and to jump on a helicopter flight to Can Tho.

Horst returned to the office from a field trip two mornings later when we heard the first shocking rumors that Thanh My might be badly hurt, and then even worse, that he was dead on a muddy battlefield south of Can Tho. While Horst did his best to console the family, Ed White traveled to the delta city of Can Tho to claim the body. Ed reconstructed events for us on his return. The Forty-fourth Rangers were hit hard in the early afternoon and Thanh My was wounded in the shoulder and was moved back through the lines to wait for medical helicopter evacuation. In the evening, before help could arrive, the Vietcong launched another major assault, overran the assembly point and killed everyone they found, finishing off Thanh My with a bullet to his neck and grabbing his cameras and other possessions, though they left his watch and his gold wedding band. The bureau was disconsolate for days, particularly Horst. He kept saying, "We have to get the pictures, that's our job, but the only way I can send photographers out there is if I also continue to go myself."

Thanh My's funeral cortege left his house late morning and at his mother's request turned down the same alley and moved along the same tree-lined streets that he took on his way to work for the AP, pausing briefly outside the bureau in commemoration of his seventeen months' employment as a combat photographer. The whole AP bureau was there, with Ed White and Hugh Mulligan and George McArthur and Horst and the rest of us. Many other friends walked in the funeral procession because the press corps was still small enough in those days to feel a colleague's loss deeply.

Monks in brown robes walked with us, chanting softly, beating mournfully on gongs and perfuming the funeral route with burning joss sticks. The slain photographer's sobbing nineteen-year-old widow was dressed in white, as was the tradition, and stumbled the whole way clinging to a railing at the back of the hearse. Other family members followed behind her, all with white scarves around their heads, one relative bearing a framed photograph of Thanh My in his proudest pose, wearing the makeshift outfit of a combat correspondent with his name on a jacket pocket and "Associated Press" stitched under it.

Nearing the Mac Dinh Chi cemetery, one of his younger sisters strewed a paper money trail along the path in a Buddhist ritual so that his soul would be able to make its way home again someday, and at the gravesite a dish of food, a flask of water and his rice bowl were placed on a bamboo mat to attend him on the journey to his ancestors. His grieving widow kissed his picture three times as the final joss sticks were burned, then she had to be restrained from throwing herself into the grave as the casket was being lowered.

As a noon bell tolled over the cemetery there was a dramatic interruption when a young man in uniform rushed through the crowd of assembled mourners and fell upon his knees at the grave, and the mother and widow broke into renewed sobbing as they consoled his younger brother, who had been in action and hadn't known of his brother's fate until he had read it in a newspaper that morning. The photographer's former CBS partner, Ha Thuc Can, pulled me aside and quietly cursed Horst. "He murdered him, he murdered him; if Cong La had stayed with me he'd be alive today." I remember Thuc Can in his misery and think how lucky the soldier who can seek revenge for a comrade's death when we can only seek solace.

Horst did his best to comfort the distressed widow. A somber-eyed youth tugged at his sleeve and introduced himself, his name was Ut, Thanh My's youngest brother. "It's best you go to your family," Horst told him, but he responded urgently, "AP my family now, I want take picture, too," and Horst turned to me with a shake of his head and told him, "Go and grow up and see me then."

Ut came around often to the office, a constant reminder to us all of the smiling brother whose picture was on the wall. We eventually started calling the kid Nick Ut and he began doing odd jobs in the darkroom for Horst, and as the years went by Horst showed him how to use a camera and sent him on some assignments in the city and eventually let him cover the war because by then Nick Ut was a hefty lad and Horst couldn't have stopped him even if he had tried.

On a late spring afternoon in 1972 I was in the office with Horst when a sweat-caked Nick Ut drove back from Cu Chi with pictures of a napalm-seared village and terrified people and a naked young girl screaming as she ran down a country road, the clothes all burned off her body. Nick Ut received the Pulitzer Prize for his pictures during that year.

182

Colleagues

WHEN MAL BROWNE QUIT the AP in 1965 he explained to me he was frustrated that our reporting was having no effect on American policy. He said the country was marching into war regardless of the daily truths that he believed showed military involvement would be long and bloody and ultimately unsuccessful. He was convinced that the printed word could no longer effectively present the Vietnam story and had decided to join the fledgling ABC television news organization as a correspondent. He was tall and slim with blond hair and an engaging smile, the all-American look. Sometimes I would see him around the streets of Saigon in his first weeks on the new job, with TV crew in tow, self-consciously practicing his on-camera closing commentaries, or "stand-ups" as they were called, as people watched with curiosity. Mal was irreplaceable; his intellectual courage and reporting skills were unmatched in the war theater and his dedication to the craft of journalism was unflagging. I was disappointed because I had learned from him and depended on him.

Horst was also unhappy to see him leave. Mal had been Horst's first convert to photography, shooting his prize-winning picture of the burning Buddhist monk in 1963 after getting a camera from Horst the previous week.

We wondered how robust a future Mal would have in television. We were not impressed with the new medium. The cumbersome technology was intimidating. The black-and-white TV film had to be air freighted from Saigon to New York, and then aired several days later. We felt this left television at a tremendous competitive disadvantage to print that it only partially made up because of the thirty-minute evening news broadcasts then newly available on each of the three networks.

We tended to ridicule the show biz aspects of TV. When CBS anchorman Walter Cronkite had visited Vietnam late in June he had spent the day with the First Battalion of the 173rd Airborne Brigade in War Zone C and used two helicopters to fly his six-man party and equipment to the command post. Sergeant Pratt said the troops had been particularly fascinated by a CBS light man who carried a battery-powered sun gun to keep the shadows off the anchorman's face—quite ironic in a war zone where soldiers applied elaborate camouflage makeup to create a shadow effect on their faces.

Pratt offered this account: "We staged some sexy footage of troops 'moving out' into the jungle, and then Cronkite did a walking interview with the battalion commander, a major. They walked side by side toward the camera talking, taking a trail through a bamboo stand that formed a tunnel over the path. A large puddle of water covered the trail and the major, like anyone with sense, stepped around it. 'Cut,' cried Ron Bonn, directing the epic for Cronkite. 'Back up and wade through the water.' The battalion commander looked at me a little odd and I shrugged and they walked through the water. 'Cut,' shouted Bonn a second time. 'Now back up and come through it again.' The major looked at me very oddly but obeyed and a cameraman closed in with a hand-held Bolex, filming only their feet and I thought about General Douglas McArthur wading ashore umpteen times at Leyte to get the picture right. 'You look disgusted, Sergeant,' Bonn said to me later, and I responded, 'I didn't mean to let it show.' Bonn explained tolerantly, 'This is what we call produced reality. When this is cut up and put together in New York it will make great stuff.' "

Those television reporters who had been very early on the scene, Peter Kalischer and Jack Lawrence and Morley Safer of CBS, and Garrick Utley and Jim Robinson of NBC, and Lou Cioffi of ABC, had been part of the Saigon press corps. They had helped us fight the censorship battles. Later television reporters swept through Saigon in a blur, barely seen because they were so closeted by bureau chiefs and producers and assistants all shaping the specialized journalism of television. They had a breezy confidence and had money to throw around on staff and parties and clothes. Some came to the war theater from comfortable bases in Hong Kong and Tokyo, and even those assigned permanently to Vietnam were only in town for six months or so. They stayed at the Caravelle or Continental hotels and tended to stick together.

Still, there were times when television captured something that we couldn't. We should have seen that such times revealed the towering future role of television news. Instead, we wrote off a scoop like Morley Safer's Cam Ne story as a fluke. I had been to Cam Ne with the marines earlier in the year when the U.S. combat troops were setting up their defense perimeter around the Da Nang air base. The marines tried to absorb the hamlet complex inside their defensive border but could not come up with enough manpower, so Cam Ne remained outside in no-man's-land, tempting fate. By early August the once prosperous community had become a battlefield, with its residents spending part of their lives in crude bunkers under their homes to escape the Vietcong guerrillas who would sneak into the hamlet to shoot at the Americans manning an outpost just four hundred yards away.

On August 3 the marines decided to do something about it, and tipped off Safer. With his cameraman, Ha Thuc Can, and a soundman he went along for the ride into television history.

For the record, the AP also had the story. Correspondent John Wheeler filed an account from Da Nang. He quoted marines saying they had orders to set fire to homes in the area if they got so much as one round of sniper fire. Then he gave graphic details of the incident, writing, "At one point about thirty women and children including one breast-feeding a child came down the path among the burning buildings. All were crying." The marines claimed to have checked the homes for occupants before putting them to the torch, but Wheeler quoted one as saying that an NCO went into one house after it began to burn and found an old man and a little girl hiding in the earthen bunker.

Wheeler had a good story but Safer a better one because he and his crew were at the scene and gathered graphic, heartrending pictures and sound. Safer was one of the best writers in television and his telexed script was read that night on the CBS Evening News. Two days later the completed television story was aired when his dramatic film arrived in New York.

His story was hotly debated across the country and President Johnson was upset. The marines tried to discredit Safer because of his Canadian nationality, in a way that I fully appreciated, suggesting that some of the pictures were faked. I spent a decade reporting from Vietnam to become a pariah within the U.S. military establishment; Morley Safer achieved similar status in just one afternoon.

The AP chose Ed White to replace Mal as the bureau chief. Our news operation was expanding as rapidly as the military. We all applauded Ed's selection because he was one of the boys, and at age forty-two a decade wiser, and far more experienced. He had worked on the foreign desk in New York headquarters, and he had helped us out frequently since the early 1960s on temporary assignments from his post in the Tokyo bureau. Ed was an even-tempered, pipe-smoking graduate of the University of Missouri School of Journalism. He liked a party and had an eye for the ladies, and like the rest of us made time for both. The intensified war and the danger and anxiety that it

185

brought gave us greater license to debauch. And Saigon catered to the tastes of occupation armies. We excused our excesses by arguing that the booze and the hookers were mainly for the soldiers who helped us in the field and whom we invited back to Saigon to relax. We understood that all this was part of the grand tradition of war reporting. I was spending less and less time at home with Nina and my son, Andrew, who was born in December 1964, and more time with the boys.

Hal Boyle, an AP columnist who spent six months with us in Vietnam writing sappy hometown tales about the "human side" of the war, reassured us we were just following in the footsteps of those who had been there before. Hal was a gentle spirit who wrote in his first Saigon column, "Any reporter who can do justice to a four-alarm fire can do well by a war, which is merely a longer fire affecting more people." His creativity was fueled by a formidable drinking habit, which is why he picked the easygoing Da Nang Press Center over Saigon. Sometimes late at night with Hal deep in his cups we would take bets on whether he would deliver his column on schedule. By morning I would invariably find under my door the three-page yarn that he had banged out sometime between midnight and dawn.

Hal had won a Pulitzer Prize for his coverage of the European Theater in World War Two. I once asked him how he had celebrated, and he said he was visiting a brothel at a military rest-and-recreation center in Belgium, "And when Bob Eunson called to tell me I had won the Pulitzer I celebrated with another blow job."

Hal's columns were published in hundreds of newspapers across the country, revealing an appetite for morale-raising accounts of the war that I was not providing. When Hal returned to New York he was replaced by Hugh Mulligan, a veteran writer from AP News Features.

Mulligan was a popular feature writer and his lengthy stories were given full-page displays by adoring editors. He had an irrepressible wit and a Napoleonic habit of striding around the battlefield with his hand tucked against his midriff. After being invited to meet some of our news sources over lunch at a Vietnamese restaurant he feigned hesitation, "I don't favor curry with the natives."

During his first tour in Vietnam he befriended the young, nubile chorus line of a visiting entertainment troupe called the German National Circus and was followed around town for weeks by his beautiful retinue. He took them to parties where our wives were not present, and talked them through their romantic crises. Half of the young ladies fell in love with him, but Mulligan maintained his fidelity to his wife,

Brigitte, back home in Forest Hills, New York. His self-denial was the press corps's gain, and many lonely reporters remain indebted to this day.

Like Boyle, Mulligan brought with him the view that whatever Americans were doing in Vietnam was probably all right. President Johnson was reassuring the country that the military commitment was legitimate and justifiable, was limited in size and duration, and was an inevitable consequence of the Cold War. There was a need to feel that if there were American boys dying in action, they were giving their lives for something worthwhile. Mulligan wanted to be supportive of their sacrifice. Hugh told me one day that he had the unquenchable belief that "the human animal is redeemable. You see more of the best of man than the worst, and war brings out the best."

I was less philosophical. Our different outlooks were evident in stories we wrote on the aftermath of the Ia Drang Valley battle in November 1965, the bloodiest action of the war to that time. Mulligan wrote of a unit's return to their base at An Khe, "The brave young boys who left their youth behind in the bitter fighting of the Ia Drang Valley came home like men to the First Air Cavalry Division base camp Sunday night," and he quoted a senior officer telling them they had met "tough, professional, capable enemy troops and you gave them a mauling they will never forget, your country is proud of you." Mulligan concluded his story, "There will be drinking and laughing and hell raising in the Second Battalion tonight, and some tears, too, tears for buddies left behind in the high elephant grass at the Ia Drang Valley, tears for comrades wrapped up in the rubber body bags and already on the first stage of their long journey to the States."

The day that Mulligan filed his story on the Ia Drang, I was in Pleiku one hundred miles away. I had covered the actual battle and I wrote a news analysis about the same action. "A new generation of Americans are being thrust into the firing line in South Vietnam. They are discovering that war is as indifferent about who it kills and who it lets live, and as brutal as the history books say all the other wars were. For the line companies at Ia Drang, it was not the elation of victory that stirred them when the battles were over; it was their elation at being alive.

"Sometimes it brought out the worst in men. One soldier shot up every wounded enemy soldier who moved as his decimated unit policed up the battlefield, because he had heard that two days earlier three American prisoners had been found bound hand and foot and shot through the head, and he was exacting revenge. It took the most compassionate of men to aid an enemy wounded after the vicious battles at the Ia Drang and there was not much compassion left.''

Both our stories were distributed by the AP that same day. Editors might have been excused in thinking that we were covering different battles. The AP foreign desk did not query the Saigon bureau over the differences in the stories, leaving it to the judgment of individual editors to chose the account they preferred. Mulligan's if they felt that Vietnam was a war the troops believed was worth fighting, mine if they doubted the undertaking.

Under the AP's big tent where everything that anyone ever wrote on Vietnam appeared on the news wires, we could tolerate different opinions of the war. We directed our competitive instincts toward UPI and not each other. I admired Mulligan's humor and generosity and I respected his talent.

But the increasing controversy over news coverage prompted AP headquarters to beef up the bureau with more mature hands. Tom Reedy was among those who arrived for a six-month tour of duty. Reedy was near retirement age, a veteran World War Two reporter and foreign bureau chief, with a roistering laugh and a talent for telling tall tales over late-night glasses of Scotch. He enjoyed recounting his exploits in the "big" war and was an unabashed booster of U.S. involvement in Vietnam.

I did not argue with Reedy because I did not have a world view of the war. I was sticking to my rule to report just what I could see. But Reedy was manning the desk and as the weeks went by I got the impression that his boosterism was leaking into the daily news round-ups. He even started referring to the troops as "doughboys," a term popular in World War One, and sometimes wrote of victories where none existed. This included a military operation by the U.S. Army's 173rd Airborne Brigade in War Zone D that I had covered where the lead battalion had been bogged down for two days at a Vietcong bunker line and had moved forward only when the enemy melted away. Reedy described this maneuver as "yet another victory for American troops" in his story roundup and I challenged him. I felt he had misrepresented the action.

"Son," he grinned sourly at me, "I was doing this thing long before you were born."

"Tom," I responded angrily, "I'll be doing this thing long after you're dead." He looked at me in startled shock and mumbled into his Scotch. Reedy didn't say much to me after that. He went home on schedule, but he did get revenge by passing on the office gossip.

Mal Browne had run a discreet bureau with no hint of scandal but now New York was getting an earful about office politics and our social habits and not liking it one bit.

While the AP's inner councils debated my abilities, Wes Gallagher went ahead and made me a star. He ordered Ted Boyle in the promotion department to launch the campaign with an 1,800-word admiring biography written by Hugh Mulligan for distribution to all American newspapers. It noted that Arnett's "cameras are always loaded, his notebooks are covered with plastic, he carries typed orders entitling him to fly anywhere in combat areas, he usually is the first correspondent on the scene."

In the November 13, 1965, issue of *Editor and Publisher,* the Bible of the newspaper industry, I saw stretched across pages eight and nine a spread featuring a black-and-white photo of me bareheaded, in combat boots, wearing a rain-slicked poncho and walking along a bomb-cratered road in central Vietnam with a company of Vietnamese marines. It was headlined in bold type: "A thousand days . . . a hundred battles: AP's Peter Arnett in Vietnam."

The caption read, "Peter Arnett went to Vietnam in July 1962 to cover a dirty little war. It's bigger and deadlier now. In October it took the lives of two photographers serving Associated Press members, Bernard Kolenberg and Huynh Thanh My. In a thousand days Peter Arnett has personally gone through a hundred battles, from the ambush-ridden delta to isolated outposts in the highlands. His datelines are Song Be and Duc Co, Zone D and An Khe, Bien Hoa and Chu Lai. And many more. Peter Arnett like other AP men in Vietnam believes the place to get the story and the picture is with the fighting troops. In doing this he has displayed courage and shown initiative and reporting skill in the highest tradition of his profession. The Associated Press. The byline of dependability."

Hugh Mulligan told me one day that he had learned that the AP was putting some of my 1965 stories in for the Pulitzer Prize in international reporting and wished me luck, but he warned that the competition would be keen. I was aware that Hugh harbored Pulitzer ambitions of his own, and I assumed that his stories would be entered into the contest; they were superbly written accounts of American boys at war and were popular with editors. The year 1965 had also been my very best and I felt I was maturing as a writer and that my stories were substantive. The AP placed much emphasis on desk editors to shape up the stream of news flowing into headquarters and from the beginning my stories had been rewritten to meet the requirements of style. But in the past year I had noted that much more of my original material was making the grade. The AP's overnight foreign editor, Harris Jackson, told me a deskman once tried to cut one of my longer stories down to three hundred words and Jackson roared at him, "If you can't improve it, don't touch it," and all 1,700 words ran on the news wire and were widely used. From then on I tried to land all my stories on Jackson's desk.

One of my stories that had survived the editing desk intact earlier in 1965 and made headlines also started a debate over writing style within the newspaper community and revealed how closely editors across the country were watching our reports, and how ready they were to pull them apart.

One early evening Huynh Thanh My had been clowning around in the office pretending to be a movie star. After he explained in his fragmentary English, we knew we had a story. His army friends at My Tho had told him that part of the Vietnamese Seventh Infantry Division was being assigned to make a movie. We set off next morning in my white Karmann Ghia down Route 1 on the My Tho highway, and beyond Tan An we watched an overloaded bus come to a halt with a jerk as machine gun fire clattered somewhere in the roadside trees.

A score of passengers leaped into a watery ditch, and remembering that snipers were not uncommon on the Saigon–My Tho road, we joined them. Motorists peered anxiously from other halted vehicles into the trees where clouds of green, red and blue smoke were rising. The firing continued determinedly but it sounded funny, like a firing range. I climbed from the ditch and walked over to the only unworried man I could see, a young U.S. Army officer casually smoking a cigarette in a jeep parked at the roadside. "Take it easy," he said casually. "This isn't war. I thought I was coming over here to advise soldiers. They may as well have sent me to Hollywood."

In the paddyfield beyond the treeline, the Vietnamese war was being filmed in full 35mm color as a United States Information Service project. A line of helmeted soldiers was staging a battle scene, standing on a paddy dike and firing into the middle-distance mud as the cameras rolled. Other troops were providing security to keep the real communist Vietcong from getting into the act.

The producers seemed surprised to see us but had no authority to turn us away and we hung around to watch. "Marvelous, isn't it," commented a USIS officer in a short-sleeved shirt as smoke from a dozen colored grenades rose in a thick Technicolor screen to enable the Vietnamese troopers to rush the unseen "enemy."

I heard someone say, "Don't talk when they use real bullets, you'll ruin the natural sound." It was the voice of the American film director, who was reluctant to identify himself or say anything about the project. By this time the onlookers on the My Tho highway could see that the Vietnamese troops had captured the "enemy" village at the other side of the paddyfield.

"Gee, just like in *Battle Cry;* how I'd like to see them do that for real," commented the U.S. adviser as he slung himself back in his jeep and took off for Tan Hiep airstrip.

The USIS official warmed up to me as the production crew began packing up its gear. The three-man unit had been hired in Washington to produce a thirty-minute show for international distribution. "We want to show the world how things really are here," he said. "What we are looking for is realism. Two days ago we staged a great attack on a little outpost. We had the men defending it like heroes and their women binding their wounds. We didn't show any Vietcong attacking it because if we did, not one of the people who saw the film would believe it."

In the three weeks the film unit had been on the job, there had been real battles within fifty miles of Saigon, but my informant declared, "We don't want to show the cruel things like bodies. We want to show how the Vietnamese fight the war as people." USIS had been critical of stories and pictures that depicted the horror of the war, including Vietnamese troops torturing prisoners. The movie would emphasize the "positive elements." But USIS officials in Saigon refused comment on just how much their positive realism show would cost.

I drove to My Tho to the old seminary that housed the U.S. military advisory team, and found them amused about the USIS project, but also a bit hostile. A battalion adviser told me, "If they want some pictures of the war come with me sometime. If they want to portray the war, do it properly or not at all." Another adviser said, "We are told there are not enough troops available for the defense of a lot of the lonely, frightened hamlets out there. But troops are found fast enough for a project like this." Back at the AP office later Horst muttered, "I hope they don't end up ambushing themselves."

I wrote the story in a low key narrative style that I thought appropriate to the material; not the usual hard sell. You had to read a couple

191

of graphs into the story before you really got the idea. I guess some editors never got that far. Some newspapers headlined the story on their front pages, but many did not run the story at all and complained to the AP we didn't hit it hard enough. Carl Rowan, the director of USIS, read my piece in the *Washington Post* and ordered the filming stopped and the film destroyed.

The editors who would make final judgment on the Pulitzer were drawn from the ranks of those editors who debated my story. Hollywood-on-the-Mekong would clearly be on my prize entry, along with Supply Column 21, the tear gas story and the reports from the Ia Drang Valley. Mulligan told me it was a strong entry, but like the dwarfs hired to whisper in the ears of conquering Roman generals that fame was fleeting, he warned me that the best journalists in the United States would also be in the running, several of whom I'd worked with in Vietnam, such as Jack Foisie of the *Los Angeles Times* and Jimmy Breslin of the *New York Herald Tribune*. He told me my chances were slim. The Pulitzer Prize was announced at Columbia University on the first Tuesday of each May. On the eve of the announcement I was in bed early, assured by my AP colleagues that if I had won I would have already been informed by our New York office. Bob Moorefield was on the desk that night, an older AP newsman from the Midwest.

Maybe Moorefield was being kind and letting me sleep, or maybe he was out in the streets researching his favorite bar girl and missed the message on the teleprinter, but he did not ring in the early hours of the morning with any news. At daybreak I turned philosophically to Nina and said there was always next year: I may have even dozed off when the phone rang. It was Moorefield. "Let me be the first to congratulate you . . ." A surge of emotion welled up in me and Nina watched tears stream from my eyes. I had never won anything in my life and I figured that the Pulitzer Prize was fine for starters. Moorefield wanted a comment for the news wire and I pulled myself together long enough to dictate a few lines.

There was soon banging on my apartment door, and Mal Browne pushed his way inside with a foaming bottle of champagne. On my way to the office I saw Charlie Mohr, then of the *New York Times,* a contender for the prize himself that year, who insisted that he host a congratulatory lunch for Mal and Horst and me, the AP's Boys of Saigon. A year earlier Charlie had approached me about working for the *New York Times* and I had been flattered by his attention but had told him I was wedded to the AP till death us do part, a melodramatic assertion that could be attributed to my youth.

A stack of telexed messages and cables were waiting for me at the office, and others came in during the day from colleagues around the world. Wes Gallagher's message said, "Of the many Pulitzer awards Associated Press men have won, none was more deserved nor gives me greater satisfaction than this one in view of the difficulties you have undergone from time to time." He later wrote, "I couldn't have been more delighted that you won the Pulitzer award, which means a clean sweep for the original trio of Mal, Horst and yourself. I am particularly pleased because it shows that the top journalists in this country recognize merit above nationality. I wish the government would do the same but that is too much to expect of any government."

I was invited to the gala fiftieth Pulitzer anniversary dinner at the Plaza Hotel in New York City. Standing on the Plaza ballroom stage amid the assemblage of Pulitzer recipients, and hearing James Reston and Archibald MacLeish talk about the responsibilities that came with the prize, I understood what Mal Browne and David Halberstam and Neil Sheehan had been seeking to accomplish in Vietnam. I was eager to return to the job.

The "Long Bloody Mile"

In 1966 I was caught up in the war's momentum. I never asked myself whether it was right or wrong, and the question did not come up in conversation, not with the soldiers or my colleagues because we were all of us too close to the action. Too many of our friends had died; we were unwilling to write off their sacrifice.

The American military authorities in Saigon professed that victory was certain, revealed no signs of doubt, and debated only when it would occur. The Vietnamese population in the secure cities had very little idea of what the American military was doing and didn't really care, comforted in knowing that the world's most powerful nation was committing its sons to the war and was recompensing them for the privilege.

The U.S. military commitment was accompanied by abundant economic assistance. Local business was thriving as never before. The faltering ranks of the South Vietnamese military were bolstered by draftees from the countryside. Prosperous Vietnamese bribed their sons out of military service or found them cushy jobs at headquarters units.

The American soldiers were unaware of the nature of Vietnamese society, prisoners of their own sequestered universe, fighting for their lives in the jungles, or isolated in base camps. Westmoreland's strategy called for totally self-sufficient American forces, needing not a razor blade, a banana nor a slice of bread from the local economy.

I often visited the Third Brigade of the Big Red One, which was based at Lai Khe near Ben Cat. There was a compelling esprit de corps among the men. The officers wanted to talk about the war, and they were interested in the abandoned Lai Khe rubber plantation where they were making their base camp. In 1962 I had visited it for a story on Operation Sunrise, when the United States was trying to corral the rural population by forcing them into fortified hamlets. When that failed, the area was abandoned and fell by default to the Vietcong. Now the army was making homes for 3,500 Americans in the tangle of scrub, infirm rubber trees and decrepit plantation factories and storage buildings. Eventually the Third Brigade became a model base camp, with neat mess halls and laundries and mobile homes for the senior officers, and even a large concrete recreation hall staffed with seventy-five gaudily dressed Vietnamese bar girls who turned tricks for the soldiers for five dollars in small rooms off the kitchen. Brigade medics checked their health regularly.

Horst and I stopped there for a drink one afternoon, and we were laughing and joking with the bar girls when I noticed a white poster that read, "Girls with tags are clean," and another, "Girls without tags are diseased." The girl on my lap had no tag and I dropped her like a live grenade.

When the base camp was being established Vietnam was called a "frontless war" because the Vietcong could pop up anywhere, but at Lai Khe their arrivals were more predictable; almost every night the sniper bullets would crack out of the gloom of the old rubber trees and thud into the homes and hides of the new plantation tenants.

Sergeant Douglas Warden complained to me that the area was not up to the standards he expected, below what the military manuals decreed. "The books talk about spacious bunkers and things like that; the bunkers we got aren't so spacious. They are so small we can only use them for fighting positions, we can't even sleep in them." The only thing worse for the soldiers than hanging around their cramped abodes was patrolling in the jungle in the heat and the uncertainty.

The Lai Khe base camp had a large swimming pool in a grove of coconut palms, built by the former French owners of the plantation, but the Americans couldn't use it because the surgeon general's office in Saigon had decreed that the water didn't come up to safety standards. I was able to help them out by persuading my pharmacist sister-in-law, Huyen Chau, to obtain the fifty pounds of chlorine needed to purify the water. But these comforts were unusual at Lai Khe and elsewhere in the war zones. While the post exchanges in the rear areas were stocked with luxuries, few such supplies were getting forward.

The most indispensable personnel on any brigade's roster were the scroungers, those soldiers with the skills to circumvent red tape and regulation and come up with needed items, no questions asked. My favorite scrounger was Captain Cosmo M. Barone of Company C of the 701st Maintenance Battalion, a natural-born confidence man who resolved to bring some comfort to the men of the Third Brigade. Barone boasted that he could fix, get a hold of or steal anything, and he proved it convincingly to me one day when he walked into our Saigon bureau and announced he had obtained twenty-five air conditioners and fifteen refrigerators for his unit. It was an amazing feat: heat was seen as a greater enemy than the Vietcong, and coolness more desirable than sex. Almost. The beaming captain explained he had gained entry to a large military supply complex near U.S. command headquarters. Armed with a can of black paint and a brush, he simply painted out the names of the intended recipients and painted in his unit's Lai Khe address. Three weeks later a supply convoy delivered the treasured goods to a cheering welcome at brigade headquarters.

The best infantry battalion at Lai Khe was the Second of the Twenty-eighths Regiment, and its men wore the unit's black lion patch with pride. The battalion commander, Lieutenant Colonel George Eyster, was a lean, laconic man who reminded me of Gary Cooper. Eyster was a West Point graduate who lived in Cocoa Beach, Florida, and enjoyed showing me pictures of his family and his wife. His father had been a brigadier general, chief information officer in the European Theater in World War Two.

Eyster invited me on several operations but I had never been able to go. I encountered the Black Lions battalion and Eyster by accident one day when Horst and I joined a combined American and Vietnamese infantry operation at Trung Lap, west of Saigon. Its mission

195

was to rout out Vietcong snipers from tunnels and bunkers in the tangle of wild rubber trees and scrub bordering Cu Chi. We stayed with the Black Lions and Eyster promised us a day of action. His Company C would be the point unit, "And they know how to kick butt."

At dawn we rolled out of our sleeping gear and suffered through a breakfast of canned C rations. Eyster and Captain George F. Dailey were planning the day's operation, and Dailey suggested his men move out along the more visible tracks and paths in the scrublands and gnarled rubber trees, even though he presumed these were mined and snipers would be observing us from hidden tunnel exits. He admitted it was a gamble, "But this way I can bring up my jeep-mounted 106 recoilless rifles and I can blast every manned bunker I find."

Eyster nodded. He had been complaining of a severe cold the night before and his eyes and nose were runny and he'd wrapped a khaki towel around his throat and tucked it into his shirt. I stayed with the colonel as Horst moved out with the infantrymen, snaking their way along a path beyond the bivouac area. There was soon a shouted warning, "Claymore, Claymore," and the colonel and I moved quickly up the path. Eyster called out to the sweating soldier bending over the plate-shaped mine, "Cut the wires, don't pull them," and we watched as he detached the mine from its hiding place near a tree stump.

The soldiers began spreading into the scrubs for security as Eyster and Dailey consulted a detailed operational map. Their radiomen stood on the path behind them, and I moved close to hear. My shoulder was touching Eyster's when a staccato of sharp cracks exploded in front of me and I felt his shoulders heave and I heard him gasp. I knew he'd been shot. I slid to the ground to save myself. Eyster slumped on his back a few feet away, his arms pressed to his chest, moaning quietly. "George, I'm hit," he muttered to his company commander, who was already on his feet, now heedless of the sniper and shouting, "The colonel's hit, the colonel's hit. Bring up a medic, bring up a medic."

Eyster was lying ashen-faced in the dust, his eyes closed, his face gray, an open wound on his neck. A medic ran up and though he told me later he thought the colonel was dying right then, that he knew it was pointless to try and save him, he did what he could, lightly dressing the neck wound. Eyster's eyes opened, he was pulling through the first, savage assault on his nervous system. His heart seemed to flutter back to life and color came to his face and he regained consciousness. "Where am I hit, how bad is it?" he rasped. Horst came into view and Eyster exhorted him to take cover, "Horst, don't get hit, don't get hit," and then he lapsed into unconsciousness.

I was filming the scene with an 8mm home movie camera. I pointed to some trees about fifty yards away and told Horst, "I think the sniper was over there. He seemed to have popped out of a hole, then slipped right back inside." Soldiers had been unable to locate the tunnel entrance and were moving deeper into the thickets. The battalion doctor ran up the pathway, and he fell to his knees to examine Eyster. He turned to Dailey and said, "I'll give him fifteen minutes more to live unless we can get him out of here." As he was speaking, rifle fire broke out nearby and Captain Dailey ordered four waiting soldiers to load the officer onto a stretcher that they rigged with a plasma bottle. The helicopter could not find the landing zone and Dailey desperately threw canisters of brightly colored smoke into the clearing and shouted into his radio until the craft appeared in the sky above him, and later came down and got him.

By the time we resumed the patrol, it was 9 A.M. and the sun was blistering hot. We bumped into a unit from Company B. The squad leader pointed up a trail and said, "The Vietcong tried to entice us up there a couple of hours ago by jumpin' out on the track and wavin' black flags at us. We brought mortars in on them."

At eleven, a private tripped a claymore mine as he moved up to our right. He saw the fuse burning and shouted a warning as he dove to the ground. The explosion was deafening. Horst and I stood rocking in shock as the dust swirled around us. When the air cleared we saw the body of the platoon sergeant ahead of us, almost split in half by the thousands of steel pellets. Another soldier lay gasping in pain, steel bits embedded in his buttocks. The private, miraculously, wasn't wounded. He crawled over to his platoon leader, who lay dying in the elephant grass. I saw an unopened letter was sticking in his helmet strap. "It was from his wife," a soldier whispered to me. "He got it this morning and planned to read it later in the day."

Captain Dailey shouted to his squad, "Be watchful, be careful, don't bunch up around the radio operators." They were prime targets. Dailey's radioman was beckoning to him; there was a call from up ahead, where sounds of firing could be heard. The scout platoon had run into a reinforced concrete bunker and they were pinned down by machine gun fire. Dailey told them to hold fast and put on their gas masks. He radioed up a helicopter equipped with rockets loaded with pellets of a caustic version of riot gas to fire into the bunker and disable the occupants.

We pulled on our gas masks. The rubber devices clung to our faces as tight as skin. The powerful gas drifted back on us and we were thankful for the protection, but as we stumbled forward a second claymore mine was accidentally detonated by a soldier as he torched a grass shack on the side of the road. Two sergeants were struck down in the blast and as the medics tore off the soldiers' clothes to treat their wounds I could barely hear their cries through the jutting noses of their masks. One man was clawing at his face trying to pull off his mask. Captain Dailey shouted to the medics to be careful, to leave their clothes on "because the gas will burn their exposed skin." By midafternoon we had barely covered a mile and we were ordered to return to Trung Lap.

I filed the story of Company C of the Black Lions the next morning. "It was a long bloody mile we walked Wednesday. At times it was a Dante's Inferno of fire and brimstone. Powerful riot gas drifted through the trees, burning where it touched a man's sweating skin. Wounded writhed on the ground, looking monstrous in their black, grotesque gas masks. It was a walk where death lurked in the trees where the enemy snipers hid, and under the ground where their mines lay."

I had not named Eyster in my story to be sure his family wouldn't hear that way. We found the colonel in a stark, uncooled hospital room draped with mosquito nets. His neck and chest were heavily bandaged, his left arm was in a sling and his skin was gray. Horst had printed a set of pictures of the patrol to give him. Eyster smiled and croaked a greeting and gazed with pleasure at the pictures, whispering, "I had a lucky escape, I nearly didn't make it." I asked him how he felt. "I'm fine," he said. "I asked the general this morning to write my wife and tell her and the children what happened. This wound is not serious enough to cable her, I don't want her to worry."

But Horst and I were worried. The next afternoon the commander of the Third Brigade telephoned that George Eyster was dead. Horst and I were invited to the memorial service the next day at Lai Khe but we were already committed to return to Trung Lap and rejoin the Black Lions because my story and Horst's pictures had received considerable newspaper play and the AP's foreign desk wanted more. Three days later I wrote Colonel Eyster's obituary. "He was the son of a general, a West Pointer and a battalion commander. But Lieutenant Colonel George Eyster was to die like a rifleman. It may have been the colonel's leaves on his collar, or the map he held in his hand, or just a wayward chance that the Vietcong sniper chose Eyster from the five of us standing on that dusty jungle path." Harriet Eyster read my story in the *Orlando Evening Star* and wrote me, "You gave his children a legacy that no one else could have by writing in such a manner that his courage and his heroism will live for them and be an inspiration to them forever."

More officers were dying in Vietnam than in previous conflicts, four times the rate of the Korean War. Captain George Dailey of Company C was killed four months later, the victim of a mistaken bombing by a U.S. aircraft.

But Vietnam was not like other wars; for many soldiers survival, not victory, was the goal. All they had to do was make it for one year. Critics said the one-year tour planted the seeds of apathy. The soldiers thought it was too long. They ruled off their pinup pictures into 365 squares and reverentially marked off each one, waiting for the magic "DEROS day," date eligible for return home from overseas, the day to catch the U.S.-bound chartered airliner out of Vietnam, the "freedom bird" with its smiling air hostesses and free drinks and journey's end in America.

At War with Westy

VIETNAM ERUPTED into a full-blown war in the summer of 1966 when General Westmoreland concluded that he could defeat the communists in battle. He traveled the countryside telling everybody that the United States would remain there until peace was assured. As Westmoreland watched his force levels climb and his combat and supply bases multiply, the idea of a negotiated peace began to fade. With the massive power now at his disposal—attack aircraft on navy carriers in the South China Sea, B-52 bombers on Guam, air force jets in bases in Thailand and South Vietnam, and a troop strength approaching and passing three hundred thousand—he grew convinced that a victory strategy was possible. It was difficult not to thrill to the war machine that Westmoreland was assembling.

President Johnson seemed to be giving him a blank check for his plan of "search and destroy" using attack and troop-carrying helicopters to give the ground forces mobility. Westmoreland conveniently looked beyond the stubborn guerrilla insurgency that was submersed in the population. He planned instead for a more conventional war against the communist armies along Vietnam's borders.

Westmoreland's operations officer, Major General William DePuy, favored risky, close artillery and air support. Sometimes I would see shell fire exploding in the landing zones just minutes before the troop-loaded helicopters lumbered in. When DePuy, who had taken command of the first infantry division, noticed my concern one day he shouted over the roar of the engines, "The trick, Arnett, is in the timing." DePuy set stiff standards for his division. His command helicopter was often hovering over forward units watching what was going on below. He did not tolerate mediocrity and would relieve platoon, company and battalion commanders for relatively minor infractions of the rules.

DePuy rewarded initiative and placed the best young officers on the fast track to rapid advancement. Lieutenant Colonel Alexander M. Haig was a favorite, singled out for promotion to brigade commander after his battalion crippled an attacking Vietcong regiment at the battle of Ap Gu. DePuy aspired to run the best division in the whole army and made no secret of it.

DePuy contended that victory had always favored the side that was able to concentrate its forces at a critical place at a critical time on the battlefield. This tactic was a cardinal principle of the Vietcong, whose units never attacked unless they fielded superior forces. With the ability to move a full battalion of troops by helicopters from anywhere at any time to any place on the battlefield, he argued, American commanders could alter the ratio of forces in their favor. With this procedure, he said, American troops would have won the battle of Dien Bien Phu. DePuy was a persuasive talker and his confidence was catching. By autumn, when after a series of large-scale engagements in War Zones C and D, he declared that he had achieved important tactical successes and had destroyed all opposing enemy forces in his operational area, Westmoreland claimed he was on the path to victory.

America had the superior military power and DePuy was using it prodigiously. But the strategy of attrition could succeed only if it broke the enemy's will and that clearly was not happening.

Westmoreland often took reporters along on his routine day-long field trips to get his views across. They would fly by helicopter and small plane to remote places like Ham Tan or Phuoc Vinh or Bao Loc, where American and Vietnamese officials would be lined up to receive him and chat about the local situation. The resulting stories were inevitably fawning, uncritical paeans to his military mastery.

Writers scrambled to come up with uncommon descriptions of what were invariably ordinary situations. He was the most photographed military officer of his era.

Tom Reedy, in an account of one such trip for the AP, wrote, "Matching strides with General William C. Westmoreland, the fifty-one-year-old commander of the war in Vietnam, on such an occasion calls for a giant. Pygmies need not apply." The writer also described the general as "a lean six footer with a lantern jaw, the energy of a tank, and the hands of a pianist." Even an acid observer like Hugh Mulligan was captivated by the Westmoreland aura. After hearing him chat with a group of Eleventh Armored Cavalry officers, Hugh wrote, "The pep talk was given with all the enthusiasm of a locker room speech before the Army-Navy game, but there was a ring of sincerity in the resonant voice and a glint of admiration in the deep-set eyes that somehow made it moving and almost memorable."

I was never invited along on a Westmoreland trip, and I never asked to accompany him. He had made it clear in private briefings with bureau chiefs that my kind of field reporting was unacceptable to him. He complained that for the first time in the history of warfare, news reports were going directly from the infantry squad to the American public, before the area commander even knew what was going on. Westmoreland argued that the Saigon press corps had to be sensitive to the morale both of the troops in the field and the public at home, and that a positive approach had to be taken in all news dispatches to avoid misleading the enemy about America's intentions, or discrediting U.S. ability in the eyes of its allies. I thought he was crediting us with too much power, but I was aware that his personal reputation could be affected by our reporting.

Press casualties mounted as the battles intensified. Photographer Charlie Chellapah from Singapore was killed on a patrol with the U.S. Army's Twenty-fifth Infantry Division on February 14. Sam Castan, a senior editor of *Look* magazine, died May 21 with troops of the U.S. First Cavalry Division on Operation Crazy Horse. The French scholar Bernard Fall was fatally wounded by a booby trap on February 21, 1967, while on patrol with U.S. marines along the central coast north of Hue, a locale he had made famous as the "Street without Joy" in a book about the French war. The ninth correspondent to die was freelance photographer Ronald G. Gallagher, killed March 11, 1967, at Rach Kien in the Mekong Delta with the U.S. Army's Ninth Infantry Division.

Our marine escort officers began demanding that war reporters wear the twenty-pound flak jackets and steel helmets favored by the grunts and we did not object to the load, as we hitchhiked helicopter rides into forward outposts near the DMZ under shell fire, often sitting astride ammunition cases, and scrambling from one sandbagged bunker to another across knee-deep gullies of mud that never seemed to dry up despite the scorching sun that alternated with the monsoon storms. Getting out of those places was equally nerve-racking, a waiting game because the priority cargoes for the few helicopters that came in were newsmen last out after the wounded and rotating soldiers.

At places like Con Thien under fire from across the North Vietnamese border, there was never more than a two-second warning of an incoming round, and AP photographer Henri Huet didn't even hear the blast of the shell that ripped fragments through his arms and legs while he was taking pictures as marine gunners returned the artillery fire. Huet was killed on assignment in 1971.

AP photographer John Nance was stumbling through the sticky mud of rice paddies along the Saigon River with First Infantry Division troops when mortar shells slapped in among them, creasing him on the arm and sending him sprawling as a machine gun opened up on the patrol, killing several soldiers around him. Nance had placed his heavy metal camera case on the paddy dike for added protection and a Vietcong gunner apparently thought it was important because he kept firing at it, six bullets bursting through the metal and over Nance's head, which was pressed for safety into the warm mud.

John Wheeler was with a lead platoon from the Twenty-fifth Infantry Division at Cu Chi when he was caught in a furious firefight and then wounded when a grenade thrown by an American soldier bounced back off a tree, killing the soldier next to him and wounding Wheeler in the lower left arm. The AP reporter drove back to Saigon with a field dressing on his wound, and pounded out his story on an office typewriter even though the blood came oozing through the heavy bandage.

The veteran military historian S. L. A. Marshall chose the autumn of 1966 to attack the integrity and bravery of the Vietnam press corps in an article in the *New Leader* magazine: "Press Failure in Vietnam—America's Sedentary War Correspondents." He concluded that journalists in Vietnam displayed a "cynical faddishness" and did not report on actual battles because "the majority of U.S. correspondents in Saigon don't give a damn about them or are ignorant of the war and do not wish to expose their innocence, or so fearful of the front that

they cannot endure the thought of staying with it." He accused reporters of trying to "cop a Pulitzer Prize by writing about demonstrations, riots, accidents or anything graphic that will make the home
front squirm." *Time* magazine devoted a page to Marshall's charges
without offering any balancing viewpoints, in accord with its persistent
denigration of the Vietnam press corps.

We were flabbergasted by Marshall's accusations. Few could recall
ever having seen him in Vietnam. In fact, Marshall had spent two
months at the First Cavalry Division's An Khe base camp, sharing
the VIP quarters of a deputy division commander, traveling by helicopter, and never once setting foot on an active battlefield. His material for the critical article and a later book he named *The Battles in
the Monsoon* was obtained entirely from after-action interviews. We
could only conclude that the once best-selling author of popular Korean War books such as *Pork Chop Hill* was seeking to get publicity
at our expense. This was later borne out by retired Colonel David
Hackworth, who had accompanied Marshall on his visit to Vietnam
and later wrote about how eagerly the historian had planned his ultimately unsuccessful return to the best-seller lists. Wes Gallagher was
one of many who wrote indignant responses to the *New Leader* article.

Despite what Westmoreland thought, I did not set out to annoy the
military establishment. I enjoyed good working relations with several
senior officers. But these didn't always work out. I had become ac-
quainted with Major General John Norton when he was on Westmoreland's staff, and I was pleased when he was given command of
the First Cavalry Division in the Central Highlands, the unit of choice
for reporters seeking dramatic action stories.

I wrote about the outfit's zealous use of Westmoreland's find and
fix tactics. It was a bold and risky technique: to dangle small American
infantry units in the jungle as bait, and pounce on the attackers and
destroy them when they took the lure. General Norton had explained
to me that the subterfuge was necessary to locate a larger enemy force
"before he cocks his real punch." Norton worried about the danger
to his troops but he believed such tactics were necessary. "Just as a
point man leads the way for his platoon and company and may well
be the first to get killed in an action," he explained, "then a platoon
and company lead the way for a battalion and a brigade."

But the severity of the risk could not be denied. The previous week
an infantry platoon had been overrun and all its members killed or
wounded before the cavalry could arrive to rescue them. A second
incident a week later prompted me to detail the general's tactics in a

news story. A First Cav infantry company was on bait duty in the notorious Ia Drang Valley when it was pounced on from three sides by an attacking North Vietnamese force. This time waiting artillery guns at nearby bases poured in two thousand shells on the attackers, followed up by intensive air strikes. A relief force arrived on the scene, dispersing the assailants, who dragged off their casualties with them. The plan worked ostensibly, but still the decoy company paid a heavy price. At least fifty Americans were killed or wounded in the action.

I had returned to Saigon when General Norton summoned me back to An Khe. I was willing enough to make the long trip. The shantytown adjoining the An Khe base was the most lurid in Vietnam, with its tinsmiths and gold stores and haggling merchants and beer parlors and B-girls. A year earlier An Khe had been only a bus stop on the Pleiku road with barely a thousand people living in its small village. Now it was a boom town providing the basics of social life for twenty thousand lonely American troops from the cavalry division.

General Norton's headquarters office was partway up a hillside with a commanding view over the sprawling thirty-two-square-mile base, with its dark green tents and wooden buildings and miles of roads. A young aide sprang to his feet and saluted as I knocked on the outer door and entered. I was soon joined by several senior division officers, all in starched uniforms. I knew most of them but they looked uncomfortably at me and said little, and I figured that there was trouble ahead. When we entered Norton's office they saluted and shouted the division slogan, "All the way, sir."

Norton rose from behind his desk and shook my hand but didn't offer me a seat. The subject was my bait story and I pointed out that I had written it three weeks ago and had almost forgotten about it. He lifted a newspaper clipping from his desktop and handed it to me. It was a tattered copy of my story in the *Columbus Ledger,* the newspaper of the Georgia home base of the division. "Goddamn it," he said. "Charlie Black wouldn't have written a story like this." Black was a Columbus reporter who had stayed for months in An Khe writing about the division.

I protested that my story was not inaccurate. "Accuracy is not the point, you've scared the shit out of the folks back home and I won't have it," Norton replied. He held up some sheets of paper that he said were a long letter from his wife. "You know what she is telling me, that the wives of these men here and others saw this story and were shocked, damnit, they think I'm trying to kill their husbands with this bait shit, and I won't have it."

I stated the obvious, that the bait strategy did risk people's lives, but the general didn't want to discuss it. He didn't want to make a deal with me. He just wanted me to know that he hated my guts for scaring the folks back home and that I wouldn't be doing it again in his area of operations.

.   .   .

Westmoreland was so convinced of the efficacy of the First Cav and the Big Red One and the six other American infantry divisions forming up in the country that he bypassed the South Vietnamese governing structure almost entirely. American troops began bearing the full burden of the war against the North Vietnamese regiments swarming across the borders. The Saigon army took on the secondary mission of pacification, securing towns and villages.

Vietnam remained a morass of special interests and regional jealousies and endemic corruption that undermined resistance to the communists. The young prime minister, Nguyen Cao Ky, was the latest of several military men to ascend to power since Ngo Dinh Diem's overthrow, and he was a hard man to take seriously. In one interview he said he endorsed "the leadership and sense of mission" of Adolf Hitler, "but not his inhuman methods." He kept saying he wanted to invade North Vietnam, at a time when you couldn't drive twenty minutes from Saigon in any direction without endangering your life. He was happiest in his role of dashing aviator, favoring a wisp of lavender silk knotted at his throat and a black flight suit. He loved to party and I watched him one evening at a Continental Hotel soiree introduce himself to Jayne Mansfield.

Ky's ascendancy had come as political rivalries drained the Vietnamese military of its effectiveness; whole infantry divisions had launched open revolt against the central authorities. American advisers attached to key Vietnamese divisions around Saigon were required to mount "coup watches" with instructions to flash a warning to the American high command if a battalion turned up a highway in the direction of the capital city. There were some who saw all this happening and were appalled that America's young men were being thrown away in a war that was supposed to be a Vietnamese affair.

The most forceful critic was John Paul Vann, the military adviser who had blown the whistle on the incompetence displayed at the battle of Ap Bac in 1963. He had resigned his colonel's commission and returned to Vietnam as a civilian official with the rural pacification program. He believed that the military bureaucrats were blundering deeper into an unnecessary American war, and he despised the armchair generals in their air-conditioned officers clubs in Saigon who were allowing it all to happen. Based at embattled Hau Nghia Province west of Saigon, Vann spent every other night in the field. He sometimes stayed in Vietnamese militia outposts where dispirited, frightened soldiers were on the verge of deserting. His presence invariably uplifted morale and drew the attention of military authorities to those low-priority locations.

Vann was charged with energy, and he was a daredevil. I sometimes got up the nerve to drive with him on his rounds in a jeep that banged over rutted roads in places known to be controlled by the Vietcong. For his personal security, Vann preferred hand grenades to a handgun, explaining in his raspy, assertive voice, "If you just hold up one of these in your hand the bad guys will run away. They know the damage it can cause." He placed the M1 grenades in his lap as he drove, where they bounced and jumped as I sat beside him in the front seat. He seemed to be toying with death at times, but he laughed whenever I brought it to his attention and he once thumped his chest and declared he was indestructible. He told me, "Last week I was flying in an army spotter plane to Bien Hoa and the weather was lousy and we couldn't see clearly where we were going, and in trying to land we struck a cluster of power lines. Now, anyone else would be dead, but my pilot skidded through those wires and brought the aircraft in safely."

I admired Vann. He knew more about the war than anyone else in the country, with lines into both the American and Vietnamese high commands. I placed great value on his information and his counsel. He made no secret of his hawkish views. He believed the war was worth winning, but he totally opposed Westmoreland's search and destroy tactics, which he judged cruel and self-defeating. He argued that the only route to victory was through the Vietnamese. He wanted the United States to strengthen the Vietnamese Army, rely less on American troops, and he asserted that if there were continued resistance from the Saigon government, America should assume command responsibility for the whole country to shape up all levels of the war effort, and utilize Vietnamese forces to their fullest.

He asked me one day, "Why should we treat so gingerly and carefully an unsophisticated little country like Vietnam when we failed to show such consideration to the feelings of Britain in World War Two?" I listened carefully to everything Vann said. His convictions were frequently iconoclastic and some of his ideas were unrealistic, but his was a voice that offered a way out of the bloody, destructive morass.

Vann was eager to be heard in policy circles though he rarely was. He knew he had no credibility left with U.S. military authorities. He said that an American army general who had wanted to hire him as an executive assistant had been told by Westmoreland, "If you really want him you can have him. But take him at your own risk." Vann then set his sights on influencing the White House. He was in occasional communication with Harry McPherson, an aide to President Johnson, and he was hoping to use his widening group of acquaintances among State Department and aid agency operatives to reach Defense Secretary Robert McNamara.

Vann was convinced that McNamara was being misled by the blizzard of statistical information fed into the systems analysis processes. He believed that if the defense secretary was aware that much of the data was unreliable he would reevaluate his support of Westmoreland's policies.

I did not share Vann's confidence in the defense secretary. I had been covering McNamara's trips to Vietnam since the early 1960s, and had seen little willingness on his part to face the disagreeable facts. He had accommodated quickly to the frequent political changes in Saigon. He was a fervent booster of whoever occupied Saigon's Presidential Palace at the time of his visits; he was particularly enamored of the most unscrupulous of the many usurpers of presidential power, Major General Nguyen Khanh, the dandified, mediocre officer who early in 1964 had overthrown the popular military group that had removed Ngo Dinh Diem from power.

General Khanh plunged the country into a year of political and military chaos, yet McNamara campaigned across Vietnam with him, attempting to bolster the general's popularity. Sometimes joined by Ambassador Maxwell Taylor, they would parade in marketplaces and public squares in Hue and Da Nang and other cities, thrusting their arms over their heads, their fingers entwined, shouting, "Vietnam Muon Nam," Long Live Vietnam. The usually cold defense secretary seemed to become misty-eyed at these demonstrations, but I rarely noticed much reaction from the crowds assembled there by the local authorities, and I presumed that much was being lost in translation. McNamara's departing press conferences in the VIP lounge at Saigon's Tan Son Nhut Airport were relentlessly upbeat, his background sessions even more so.

At one press conference early in 1965 I had asked McNamara how he reacted to charges that Vietnam was becoming "McNamara's War." He stared at me for a second, then brushed his hand across his sleek

207

black hair and adjusted his glasses and straightened his shoulders and responded, "McNamara's War? I'll have you know I am proud to have my name associated with this venture, proud of it, I tell you," and then he was off in a whirl of hurrying aides and banging doors and the scream of jet engines warming up for the long flight back to Washington.

I felt that McNamara was unreachable. I had seen generals risk their lives, and some weep when a soldier died in battle. I could not imagine McNamara crying over such things, though he became sentimental at expressions of patriotic fervor. I told Vann that I doubted that McNamara cared. Vann went ahead anyway, deciding to make a direct approach to McNamara using a former staff member of the secretary of defense, a man who had become Vann's favorite companion, a brilliant, quirky former marine officer named Daniel Ellsberg.

I first encountered Dan Ellsberg in January 1967 at the northern Mekong Delta town of Rach Kien twenty miles south of Saigon, a place typical of the hundreds of once prosperous farming communities that had been abandoned to their fate on the front lines of the war. Now Rach Kien had become a desolate ghost town. I had driven with Horst and John Nance and along the way we passed horse-drawn carts loaded with family possessions and two rusted, creaking buses packed with people. Some of the displaced population was returning from refugee camps. Under a new pacification program Rach Kien was to be restored and they hoped they could resume their former lives.

A few trestle tables had been set up in the market square on the sidewalks where vendors hawked the abundant produce of the Mekong Delta. A squad of perspiring American infantrymen was sitting on the curb with their fatigue shirts open and their sleeves rolled up, drinking from Coca-Cola bottles. This was the third time in six years that the Saigon government had attempted to revitalize Rach Kien and the neighboring districts, each time financed by millions of dollars in American aid. We were looking for the headquarters group when we noticed some soldiers in an abandoned house and stopped to ask directions.

As we walked inside we saw a slim, pretty farm girl who looked in her early teens being threatened by a Vietnamese soldier. Her hands were bound behind her back and her eyes were frozen in fear as the soldier swished a knife from side to side and then flashed it toward her, stopping inches short of her chest. He snarled questions about her name and background, and she stuttered answers in a whisper as several Vietnamese soldiers jeered and laughed.

I asked a young American soldier standing uncomfortably in the background what it was all about and he said his patrol had found her working in a paddyfield near the town and had brought her in because she carried no ID card. They had handed her over to the Vietnamese troops assigned to work with them, a provincial reconnaissance unit, part of a special command, the PRU, created to seek out Vietcong operatives. The units had become notorious. On the pockets of their camouflaged shirts, the PRU soldiers wore the skull and crossbones emblem, and their ranks included former criminals and Vietcong defectors upon whose chests the government had tattooed the phrase "Sat Cong," meaning "kill communists," to prevent them from returning to their old allegiances. Horst Faas had found one PRU outfit that used a twelve-year-old boy as an executioner. They had dressed the child up in a cowboy hat and a tailored uniform and armed him with a revolver that he wore proudly on a holster hanging around his waist. When Horst photographed him the boy had already scratched thirteen notches on his gun barrel.

We persuaded the Americans to take the frightened young girl with them to their own base in an old concrete schoolhouse in another part of town. After sending her by helicopter to provincial headquarters they found she was not yet old enough to require an identification card, and she was released back to her family.

The American soldiers were supposed to further the pacification process. Sometimes this meant negotiating settlements between fighting neighbors. Sometimes it meant retrieving stolen chickens. In Rach Kien, the Vietnamese, however, were not always so quick to join the peace-making efforts. Vietnamese soldiers brought back something more than chickens from their morning outing. They carried four severed human heads still dripping with blood, trophies from alleged Vietcong sympathizers they killed earlier in the day. We saw the trophies stuck on spikes south of town, a ghoulish warning to Rach Kien's returning population.

Then we found Ellsberg in combat uniform and a floppy khaki hat, waist deep in a rice paddy, pulling himself through the muck, a submachine gun in his left fist. He was shouting at a dawdling squad of American infantrymen, "Get up here, damn it." They seemed reluctant to move forward, and a lieutenant explained to us, "He's not one of us, he's from the embassy, and he's here playing soldier." A bullet cracked over our heads from somewhere up front and we dove into the mud and crawled forward to where Ellsberg was peering through the rice shoots at several patches of trees ahead, looking for a sniper.

The infantry squad moved ahead of our group into a grassy, swampy flatland and Ellsberg relaxed. Vann had told me a lot about Ellsberg, who had become a strategist for the Defense Department and then volunteered for Vietnam, joining the staff of Major General Edward G. Lansdale, the celebrated counterinsurgency expert. I asked Ellsberg if it wasn't unusual for an armed civilian to be on the front line with the troops and he said, "I'm trying to see if this sort of thing works and what better way to find out than at the place where it is happening."

When I informed him of the gory bridge decoration, he grew angry, declaring that the whole point of the pacification program was to do everything possible to avoid hurting civilians, to avoid alienating them.

We left the infantry unit maneuvering in the mud of the paddyfields, and walked back to the town. Ellsberg raised his submachine gun and posed for pictures under an archway that had just been newly erected for an upcoming festival. Clearly he still had a foot planted firmly in the military. He shouted to Horst, "Don't forget to send me over a few copies of that picture, eight-by-tens," as we loaded into our vehicle and left Rach Kien for the ride back home.

Vann and Ellsberg were in agreement that the only way to convince McNamara of the error of his ways was to lay before him a detailed argument that the U.S. war policy of using American troops to bear the brunt of the action was tragically mistaken. They knew they had to get around his personal staff to get his ear, and Ellsberg undertook to do that by using his connections to get aboard McNamara's plane on his next visit to Vietnam. The secretary would be a captive audience for the thirty-hour journey to Vietnam. Vann attributed McNamara's rapid change of heart on the war partly to Ellsberg's efforts.

I would include Vann's views in my analyses. I wrote an unflattering assessment of Westmoreland for the papers of January 27, 1967, and it was widely used. I pointed out that in the three years he had been in Vietnam the war had changed dramatically, that it was fifty-seven times more costly per day, that American casualties had increased fiftyfold, and that the four-star general had the ear of the president of the United States, who was trusting him to deliver on his promises of victory.

I quoted critics who complained that Westmoreland had displayed a ruthless ambition, shoring up his base of power by calling for more and more American troop deployments when his job had originally been to build up Vietnamese capability to fight their own war. The joke going around town was that he had aspirations to become "C-in-C World," commander in chief, world.

My relations with Westmoreland reached a low point when I was assigned with Kelly Smith to write a lengthy story for the AP news features department comparing a day in the military commander's life with that of a typical soldier. Kelly was to breakfast with the general and spend the rest of the day with him; I was given the field assignment and joined up with an infantry company from the Twenty-fifth Infantry Division operating northwest of Saigon. The story seemed fine to us. The final version began,

"Dawn breaks over a sleeping city, its first pink tones paint the red-tiled roofs of suburbia and wash the roof gardens of tall hotels lining the Saigon River. Traffic barely stirs on the shadowy streets; a helicopter, its rotor blades slapping the cool morning air, drones overhead toward the still mountains of the north.

"In the whitewashed mansion at 19 Doan Cong Buu Street, typical of those occupied by Americans in Saigon, a sleeper turns restlessly at the noise but doesn't awake. Then General William C. Westmoreland reaches over to turn off his alarm. It's 6:15 A.M. An aide knocks on his door to make sure his boss is awake. The tanned, lean-faced general gets up, brushes his teeth and shaves.

"Thirty miles northwest across the canal-laced paddyfields now brightening with morning light, Lieutenant William Howard of Cordele, Georgia, crawls out of a shallow foxhole dug into the bank of a country road. He brushes the caked mud off his wet fatigues and yawns."

It was Kelly's midpoint in the story that upset the general. "It is 2 P.M. at the Cercle Sportif, the last stronghold of the country club set, an oasis of gracious living in a sea of drabness. Westmoreland arrives for a fifty-minute tennis game on court number five, one of fifteen at the club. As Westmoreland lines up his first serve against his Vietnamese instructor, the first vehicle in a ninety-two-truck convoy on a lonely road forty miles northwest of Saigon gets mired in thick mud, and within minutes the whole convoy is up to its axles in slime, throwing all the operational planning of the Twenty-fifth Infantry Division out of balance and threatening the success of a series of assaults planned later that day and on Sunday."

When our story was published in newspapers across the United States the Pentagon cried foul for our even mentioning his tennis game. A few weeks later, I was waiting for the arrival of Vice President

Hubert H. Humphrey for an inspection visit to a Mekong Delta riverine force base when Westmoreland accosted me.

"Well," he declared, "you'll be happy to learn that I have quit the Cercle Sportif and tennis." I was genuinely surprised. But I couldn't help but blurt out that at the entreaties of my wife I had joined the club. Westy looked at me with narrowing eyes, and said, "Well, maybe they gave you my slot," and turned away.

Merton Perry, now of *Newsweek,* had overheard our conversation and sent it verbatim to his magazine, which published the item in its gossip column the following week. Westmoreland's press officer, Colonel Winant Sidle, informed me that the commander was convinced that I had planned the whole thing and did not wish to have anything to do with me again.

By the spring of 1967 President Johnson was picking out military targets on maps in the White House war room and ordering his land- and sea-based fighter aircraft to bomb them. He also launched strikes against his perceived critics. We were told in distant Saigon that Johnson was our most avid antagonist, brooding over the media's depiction of the war in front of a row of television sets tuned to the network news, checking on the three telex machines clicking out the product of the AP, UPI and Reuters wire services, and scrutinizing a dozen or so important newspapers each morning. Johnson did not hesitate to arm-twist reluctant editors to "get on the team." His long arm reached to the war front, where in telephone calls and cables to the bureaucrats he and his personal staff rode herd on the daily information flow. If the press was generally beyond Johnson's reach, his officials were not and he vented his displeasure swiftly upon them.

His information chief in Saigon was Barry Zorthian, an experienced United States Information Service official, who relished telling colleagues of a humbling encounter with Lyndon Johnson at a White House staff meeting in 1965 called to discuss war coverage. Before Zorthian could begin his presentation, press secretary Bill Moyers whispered into his ear, "The boss wants to see you upstairs right away." The two proceeded to the family quarters, where Johnson was sitting in bed. When he caught sight of Zorthian, Johnson "started taking off on the press in a nonstop monologue," and then turned on Zorthian. "Goddamn it, what's wrong with you? Why can't you handle the press out there better? Why do you let them write that? Why don't you straighten them out . . . ." Zorthian returned downstairs, shaking.

President Johnson wanted from Zorthian and other officials in the field what he himself was unwilling to effect, an unofficial censorship that would shape news dispatches to conform to his view of how the war should be proceeding. Johnson sometimes got as involved in the news coverage as the bombing missions, at times listening to Saigon's Five O'Clock Follies briefings, which were piped into the White House by telephone in the early-morning hours, and not hesitating to call in his views afterward.

One day spokesman Jack Stewart was "no commenting" a question from the press corps on a Saigon political development. The president grew annoyed. "Who's that damn fool saying 'no comment' like a parrot?" he declared angrily to an aide. The next day Stewart received a cable from his superiors at the U.S. Information Service, ordering his immediate transfer to Léopoldville in the Congo. When Stewart protested the decision, the USIS director told him of the president's reaction and that nothing could be done to change it. Stewart threatened to go public with his complaints, and the transfer was shelved.

I had as little as possible to do with information officials, and they with me. To Stewart and Zorthian and the others who were feeling the president's hot breath, I was their worst nightmare: a field reporter who came up with controversial information that was beyond their means to control, and which when published almost invariably meant censure for them from the White House. Zorthian and I got along for some time after his arrival in Saigon in 1964 to shape up the U.S. Embassy information operation, and it was clear he was a man of great savvy. But my relations with him soured after I wrote my story on the phony war movie and got worse with my story of the South Vietnamese military's experimentation with nonlethal gas. We were barely civil with each other after that.

When early in 1966 I had complained to Zorthian about being pushed around by American military police he grinned at me like he was enjoying my discomfort. During a weekend of Buddhist demonstrations against the government in the streets of Saigon, two American military police jeeps pulled up alongside a group of reporters and ordered us to leave the scene. I was with Bob Schieffer, then of the *Fort Worth Star Telegram,* and Bob Keatley of the *Wall Street Journal,* and I told the policemen, "We are newsmen, leave us alone." One of them answered, "I know, but our orders are to clear all Americans off the streets, including newsmen, that's our orders." We objected strenuously, aware that Saigon security was in the hands of the Vi-

213

etnamese police and that American jurisdiction extended only to U.S. soldiers and installations.

"I'm not an American," I said, "I am from New Zealand," and when asked to prove it I responded, "Isn't my accent and haircut enough?" Eddie Adams said, "You have no right to order American newsmen off the streets, you have no jurisdiction over us." The military police thought about this a minute and then drove off.

They soon returned. "You're coming with me," one told Adams. "All Americans off the street." I again protested that I was not an American and the policeman angrily pulled out his black .45 pistol and pointed first at the midriff of Adams, then at Keatley and Schieffer, waved it toward some *Life* magazine photographers nearby and then focused on me. "You're coming with me," he said belligerently. "You're an American."

Bob Keatley broke in, "I am American but I deny you the right to force me away from here. The U.S. command has no jurisdiction over me." At this point the conversation became even more heated and several obscenities were exchanged, with the pistol of the flustered military policeman wavering between us all. When two Vietnamese police came by they refused to intervene. The confrontation was resolved only when a group of young American servicemen, partying at a brothel above a nearby bar, were rooted out by a crowd of demonstrators and had to be rescued by the MPs and driven away.

Zorthian heard out my story and declared, "You say an American MP pulled a pistol on you? No way that could happen." I produced a series of eight-by-ten photos by Eddie Adams of the encounter. "See?" I demanded. "What are you going to do about it?"

"Well," Zorthian responded, "you were abusive and obnoxious. Maybe we'll charge you with assault on that poor MP, assault with a pen and pencil." He was still grinning when I left, but I had the last laugh. The AP distributed on the photo wire a picture of me held at gunpoint and the next morning's *Washington Post* used it across three columns on an inside page. Secretary of State Dean Rusk was apparently not amused.

No prisoners were taken in the rough and tumble of the information war and accusations flew on both sides. When David Halberstam was visiting Saigon in 1967 he told me that Zorthian had told some visiting congressmen that I was a communist. Halberstam said he was going to call Zorthian on it. The telephone soon rang. It was Zorthian, saying that Halberstam was in his office. "I want to tell you, Peter, that I've called you many things including an SOB but I've never called you a communist because I don't believe that."

Zorthian's main preoccupation was with positive stories. He would advise newly arrived officials, "Tell the truth, but don't blurt out everything you know." He was a member of the U.S. mission council, the group of senior-ranking officials who met to discuss and establish policy. Zorthian tried to include the government's spin in my stories, and he would sometimes rail at me, "Peter, you have got to get the viewpont of the mission in your war analyses, you owe it to us. We know more than you do about what's going on," to which I would respond that I gathered my information in the same places the government did and that my assessments were as valid as theirs.

The media manipulation began to slip in 1967 when the real cost of committing American troops to Vietnam became impossible to conceal. The war strategy was implausible and the bloodshed and brutality that accompanied the troops into action was difficult to justify. Zorthian and his information team were overwhelmed by bad news; they did not have enough fingers to stick in every leaking dike. Questions were asked each day about how close victory was now that U.S. forces had been in action for two years and had taken over the battlefield from the South Vietnamese. Even General Westmoreland was tongue-tied: "It is impossible to say how long the war will last; I can't see any end in sight," he told an AP reporter in early spring.

Overwhelming firepower was the primary American battlefield tactic. U.S. forces were firing more than one million artillery rounds every month, and the heaviest bombardments in the history of aviation were being dropped by B-52s and fighter-bombers in both North and South Vietnam. Infantry commanders were under rigid instructions to safeguard American lives and were calling in air strikes and artillery blitzes even on single Vietcong snipers.

"This is the first war where the infantry has supported the air and artillery," a First Division company commander told me after a frustrating action where his unit had waited for hours for tactical air support and lost track of the enemy. He added, "Chasing the communist forces behind a wall of firepower is like punching a balloon because when you thrust into them in War Zone D they bulge into Cambodia or sink into War Zone C."

The virtually unrestricted use of bombing in some areas resulted in inevitable accidents, and the March 4, 1967, military communiqué listed a series of erroneous attacks on civilian communities in the

Mekong Delta. But the communiqué made no announcement of the mistaken bombing and rocketing two days earlier by two delta-winged aircraft against the friendly village of Lang Vei northwest of Da Nang, where the AP's Bob Gassaway reported that one hundred civilians were killed and 175 wounded in the twisted wreckage of their homes. The aircraft were later identified as American planes misdirected by an air controller.

A "scorched earth" policy was the favored tool of American planners in areas outside government control, and graphic reports of its implementation brought chills to the spines of officials who had to justify it. John Wheeler quoted a Twenty-fifth Infantry Division soldier exclaiming during an operation at Giong Dinh in the northern Mekong Delta, "God, my wife would faint if she could see what I'm doing now. Killing ole Charlie is one thing but killing puppies and baby ducks and stuff like that, it's something else, man."

The unit had been ordered to burn the village to the ground, and Wheeler noted the hate-filled eyes of the rural Vietnamese residents as Americans torched their homes and even their family religious shrines, and blasted away at water buffalo and chickens. And Wheeler described a scene four miles to the west where "more sullen, hate-filled eyes were watching the smoldering ruins of a farmhouse. They belonged to the bearded, sunburned members of a Twenty-fifth Division unit clustered around the riddled body of a dead Vietcong. The black pajama-clad communist guerrilla had emerged moments before from a hidden tunnel, his hands raised in surrender. As the American infantrymen closed in, the Vietnamese suddenly whipped a grenade from his waist and pitched it into the center of his captors. An explosion, a burst of rifle fire, then silence and hate. 'Dirty, stinking war; dirty stinking communist bastard,' an officer exclaimed. Nearby a rifleman knelt in the bush with his back to the scene, one hand over his eyes and the other clutched to his throat as he fought to control his emotions. More minutes later and a rifleman grabbed the riddled body of the Vietcong and threw it into a canal, the guerrilla sharing his watery grave with a brace of dead ducks killed earlier by the Americans."

There was the institutional brutality, and the personal. The U.S. Marine Corps released the trial record of a young soldier who admitted shooting a Vietnamese civilian and cutting off his ear because he had heard about such behavior in boot camp and thought "it was the common thing to do in Vietnam after a kill." His squad was moving through a village near the Chu Lai marine base camp when they saw a Vietnamese man and opened fire on him even though he was not armed and showed no hostility toward any of them. The soldier was given a ten-year prison sentence.

A few weeks later the Marine Corps revealed that in the same incident it had sentenced a corporal to hard labor for life for murdering an elderly woman. The marine had asked a buddy, "How big a hole do you think I would make in there?" and reportedly fired at the old lady with a .45 pistol; then he aimed and fired again and then a third time, the final bullet entering the right side of her head. The troops covered her body with straw and burned it.

Another controversy was the destruction of hamlets and villages in populated areas outside government lines designated as "free fire zones" as soldiers confusedly implemented Westmoreland's search and destroy policies, which were being modified because of international criticism. I watched it happen on a First Cavalry Division operation with Michel Renard and French freelance photographer Catherine Leroy in the Crow's Foot area of the central coastal plain. Troops began burning down a village despite specific orders not to from company commander Captain Nelson Newcombe. When he saw wisps of smoke spiraling over the cluster of brown thatched huts that made up the hamlet of An Huu, the bespectacled, unshaven captain barked into his radio, "Who the hell's burning down those houses? There'll be no burnings today, that's an order."

Just the previous day his platoon had torched the few unbombed homes left in nearby Linh Hoi hamlet, an incident reported by a UPI correspondent that set alarm bells ringing and requiring explanations right down the line from Washington. I asked Newcombe what had happened and he explained that directives from Saigon command headquarters clearly stated that the burning of civilian homes was forbidden. The view from division headquarters was that only homes provenly occupied by armed Vietcong could be destroyed, while brigade was more permissive, allowing soldiers to destroy any village or hamlet from which gunfire was received.

At battalion and company level the temptation was to shoot anything that moved and destroy that which didn't. In earlier wars military censorship might have delayed or deleted such negative stories because they could have harmed morale at home, but in Vietnam neither the White House nor the Defense Department was willing to face the responsibilities of such control. Zorthian and his troupe had little choice but to try and put the best face possible on what was going on.

Da Nang

IN THE SUMMER OF 1967, Horst and I celebrated our fifth year in Vietnam with a party for three hundred at the Hotel Royale, a decaying, turn-of-the-century lodging house at the corner of Nguyen Hue and Nguyen Thiep streets, two blocks from our office. In its heyday in the 1920s and 1930s the Royale had attracted French colonial bureaucrats to its cozy bar to sip absinthe or chilled champagne; haute cuisine was served in the dining room. Upstairs in the guest rooms, French planters visiting from the countryside would have discreet meetings with their Annamese mistresses and sometimes avail themselves of the services of an equally discreet opium dispenser.

Horst and I had made the Royale our retreat, though all that was left of the colonial era were the creaky floorboards and noisy plumbing and an old recruiting poster for the French Foreign Legion. The shabbiness of the bar preserved its serenity in a city bursting with noisy clubs and B-girls and carousing Americans. The restaurant was similarly unappealing, with a menu that promised filet de flétan a la moutarde and soupe de poisson avec palourdes, but delivered greasy Corsican style fare, heavy on the olive oil and garlic. The wine list favored cheap Algerians that were so new that they featured not the year on their labels but the day of the month they were bottled, and were drinkable only when drowned with seltzer water. The decline of the Royale paralleled that of its proprietor, Monsieur Jean Ottavi, an aged Frenchman usually impeccably dressed in a white shirt and tie. M. Ottavi hobbled around his hotel on a cane that he thwacked on the floor imperiously when the Vietnamese staff failed to jump to his bidding, which was not infrequent because most had grown old in his service. We discovered that M. Ottavi's haughty manner hid a tolerance toward steady customers of which we took full advantage; he would allow us to drink and dine long beyond closing hours, and for special occasions he would have his chef prepare exotic foods of our own choosing. At our party the staff marched around the ballroom carrying lamb and goat roasted on spits and stuffed with exotic fruits and vegetables.

Some of our American colleagues could not understand our preference for the faded charms of the Royale when other establishments seemed to offer more; the Aterbea just up the street and the Guillaume

218

Tell on Trinh Minh The Street, and the restaurants in the Caravelle and Majestic hotels all had superior food and wine. But the discreet style and location of the hotel served us well in meeting with sensitive news sources. Lieutenant General Julian Ewell would sometimes drive into Saigon from his Third Field Forces Command at Long Binh to dine with us at the Royale, his only condition that he arrive incognito in civilian clothes and dine concealed behind a Chinese screen in a quiet corner of the restaurant.

By mid-1967 the Saigon press corps had grown to more than four hundred, most single and sharing apartments or living in hotel rooms. Some served almost permanently in the field with the troops. Some twenty or thirty had their wives in Saigon. Among them, R. W. Apple of the *New York Times,* and Tom Buckley also of the *Times,* Maynard Parker and William Tuohy of *Newsweek,* Lee Lescaze and Robert Kaiser of the *Washington Post,* Robert Pisor of the *Detroit News,* and Joe Fried of the *New York Daily News,* and me.

Life was comfortable enough in rented colonial-style homes with affordable maids and cooks, and there were diplomatic cocktail parties and dinners and press parties and afternoons at the Cercle Sportif club and even water skiing on the Saigon River, a sport that Ursula Faas enjoyed even though she risked being shot where the river coursed outside of town.

You could still pretend that the capital was at peace; the war had not yet come to Saigon. But it echoed in the terrorist blasts that sometimes ripped through the city, and in the clamor of the helicopters and the booms of artillery shells and air strikes from the surrounding countryside. There was no real escape from talk about the war other than fleeing for a vacation to another country. The most dramatic news stories would almost always be found in the battlefield but Saigon was the clearing house for all information and assessments of the war and the pacification programs both Vietnamese and American.

The high command's grand conspiracy to control the information flow collapsed not only in the war zones but at every cocktail party and dinner gathering. Candid remarks about the war's frustrations found their way into the news analyses and magazine articles of the morning. The city leaked like a little Washington. A stream of ruinous detail underlined the bad news from the battlefield—that the war was at best a stalemate and at worst being lost, that the Westmoreland strategy, centered on vast, expensive base camps, complex supply depots, elaborate search and destroy military operations, was not ending the war quickly nor was it bringing the communists to the peace table. But understanding what was going on did not lead directly to clear communication. The Johnson White House kept insisting that the war was being won, and many in the United States were still not ready to disbelieve a president.

The Vietnam press corps was a male bastion that women entered only at the risk of being humiliated and patronized; the prevailing view was that the war was being fought by men against men and that women had no place being there. Some of the women reporters who emerged from the war were Georgie Anne Geyer, Liz Trotta, Gloria Emerson and Beverly Deepe. The military made few concessions to the special needs for privacy of women reporters and photographers. We reporters tended to disparage the abilities of the women and gossip about them and their relationships, and were uninterested in helping them out with the authorities.

The women most welcomed by the soldiers in the field were those who acted like men. After the renowned photographer Dickie Chapelle died from wounds from a booby trap explosion late in 1966, Hugh Mulligan quoted a corps commander: "Whenever any other girl reporter came up here, we always had to run a colonel out of his room because it had a private toilet. But not Dickie Chapelle. She never asked for the slightest concession because of her sex. She'd spread her poncho in the mud like the rest of them and eat out of tin cans like she hated it, the way we do, and not because it was something cute. In fatigues and helmet you couldn't tell her from the troops and she could keep up front with the best of them."

The diminutive French freelance photographer Catherine Leroy walked into the AP bureau in 1967 and she was immediately enlisted into Faas's army of stringers, with the same promise of fifteen U.S. dollars per usable picture that everyone else got. She made enough to rent a one-room coldwater flat in a crowded residential part of Saigon. At twenty-two years old, Catherine still wore her blonde hair in braids, but she quickly discovered that politeness opened no doors for her and soon mastered an earthier vocabulary that she used with gusto whenever her path was blocked by battlefield bureaucrats.

I was with her at the Dong Ha U.S. Marine forward base one day when a press officer tried to dissuade her from joining a company of marine scouts on a parachute mission into a border region. Such missions were off limits to the press, but Cathy was not to be denied. The litany of high-pitched profanity that the eighty-five-pound photographer delivered shamed me into retreat and so infuriated the marine officer that he filed an official complaint with headquarters.

Da Nang

Catherine eventually won the grudging respect of the marines and a worldwide reputation for her dramatic pictures. On one assignment she received a severe wound to her stomach, but thrust her blood-stained film canisters into the hands of a marine officer before passing out. She learned in the hospital that the battle pictures she had taken had made her internationally famous.

The willingness to allow women to serve on the news staff came late in the war, and none were permanently assigned to the AP Saigon bureau until the early 1970s when two—Edie Lederer and Tad Bartimus—were sent in a belated recognition of the competence of our female colleagues.

But most of the AP reporters were bachelors and they hung out at the large apartment rented by photographer Al Chang in the same building as the bureau. We called it the Pineapple Suite in recognition of Al's Hawaiian roots. It was a place to unwind from the war: sparsely furnished with three double beds, a few chairs and a beer cooler, with a view overlooking Lam Son Square. Often the stereo bought at the PX would be playing "Tiny Bubbles" or "Blue Hawaii" or some other Don Ho melody for the homesick listeners. The few tables were strewn with cameras and lenses, and along the walls were military packs and web gear and dirty uniforms.

The apartment was also a second home to soldiers we had befriended in the field who had scored passes to Saigon and were taking us up on our promises to put them up for a night or two and show them a good time. They arrived dusty and sweaty to climb into their first hot shower in weeks and emerge to grab a cold beer and embrace any or all of the hookers assembled for the occasion. Unlike Saigon's bars there was no curfew and a soldier or a reporter fresh from the war could drink himself into happy oblivion and often did. No one got into trouble going home because they stayed where they fell.

We broke that rule rarely, once venturing out in the early-morning curfewed hours in a convoy with several horny soldiers to visit a cemetery in Cholon that was inhabited, it was rumored, by a family of prostitutes who had nowhere else to ply their trade. George McArthur, the most experienced among us at this sort of thing, insisted on riding on the hood of the lead vehicle as a spotter but the driver was as inebriated as he and as the cemetery headstones came into view and the girls materialized between them, the vehicle lurched and George was thrown forward onto the hood ornament. Ed Meade, a visiting publisher from Erie, Pennsylvania, who had learned first-aid as a football player in college, patched George up and we got him back to

221

his room at the Caravelle Hotel without further incident. Fortunately one of our acquaintances, Dr. Tom Durant, the medical officer for Saigon, stopped in from time to time to check the wound and finally ordered him to the hospital, where the surgeons had to remove three feet of intestines.

One early morning I was unwinding in the apartment with the rest of the crew when AP photographer Rick Merron came down from the bureau with some slides he had made from a pornographic magazine someone had purchased in Hong Kong. Rick projected the images onto the front of the Caravelle Hotel across the street and genitalia two stories tall appeared on the wall, much to the amazement of the Saigon policemen pulling security duty in the square below.

The carefree camaraderie masked foreboding. The AP bureau operation remained singularly free of petty rivalries and staff jealousies, even though underneath the surface our nerve ends were frayed by the tensions of the war. Hal Boyle wrote that one reason for this was that "Vietnam is the one story in the world where there's plenty for everybody. You never have to worry about anyone stealing your stories because even better ones are out there waiting." Each day, we filed eight to fifteen news dispatches over the office telex machine to New York, forty or fifty pages of copy, contributions phoned in from reporters covering the marines in Da Nang in the north, the two U.S. infantry divisions in Pleiku in the Central Highlands, plus Saigon with its headquarters briefings and political crises.

But there was another reason for our camaraderie, and that was the awareness that on any day a colleague could be wounded or even killed just trying to do his job. You can forgive a lot under those circumstances.

When Ed White left for home his replacement as bureau chief was Bob Tuckman, a beefy veteran of World War Two and Korea. We performed a small change-of-command ceremony. I placed a toy crown on Bob's bald pate and Horst handed him his "scepter," the bamboo Vietcong water container given Mal Browne years earlier after a bloody ambush, a reminder of the time when Saigon was a one-man AP bureau, not the thirty-staff operation it had become. Other symbols and artifacts reminded the new leader of the burdens and glories of the past: a plaster bust of Ngo Dinh Diem, acquired on the night he was overthrown, from the days when the staff was all "coup-qualified," and a bazooka Horst found in War Zone C in 1964 when Vietnam was just a dirty little advisory war. Ed White was accompanied to the airport by a Chinese band that Horst and Al Chang had hired that morning. The wispy-bearded leader of the orchestra bore such marked resemblance to Ho Chi Minh that the MPs turned the procession back at the airport gates. We conducted the departure ceremony on the spot and poured champagne as a taxi waited to take Ed the rest of the way to the terminal. That evening Bob Tuckman wrestled with his first bureau chief's decision: how to justify the Chinese band's two hour performance on the office expense account.

.   .   .

Around this time, Gallagher wrote to Horst and me offering us other assignments. "You are entering your fifth year in Saigon, which is a long time in any war zone, particularly one as physically difficult as Vietnam. I would like to know if you want an assignment elsewhere, at least for a period of time. I know that you want to be where the action is but it looks as though the action is going to be there for a long time to come." I took some months to respond to Gallagher's letter because I did not take his offer seriously, but when he pressed me for a response I wrote him, "Physically I feel in fine shape and I have not taken off one day because of sickness since I arrived here. Mentally, I like to think that I am as adjusted now as I ever was. Professionally, I feel my best work is still ahead of me."

I admitted that Nina and I had discussed leaving, but I told Gallagher that I wanted to stay for a couple more years.

Saigon was a headquarters city and it was possible to go about our business and pleasure in relative privacy, but not so Da Nang, where the inquisitive news organizations collided with the frustrations of the military at the marine press center. Everyone, it seemed, eventually visited the city, congressmen, news executives from the United States, even human rights activists, because the old port had been reborn as U.S. Marine headquarters and was the gateway to the northern war zones. By going to Da Nang they could say they had visited a front without actually venturing to one.

I went up there often, flying in on U.S. Air Force C-130 transport planes on the space-available basis that our military accreditation entitled us to, and disembarking at the Twelfth Aerial Port office, a newly erected prefab wooden building where soldiers from the United States arrived weary and apprehensive to begin their Vietnam duty, and from where they departed a year later, grateful to have survived the war. There was usually a straggling line of sweaty soldiers leaving the aircraft with me, and we would pass rumpled uniformed men and American civilian workers and officials in shirtsleeves waiting to take the ride back to Saigon.

If I was lucky a jeep would be waiting from the press center driven by a friendly marine who would head out the main gate into the sights and smells of Da Nang, horn blaring, as he threaded along a highway noisy with heavy traffic, cyclos peddling along the gutters, crowded buses and overloaded cars threatening to push each other off the road. We would join the river route into town and then take a right turn around the Cham Museum, a handsome, open-balconied masonry structure containing exquisite Hindu-Buddhist sandstone sculptures, all that was left of a people who had lost a war to the death with the Vietnamese five centuries earlier.

Just beyond the sublime would be the ridiculous, a ramshackle tin roofed motel surrounded by a high fence. The main gate was guarded by a wizened Vietnamese we called Shorty. A yellow and red sign hanging from the gate read, "111 MAF Press Center," the acronym of the Third Marine Amphibious Force. At the center of the compound was a tall water tower and beneath it a sandbagged bunker. At the river end was an A-frame shack called the Dickie Chapelle Memorial Chapel, not a church, of course, but an operations center where the marines cranked out war communiqués, and reporters could attempt, if they could make themselves understood through the shouting, to telephone their Saigon bureaus. Behind the shack at the river's edge was a rickety wooden dock surrounded by rusty barbed wire, and underneath it the placid Han River. Across the river was the bulky outline of the marine headquarters buildings and, beyond that, China Beach and its beckoning sands and warm blue waters.

The AP hootch, as we called it, accommodated three, on single beds that were always unmade, their dirty sheets dragging on the dusty floor amid the debris of empty beer cans and whiskey bottles and cigarette butts. The compound provided maid service but it was rarely used because someone was usually in bed with the door locked, sleeping off a tough field trip or hangover or both.

The Da Nang press center was run by marine officers who clearly would have preferred being somewhere else. We sometimes wondered what these men had done, what fall from grace had forced them into this position. Working with us was clearly no promotion. And none had any previous experience working with the press. If ever there was a hell on earth for a marine officer in time of war, this was it. Unlike the marines, we often slept late, rarely shaved and were usually ill-dressed and undisciplined, were frequently drunk by early evening and argued and fought over trivial matters. To top it off, we were often, it must have seemed to them, critically unpatriotic about the war and the marines' role in it.

An early press center officer, Major Joel Martin, who had commanded troops in the field, used to get so angry with his media clients that he took to discharging his handgun in the bar, one afternoon shooting up the slot machine as he shouted, "Take this, Morley Safer, you son of a bitch." I sympathized with Martin and after his wrangles with me and my colleagues we would sometimes sit late into the night on the wooden dock drinking beer and talking about the war, and as he mellowed he might break into the Scots ditty "I Belong to Glasky" in a raspy voice that roused the security dogs at marine headquarters across the river.

Eddie Adams, who had come back to Vietnam, tried his best to smooth the roiling waters of the Da Nang press center by including marines in a goofy club he formed called the TWAPs, the Terrified Writers and Photographers. He collected five-dollar fees from scores of colleagues, wore a GI can opener around his neck engraved with the words Head Twap, and demanded secret signs and catchphrases from members. He decided to swear in as an honorary member the marine commander, Major General Lewis Walt, who was known as a good sport. Eddie organized a steak dinner on the banks of the Han River, with tables from the press center restaurant forming a large U shape and set with white linen cloths. General Walt was late and by the time he arrived with two lower-ranking officers it was dark, most of the media guests were drunk and disorderly, and the sky over Marble Mountain in the middle distance was ablaze with streaking white light as helicopter gunships fired on Vietcong guerrillas.

Eddie was wearing a red satin happy coat pinned with four dozen cheap military medals purchased on the Da Nang black market, his steel helmet pushed down over his ears. He asked General Walt to rise and raise his right hand and repeat after him, "When under fire I must shout Bao Chi [Vietnamese for journalist]," and the general obliged. Eddie continued, "When I contract a social disease I must inform all other TWAPs the name of the carrier. . . ." The general laughed at this point but Eddie with straight face declared, "This is serious," and the officer cleared his throat and repeated the line. Eddie then presented him a gold tie bar engraved with the TWAP emblem, which he promised to wear with pride. We all got to shake the general's hand that night and even though there was no immediate improvement in our relations with the press center staff we all did enjoy the free steak dinner.

"The Light at the End of the Tunnel"

IN 1967 THERE SEEMED TO be two Vietnam wars going on, one being fought in the comfortable air-conditioned headquarters buildings in Saigon and Long Binh and Da Nang, and at the Pentagon, where crew cut briefing officers waved slick brass-tipped pointers toward computer-generated statistical charts of kill ratios and desertion rates and pacification programs and bombing tonnages. In those arcane estimates, there was the siren song of victory, tempting General Westmoreland and the new ambassador, Ellsworth Bunker, and the president of the United States to proclaim to an anxious nation that there was "light at the end of the tunnel" and that American boys could start coming home soon.

Then there was the other war that also made the headlines, a war that was increasingly bloody and destructive, of battles fought time and time again over the same hills and valleys, of flag-draped coffins flown home to sad-eyed relatives, of tumbling napalm canisters bursting over thatched-roofed villages, of blindfolded prisoners and fields of uprooted peasants, of an enemy defying the American strategy of attrition that at its simplest contrived to kill so many of them they would eventually give up, that Asia would run out of Asians.

The AP covered both those wars, and I often worried about how confusing our stories must be to our readers. My assessments would appear on newspaper front pages alongside AP reports of the positive views on the war from the State Department and the Pentagon and from President Johnson's frequent Oval Office televised speeches. The AP did not interfere with the disparate news flow, embracing the ideal of news freedom. But there was a vast, unbridgeable credibility gap materializing that would surely ruin someone's reputation.

In the spring of 1967, I followed Operation Junction City in War Zone C where General DePuy's First Infantry Division and the 25th Tropic Lightning Division teamed up for the biggest military mission of the war, deploying 45,000 American troops across the jungled landscape in a search for the elusive headquarters of the communist command. But as the mission drew to a close, Major General Jonathan Seaman, told us at a press conference, "We didn't catch their Mc-Namara but at least we were on the outskirts of their Pentagon." His analogy revealed an emerging problem, that even the most over-whelming American military operation was unable to score decisive victories against the communist side, and no manipulation of statistics could compensate for that failure. General Seaman was an admirable officer, who encouraged us in our news coverage, and I wanted to believe him when he declared that the deaths of 143 American soldiers in Operation Junction City had been well worthwhile because they had penetrated a communist sanctuary and killed 1,243 enemy sol-diers. Westmoreland had said in an interview with the AP that the U.S. would "go on bleeding them until Hanoi wakes up to the fact that they have bled their country to the point of national disaster for several generations." It was becoming clear, though, that in this mas-sive operation—and in the others that preceded and followed it—even if the enemy body count was accurate, the sacrifice of the Americans was barely moving the goals of the war forward. John Paul Vann, of course, but other war watchers, too, were convinced that the United States risked bleeding internally if its war strategy continued. Vann's arguments were convincing: that the communist side was enticing American forces into battle and willingly taking heavy casualties; their intention was to nickel-and-dime United States policy to death, to undermine the credibility of the war at home. Vann would produce his own flow charts that showed the Vietcong and North Vietnamese regiments picking the time and the place for battle, and when their casualties became exorbitant pulling back into their jungle bases near and inside Laos and Cambodia, where they could retool and re-emerge to fight months later. Vann had determined that as a North Vietnamese regiment went into action in the south, its reinforcements for its next battle would already be leaving Hanoi and heading on the long journey down the Ho Chi Minh Trail. These were soldiers confident that they were instruments of the revolution, that they were "born in the north to die in the south." The flow of men was unremitting and abundant and the demographics were chilling and undeniable. Despite the vast bombing campaigns in the north and the massive use of firepower in the south, fewer Vietnamese soldiers were being killed than male children born. According to Vann, the war could go on indefinitely unless it was enlarged—to a degree that would be unacceptable to the American public—or its direction fundamentally altered.

Vann, who had been plotting for a year to present his views to

227

Robert McNamara, told me he succeeded in July 1967, on one of the last of the defense secretary's fact-finding trips to Vietnam. Vann revealed that his pal Dan Ellsberg had joined the secretary's flight to Saigon and had briefed him about an alternate policy. We were surprised to learn that McNamara was losing his enthusiasm for the war, that he had refused to implement a request by Westmoreland for another large troop increase beyond the 466,000-man organization already assembled, and that he had encouraged more participation by Vietnamese forces in military operations.

But the dogs of war that McNamara had long ago unleashed would not be muzzled by his second thoughts. Nor were they about to be held in check by a White House about to enter an election year.

In the fall of 1967, I wrote an account of battlefield stalemate. "Thirty months of hard, inconclusive fighting in Vietnam has forced American military commanders to acknowledge a crucial fact: unless the dispirited Vietnamese armed forces can be revitalized into a fighting army, United States troops will be tied down for at least a decade just holding the lid on the communists all over the country." I said Westmoreland had tried to go it alone, "pulling the Vietnamese army along by the bootstraps as the enemy was crushed by U.S. infantry and marines" but that such tactics had been thwarted by the resilience of the communists. The hopes of quick success had "died with the nearly thirteen thousand Americans already killed."

My contribution was just a breeze in a blizzard of commentary circling the globe about Vietnam, but I wanted desperately to believe it had some significance. Much of the world was questioning the American role in Vietnam, as well as many within the United States, who did not believe Vietnam was worth the money and the blood that America was committing to it. I was not so much against the war as much as I was for accuracy. I believed that the truth was to be found in the battlefield and not in the briefing rooms.

I continued to follow American troops into action, joined by an impatient throng of reporters all competing for stories.

General DePuy had pointed out to me a phenomenon that he had discerned on the battlefield, that the war was characterized by cycles of communist actions that would peak and then diminish, but with each new cycle the peak would be higher than the time before. At Dak To in the distant highlands on a rainy November, the peak rose to its highest and it lured me into the most unnerving experience of my life, the battle of Hill 875.

The North Vietnamese picked the time and the place for the battle, and Westmoreland's strategy led him to fight the war there on the enemy's terms as certainly as the monsoon rains always followed the dry season.

Once the mountain valley of Dak To and the territories around it, far from the populated coast, were privileged preserves for big-game hunters who enjoyed open season on the wild animals abounding there, stalking the leopards, the tigers, the panthers, the elephants and the gaur that made up the rich fauna of the Central Highlands of Vietnam. Entomologists sought the rare butterflies and curious insect life, and anthropologists wrote learned studies on the primitive peoples who lived there, the Jarai, the Meo, the Rhade, the Koho and the Bru. Its remoteness had made it a valuable stronghold for the resistance movements that opposed the governing colonial French. Its continued isolation assured its use by the North Vietnamese forces streaming into the south.

Two years before, the communists had destroyed the government's only two strongpoints in the valley, the district town of Tou Morong and the American Special Forces camp of Dak Sut, and they remained a threatening presence to the few tentacles of government presence that still clung on. Westmoreland had often publicly reaffirmed his tactics to find and fix the enemy and destroy him with his superior forces, and the North Vietnamese took him up on his boast, methodically preparing Dak To's hilltops and ridge lines for war. Under the shelter of the triple-canopy jungle, out of sight of satellite photography, the Vietcong dug extensive bunkers and trench systems and tunnels leading into caverns lined with log floors and woven bamboo walls for comfort; each hilltop bunker system was built to withstand the severest bombing, some thirty feet deep with six feet of earth and log cover on their roofs, and their twisting entrances were designed to seal the inhabitants against the most horrifying of America's weapons of war used in Vietnam: napalm.

Westmoreland's find and fix strategy could only lead him into this well-laid trap. The only way to win in Dak To would be the most exacting way, to meet the enemy face-to-face and kill him. The communists had prepared the battlefield and then they set the lure, a small ambush launched from a bamboo thicket against an American paratrooper platoon early in November that attracted the attention of the high command. The ante was raised on November 6 when they killed and wounded almost everyone in a paratrooper company from the 173rd Airborne Brigade. Westmoreland took the bait, authorizing the U.S. Army's Fourth Infantry Division to join the fray under Major

General William R. Peers, who had been waiting impatiently for a sign that the communists wanted to fight.

I flew to Dak To in mid-November, joining an AP reporting team already assembled there. By this time four North Vietnamese infantry regiments had been identified in the surrounding hills, around twelve thousand men, the largest force ever gathered against the Americans, and I watched in amazement as the skyline all around me erupted with the smoke and fire of artillery barrages and air strikes directed against them. My colleagues told me of brutal hill battles that were swallowing up infantry companies. But the actions had been difficult to assess because the communists were usually able to remove their casualties from the battlefield and there was even speculation that the whole battle was a decoy to get American units away from population zones so these could be infiltrated and exploited.

On November 18, we learned that three paratrooper companies from the Second Battalion of the 173rd Airborne Brigade were outflanked to their east and west near the crest of Hill 875 and had suffered heavy casualties. The following morning AP reporter Lew Simons, Al Chang and I hitched a ride in a jeep to the brigade field headquarters, a cluster of tents about two miles beyond the airstrip. The dew was drying off and the dust was rising as we bowled along the dirt road, scattering mountain tribesmen in loincloths who were sucking on large cheroots and carrying loads of fruit on their heads. We pulled up outside a tent with the sign "PIO" painted on a cardboard meal-ration box, the public information office, and inside a CBS crew was trying to get Saigon on the field telephone, the frustrated correspondent—with the latest on the story—bawling impatiently into his mouthpiece.

Thirty-five reporters and photographers had assembled by the time a briefing officer arrived to inform us that the situation had worsened considerably on Hill 875. The communists were in bunkers that resisted bombing. The American unit was fighting for its life and an accidental bombing by an air force aircraft had killed twenty soldiers previously wounded in action. Eight helicopters had been shot down trying to evacuate the other wounded that morning and the attempt had been suspended. There was no way to get the wounded or anyone else out of there.

The brigade was assembling a relief mission, sending in three infantry companies from the Fourth Battalion on foot through the jungle with orders to fight its way up the side of the hill to their embattled buddies. There would be room on the mission for three of us if anyone wanted to go. As the officer concluded his remarks, I knew I had to be on that mission. I pulled rank, asserting my rights as the senior man present, and as a representative of the AP. Tom Cheatham of UPI demanded to be included, and after some grumbling the group also agreed that a Vietnamese freelance TV cameraman be the third man. I saw a trace of jealousy on a few of the faces of my colleagues, but on most there was relief.

We three were loaded into a waiting helicopter and flown to Fire Base 16, a forward artillery position in a forested side valley off Dak To, two miles from the Cambodian border, where the air reeked of cordite, and smoke drifted from the ridge line of a jungled knoll to the south. "Hill 875, burning," said our escort sergeant. We walked over to the brigade command group, which was examining a map spread out on a sandbagged bunker, and instead of a greeting we heard, "You're too late," from the brigade commander, who was waving his arm down the hill. "They left an hour ago." I knew Brigadier General L. H. Schweiter, who had run the outfit for three months, did not dislike reporters and I appealed to him for help. He agreed to send a lone paratrooper escort with us along the same jungle trail taken by the ill-fated soldiers the previous day and by the relief column that had followed them. We took off at a run: it was around noontime and there were several miles to travel.

Beyond the fire base, the trail disappeared along a shallow ravine and we turned up a ridge line overgrown with thick bamboo trees and low underbrush that made for slow going. We pressed on and by midafternoon we had stumbled and crawled our way to the rear elements of the relief column. I was sweating and thirsty but reluctant to suck too frequently on my water bottles because there would be no refills where we were going. We moved up to the company command group, where the officer was conferring by radio with units ahead and we began proceeding cautiously, fearing ambush.

By late afternoon the landscape changed into high forest with towering teak and mahogany trees, and we were stepping across branches torn down by H&I fire, the random harassment and interdiction shooting missions favored by American artillery units. At dusk we were still two miles from Hill 875. The lead company found a narrow trail and all five hundred of us began moving along in single file, terrified of an ambush and holding on to each other's belts so we would not separate and be lost in the dark. Hidden gunners opened up with antitank rockets that howled over our heads and exploded in the trees around us in balls of fire. We scattered into the underbrush and hugged the ground, and pushed on only when the barrage subsided.

Live from the Battlefield

The darkness was so thick that the battalion commander called for artillery-fired parachute flares from Fire Base 16, and we negotiated the rest of the journey in eerie illumination that was projected through the tree canopy by the flare lights drifting high above. By nine we reached the slopes of Hill 875 and began using the thick vines that hung from the trees to pull our way up. Ahead the jungle had been seared by bombing and shelling; the splintered tree trunks stood stark in the moonlight.

We began to see the shapes of dead bodies in the shadows around us and a soldier near me cried out, "Ah, look at the gooks, they're all killed," but after a few moments it became clear they were not Vietnamese but American dead, victims of the previous day's battle left lying there, their uniforms, boots and weapons stolen by their attackers. At ten o'clock our advance company reached the remnants of the Second Battalion, and we covered the last few hundred yards even more cautiously and in silence, all aware we were in the killing zone on a forsaken hill.

We moved further on and gasped at what we found: mounds of dead paratroopers spread-eagled where they had fallen, and behind pitiful barricades of tree branches, the wounded. There were scores of them, some with head and chest wounds crudely bandaged and others with untended arm and leg wounds, the blood seeping through their sleeves and trousers. One made a whispered request for water and I handed him a bottle. He told me he had been there for thirty-six hours, lying on a carpet of leaves waiting to be evacuated, that he had seen the errant bombing that killed thirty of his buddies, that eleven of the twelve battalion medics had been killed trying to help the wounded. He was sure he would die.

The defenders still able to do so had gathered themselves together as best they could, withdrawing everyone into a circle about fifty yards across for greater safety, manning bunkers abandoned by the North Vietnamese, and fashioning new foxholes in the raw earth. The soldiers in the rescue mission I had come with joined them and promised to hack a helicopter landing zone out of the jungle in the morning to get out the wounded, if the North Vietnamese soldiers, in firing positions less than a hundred yards away on the hill's summit, could be driven off.

I found an open patch of dirt and borrowed a soldier's entrenching tool and started digging a shallow foxhole to spend the night, but the metal struck at human flesh, a body buried there by a bomb explosion earlier in the day. I recoiled in horror and stepped back on something soft and discovered it was a detached arm from another corpse. I looked about me and felt ill. I was an interloper, a voyeur on desperate ground. I had been proud of a certain professional detachment, but now I felt ashamed of my neutrality, useless with my notebooks and cameras and water bottles. I didn't even carry a gun, so I was just one more liability for the surviving defenders.

I slept as best I could in a shallow hole I scraped out with my fingers. When I woke, the stench of the dead was strong in the air. I had barely rubbed the sleep from my eyes when I heard the pop of mortar tubes firing from nearby, and the roar of violent explosions around us. Soldiers ran to their bunkers for cover; I saw the wounded crawling to the shelter of tree branches and dirt mounds. Metal fragments whistled over my head as I dropped to the ground. A group of soldiers I had exchanged greetings with minutes earlier had not been so lucky. They were writhing wounded in the dirt.

As the barrage continued I scrambled into a bunker where three paratroopers were hunched. One of them said he was Private First Class Angel Flores from New York City. "If we were dead like those out there we wouldn't have to worry about this stuff," he murmured as though to himself, fingering the plastic rosary around his neck and kissing it reverently. One of his buddies asked him, "Does that do you any good?" And the private responded, "Well, I'm still alive." His buddy responded, "Hell, the chaplain who gave you that was killed on Sunday," and Flores nodded but still kept kissing the rosary.

The mortaring ceased and rockets began whizzing through the trees, and I forced myself to leave the bunker and look around. I joined a platoon leader, Lieutenant Bryan Macdonough, at his bunker facing up the hill. He said eight of his fellow officers were dead and the other eight wounded, and that he had started out with twenty-seven men thirty hours earlier and had only nine left. They were in firing positions around him, waiting for reinforcements to bring in flamethrowers, and they were resigned to making a final charge up to the summit. While I sat with them a helicopter attempted to land in our vicinity and a machine gun opened fire on it from about fifty yards up the hill and a soldier yelled excitedly, "There they are, they're closer" and began returning the fire with his M-16.

The lieutenant got on his radio to his headquarters at Fire Base 16 and called in an air strike—the first of a score that day—which came in low over our heads and tumbled napalm and bombs on the North Vietnamese with no discernible effect. When the aircraft departed the shelling resumed and the casualties mounted. I returned to Private

Flores's bunker and noticed its roof was thin. While an air strike distracted the enemy, I climbed outside with a shovel to throw on another layer of dirt. I watched a Navy A-3 jet come in for a low run and saw two black projectiles hurtle out from its bomb racks; they looked like 250-pounders. I waited for them to fly overhead but they kept on coming in toward me and I knew right then that I was looking death in the face and I didn't have time to be frightened but wondered what my corpse would look like, splintered into a thousand pieces by the explosions. The bombs came in together, one landing far to my right in an empty bunker and exploding harmlessly. The other bomb embedded itself fifteen yards in front of me in the roots of an old tree. Miraculously it did not explode. It just stayed there.

Cheatham and I and our Vietnamese colleague decided we'd had enough by late afternoon and moved back down the hill to a landing zone being hacked from the forest. The wounded were assembled in long lines, the most grievously hurt wrapped in ponchos and attended by medics. "It's a goddamn shame they haven't got us out of here," gasped a sergeant with tears in his eyes who had been lying on the hill for fifty hours with a serious groin wound. Others had ceased moaning; the blood had clotted on their bandages and their eyes were glazed. The evacuation helicopters began coming in even though the shell fire continued.

We waited our turn to get out, squeezing into a small foxhole as the hours went by. I was praying to get off the hill, to get out of there with my story and my life intact—in that order—and eventually we got the call and dashed down to the landing zone where a chopper was hovering above us. The loadmaster yelled at us, "This is the last one of the day. We moved one hundred and forty wounded, ninety dead and three newsmen outta here," and I waved at him gratefully and scrambled aboard, lying on the floor as we lifted up and out, and I stayed that way for a while because I was crying.

The helicopter dropped us off at the northwestern end of the Dak To airstrip and I looked thankfully at the familiar army tents and sandbagged walls of the headquarters barracks. Inside there would be sleeping cots and drinking water and food rations.

As we approached the barracks we heard someone shout "Incoming" and there was the whoosh and roar of an explosion; we were under mortar attack from the hills. There was crashing and banging. Any other time I would have dashed for cover but on this particular night I felt I had seen it all and survived, and I casually walked to the nearest bunker and joined the soldiers huddling inside. I found AP reporter John Lengel later in the evening at the Fourth Division press tent and he told me that communications were impossible with Saigon because of priority military telephone traffic. I didn't even try to get through. I rose at daybreak and walked over to the flight line, where a light mist was hanging like a curtain from the neighboring hills. I saw the remains of two transport planes lying at the far end of the strip, victims of a shelling the previous afternoon. Within an hour a U.S. Air Force C-130 supply plane arrived, slicing down through the clouds and pulling up with a roar and unloading its cargo of ammunition crates. Its propellers kept revving, understandably impatient to leave the region in a hurry. I flashed my press accreditation to the crew chief as I scrambled across the ramp and into the aircraft, and he pulled off his earphones and shouted to me, "Don't you want to know where we are going?" and I answered, "I don't care, just take me anywhere there is a telephone."

We landed at Qui Nhon, the coastal supply hub for the Central Highlands, where I knew there was a military press office. The army sergeant in charge lent me the office typewriter and I sat there for a long time, wondering how to describe the drama that I had witnessed on Hill 875, how to give justice to the reality of the war, to the sacrifice and the bravery of the paratroopers and the stubbornness of their North Vietnamese adversaries. I started typing and I called over to the sergeant to help me out by calling the AP bureau in Saigon and dictating my story page by page, so I could meet the noon deadline. He obliged and started to read the first page over the phone as I began writing the second.

"War painted the living and the dead the same gray pallor on Hill 875," the sergeant began reading. "The only way to tell who was alive and who was dead amongst the exhausted men was to watch when the enemy mortars came crashing in. The living rushed unashamedly to the tiny bunkers dug into the red clay of the hilltop; the wounded squirmed toward the shelter of trees that had been blasted to the ground. Only the dead didn't move, propped up in the bunkers where they had died in direct mortar hits, or facedown in the dust where they had fallen to bullets."

I heard the sergeant gasp as he read my account, but he persevered through the eleven typewritten pages. Afterward I returned to the airport, seeking a ride back home to Saigon with my film. The first flight available was a transport aircraft loaded with black rubber body bags containing a hundred dead soldiers from Dak To. I was the only living passenger, sitting up forward in the cargo cabin. The bags were leaking on the deck. As we began our steep descent the viscid liquids surged over my ankles before the plane leveled off and landed at Tan Son Nhut Airport.

I hailed a taxi outside the terminal. The driver, assuming I was a soldier looking for fun in Saigon, offered me a bag of marijuana for five dollars. When I turned that down, he suggested I meet his sister. He began to ridicule my disheveled appearance so I cuffed him hard on the ear and cursed him with the few Vietnamese swear words I knew. I realized I was more stressed by my experiences than I supposed. Ed White and John Lengel stayed with the Hill 875 story and reported that the summit finally fell to American troops at noontime on Thanksgiving Day, but that instead of the 120 dead they had expected to find, there was only one North Vietnamese body left at the top.

The Dak To action had cost more American lives than any previous engagement in the war, but still the authorities chalked it up as another victory, reinforcing the message delivered by General Westmoreland to the National Press Club in Washington late in November when he declared that 1968 "will be the year when the end begins to come into view." Merton Perry of *Newsweek* came by our bureau at Christmastime in partial shock; he said he had received the most positive briefing of his five-year Vietnam career from the U.S. Army's Second Field Forces headquarters at Long Binh. A senior general had asserted that all major enemy units in the vast region around Saigon had been dispersed and had fled into Cambodia and that the security situation had greatly improved.

In the year-end assessment the AP asked me to provide, I seemed to describe a war on another planet. As I looked back over the year, and the battles I had covered, and the conversations with John Paul Vann and some candid military officers, I concluded that 1967 was a curtain raiser to a military showdown in Vietnam in 1968. I quoted knowledgeable Americans predicting for the new year "the biggest and bloodiest battles still to be fought despite a long year of mauling, brawling actions from one end of the country to the other." I wrote that both sides were optimistic, "which from their viewpoint made sense because American commanders still analyze Vietnam in terms of World War Two, and the communists analyze the war in terms of the fight to oust the French in the 1950s." Hanson Baldwin, the prominent military writer of the *New York Times,* was also preparing an assessment of the war. He was close to Westmoreland and consequently his piece reflected the rosier confidence of the high command.

New Year's Eve brought a brief truce to the battlefield and a calm to the bureaucratic rivalries in the capital. Some young Americans from the embassy and the other U.S. agencies threw a "light at the end of the tunnel" party to poke sly fun at the official optimism, calling themselves "the flower people of Saigon" on the neatly printed invitations.

When Nina and I and her sisters arrived at the rambling embassy villa at 47 Phan Than Gian Street on the Saigon side of the Bien Hoa bridge, the affair was well under way. A Vietnamese dance band from one of the downtown bars was playing fox-trots, and officials with sunburnished faces on leave from their posts in the countryside were cheek to cheek with secretaries from the embassy in the city. Several representatives of the new administration of President Nguyen Van Thieu glided suavely through the crowd. Journalists were gathered at the bar around Barry Zorthian, who sported a bright Hawaiian shirt, and in a hallway around John Paul Vann, who held court with a senior embassy official. I marveled that the function was held at all, that so many key people would gather so openly in wartime Saigon. But I could play at denial myself; I drank and danced the night away with the others and by morning, I, too, wanted to believe in the light at the end of the tunnel.

The Tet Offensive

I HAD WATCHED SAIGON change from a charming city with leafy parks, shady, narrow sidewalks and louvered, whitewashed buildings into a gaudy garrison town. Walking to the office along Pasteur and Tu Do streets became an obstacle course across uncollected garbage, around sandbagged guard posts, and past engine-revving, horn-blasting military trucks. The beauty was gone: the graceful young girls in their silken ao-dai dresses had long ago surrendered the center of the city to the rabble of the war, to the crippled veterans who hobbled forward on crutches, brandishing their stumps of arms and legs as they demanded food and cash, "Chop chop, gimme chop chop," or, "Hey, you, me baby sick, me baby hungry, please give money." Aggressive touts were underfoot, plucking at your shirtsleeves and offering black market deals and drugs; street kids with tattered clothes

237

and grimy faces begged, "Gimme five piasters, me hungry, please number one, please give me five p's," and simultaneously trying to steal your wallet.

Early in the war the authorities had tried but failed to protect Saigon from the impact of the vast military buildup in the countryside. From the squalor of a soldiers' town flowed the largesse that enriched many. There was a tide of tape recorders and soda pop and air conditioners and other basics of American life—all adopted by newly prosperous Saigonese who were casting aside traditional Vietnamese society.

By January 1968 Americans were an overwhelming presence on and off the streets; legions of political advisers at many levels of government determined the nation's future. The Joint Public Affairs office hired a professional astrologer named Thai Son to make designer predictions for the coming year "favorable to the government side and unfavorable to its enemies," while other American officials helped decide what colors the lights of the fountain should be in downtown Saigon, what trees should be removed for parking meters, and whether or not the library of the National Museum should adopt the Dewey decimal classification system.

The city fathers made a timid attempt to fight back, decreeing that all storefront signs should be in the Vietnamese language, or at least three times larger in Vietnamese as in English, so Botany Tailors became Bo Ta Ny, the Dolly Bar became Da-Ly, the Texas Bar the Te-Xa and the Ohio Bar the O-Hai-O.

Saigon was still a preferable watering hole to the cities further north and to the battlefields where I spent much of my time. There was a comforting sense of security in the mayhem of Saigon. Even though the blasts of artillery shells and bombs echoed from not too far in the countryside, the carnival air of the capital kept at bay the sense that the war must one day come to town. I figured that the corruption of Saigon was the necessary price we all had to pay for the umbrella of American power that sheltered us, and my Vietnamese in-laws and their friends seemed to feel the same, despite the undermining of their traditional culture and the disappearance of the post-colonial lifestyle they had grown to enjoy.

I was so confident of the security of Saigon and my own powers of survival that I had fathered two children, Andrew Kim, and Elsa Christina, born in October of 1967. I was out of town when Andrew was born, but at home when Elsa was due, and I drove Nina and her mother to the third-floor maternity ward of the Catholic St. Paul's

Hospital in the early-morning hours, waiting with Nina in an anteroom until the contractions became strong, and racing her into the delivery room.

I was looking forward to spending a few days with my children when I returned to Saigon in January 1968 from a reporting trip just before the celebration of Tet, the Vietnamese lunar new year. In the past, the holiday had signaled a break in the fighting, and again both the communist and Saigon governments continued the tradition by declaring ceasefires.

The capital was already closing down on the afternoon of the twenty-ninth. Even the street vendors had gone home, and the touts and urchins were clustered in shop doorways counting their money, or stretched out lazily on the pavement. I drove down Nguyen Hue Street and across the Khanh Hoi Canal and along Trinh Minh The Street. The Guillaume Tell restaurant was decorated with colorful streamers, and rows of firecrackers were hanging from its front porch. At private homes elsewhere in the capital I saw fireworks and flags. People were prepared to celebrate their most prosperous Tet ever, convinced by government propaganda that the communist military threat had receded to the nation's borders and that victory was near.

That evening I wrote a news analysis about the developing crisis at the marine base at Khe Sanh where I had spent the previous week. Some were comparing its vulnerability to the French garrison at Dien Bien Phu, and the future of the remote base was the American high command's focus of attention. The next morning, their anxiety was further heightened by big, unexpected communist attacks on six Vietnamese cities in the central and northern area that terminated the truce in those regions. But the Saigonese were not deterred from their celebration; the lifting of the nighttime curfew spilled thousands of revelers onto the streets as midnight and Tet Mau Than, the Year of the Monkey, neared.

I joined in my family's preparations, and we had fun following the instructions of Nina's father, the repository of traditional lore and the director of family religious ceremonial activity. Nina and her sisters were required to dress in high Mandarin collars: all were self conscious because they preferred Western clothes. We assembled in the late evening at their parents' comfortable living room, bright with fresh flowers. Nina's father was wearing a gray robe over his best suit and as the family bowed and prayed he chanted Buddhist benedictions at a small altar with burning incense sticks and surrounded with dishes of delectable sweets and fruits, offerings to the spirits of their ancestors. Outside on the yellow-tiled terrace we lit strings of firecrackers hanging from the branches of an old mahogany tree.

The noises in our backyard blended with the cacophony of explosions from the immediate neighborhood, from the entire city. It was the first time in years that firecrackers were permitted in Saigon. We then exchanged red paper envelopes containing new money for good luck, and we sipped champagne and bade each other success in our ventures and ate a festive dinner. When we left for home, Nina's father directed us to follow strict rules of navigation, determined by our astrological charts, and I drove tortuously around and about with Nina watching carefully to see that at no point did I drive due west and risk offending the propitious spirits.

The bangs of nearby firecrackers woke me and I called Ed White at the office. He had just completed the evening news roundup and was too tired for small talk. He said, "Peter, it's 1:15 in the morning and I'm going home." I dozed fitfully for a while, our bedroom air conditioner grunting and wheezing and drowning the outside sounds until a loud, methodical rat tat tat jolted our windows as though someone were banging on the shutters with a hammer. I knew that this was no string of firecrackers but an intruder from the battlefield, a heavy-caliber machine gun that seemed to be firing up Rue Pasteur just three room lengths away. A weapon that lethal had not been discharged in Saigon since the overthrow of President Ngo Dinh Diem four years earlier. I bundled Nina, Elsa, Andrew and the Vietnamese maid into our tiled bathroom, which I hoped was safer than the rest of the apartment, and covered them with the mattresses from the beds.

I opened the bedroom window and watched the war come to the capital. Red tracer bullets zipped through the sky near the Presidential Palace and the American Embassy, and the muffled roar of hand grenades or rockets or both vibrated through the night. I phoned the office and Bob Tuckman answered, his voice high-pitched and excited. "They're shelling the city, for God's sake," he said. I told him I was on my way. I looked back into the bathroom and realized that my wife and children were as vulnerable as the people I had often photographed in the war-torn villages in the countryside, and I hesitated for a moment, reluctant to leave them there alone until I reasoned there was nowhere for them to go anyway until daylight. I told Nina I would be back for them later; she was quieting three-month-old Elsa as I left. As I gingerly opened our apartment door, a heavy machine

240

gun opened fire again, spitting its load in the direction of the Presidential Palace on Cong Ly Street, two blocks away.

I waited for a break in the shooting and stepped out into the lamplight, raising my arms in a friendly gesture to the invisible machine gunners behind the sandbags a block down the street. I was in shirtsleeves and slacks and I smiled and shouted, "Bao chi, reporter," and walked toward them. There was no reaction so I kept on going, down Rue Pasteur to Le Thanh Thon Street, where I walked carefully by a guard post outside City Hall and over to the Eden building, where a nervous Indian lookout quickly opened the iron gates and let me in.

Ed White was in the office along with Tuckman and George Esper and they were all working the phones and telexing additional news to the New York desk. We needed eyewitness information, so I grabbed the keys to the office minijeep and set off with photographers John Nance and Joe Holloway. I drove up Tu Do Street to the Catholic cathedral in John F. Kennedy Square. Our path to the American Embassy was blocked by jeeps filled with nervous U.S. military policemen. One of them ordered us to leave and we didn't stay to argue. We turned around but devised an approach from another direction, spinning down the deserted city avenues and past the central market and up Le Van Duyet Street until we neared the Club Hippique restaurant. There was a firefight in progress at the Presidential Palace. We swung down Nguyen Du Street for a closer look and came under attack ourselves.

Long bursts of automatic weapons fire raked over our heads as Holloway and Nance shouted at me to stop. I flipped off the lights and the three of us squeezed under the vehicle as bullets slapped at the sidewalks and the sandbagged defenses of the Meyerkord bachelor officers quarters behind us. We stayed there for half an hour, in fear for our lives, until a jeepload of Australian military police came to the rescue, covering us with return fire long enough for me to reverse the minijeep and depart. We learned that our attackers were a squad of Vietcong commandos who had retreated from their unsuccessful assault on the south gates of the palace, and were holed up in a half-finished residential hotel on the opposite side of the street.

When I returned to the office around 4:30 A.M. there was a call from USIS information chief Barry Zorthian, who told me he wanted us to get an accurate story about what was going on, and that I should phone the veteran American mission coordinator George Jacobson, who was apparently trapped by Vietcong guerrillas in his villa on the grounds of the embassy. Jacobson told me several communist commandos had penetrated the compound's concrete walls and were roaming the embassy grounds and firing bazooka shells at the facade of the shiny new eight-story chancery building, trying to get inside.

Jacobson's bedroom windows had already been smashed by a rocket, and he said he had armed himself with a hand grenade for a last-ditch stand. Still he was a cool one, a veteran of nine years' service in Vietnam, and his last comment to me was that the Vietcong "are calculating a big splash all over the world with their activities." I was intrigued by these comments from a senior official crouching in his bedroom fearing for his life but already figuring out a credible explanation for what was going on, that it was a communist publicity stunt.

As I wrote the story I could hardly believe the audacity of the Vietcong, who were not only assaulting the American Embassy but, as we were learning from phone calls from around the city, also launching vigorous attacks against a dozen other targets across Saigon, all this at a time when the conventional wisdom had them pushed to the ropes.

In my year-end forecast for 1968 I had bucked the optimistic official view of the war and predicted that "the biggest and bloodiest battles are still to be fought" in Vietnam, but never in my wildest imagining did I expect to see combat at my doorstep. It might well be a publicity stunt as Jacobson had advised me, but it was certainly a story we could not ignore, and we soon set off for the embassy again, this time on foot to slip through the park in front of the Presidential Palace and avoid the military police sentinels. We barely noticed the security men in the darkness, taking cover behind the park's trees, and they made no effort to stop us as we rounded the red-brick Catholic basilica, ran up toward Duy Tan Street to the broad expanse of Thong Nhut Boulevard, and turned northeast toward the American Embassy.

The bursts of rockets and crack of small arms fire drew us further down the boulevard, past the headquarters office of the Texas construction giant RMK-BRJ, to Hai Ba Trung Street and the corner of the block, where the six-story embassy, behind an eight-foot concrete wall, towered over us in the darkness. We edged along the street and crouched beside the fence as small as we could make ourselves. The boulevard was a shooting gallery; gunfire crackled over our heads and thudded into tree trunks and walls. American military police from the 716th Battalion had occupied an upper floor of an apartment building across the street and were directing their bullets into the embassy grounds; the Vietcong inside were returning fire of their own.

The first glow of a gray dawn lit the scene. In the middle of the street was a bullet-ridden black Citroën sedan, its driver slumped over the steering wheel. Nance ran to shelter behind it for a better look at the embassy building but scurried back for cover as the shooting came near us. Outside the embassy gate were two other immobilized vehicles. There was concrete rubble scattered near them and a haze of dust in the air from the blasting the Vietcong had done to make their entryway to the embassy grounds.

I wondered what happened to George Jacobson, if he was still cornered in his villa inside the wall, and I slipped back to Hai Ba Trung Street and explained his predicament to a young U.S. Marine captain named Robert O'Brien who had arrived with marine guard reinforcements and was manning a radio in his jeep around the corner. He said he already knew of the problem and was in radio communication with embassy staff inside the chancery, and had relayed to them the word from command headquarters that they would have to hold out because a counterattack would be too dangerous in the darkness.

I saw military policemen crawling along the exposed gutters and the sidewalk next to the embassy wall up ahead of us, moving into position to attack, while others were gathering in formation to assist them. I suppressed an immense desire to rush to the nearest telephone to report to the office, instead holding my place. At this point, only correspondent Don North of ABC-TV had joined us and he was not competing with the AP. A dozen Hueys came in low over the gardens of the Saigon zoo at the end of the boulevard. They were heading toward us and I realized they were going to attempt an infantry assault against the embassy.

Nance was back at his automobile vantage point as a private rose to his feet and slammed his shoulder against the wrought iron embassy gate. It swung open and the military policemen poured inside as the roar of hand grenades and automatic weapons erupted. We could see the first of the helicopters hovering above us, trying to land on the embassy roof. In a barrage of gunfire it pulled away and was gone, and soon many of the soldiers who had stormed into the gate were back out on the street with us, pointing to the middle floors of the chancery building.

Not only were the Vietcong inside the grounds but they apparently had penetrated the embassy itself and were upstairs. I asked a disheveled officer if he was sure and he responded, "My God yes, we're taking fire from up there. Keep your head down." I ran to the construction company office along the street, where the Indian night watchman let me use the lobby phone.

Ed White calmly took my dictation. I needed no reminding that I was witnessing one of the most sensational actions of the whole war, and I was quickly back at the corner of Hai Ba Trung, where a dozen of my colleagues had assembled, including Tom Buckley and Charles Mohr from the *New York Times,* Peter Braestrup and Lee Lescaze from the *Washington Post,* and François Sully of *Newsweek.* We exchanged what information we had and chatted with soldiers and officers, waiting for the next development.

It did not come for another hour. A second helicopter assault was launched, and this time we glimpsed troops from the 101st Infantry Division jumping to the embassy roof and beginning their descent through the building. I saw correspondent Howard Tuckner of NBC and his cameraman, Vo Huynh, follow a military police squad through the front gate into the embassy grounds and we were all soon inside with them, gasping at the evidence of the fierce struggle inside. A large hole had been blasted through the protective wall, the Great Seal of the United States was bullet-ridden and knocked down from above the door, the lobby a tangled wreck. There were a score of dead Vietcong in green and brown clothing and red armbands, and several dead Americans, their blood splashed on the pathways and walls.

We were then startled by a series of gunshots from behind the embassy building, and we rushed to the rear to see George Jacobson emerge pale-faced from his villa, the victor over a lone Vietcong who had entered his house and hidden in a bathroom and then attempted to shoot him with his automatic rifle. Jacobson had killed his assailant with two shots from a pistol that had been thrown up to him as he had leaned out a window of his second-floor bedroom.

General Westmoreland soon arrived, his confidence as unwrinkled as his tropical khakis. He told reporters that the Vietcong attackers had brought in with them a large quantity of powerful explosives to blow up the embassy, but that "the enemy's well-laid plans went afoul." It was a measure of the low regard in which many of us in the press corps regarded the general's opinions that we didn't completely believe him when he asserted that no Vietcong attackers had obtained entry to the main embassy building. We quoted his comments in full in our stories, but also retained what we had learned from military policemen at the battle scene, that there was firing coming from upstairs rooms. Technically the general was correct, and eventually we confirmed that nineteen Vietcong guerrillas, from a citywide force of ten thousand, had driven unchecked through the capital city, surprised the embassy guards, killing five of them as they blasted their way through the defensive walls, and held the grounds for six hours, but did not actually get inside the main building.

As I listened to Westmoreland confidently proclaim that American forces were on the offensive and the enemy was on the run, I heard in my memory the words of his predecessor, General Paul D. Harkins, at the Tan Hiep airstrip in January 1963 when he had told David Halberstam and me that the battle of Ap Bac, with its high South Vietnamese and American death toll, was a victory for our side because "the enemy is on the run."

Six years and half a million American troops later the battle of Ap Bac had suddenly come to Saigon and every city in the country, and the response from the American high command was still the same stonewalling optimism. But unlike the earlier battle, when Vietnam was an obscure problem in counterinsurgency, the Tet Offensive was being fought in an American presidential election year in the glare of television news, and the old answers would no longer suffice.

Destroying the Town to Save It

THE SURPRISE WAS COMPLETE. The Tet Offensive rolled across Saigon like a tidal wave over a landfill. The four million people of the panicked capital retreated behind locked doors and shuttered windows. Armed Vietcong guerrillas moved into crowded neighborhoods and took over the streets and private homes and pagodas, prepared, it seemed, to fight to the death.

The AP staffers made their way to work with harrowing tales of close encounters. Three people were killed on the street outside the Cholon home of a radio photo operator. Photographer Dan Van Phuoc sat terrified in the dark at his house in Gia Dinh, while the Vietcong pounded on his and his neighbors' doors, ordering everyone out into the streets and firing guns into the air with announcements that they had liberated the city. A darkroom technician walked around the corner of an alley near the An Quang Pagoda and into the startled embrace of several dozen armed Vietcong soldiers, but they let him go after lecturing him on the evils of the government.

Ursula Faas called Horst from their home in Cholon to tell him that a policeman had been shot dead in the driveway. Horst told her to fasten the window shutters, lock the doors and wait out the crisis. Like the rest of us, he was impatient with personal responsibilities.

I had picked up Nina and our children from our apartment and driven them to her parents' home, but then had little time to visit. We knew that we were covering the biggest event of our careers.

We learned that four thousand communist combatants had been committed to attack Saigon's center, and twice that number were fighting in the outlying suburbs. Like the Greek soldiers of legend, who had hidden in a wooden horse to infiltrate Troy, the Vietcong had used surprise and deceit to launch their attack. Some had concealed themselves and their weapons in truckloads of flowers and farm produce bound for city markets; others had ridden in on buses and motor scooters carrying forged documents and picking up weapons previously hidden in safe houses.

American officials accused the communists of blasphemous indifference to the sanctity of the Tet holiday and predicted a backlash of public anger. But the Vietnamese population was too scared to be angry and they kept their heads down.

At his headquarters in Bien Hoa, John Paul Vann told me, "Christ, we knew the VC were up to something, but nothing this extensive, nothing," and he mopped his face and shook his head in wonder. The Tet Offensive had confirmed his warnings. He had always argued that the fate of South Vietnam rested on improving the motivation and ability of its own armed forces, but the Vietcong had exposed the perennial weaknesses of the South Vietnamese military, particularly the hopelessly inadequate security cordons around Saigon and the forty-three provincial capitals.

As we struggled to cover the offensive and to fathom its meaning, the full scale of the assaults became apparent. We moved out onto the streets at dawn and spent the days riding jeeps with military policemen along body-strewn streets, ducking across intersections with Vietnamese soldiers, through burning, rocket-scarred neighborhoods aboard American tanks and armored personnel carriers.

I spent a day with the Vietnamese Eighth Airborne Battalion at the Saigon golf course, where vicious fighting had stained the fairways with blood, and pitted the rough with holes from exploding mortar and rocket rounds. I wrote that evening, "From the seventh tee of

Saigon's only golf course you could drive a two-iron shot into the headquarters of a Vietcong infantry company."

I felt I knew the city well enough to take off by myself, sometimes driving along side streets and alleyways to visit friends and acquaintances who were isolated by the fighting and fearful. A psywar operative I knew, Ron Fleming, let me through the fence of his Chi Lam home after I had leaned on my car horn for a few minutes. He cautioned me to be careful as we crept around the wall. Fleming's clothes were dirty and he hadn't shaved for a few days. He had a pistol strapped to his thigh and carried a high-powered M-14 rifle in his hands. "There's no law out here, it's every man for himself," he whispered, rising to his full height and aiming his rifle carefully over the wall and pulling the trigger. There was a Vietcong soldier hiding in the next building, "the friendly neighborhood sniper" who had been harassing his home. The crack of the report echoed around the small cluster of neat concrete buildings in the compound. I was intrigued by Fleming's adeptness; he was a civilian who had graduated from Harvard University three years earlier, and now he walked around with the stance of an Indian fighter. As I was leaving, the neighborhood sniper had resumed shooting and Fleming was stalking him again.

By the end of the third day of the offensive the city was still closed down under a twenty-four-hour curfew, and I wrote a report: "The only shops open in the whole of Saigon Friday were the coffin makers." The craftsmen were sawing and hammering wooden planks on the streets outside their storefronts to keep up with the demand from a steady stream who braved the curfew and arrived in small trucks and cars to load up the coffins gaudily decorated with religious symbols. I knew that in the heavy fighting there would have to be numerous unidentified dead, who would be unlikely to receive the dignity of a decent burial, and I eventually discovered their final resting place, three huge mass graves excavated by bulldozers in an abandoned old cemetery in the western edge of Saigon.

One grave was a block long and filled with six hundred corpses stacked five layers high. In an unsuccessful attempt to keep down the rancid smell a mantle of quicklime had been placed over the remains. It looked like the work of a ghoulish cosmetologist. Cemetery officials said most of the dead were Vietcong insurgents, but I noticed in two other large graves the bodies of women and children lying beside the males, and officials said these were whole families wiped out in the fighting whose remains were unclaimed.

A sobbing woman tugged at my arm and said she had lost her son but could find no volunteers to help her wade through the hundreds of bodies to find him, and I too lacked the stomach to assist her. Several street urchins were hanging around with handkerchiefs knotted around their faces to shield against the smell, their pockets bulging with items looted from the bodies. They were eyeing the garbage trucks that were arriving with more corpses.

Bob Tuckman had complained that he was stuck in the office so much he never got to see what was going on, so I invited him to join me for a tour of the city. He squeezed himself into the AP minijeep and we drove off along the deserted expanses of Le Loi and Trung Hung Dao streets toward the Chinese area of Cholon, where the fighting was continuing. No attempt had been made to restore order there. We drove past a gas station at the corner of Bui Huu Nghia Street where six dead men lay rotting in the noon sun. The blood from their wounds had dried into a black crust on the pavement and their bodies were bloated beyond recognition.

I explained to Tuckman that Saigon's police force had disappeared the night the offensive began, and had not reappeared. The priority of the military forces was to clear the Vietcong from the area before they cleaned up the streets. We pressed on along Cholon thoroughfares normally alive with business, now empty. Eventually we approached the racecourse on a street where the houses had been entirely demolished. The captain of the Sixth Vietnamese Marine Battalion complained, "It is much easier fighting in the countryside than here. Too many people in our way."

Tuckman mentioned that it must be worse in the Vietcong-controlled area of the city; he blanched when I told him we had just been through part of it. "Goddamn it," he muttered, "we're risking our lives out here." I concurred, "At least you're a bureau chief who shares our risks, however inadvertently."

I was, in fact, fascinated by the prospect of actually encountering communist combatants in Saigon, an opportunity never available in the countryside, where both sides fired first and asked questions later. Several journalists in the capital and in Hue had already stumbled into the hands of the Vietcong. Korean reporter Kim Kyung-Kuk was executed in Saigon along with one of his embassy officials. But one of the newsmen taken, Italian Alessandro Casella, told me later how he and three French television correspondents had spent four hours in captivity in a house in Cholon, and were treated politely and served tea while under guard. Before being freed they were briefed by a man describing himself as the press representative of the National Liberation Front.

This was clearly another side to the picture we were not encouraged to discuss. We were again forced to examine battlefield reverses in terms of American and South Vietnamese inadequacies, rather than the communists' competence. There were no limitations on our reporting on the courage or the transgressions of the American soldier, and we could praise or ridicule the tactics of U.S. commanders as factors in the pursuit of victory, yet it was understood that while we could be negative about the enemy we would not dwell on his military virtues, which were now as much a factor in the escalation of the war as incompetent American strategy.

It would still have been professional suicide for us in the AP to suggest that the Vietcong insurgents and Hanoi's regular forces were generally superbly trained and well motivated and seemed to believe in their revolutionary cause. We were dissuaded by our editors from suggesting that the Vietnam conflict contained significant elements of a civil war, even though every Vietnamese knew the truth of that description.

I understood the confusion of the American public over the course of the war. Their government was telling them that the communists were on the ropes and their boys would soon be coming home. Then came Tet. I was surprised myself by the vast scale of the offensive but not by its tenacity and boldness. The skill, perseverance and rise of the Vietcong insurgents under the most difficult conditions was never properly acknowledged until the Tet Offensive, when their formidable capabilities could not be ignored.

I was talking with Nina's family of their fears about being apprehended by the Vietcong. They were potential targets because they had fled from Hanoi years earlier to escape the communists. Then their youngest maid, Thao, piped up in a confident voice. She said she wasn't scared because the rebels were interested only in attacking "the rich people and the Americans" and that she would be unharmed because of her poor station.

She was not an active supporter of the insurgents and I wondered if the millions of other people of quite modest means in Saigon felt similar sympathies for the communist side. I never pursued that story because its premise would have been unsuitable in the political climate of the times.

The U.S. military leadership was unable to provide any sensible explanation for the Tet Offensive because they were hobbled by the practice of expressing only contempt toward Vietcong and North Vietnamese military abilities. The growing respect of the American infantryman for "Mister Charles" as he was beginning to call the previous Charlie, the communist soldier in the field, was not reflected at command level. In an interview with Wes Gallagher, who rushed out to Saigon in February to rally the staff, Westmoreland called Tet a "Battle of the Bulge," a reference to the German army's failed counteroffensive against Allied forces at Bastogne near the end of World War Two.

To Westmoreland, Tet was a last desperate gamble by the communists before inevitable defeat. His confidence was not shaken in the least; victory would come, he believed, with one more escalation of the war.

Because the curfew made moving around the city in darkness too risky, the AP staff camped as best it could in the office each night. We slept on cots and tables, and chewed on packs of army field rations that Bob Tuckman brought in each day from the U.S. military information office at the Rex Hotel across the street. We learned that newspapers and television stations in the United States and much of the rest of the world had been jolted by the drama unfolding in Vietnam.

The AP foreign desk was asking for analyses, interviews, eyewitness stories and features. Saigon was one center of the story. In Hue, communist troops had occupied most of the old city at the start of the offensive and were engaged in fierce battle with the U.S. marines who were trying to seize it back. The third major story was at the marine base at Khe Sanh, which John Wheeler was covering singlehandedly under the most difficult circumstances.

We relayed thousands of words each day to New York headquarters accompanied by photographs. Horst was running the photo side even though he was recovering from severe leg wounds received on patrol with First Division infantrymen two months earlier. His left leg was still in a heavy plaster cast. One day a tough-looking Vietnamese wearing army boots and trousers and a civilian shirt came in off the street with four rolls of film, introduced himself as Huynh Cong Phuc. "I hear the AP pays dollars for pictures," he asked. "I have pictures from big fight." Nobody had seen him before but on one roll of his negatives Horst found a picture of a weeping South Vietnamese colonel holding his child in his arms, murdered hours earlier by Vietcong attackers. It was one of the most memorable images of the offensive. He returned several times with pictures but apologized one day for having to return to his regular job. "What do you do?" Horst asked, and Mr. Phuc responded, "I have very easy job. I make the white spots in the Vietnamese newspapers. I am the government's censor."

The pictures of the Tet Offensive reinforced the impression that American policy was in ruins. The images sent to newspapers and shown on television were shocking.

Each day cameras captured extraordinary pictures of the casual brutality on the streets. AP photographer Le Ngoc Cung returned one afternoon with a roll of film showing grisly images of the execution of a wounded Vietcong at the Binh Loi Bridge. A band of Vietnamese marines had gunned him as he lay wounded in the wreckage of a wooden hut. An even more sensational series of pictures came from the camera of Eddie Adams. I was in our office when Eddie rushed in, his flak vest flapping. "Goddamn it," he said. "General Loan shot a man right in front of my eyes," he gasped. He held up the roll of film. "I think I may have got it right here; heh, I hope so."

Brigadier General Nguyen Ngoc Loan was the commander of the Vietnamese National Police, a feared man running a feared organization, with a flamboyant manner and a hair-trigger temper. As we waited for his film to be developed, Eddie told us that he had been traveling with an NBC crew in Cholon. They were at an intersection near the An Quang Pagoda when they saw Vietnamese marines escorting a disheveled prisoner with his hands tied behind his back toward General Loan. The journalists approached the police chief. As they got near he raised his snub-nosed revolver to shoulder level and shot the captive in the head. As he lowered his gun, Loan turned to the journalists and commented with a thin smile, "They killed many Americans and many of my people," and walked away.

A few minutes later the darkroom attendant emerged and handed the strip of film to Horst, who inspected the frames with a magnifying glass. There was professional rivalry between Horst and Eddie but it was not apparent this day. Horst muttered "Damn," and handed the film to Eddie, who looked at it and then let out a whoop. It was there, the moment of death, the cruel expression on the general's face, his extended arm and revolver at the moment of firing, and just inches away the victim's face twisting in the impact, his shoulder turning as he began to collapse. NBC cameraman Vo Suu had captured the whole sequence on color film, but it was Eddie Adams's picture that was published on the front pages of the most important newspapers in the world.

Eddie was never entirely comfortable with the fame of the picture

251

that won him a Pulitzer Prize and secured his place in photographic history. He felt he had betrayed his country's war effort and ruined the reputation of the Vietnamese police chief, who he felt had been pushed into his impetuous action by the pressures of the Tet Offensive. I disagreed. His picture captured the brutality that was common to General Loan and the war.

The chaos on the streets of Saigon and the extended battle in the citadel at the old capital of Hue frustrated efforts by the American military high command to control the propaganda flow. In the same way as the Buddhist crisis in 1963, and the coup d'etat epidemic of 1964 and 1965, the situation got totally out of hand and the image-makers were unable to stop the negative impact. On the grounds of the embattled American Embassy on the morning the attacks started, General Westmoreland had insisted that all was well but no one was listening. Subsequent efforts to claim a high ground of victory were derided.

The AP attended all the Saigon briefings and reported on the official view of events, including intelligence assessments that the communists had made gross errors of judgment. The communist side was clearly taking tremendous casualties on all the battlefronts and giving ground to allied forces. While there was grim satisfaction among American combat units that they were clearing the cities and winning the day, the civilian population did not share this sense of victory. Numb with fear, hiding in their homes, there were a hundred thousand refugees in the Saigon area alone.

Almost as injurious as the communist attacks were the severe measures taken to repel them. We watched whole city blocks in Saigon become free fire zones for gunships and tanks. From a helicopter overhead the patches of ash and rubble scarring the city looked like the footprints of some giant wearing hobnailed boots. Small slashes of wreckage were visible in almost every sector. Ugly holes gaped from the city floor where there had once been clusters of houses, shops and offices. The heaviest fighting was in the rabbit warrens of lanes and homes where Cholon merged with Saigon and near the Cong Hoa soccer stadium and the racetrack. The American forces brought the tactics perfected in the countryside. U.S. Army helicopters sought out the Vietcong, roaring low over the city with machine guns, spitting bullets and rockets into the crowded communities below. Vietnamese Skyraider dive-bombers flattened the tarpaper shacks of the poorest residents along canals. Tanks and armored troop carriers and their wide-eyed American crews just in from the paddyfields and jungles were facing unfamiliar combat in the narrow back alleys of those communities.

.   .   .

The Tet Offensive stretched beyond Saigon across the whole country-side, enveloping thirty-six provincial capitals and sixty-four district centers. Communist insurgents had emerged from the jungles and paddyfields and streamed past government security forces into the population centers. Just a few days earlier, the U.S. mission's pacification chief, Robert Komer, had bragged to reporters that the primary highway, Route 1, was open from Saigon all the way to the DMZ border with North Vietnam. When I saw John Paul Vann in Bien Hoa the day after the attacks began he made a joke of it. "The highway might be open, but watch out for the cities and towns en route; they're dangerous."

The reports coming in from the countryside told of unprecedented destruction. Eddie Adams visited the Mekong Delta cities of My Tho and Vinh Long and returned with photographs of the battle scenes. He told me, "The damage was devastating, man. The ruins were still smoldering, the population was silent and were looking angrily at us, us Americans, they don't like us down there because of the bombing and the gunships." I wanted to see it for myself. On February 7 I climbed aboard a U.S. Army Caribou transport aircraft with a dozen other reporters to visit Ben Tre, the capital of Kien Hoa province, a sleepy city nestling on a meandering finger of the Mekong River where the vast waterway spilled across the delta, its last terrain obstacle, into the South China Sea. Kien Hoa had always been a bellwether province for the evaluation of American counterinsurgency programs and government performance. I had been there in January before the offensive began.

Our transport aircraft climbed noisily into the thin morning air on its twenty-minute trip south and I quickly noticed that we were flying at the wrong height, about two thousand feet, well within range of anyone on the ground below who might be interested in trying to shoot us down. The usual procedure was for pilots to travel either at treetop level or much higher, beyond rifle range. Dick Swanson, a *Life* photographer who was strapped into his seat beside me, began making slitting gestures across his throat as he looked out the porthole window. Ten minutes later, there was the loud bang of an explosion in the passenger compartment. The crew chief was standing at the entrance to the pilot's cabin and he collapsed. I assumed that he had been hit.

The pilot looked back to assess the situation as the aircraft lurched and fell into a steep dive.

I immediately thought the engine had been disabled and we would crash. Similar expressions of fear were on the faces of my colleagues, with one exception, Jack Foisie of the *Los Angeles Times,* an ebullient, prematurely balding reporter who shouted his favorite exclamation in times of joy and crisis, a full-throated "Yahoo" in harmony with the roar of the aircraft engines. Somehow we leveled off safely and proceeded on our way to Ben Tre. It turned out that the crew chief had only fainted. But when we landed Swanson dug a rifle slug out of his camera bag, which had been resting beside him on the floor.

Jeeps were waiting at the palm-fringed blacktop airstrip to take us into the city, but I let my colleagues go on ahead and walked over to the wooden control tower near the terminal shack where I had seen the familiar face of Major Chester L. Brown, an air force officer, who had flown me around in his tiny L-19 spotter plane on my previous visit. Brown agreed to drive me to the city in his own jeep. He warned me that I would be shocked at what I saw, that Ben Tre was in ruins and that many people had died. "It is always a pity about the civilians," he explained. "In the mass confusion of this kind of thing, the people don't know where the lines are, they don't know where to hide, and some of the weapons we were using were area weapons instead of against specific targets, and that way people get hurt."

At the outskirts of the city we saw rows of ragged palm trees with their tops burned off, and the blackened wreckage of roadside homes and small shops. As we drove along the main street toward the commercial center, Major Brown said he had used the thoroughfare as a bombing marker during the nighttime attacks. "The streetlights never went off," he said.

We passed the gaunt concrete shells of two- and three-story office buildings. The once handsome Kien Hoa marketplace where I had purchased durian and star fruit three weeks earlier was a crumpled ruin. We arrived at the administrative center of the city along the riverside where the U.S. Army Advisory Team 93 compound was buried in protective sandbags; the province chief's home and the Vietnamese tactical operations center were similarly shielded across the grassy compound. From a wooden landing inside the base I looked across the river to the opposite bank, where a two-mile stretch of thatched-roofed homes had been reduced to ashes; the squatter district and lower-class housing at the western and northern sides of the city were similarly leveled, now just piles of jagged rubble.

I asked the army advisory team commander how many civilians had died, and he estimated five hundred to a thousand. "But we will never know for sure, many families are buried permanently under the rubble." I had met him before and I liked him. I asked him how it could have happened that so many civilians had died that way in a city of only thirty-five thousand people. He looked at my notebook, shook his head and responded, "None of us can talk about that, you know that, we can't go on the record criticizing our Vietnamese counterparts, not at a time like this."

There was a murmur of assent from the crowd of American officers around him and I made an exaggerated gesture of placing my pen in my shirt pocket and stuffing my notebook in my trouser belt. I said, "Now, you know me, I've been down here before, talk to me, trust me and I won't quote you on anything that'll hurt you, I never do that." Most of the group wandered off to their duty posts but the commander stayed to chat, and during the morning I was able to catch up with the rest of the officers over coffee or walking with them around the post.

A picture emerged of chaos and ineptitude in the defense of the city. The Vietcong had sneaked in as they had in Saigon, and launched their attacks against an unprepared defense force, half depleted by holiday passes. Ben Tre's commercial center and residential areas were under the insurgents' control by dawn and the guerrillas were threatening the administrative center, including the American advisory compound and the Vietnamese barracks, whose troops were unwilling to launch counterattacks. Another of the majors who had helped defend the American compound told me that the decision to use the heaviest of firepower against the insurgents was not taken lightly. "They are our friends out there, we waited until we had no choice," he insisted. "The Vietnamese chief of staff had to bring in an air strike on the house of his neighbor because the communists had occupied it. Our own positions were being threatened, the government center nearly overrun. It became necessary to destroy the town to save it."

An American captain said there was initial reluctance from the corp headquarters at Can Tho to authorize the extraordinary use of force within the city. "We had to argue with them; they didn't like the idea," he said, but when the stratagem was finally approved, the fighter-bombers came in dropping napalm and heavy projectiles, and were followed by armed helicopters and artillery barrages.

An American lieutenant who watched the bombing told me, "The only places they weren't hitting were the American compound, the province chief's headquarters area and the hospital; everything else was fair game." American troops from the Ninth Division eventually came into Ben Tre to secure the city after two days of fighting.

When we drove back to the airstrip I gave Major Brown the same promise that I had given the others. I wouldn't quote him on anything that would harm his career. He thanked me. It wasn't all bad, he said, "There could have been many more dead, I think I saved hundreds of civilians." He told how in the midmorning hours he had been ordered to guide air strikes on what he was told were "a thousand Vietcong" retreating north from the city. He buzzed down low in his spotter plane and saw scores of women and young children carrying bedrolls and household goods, clearly fleeing from their destroyed homes. "Some Vietcong may have been among those people but most of them were refugees and I wasn't about to bring napalm down on them so I called off the planned air strikes."

On the return flight to Saigon I thought about what I had seen and heard in Ben Tre; the phrase in my notebook, "It became necessary to destroy the town to save it," leaped out as a comment on the essential dilemma of the Tet Offensive. The authorities had not only to defeat the attackers, but protect the civilian population. At the AP office I sat at my typewriter long into the night. Eventually I began, "At what point do you turn your heavy guns and jet fighter-bombers on the streets of your own city? When does the infliction of civilian casualties become irrelevant as long as the enemy is destroyed? The answers to both these questions came in the first few hours of the battle for Ben Tre, a once placid Mekong Delta river city of thirty-five thousand people. 'It became necessary to destroy the town to save it,' a U.S. major says. The destruction of this provincial capital was drawn out over fifty hours."

I wrote eight pages of copy and at 3 A.M. passed them over to the telex operator, who punched the material directly through to our New York foreign desk. I lay down on a cot in the bureau chief's office and slept until Tuckman came in early to start the news day. Late that evening Tuckman had a telephone call from a staffer at the U.S. military information office asking me to identify the major who had made the comment I had highlighted in my story, a request that I rejected out of hand because we routinely gave anonymity to our many nervous sources who requested it.

This was my first inkling of how controversial the story was becoming. The next day, the AP foreign desk advised me that the quote had echoed from Fleet Street, London, to Seoul, South Korea, and was the subject of editorial comment in the United States.

A secretary in Barry Zorthian's office said the message traffic indicated that President Johnson himself had demanded to know the name of the major, and a few days later the *Wall Street Journal* correspondent, Peter Kann, told me that a helicopter full of senior American officers had descended on Ben Tre while he was visiting there, demanding the name of the culprit.

At least the military command believed that the major who made the quote actually existed. Some of my news colleagues expressed doubts about its authenticity. Bill Tuohy of the *Los Angeles Times* wrote after a visit to Ben Tre that Americans there "doubted that the statement was actually made in that form," and ironically quoted an unnamed U.S. civilian adviser as saying, "It sounds too pithy and clever to have been made on the spot." But my AP superiors expressed no distrust of my information.

I returned to Ben Tre several weeks later and found that nothing much had changed. The city was still in ruins. Few of the resident Americans were willing to be quoted on the record. Several of the officers I had talked with on my earlier visit took me aside and asked me if they had been responsible for the famous quote, each noting that the comment accurately summed up their feelings at the time. They said the quote had become so notorious in military circles that the consequences to the career of its author would be disastrous should his identity become known.

Joseph Alsop weighed in with criticism of my Ben Tre account, not unexpectedly because he rarely lost an opportunity to criticize the Saigon press corps. He wrote that we were between what he called "the rock and the hard place," to be blamed for complicity with the enemy if the war was lost and ridiculed for stupidity if it was won.

Alsop's views on the war that he only occasionally visited, and then only in the company of the most senior government and military officials in the country, veered so widely from what we reported that we never took him seriously. I encountered Alsop at a dinner party for a few reporters given by American Ambassador Ellsworth Bunker, who'd been appointed the previous year. The columnist was a guest at the ambassador's residence and was looking bored as he sipped his wine.

After I made a few comments about the military situation Alsop looked at me across the table, and said, "You're the fellow who makes up the quotes, aren't you?" I was not familiar with the protocol of honored guests in the patrician world that Alsop inhabited, but I knew what I had to do. A direct attack required a direct response, a lesson I had learned as a kid on the streets of Bluff. I pushed my chair back and advanced around the table with my right fist raised menacingly, and I heard the encouraging laughter of my fellow diners.

Alsop rose unsteadily to his feet. He may have seen the anger in my eyes. Before I could decide whether or not to swing at him, Ambassador Bunker was standing between us. "Peter, go back and sit down," he ordered me, his hand pressing on my shoulder. And he turned to Alsop and said, "And Joe, tut, tut and shut up."

President Johnson named General Westmoreland Army Chief of Staff on March 23, just seven weeks after the Tet Offensive. Few were fooled into believing it was a promotion; the Vietnamese-owned *Saigon News* headlined the announcement, "Westmoreland Kicked Upstairs," and there was little disagreement that the American field commander would leave the war theater with little glory and with much to be accountable for. Just nine days earlier on March 14 the American death toll in Vietnam had passed the twenty thousand mark; there had been 3,500 helicopters and airplanes lost. Westmoreland's removal brought interesting responses from the officers on his staff we were in contact with. They viewed his replacement, General Creighton D. Abrams, a former tank officer, as a superior soldier and a wiser tactician, "a leader we should have had here years ago," commented a colonel much to my surprise. The colonel had spent the previous two years promoting the merits of Westmoreland.

Gallagher asked Faas and me to assess the Vietnam situation in an address to the annual meeting of the AP board of directors in New York City in April. I was looking forward to the trip. I had little inkling of the real measure of American public opinion because I had been buried in the day-to-day minutiae of war coverage, but I was aware of the anti-war demonstrations in American cities. Gallagher had startled me by asking for some advice about his son, who was considering going to Canada to avoid the draft.

The day before I arrived in New York, President Johnson had announced that he would not seek a second term in office; he had halted all air and sea action against North Vietnam in an effort to end the war. The AP executives I met seemed convinced the war was over, but the passions of the antiwar movement were not dampened by the peace offerings, as Horst and I saw at an antiwar rally in Central Park.

At Sheep Meadow, thousands of protesters were carrying banners and chanting, "Hell no, we won't go" or "Peace now, peace now" and "Hey, hey, LBJ, how many kids have you killed today?"

Horst noted that the protesters were carrying huge blowups of AP pictures from Vietnam, including Eddie Adams's street execution photo. What astounded me were the scores of young American draft resisters marching through the park carrying large Vietcong flags. In all my years in Vietnam I had never seen a Vietcong flag flying freely other than as a captured souvenir fluttering from a tank or from a soldier's backpack. In America, it had a place in the parade.

Senator Harry Byrd from Virginia, a conservative Democrat, was a member of the AP board of directors. He asked me to testify before his Senate Armed Services Preparedness Committee. I had no desire to become publicly involved in the war debate so I turned him down. Soon afterward I received a telegram from Robert Kennedy, who was campaigning in the presidential primaries, asking me to brief him on the war. I was flattered and eager to comply because I thought I could count on his discretion.

Gallagher contemplated my proposal with some amusement and declined his permission. "You would turn down an opportunity to do a favor for a member of the AP board of directors and yet expect me to approve this?"

The evening before I was to return to Vietnam, I walked out of the Americana Hotel in Midtown Manhattan and down Broadway. I heard a newsstand attendant shouting, "Saigon killings, Saigon killings, come and get it." I walked over and he handed me a copy of the bulldog edition of the *New York Daily News,* which displayed a gruesome picture across its front page of bloodied bodies draped over and near a minijeep. One of the victims was my old Bangkok pal John Cantwell who had left the AP for *Time* magazine a year earlier. He was dead on the streets of Cholon along with three of his colleagues, victims of a Vietcong ambush.

I was shocked again. They were young and enthusiastic. I wondered at myself. I was husband to a trusting wife and father of two young children, and bent on returning to the war. I had learned from the AP personnel chief, Keith Fuller, that President Johnson was after me again. He had invited the AP executive to the Oval Office in March and after serving up a lunch of hamburgers and milk he mentioned that he had decided to pull Barry Zorthian out of Vietnam "because he has been there too long."

259

The president had then asked, "Now hasn't that Australian Pete Arnett been in Vietnam too long, too?"

The next morning, I climbed on the Pan Am Clipper flight to Saigon.

The Forgotten Men

I RETURNED TO VIETNAM in the late summer of 1968 believing that the war would soon end because the peace talks had started in Paris and the bombing of North Vietnam had been halted. Nixon campaigned on the promise of a "secret plan to end the war," which helped get him elected. As I traveled the Vietnamese countryside I saw that both sides were scrambling to claim territory in the expectation of a ceasefire that would end the shooting war and begin a political struggle. I wrote about an expected "flag war" that would come on ceasefire day, with both the Saigon government and the communist side competing politically for attention in villages and hamlets that had been locked in bloody conflict for most of the decade.

The general ceasefire never came. Instead of trying to end the war quickly, the Nixon administration attempted to bring the American chapter to a close gradually by withdrawing gracefully and saving face, and building up the South Vietnamese side to fight on.

Retreat was judged the most difficult of military tactics and we began writing about the morale of the remaining American soldiers and the plight of those left behind to support the Vietnamese forces. Late in June we heard that the Special Forces camp of Ben Het was under siege and that American engineers and artillerymen were trapped there.

On June 26, 1969, the seventh anniversary of my arrival in Vietnam, I managed to visit the camp by hitching a trip on an American army helicopter out of Kontum, riding in with Ollie Noonan, a photographer freelancing for the AP, and TV correspondent Don Webster of CBS and his crew. The remote camp on a hill near the Laos border was a shambles of rusting barbed wire, rotting sandbags and muddy pathways, and we were barely through the main gates when the roar of exploding incoming mortar shells sent us cringing into a ditch for shelter.

The CBS team moved through the camp to interview the Special

Forces team, but Noonan and I stopped off at the American artillery battery on North Hill, where we were confronted by a dozen grimy, unshaven men who said they had been forgotten by headquarters and had been out of fresh water for five days and were drinking the cordite-flavored dusty liquid they caught in their ponchos in the monsoon downpours. Their angry complaints covered shortages of ammunition and food and lax security and were the most serious I had ever heard in Vietnam. The Americans felt they had been left hanging on a limb because the U.S. high command saw Ben Het as an opportunity for the South Vietnamese military to show responsibility and had chosen not to interfere.

The battery commander, Captain John Horalek, said that despite everything, they were trying to do their job, but morale was deteriorating. "If we weren't here to help the defenses, there would be nothing left of Ben Het," he said, as another flurry of incoming mortar rounds fell among his six self-propelled artillery tubes, and the hoarse cry of "Medic" could be heard. Soldiers peppered with metal fragments were carried or staggered in on their own to a murky bunker that served as the first-aid station. Under the light of a candle augmented by occasional flickers from a generator-driven lamp, Horalek and the medics worked over the wounded, hoping that the medical evacuation helicopters would not be too long in coming. Later as we were about to leave the artillerymen lost their last luxury: an incoming artillery shell disintegrated the bunker where they stored their twelve-inch black-and-white TV set.

The disenchantment in the camp seemed to reflect a wider crisis in confidence as America tried to pull out of the war, without seeking a solution or admitting defeat. I titled my story "The Forgotten Men of Ben Het" and tried to document the bitterness that pervaded the place. The chairman of the Joint Chiefs of Staff, General Earle Wheeler, complained personally about the story to Senator Harry Byrd, and he in turn passed on the complaint to Gallagher, who was satisfied with my account. The final word on the incident came from the Ben Het soldiers in a letter to me addressed to the AP in New York dated July 7:

"We the men of A Battery, Third Battalion, Sixth Artillery wish to express our deepest gratitude and thanks to a reporter who turns darkness into light. While you were at Battery A, though it was but for a short while, you saw our desperate situation. A few days after you left to publish your story we received mail and newspapers from home, and the men of A Battery finally got to read their own story.

261

You wouldn't believe how high our morale went, to know that the people back home knew the hell we were going through, to know that we were no longer the forgotten soldiers. This has given us new hope and faith in our country. Two days after you were first among us the results came pouring in; the results to us were comparable to the Berlin airlift, for we received tons and tons of munitions, supplies and the all but forgotten hot meals. Newsmen like yourself who fight their way into the hot spots to get the facts and then fight their way out again to get the news published deserve the faith and gratitude of the men of A Battery. Thank God for men with courage and stamina like yours."

The perception that the American military effort in Vietnam was disintegrating was made forever clear by the revelation of the My Lai massacre, and further by disturbing rumors of disobedience and drug abuse and the murder of some officers. Horst and I encountered an example of crumbling troop morale when we went on the cheerless mission of recovering the body of Ollie Noonan, who had been killed in a helicopter crash late August in the remote Song Chang Valley south of Da Nang.

Horst joined the Third Battalion of the 196th Light Infantry Brigade as it moved down the jungled, rocky slopes of the Nui Lon Mountain to the crash site. I remained at the battalion base camp at landing zone center on the ridge line above, with a radio to keep in touch with Horst, and report back to the Saigon bureau when Ollie's body was recovered. The battalion's A Company was spearheading the search. They had pushed through a labyrinth of North Vietnamese bunkers and trench lines, taking heavy casualties.

But after five days, the men finally had enough. Colonel Robert C. Bacon was ordering the company commander, Lieutenant Eugene Shurtz, Jr., to move forward to the objective. "I am sorry, sir, but my men refuse to go. We cannot move out," Shurtz radioed back. As Horst listened, Colonel Bacon asked, "Repeat that please, have you told them what it means to disobey orders under fire?"

The response came, "I think they understand but some of them have simply had enough, they are broken. There are boys here who have only ninety days left in Vietnam. They want to go home in one piece. The situation is psychic here."

Colonel Bacon broke in, "Are you talking about enlisted men or are the NCOs also involved?" and Lieutenant Shurtz responded, "That's the difficulty here, we've got a leadership problem; most of our squad and platoon leaders have been killed or wounded."

Colonel Bacon advised him quietly, "Go talk to them again and tell them that to the best of our knowledge the bunkers are now empty, the enemy has withdrawn. The mission of Company A is to recover the dead. They have no reason to be afraid. Please take a hand count of how many really do not want to go."

The lieutenant came back on the line a few minutes later. "They won't go, Colonel, and I did not ask for a hand count because I am afraid that they will all stick together even though some might prefer to go." The colonel finally ordered him, "Leave the men on the hill and take your command post element to the objective."

I was waiting at battalion headquarters when Colonel Bacon radioed for help, ordering two of his staff to the scene to talk sense into Company A, to, "Give 'em a pep talk and kick 'em in the butt." The emissaries were the battalion executive officer, Major Richard Waite, and a seasoned Vietnam veteran, Sergeant Okey Blankenship from Panther, West Virginia; they wouldn't take me along with them on the helicopter but agreed to talk with me afterward.

They found the infantrymen sitting exhausted in the blackened elephant grass, some with peace signs scratched on their helmets and others with beads around their necks. Their faces were bearded and their uniforms were ripped and caked with blood. One was weeping and others poured out their frustrations and explained why they wouldn't move, that they were sick of the endless battling through the jungle in the heat, the constant danger of sudden firefights by day, and the mortaring and enemy probing attacks at night. They said they were denied sleep and were being pushed too hard, that they hadn't had mail in weeks, and there was no hot food and the other little things that made patrolling bearable.

Sergeant Blankenship told me that he looked at the eighteen- and nineteen-year-olds, becoming aware that there was a generation of difference between them not only in age but in attitude. One young man argued that his unit had suffered too much and should not have to go on. But Blankenship, a quick-tempered man, responded angrily with a white lie—another infantry company was down to fifteen men and was still on the move. When someone asked why they were doing it he responded, "Maybe they have got something a little more than what you have."

The soldier shouted angrily, "Don't call us cowards, we are not cowards," and ran toward the sergeant with his fists raised. Blankenship turned his back and walked down the bomb-scarred ridge line to where Lieutenant Shurtz waited disconsolately. He looked back and saw that the men of Company A were stirring, picking up their rifles and falling into a loose formation and following him down the cratered slope and back into the war.

Company A reached the helicopter crash site later in the day and recovered the bodies of Ollie Noonan and the others. Horst and I flew out to the U.S. base at Chu Lai and I scribbled the story in my notebook while Horst attempted to get the AP Saigon bureau on the phone. When he finally got through I was able to dictate a thousand words on the travails of Company A. The story touched a nerve in America. There was considerable editorial comment about what columnist James Reston called the "whiff of mutiny" in the army and the need finally to end the killing of American boys in Vietnam and bring them all home.

Lieutenant Shurtz was relieved of command of Company A but not formally charged and was assigned to duties of less responsibility in the division. No action was taken against any of his men. But the story of the reluctant soldiers of Company A was becoming the story of the war.

Clashing with Gallagher

FIFTEEN MONTHS AFTER Richard Nixon took office, he authorized the invasion of Cambodia. He not only surprised protesters in the United States, he astounded the Saigon press corps by departing from the long-held strategy of limiting the ground war to Vietnam. On the first day of the invasion, May 1, 1970, I flew to Cambodia with the Vietnamese regional commander, General Do Cao Tri, in his Huey helicopter. By noon the dust trails from the armored vehicles below were twenty miles over the border, advancing across the expanses of rubber plantations and rice fields.

General Tri was a flamboyant young officer who wore a red beret and carried a swagger stick under his arm. He was well regarded as a field commander, and more important, he was fond of showing off to Western reporters. In midafternoon he swooped down on a Vietnamese tank column stalled by snipers and demanded that they get moving. He assumed command of the lead vehicle, scrambling on top of the armored personnel carrier, pointing his stick toward the sniper positions in a small farmhouse ahead, and shouting the order to charge. Only when he was forty yards ahead of everyone else did he realize that his had been the only vehicle to move forward. He ordered a halt and scrambled down into the gun turret until the others caught up with him.

The border region was not guarded by the Cambodian government and had long been identified as a base area for the communist side. It was frequently penetrated by South Vietnamese forces. The previous week I had joined Steve Bell of ABC News and his crew on Route 1 looking for a South Vietnamese infantry battalion we thought was ahead of us. We had driven until we came to the Cambodian provincial capital of Svay Rieng. It was deserted and looked dangerous so we drove back the way we had come.

But the full-scale invasion had clearly caught the communists by surprise and they had fallen back toward the interior jungles, leaving behind underground storehouses of rice and ammunition and weapons. The initial resistance was so weak that a picnic atmosphere prevailed among American forces. At one forward fire base in the "Fishhook" zone of operations I signed autographs for young officers who had recently arrived in Vietnam and recognized my name from news dispatches. The controversial Cambodian invasion was the biggest story in Vietnam since the Tet Offensive. Competition was keen to meet the demands of newspaper editors anxious to illustrate this first major crisis of the Nixon administration. Reporters and photographers spilled across the war zones in search of scoops.

On May 3, I climbed aboard a U.S. Air Force C-130 transport plane at Tan Son Nhut Airport, headed toward Loc Ninh, that was so loaded with American soldiers that we took off standing up in rows holding guide ropes strung across the cabin. We encountered serious monsoon turbulence that bucked and rolled the aircraft leaving most of the passengers, including me, vomiting up their breakfast.

Later, I jumped off a helicopter at a Vietnamese Ranger forward base and was confronted by a sweating, bare-chested American officer who was obviously suffering battle fatigue. In a string of shouted obscenities, he told me what he thought of the press and he pulled out his .45 and placed it to my temple and demanded that I leave immediately. Luckily I was saved by a few Vietnamese officers. I was convinced I had been next in line for execution.

Under the circumstances, I was happy to be taken away by a medical evacuation helicopter to an American armored task force that had been stalled outside the town of Snuol by entrenched communist troops and was waiting for air strikes to clear the way ahead. The unit commander said the tank column had been forced to retreat from Snuol earlier in the day and would counterattack in the morning. "I was told to come in here Monday because this was a hub of North Vietnamese activity; it is a crossroads for them, for their supply line. We have no choice but to take it." The colonel even allowed me to use his helicopter to roundtrip it to Loc Ninh to file a story on the developing battle. By evening I had returned to prepare for the morning attack.

At daybreak a wave of air strikes crashed through the rubber trees and into the town a mile ahead of us. Red dust from the rubble and black smoke from the tires billowed into the sky. During a break in the assault we were joined by Leon Daniels of UPI and an NBC crew and at 9 A.M. we climbed aboard tanks and moved forward down the road. The troops were tense, not certain that the communist defenders had fled even though all agreed that the air strikes were so devastating that few could have survived.

Snuol was only two city blocks in size. Probably once it had been picturesque with its few tree-lined streets and flowers in the front gardens, but all the two-story concrete homes and stores had been destroyed by the bombing and only a line of wooden shops remained, the doors padlocked and the windows barred. The Americans relaxed and began searching through the ruins and I saw one soldier run from a burning Chinese noodle shop with his arms full of Cambodian brandy. A Vietnamese interpreter was behind him dragging a case of sodas to a tank. We watched other soldiers smash open the doors to the remaining shops, pocketing clocks and watches and carrying out electrical equipment before setting the buildings ablaze. One soldier carried a suitcase filled with new shoes to his tank and two others wheeled out motorcycles and tied them to the turrets of their vehicles. After about an hour of looting and merrymaking an officer came by and yelled, "Get your hands off that stuff, we're moving on." The soldiers laughed and mounted their vehicles.

I was shocked by the spectacle. For the previous decade the excesses of the South Vietnamese Army in the field had been a constant worry to their U.S. advisers. Now Americans were disregarding the basic rule of counterinsurgency warfare that you don't abuse the civilian population. The worst habits of the student were being adopted by the teacher. There was another scene that was seared on my brain in Snuol. The unit commander told me that he was under the impression that all the civilians had left before the fighting began, yet at the mouth of a large bunker in the town square were the remains of a woman and a young child and two men, their bodies fused together by the fire of an explosion, probably a napalm bomb.

Leon Daniels and I hitched a ride out in the early afternoon in a supply helicopter that headed south and set down in Tay Ninh. There was a U.S. Army Caribou transport plane already revving up its engines to fly to Saigon, and by late afternoon we were in a taxi heading through city streets to our offices. We didn't say much to each other on the ride home. I knew Daniels was busy planning his story. He was a skilled reporter with a reputation for a colorful turn of phrase. I knew I had my hands full that day. The taxi stopped at my office first. I said goodbye and walked nonchalantly into the building but as the taxi disappeared around the corner I bolted for the elevator and was soon at my typewriter. I wrote the story with plenty of detail and immediately it came clattering back over the international wire. To go with the article, Horst radioed three photographs I had taken at Snuol in plenty of time to make the morning newspapers in the United States. I headed home exhausted.

I slept late and was back in the office around noon. The staff did not offer their usual greetings. I knew something was very wrong when Horst came over to me, put his arm around my shoulders and said, "I can understand it if you quit." The current bureau chief, Dave Mason, handed me a message from foreign editor Ben Bassett that spelled out New York's unhappiness with my reporting. I was used to this attitude from the authorities but never expected it from the AP. Bassett's message read, "We are in the midst of a highly charged situation in the United States regarding Southeast Asia and must guard our copy to see that it is down the middle and subdues emotion. Specifically today we took looting and similar references out of Arnett copy because we don't think it's especially news that such things take place in war and in present context this can be inflammatory."

Kent State was the "present context" Bassett was referring to. Four students had been shot and killed by the Ohio National Guard. My colleague Richard Pyle was looking at me, waiting. I was known to have a fiery temper when roused and surely this was reason enough to be furious.

I did not explode. I knew the decision had been made hastily. I had lost the battle but hoped to win the war. Somehow, I would make clear to the AP the significance of all we had done in Vietnam over the long years, from Browne's battles with the Diem administration, through the histrionic days of LBJ and the deaths of our staffers.

The Saigon staff couldn't believe that we were being ordered to depart from decade-long news guidelines. Dave Mason phoned Gallagher and told him that there was a "crisis of confidence" in the bureau.

I sent my own bitter cry from the heart: "I was professionally insulted by New York's decision to kill all my story and picture references to the Snuol looting on grounds that it was inflammatory and not news. I was also personally upset by the suggestion of foreign editor Bassett that this was emotional reporting. To ignore the sordid aspects of America's invasion of Cambodia would surely be a dereliction of a reporter's duty and I find it impossible now to compromise my reporting to suit American political interests. I intend to continue to report the war the way it is and will leave the responsibility suppressing the news with New York." To make matters worse, Leon Daniels's story, which included the looting, ran all across America and was used by the *Washington Post* as its lead editorial on the banality of Vietnam policy.

I leaked the story to Kevin Buckley of *Newsweek* magazine to force the AP into the open, and the following week an article appeared in the magazine that quoted Gallagher as admitting he had made an "error in judgment."

Gallagher said six years later when he retired from the AP that spiking my story was one of the biggest mistakes he had made.

End of the Obsession

AFTER THE CAMBODIAN INVASION, I felt my detachment toward Vietnam cracking as I watched the administration expand the war. I feared that I would no longer be an unbiased observer, that my reporter's values were swamped in the bloodshed. Like others who had become disenchanted before me, I felt anger that the war seemed impervious to solution, that the reporting and terrible sacrifices seemed to do so little to end it. I wanted to leave. I was ready.

Horst seemed to feel the same way, and we decided that we would leave together, just as we had arrived together more than eight years earlier. Nina was eager to live in New York City, where she had once been a medical librarian, but the AP had other ideas, suggesting that we move to Hong Kong or, as Gallagher told me, "Somewhere in the British Commonwealth like Canada to accommodate your nationality." But Nina would not give up, and I had ambitions, born out of the success of colleagues like David Halberstam and Neil Sheehan, who were building substantial careers.

The AP eventually acceded to our request, and we made plans to leave. I was eager that Horst and I continue the collaboration that had served us so well and suggested we team up permanently, but the AP was not interested in that idea and Horst was in the end unwilling to break the ties that bound him to Asia. He decided to move to Singapore. There was a final group picture with the whole AP staff and a champagne-drenched farewell at the airport. And then we were gone for good, I thought.

I left Saigon in the summer of 1970 believing that at thirty-six my war-reporting days were over. We stayed over in Hong Kong for a week where I ordered some new suits. I had them made two sizes larger than usual to fit what I assumed would be my more portly presence on the less hectic New York scene. I startled the AP head office by checking my family into the Pierre Hotel on Fifth Avenue in Manhattan, a place I had been led to believe was a small French-style lodging but which turned out to be a more desirable and much more expensive residence, as we realized on our arrival when we rode up in the elevator with Tricia Nixon, the president's daughter.

The AP personnel chief, Keith Fuller, sat in our lavish suite sipping a Scotch and soda with a bemused look on his face. "I've often wondered what this place really looked like inside," he said. We stayed a short while at the Pierre before renting a comfortable apartment in Riverdale. Some news colleagues from Saigon were my neighbors, and we endeavored to settle into a life without the war.

Wes Gallagher had warned me that I would "take a bath" financially by leaving the easygoing lifestyle of Southeast Asia for the United States, and he was right. I had to pay income taxes for the first time in my life and master the mysteries of commuting to work and functioning in a professional environment. Tom Buckley, back at the *New*

York Times in New York, wrote me, "Welcome to the only city in the world that's tougher to live in than Saigon." The AP headquarters was located at 50 Rockefeller Plaza. The fourth floor was devoted entirely to the gathering and dissemination of news, where pale-faced editors pored over copy on around-the-clock shifts. Sometimes I would walk over to the foreign desk, where a bank of telex machines brought in raw news from the AP's overseas bureaus and I would peek at the Saigon stories, just to be certain that nothing much had changed.

Gallagher decided that my first assignment should be to write a series of stories on the United States, and he asked Horst to come over from Singapore for three months to take the pictures. Horst and I approached our "Meeting with America" assignment as we had covered the war: we rented a car in San Francisco and followed our instincts. In our first few days we visited hippies in the Haight-Ashbury district and talked with winos on skid row and met with the Indian activists illegally occupying Alcatraz prison. We intended to prepare regular dispatches but quickly ran into trouble with Gallagher, who did not like my first report. His message was: "Stay out of skid rows and Indian reservations, that's not the America I want you to meet."

We ignored his advice. In our three months of travel we were able to photograph more raw beauty and meet more upstanding citizens than I had imagined. I compiled twenty-seven notebooks of interviews.

Sorting all our material into a readable series took the efforts of several news and photo editors and led to much argument and debate. Two days before the series was to begin, Gallagher called me to his office. He had invested a lot of money and a lot of staff into the series and it had not turned out the way he had expected. He seemed particularly bothered by the opening paragraphs of the main Sunday story that I began in the form of a letter: "Dear Horst, We were one hundred days older when our tour of the United States ended, experts on motel bathrooms, rental cars and airline schedules. But how much had we really learned? I remembered your comments at the end: 'Good luck, you'll need it,' you said shaking your head and my hand simultaneously as a chill wind whipped across Rockefeller Plaza in New York. You had finished your pictures and you were heading back to Indochina that night to cover the war. But you sounded sorry for me because I was staying in America, where to your mind the concrete jungles contain a more dangerous yield of uncertainties and insecurities than the green jungles of Vietnam."

Gallagher did not tell me so directly but I believe he had expected Horst and me to be more positive about the States, more optimistic.

But he said, "It's not your fault, I just should not have assigned you to a story like this." I hastened to reassure him. "Wes, it's out of our hands now, but I think America's newspaper editors are more realistic about your country than you think." Late Sunday morning I drove down the West Side Highway to the Forty-second Street exit and found the magazine store in Times Square that sold out-of-town newspapers. I searched through the Sunday editions from around the country to see how cordial America's editors were to foreigners who criticized their country. The *Boston Globe* played the story on page one, and so did the *Indianapolis Star* and the *Binghamton Press*. I drove over to AP headquarters, where they were compiling a log of the story usage: the front pages in Houston, Omaha, and Lincoln, Nebraska, Tulsa; in the feature sections in Chicago, Philadelphia, Kansas and Detroit.

Gallagher, however, was still not sure what to do with me. He assigned me to the News Features Department, a privileged enclave of talented writers on the sixth floor. I enjoyed the company of Saul Pett and Hugh Mulligan and other witty colleagues, but I just couldn't stand the slow pace of the place. One of the news features reporters scolded me one day for typing too fast. "You're creating a precedent," he complained.

My first assignment was to compile a feature story on the state of the American magazine. Os Elliot, editor of *Newsweek,* sat through one of my interviews, then exclaimed impatiently, "What the hell are you doing stories like this for, Arnett? You're an action reporter."

My growing discomfort reached Gallagher, who called me into his office one day and told me I wasn't working out well and assigned me to the general desk on the fourth floor, reporting to the senior news executives. The clatter of telex machines made me feel better and I had genuine news assignments, including the prison rebellion at Attica in upper New York state. Helicopters came in with combat troops and the bullets were flying and the casualties mounted up like in a war, thirty prisoners and ten hostages dead in just four minutes. It felt familiar.

In October of 1971 Gallagher named me a special correspondent, "In recognition of the fact that you are showing the same high competence as a domestic reporter that you did in the foreign service." I folded up my oversized Hong Kong suits and packed them in a trunk for a later time; I did not intend to be gaining any extra weight in this new job.

271

Journey to the Other Side

I HAD FOLLOWED THE COURSE of the war with continuing interest and was eager to get back when Gallagher sent me to Saigon early in 1972. I covered a new military assault by the North Vietnamese that had slashed across the Demilitarized Zone and the Central Highlands and become known as the Easter Offensive. By this time all American combat troops had been phased out of battle and sent home; the Cambodian invasion two years earlier had increased political pressure on the Nixon administration to end American fighting in the war. Only supply and support units remained. Attempts had been made in Paris for three years to negotiate a settlement but they had failed, and U.S. military advisers were still in the field with Vietnamese troops; still risking—and losing—their lives.

The press concentrated on covering the few Americans that remained and tended to congregate around the most amenable officers, just as in the earliest days of the war. One such soldier was Lieutenant Colonel Burr M. Willey, who was advising Vietnamese forces on Route 13 north of Saigon as they attempted to drive attacking communist troops from the An Loc region. I made the hour-long drive up Route 13 every day to the battle area to visit Willey, and it was not unusual at times to see a dozen of the best-known news byliners in Vietnam with their faces in roadside ditches hiding from mortar and shelling attacks.

On June 19, Colonel Willey walked into an exploding rocket as Moose, his gray mongrel dog, trotted behind him. Both were killed. His death seemed pointless to me, given the circumstances of America's withdrawal, which made it clear that Vietnam was of little strategic importance to the United States. A few days later John Paul Vann died in a helicopter crash near Kontum, a decade after I had first met him in the Mekong Delta. I had watched his dire predictions come true and his stature rise until he had become the senior American in the Central Highlands region. I had lost my best news source and also a good friend and I had difficulty coming to terms with his death. Two weeks earlier, Vann had flown me in his Huey helicopter from Pleiku to Qui Nhon on the central coast. He had circled the steep hills around the Mang Yang Pass, where the French combat unit Group Mobile 100 had been destroyed in a historic ambush by the Vietminh in 1953.

He had told me, "If I die here I want to be buried in Vietnam like the dead Frenchmen were, standing up and facing home." But Vann was buried at Arlington National Cemetery just outside Washington, D.C., with full military honors. And the press was continuing to take casualties in Vietnam and Cambodia. My photographer friends Larry Burrows of *Life* magazine and Koichi Sawada of UPI were among the dead.

My 1972 assignment stretched into seven grueling months covering and assessing the military situation in both Vietnam and Cambodia. The United States finally negotiated a settlement with the North Vietnamese, in public and also in secret, and officials were suggesting it would be in place before the November presidential elections.

Nothing had yet come of the talks when I was on my way home in September. I spent a weekend in Paris, where Henry Kissinger was rumored to be negotiating secretly with the North Vietnamese official Le Duc Tho. I had enjoyed the view from the balcony of my room in the Claridge Hotel on the Champs-Elysées, had eaten a fine dinner and was sleeping, when the AP foreign desk supervisor called me from New York at 4 A.M. Paris time with urgent instructions to telephone Gallagher. I knew my brief vacation was over; the call had to be something important because our executives rarely allowed themselves to be disturbed over the weekend. Gallagher got straight to the point. "Do you want to go to Hanoi?"

I breathed in sharply. Despite the hour I felt the familiar surge. Hanoi was the stubborn hub of a war effort that had defied the most powerful nation on earth for a decade. Few Westerners had ever visited it. It was still a mystery. Gallagher explained that three American prisoners of war were to be released in Hanoi to an antiwar delegation as a goodwill gesture, and I had been invited to join the group as the sole journalist. Clearly the communists were making a public gesture to influence the peace talks. He told me to get home immediately, talk with the sponsors and then report to him. He said he had grave reservations about the project and the people involved. The State Department was critical, fearful that a private initiative might threaten the peace process.

I left Paris on the first TWA flight, realizing that if the trip came off I would be an eyewitness to the beginning of the end of the war. Though the U.S. government was suspicious of the venture, the release of American prisoners would be seen as evidence that the North Vietnamese were willing to compromise on the central issue of the peace negotiations, the fate of the many American POWs.

273

I arrived in midafternoon and took a taxi to Waldo Avenue in Riverdale to the home of Cora Weiss, who, with other antiwar activists, would make the journey to Hanoi. Two members of the delegation, peace activist David Dellinger and Yale University chaplain Rev. William Sloan Coffin, were national figures. Mrs. Weiss was less publicly known. But I knew right away that she was the inspiration for the journey. "You are on trial here," she told me bluntly after she led me to the dining room, where her three young children sat and her husband, Peter, was preparing pizza.

Cora Weiss was a handsome woman with curly brown hair and a bright smile that could twist quickly into scorn. The phone in the kitchen rang often. Cora told me that it was bugged by the FBI and other government institutions. "In Martha's Vineyard [where she had a home] the tap was so loud the phone spluttered and jumped on the hook all night long, and imagine that when you're lying in bed with your husband," she said. She had protested to a State Department security officer, who told her, "That's not my bug, mine's not so powerful, that's Laird's." Melvin Laird was secretary of defense.

Cora told me that her group had originally invited CBS correspondent Mike Wallace. When he turned it down they had offered the trip to *New York Times* reporter Gloria Emerson, but she told them she could not guarantee extensive coverage. Gloria had recommended me. Informing me that I had been their third choice, she said, "They tell me you're a good reporter, a fair reporter, but with us you also have to be an agreeable companion; we have a long way to travel."

She said that if I was chosen, I would have to be a member of the official party to satisfy North Vietnamese bureaucratic regulations. The group, I learned, would include Minnie Lee Gartley, the mother of one of the navy pilots to be released, and Olga Charles, the wife of another pilot. Under the circumstances, I would have unprecedented access to all the participants and their activities.

Cora thrashed out a set of ground rules that would allow me to function professionally without violating their privacy. "I mean I don't want you talking to the CIA and I don't want you endangering any future prisoner exchanges, do I?" she said. "I don't expect your political sympathy for our cause but I would expect your personal sympathy for what we are doing."

I asked her what stories I could expect to write and she responded, "An accurate, full account of the journey." I was desperate to go. I tried to persuade Cora that I was both professional and amiable. After two hours of conversation I seemed to have convinced Cora, her children and her husband, but she insisted on one more requirement, a meeting with David Dellinger. He would make the final decision that night.

I was aware of Dellinger's fervent anti-establishment stance and I half expected a confrontation, but he turned out to be a gentle man with a wry sense of humor. When he came to my apartment, I offered him a beer, which he glady accepted. He had just come off a long antiwar fast. After a short conversation he said he felt that accurate, honest coverage by an independent newsman would be in the best interests of everyone on the trip and he agreed I should go. He only wondered how the North Vietnamese would react. Next day Wes Gallagher counseled me to be cautious about how I acted and what I wrote. Both Anthony Lewis of the *New York Times* and Jane Fonda had incurred storms of criticism on their visits to Hanoi earlier in the year. Wes looked at me from under furrowed brows: "Peter, it's your reputation and mine on the line this time."

Cora Weiss impressed upon me the need for secrecy in all arrangements. She was convinced that the FBI and other government security agencies would try to thwart them. She was so concerned about telephone taps that she handled most of her arrangements by written note, particularly with travel agents, who were asked to use pay phones. She had agreed with the North Vietnamese to escort the three released pilots all the way back to the United States, but she was worried that the U.S. Defense Department would intervene and try to gain custody of the pilots somewhere during the return journey home. Thus she devised an unusual route back, from Hanoi through Beijing and Moscow, and then Copenhagen en route home to New York.

To win acceptance, I ordered champagne for all as we lifted off from Kennedy Airport, and I kept it flowing for the rest of the trip. The group included Richard Falk, an expert on international law who revealed a quiet wit. Reverend Coffin was an energetic, boisterous traveling companion who believed the American antiwar movement enjoyed a unique entrée to the North Vietnamese. "We are closer to them than either the Russians or the Chinese because we want the war to end, and they know it."

We flew the final leg of our journey aboard the regular International Control Commission flight from Vientiane, climbing over the purple hills of Laos and across the bomb-pitted river valleys of North Vietnam to a bumpy landing at Giam Lam Airport on the outskirts of Hanoi.

Our plane was the only one on the ground. The terminal buildings were modest and rural, in stark contrast to the sprawling complex of hangars and maintenance buildings and terminals at Saigon's Tan Son Nhut, at one time the world's busiest airport. We were met by a small delegation of Vietnamese officials who came out to the aircraft accompanied by soldiers with red stars on their pith helmets and AK-47 assault rifles over their shoulders.

When the plane doors opened I dashed from the aircraft to the terminal building and began typing a news bulletin about our arrival on my portable typewriter. I had noticed correspondent Richard Dudman of the *St. Louis Post Dispatch* about to leave and figured that he could be my courier. Vietnamese officials and security troops gathered around me in surprise as I typed and made a half-hearted effort to stop me from handing my dispatch to Dudman, insisting they read it first, but the plane was about to leave and Dudman placed it in his jacket pocket and boarded for the return flight to Vientiane.

Sheltered in a sandbagged bunker at the airport from a distant bombing raid, Cora Weiss upbraided me politely, explaining that I was now officially part of the delegation and we were required to follow procedures. I agreed to be more considerate, but I felt that in my determination to be a reporter first and an emissary second I had won the first round.

The drama of traveling to an enemy capital was an engrossing news story, though a few reporters had already broken ground in that department. But I had additional emotional elements: the release to our care of three American POWs who had been held in the notorious "Hanoi Hilton" prison, and the presence of the mother of one of them and the wife of another, who were trembling with happiness but concerned about the dangers of visiting a war zone.

Security men ordered us into roadside shelters twice in the two-mile drive into Hanoi because of distant American air strikes, and there were two more alerts on that first afternoon after we checked into the Hoa Binh Hotel. Olga Charles's flowery silk dress was soiled and crumpled from the dirt of the shelters when she arrived at the hotel and she was about to step into a bath a little later when the alert sirens sent her in a bathrobe down the labyrinth of back rooms and corridors to a concrete basement room for shelter. As we sat there she said, "And I was silly enough to think that Washington would stop bombing while we were here."

I was assigned a young woman named Lien as an escort when I left the hotel for a walk around the city. She complained to me of getting too little to eat. She blamed the American bombing for cutting off the supply from the countryside. The hardships made her look older than her years, and when I asked her if she had a boyfriend and if she wanted to get married, she said no to both questions: she was practicing "the three delays, delay love, delay marriage, delay babies," until the war was over.

Hanoi looked as worn as she did; dust seemed to have settled over the city like a plastic wrapper, sealing in the past. The grand old French colonial buildings were tidy but faded. In the little shops in the densely populated quarters, the paint was peeling off the walls and the timbers were rotting. An old French tram clanked along as bicycles meandered by. The few automobiles honking through the streets were relics from Soviet Union used-car lots.

The people were dressed in somber garments, usually black trousers and white or gray shirts and blouses. I thought of Saigon, where I had been just a week before, a city that wore the veneer of a desert vacation boom town with flashy motorcycles, sporty cars, perfume, hair spray and sharp differences on the streets between the rich and poor. The barmaid at the Hoa Binh Hotel told me that she owned only one white blouse and one pair of black trousers, "And I wash them each night to wear the next day." I thought of the maids I employed in Saigon who wore silk ao-dai dresses and carried beaded handbags.

For the most part, the people of Saigon lived with a war that was distant in the countryside. In Hanoi the war came screeching in on the wings of fighter-bombers. I noticed a large billboard in the main city square with a map of South Vietnam emblazoned with red victory stars over the battle zones and I realized with a start that a similar map decorated Saigon's Lam Son Square and claimed victories in the same places. I could see fear tearing at Hanoi with the first squawks of the loudspeaker systems hanging from the main street intersections. People would look urgently for a shelter as they listened to the voice proclaiming, "American planes seventy kilometers out." Soon afterward, the announcement, "American planes fifty kilometers out." Then the sirens wailed when the attacking aircraft were within forty kilometers. People searched out individual bunkers built like cisterns along every street, or were pushed by wardens into larger, roomier shelters beside Reunification Lake in the heart of the city. Then a quiet would settle over the city, a silence as people waited to see how close the bombers would come.

My wife Nina's siblings lived in Hanoi; a younger brother about my age was a math teacher in the grade school system with a wife and young family, and an older sister worked as a medical doctor in the military services. Another brother living in Hanoi had died several years ago from illness. They had been left behind eighteen years earlier when Nina's family had fled south. Nina was worried that the communist authorities would learn the two were related by marriage to me, and would receive unwelcome attention. She feared it would endanger her relatives to be even remotely connected with a foreigner. During a reception soon after I arrived in Hanoi a middle-aged Vietnamese man introduced himself as an assistant at the Indian Embassy and said he knew my brother-in-law. I quietly asked him to pass on my regards. (But it would not be for four more years, on a return visit to Hanoi after the war was over, that I was able to contact him directly, and then only for an instant—by photographing him and his daughter as they rode a bicycle past a prearranged spot near the post office. That's how suspicious the communist authorities remained of foreign bonds with their citizens.)

We received the three American pilots at a large press conference the day after our arrival, in a hall crowded with reporters and television cameras from communist news organizations. The event was produced to gain the maximum propaganda. The pilots appeared on stage smiling, in newly made suits, spoke appreciatively of their captors and hoped that their release would soon lead to peace. Both Minnie Gartley and Olga Charles had spent the morning at a beauty salon in downtown Hanoi. Mrs. Gartley embraced her tall blond son, Lieutenant Mark Gartley, who had been imprisoned for four years. Olga Charles kissed her husband, Lieutenant Norris Charles, who had been ten months in captivity. The third pilot, Air Force Major Edward Elias, was the most recent of the captives, shot down four months earlier, and he had been expecting his wife or father to greet him. He seemed disappointed. I was his consolation prize and we were bunked together at the hotel. Major Elias was the most reserved of the three and became even quieter when he read his mail and learned how controversial this trip had become, and that his family had not traveled to Hanoi because of Defense Department objections. I think he was unsettled having a correspondent pounding out news stories in his room late into the night, but he kept his concerns to himself. After a few days Major Elias became more talkative and told me about prison life and how he had compared dreams with his buddies. For the first two months of captivity no one dreamed at all. In the third month they began to dream of food. And after the fourth month they dreamed of sex.

On a field trip we traveled the path Jane Fonda and former U.S. Attorney General Ramsey Clark had taken earlier in the year, driving south to Nam Dinh city and the Phat Diem Cathedral, both heavily bombed by American planes. As we bumped along narrow highways in the dark hours before dawn, all the clichés about communist Vietnam's "ant power" and the unique adaptability of the people to adversity came alive before our eyes. Where bombs had scored direct hits on railway cars or on the tracks paralleling the road, we could see dark shapes of people hammering at twisted wreckage. Others carried filler material and dumped it into the bomb craters. As dawn came and we passed through the railroad junction of Phu Ly we saw that the dark shapes were women. They weren't even using buckets; they were carrying the mud in their bare hands to fill the craters. When the old Russian Volga sedan we were traveling in bogged down at one point, women swarmed out of the mud and gathered around us, laughing and pointing and pushing us on our way. Major Elias rode alongside me, and it was an education to see the countryside through his eyes, an experienced American pilot who had flown reconnaissance regularly.

"See those grave mounds over there?" Elias asked as we waited for a ferry to cross a river whose bridge had been destroyed. I saw a bucolic scene with cows grazing on the gently rolling land. "They're anti-aircraft pits with the muzzles down," Elias said. "Let a plane come over and they'll stick up their snoots and blast away. And those things are difficult to spot in pictures. It would take an expert and a very lucky photo interpreter to see them." As we sped into the rising sun, Elias's head turned left and right. "See that flak site? They're 85s. There's another one, half a dozen .50 calibers." To me they all looked like banana trees.

What was startling to the pilots was the extent of North Vietnam's visible supply chain, manifest evidence that the years of American bombing had failed in its goal. From the time we left Hanoi at four o'clock one morning, until our return at eight o'clock the next night, we repeatedly encountered vehicle convoys, rows of stacked ammunition alongside the roadsides, and piles of full gasoline drums. During daylight hours we passed scores of transportation trucks casually parked under trees. They looked vulnerable but Norris Charles told me, "We could never see those things from the air and the moment someone comes down to get a better look, blam blam, man." Mark Gartley recalled flying over the area the previous year: it had seemed uninhabited when it was actually teeming with life. Elias remarked that it was technology against ideology: "I just wonder how far technology can go because the Vietnamese habitually beat it."

A day after our return to Hanoi the North Vietnamese official I knew as Mr. Lieu waved me to a table at the corner of the Hoa Binh Hotel lobby. He was clutching three copies of the news dispatch I had filed eight hours earlier on the field trip. Normally Mr. Lieu wore a broad smile and spoke Vietnamese but now he was grim-faced and used broken but identifiable English, in short, staccato bursts.

"Mr. Arnett," he began, "you know you are perfectly free to write anything you wish about the Democratic Republic of Vietnam. However in this message there are some references that disturb us greatly," and so began an hour-long haggle over the dispatch, which he insisted put too much emphasis on the negative. "You have suggested that we forced the pilots to make statements condemning the damage," he said. I saw that was the interpretation he had put on my reference to the constant presence of government photographers and radio reporters, and the queries from provincial officials and from people who said they were bombing victims who asked group members loaded questions like, "What do you say about this destruction by your imperialistic government?"

I finally narrowed down Mr. Lieu's area of concern to two passages in my dispatch. In one I had written that local officials seemed to be pushing the questioning too far and were upsetting the American women. In the other, I quoted Mark Gartley; he felt the North Vietnamese were disappointed when he did not publicly condemn the war. I finally agreed to delete the reference to pushing, because Mr. Lieu interpreted this literally as meaning forcing, but I insisted that Gartley's quote remain. Mr. Lieu was apparently satisfied with his small victory and shook my hand and said the dispatch would be telegraphed to the Paris bureau of the AP immediately. Similar negotiations surrounded each of the stories I wrote but the North Vietnamese did not insist on any changes that would have compromised professional standards.

Communications from war-torn Hanoi to the outside world were limited to a few hours a day, to Paris and Hong Kong. My long dispatches tended to accumulate at the post and telegraph office and when I complained about the delays, Miss Lien told me, "Firstly, you send far too much, and secondly this is an agricultural society not an industrial one so don't expect marvels from us."

One afternoon we were granted a meeting with Prime Minister

Pham Van Dong at his official residence near Ho Chi Minh's tomb. We sipped tea and talked for an hour, and afterward we walked briskly around the grounds together oblivious to the late-afternoon heat. I was interested in the cordiality between the members of the antiwar group and the Vietnamese leader. Caught up in the spirit of the moment, Premier Dong even clasped my hand and praised my reporting from the war front, although I doubt he could have seen much of it.

Later, back at the hotel, I discussed with Cora Weiss the irony that she and her party trusted the North Vietnamese government's views on the war more than their own. Cora responded that America's policies were opposed to world peace and that the future of Vietnam should be entirely in the hands of the Vietnamese; America had no right being there and that total withdrawal from the war effort was the only solution.

Before we left Hanoi, we were summoned hurriedly to a downtown government building and into a bare room set up with rows of chairs and with bottles of local beer and glasses on the large coffee table. Seven Americans came in dressed in prison garb, with their hands outstretched and faces beaming. They bear-hugged us and shouted greetings. They were a few of the more than four hundred American pilots known to be held in Hanoi and they all wanted to go home. They could hardly contain their feelings, and talk spilled out—letters from their families, prison life, criticisms of the war. They were all willing to attack their own government's policies. I had no idea how many other prisoners felt the same way, or the constraints they were under. The conversation flowed on. The beer glasses clinked and you could almost forget that these men were prisoners until you realized that even though you could touch them across the table the gulf was immeasurable. We would leave that room and climb on a plane for home. They were hostages to peace negotiations that neither side was willing to conclude. A North Vietnamese official soon stood up and announced that our plane was departing. The prisoners drained their glasses and were gone.

The journey back home with the freed pilots was, in a political sense, as perilous as the flights that had originally got them captured.

Beijing was our first layover; it was made clear that we were not entirely welcome. We were placed in a bus and driven to a modest hotel for an overnight stay. We were told not to leave our rooms and guards were placed in the corridors to enforce the restriction. But Beijing was cool to Washington, distant from the Pentagon, and thus safe.

Cora saw Moscow as the first danger point because of the cordial relations between President Nixon and the Soviet leader, Leonid Brezhnev. She was worried that the Soviets would allow the pilots to be claimed by U.S. officials and flown home independently, deflating the balloon of publicity that I, in part, had created.

During a stopover at the Siberian city of Novosibirsk an In-Tourist guide boarded with the information that a delegation of American Embassy officials would be meeting our plane when it landed in Moscow. Cora expected them to immediately demand that the pilots turn themselves over.

Everyone gathered in the airport coffee shop to confer on a plan of action. At first, Major Elias had been adamant about obeying orders: when we left Hanoi he had told everyone, "I will go with the first American official who requests it." Mark Gartley was influenced by his mother, and thus was the most cooperative pilot. Norris Charles and Olga generally avoided the debate. Richard Falk, the lawyer among us, was of the opinion that none of the pilots were at the time legally bound to follow the orders of a superior officer and would therefore not be obligated to respond to embassy officials if they did not wish to do so. But that was only his opinion. The fliers worried that refusing a direct order to report to the American Embassy was a military offense. The issue was a cloudy one. In the end lawyer Falk won everyone over.

The Moscow international airport was usually one of the most secure installations in the world, but on that evening the Soviet authorities had unaccountably withdrawn the guards. We stepped off the plane into the boisterous embrace of the international press corps, assorted Western officials, airline executives and bystanders who milled around us shouting and pushing. I recognized Murray Fromson of CBS News in the crowd and I felt him clutch at my shoulder as he yelled a question I could not hear in the roar. We surged toward a terminal entranceway and were jammed in a corridor when I heard my name spoken in a deep voice and turned and saw Brigadier General Sam Wilson, the American Embassy military attaché I had known in Vietnam. He invited me to spend the night in the comfort of the embassy but I remembered Cora's injunction to avoid confiding in the authorities and I turned him down.

An official who described himself as the American chargé d'affaires attempted to block the path of the pilots but was pushed aside by Coffin. Falk glared at the official and shouted, "You have no legal right to order these men around on foreign soil," and then we were all swept further into the terminal, until we ended up in the SAS airline office. The embassy official explained that he had been instructed to offer the pilots a comfortable ride home on a U.S. Air Force aircraft and that it would be in their interests to take it. Olga Charles looked toward Norris and clenched her teeth and slowly shook her head as though her husband might be tempted to accept the offer but he stayed firm. "It is in the best interests of all of us to return the way we had planned, on a civilian plane all together."

The embassy official looked disappointed but did not issue a direct order. Instead, he remarked quietly before leaving, "I will respect your wishes and inform Washington of them." Inside the little room the tension began to melt away and Cora Weiss broke into a broad smile and exclaimed warmly, "I'm just so proud of you guys, you came through," and she shook hands all around.

We left for Copenhagen the next morning where a brief press conference was planned. A few officials from the American Embassy rode on the plane with us, including an officer who identified himself to me as a medical doctor who had come aboard carrying a large suitcase of a size that would normally be stowed in the cargo compartment. I told Coffin that the suitcase probably contained military uniforms. I was right. How the officer convinced them I am not sure, but our three men changed an hour out of Kennedy Airport, much to the chagrin of Minnie Gartley, who wept with anger when her son left the plane in the company of the other two pilots and a military escort. By this time I was exhausted. I handed off my story to an AP reporter as I cleared immigration. As I made my way through the crowd I felt a hand at my shoulder; a photographer was looking at me and then saw the New York press card around my neck. A colleague called to him, "He's not one of them, is he?" and the photographer responded, "Nah, he's one of the good guys," and I knew then I was back home in New York.

The Beginning of the End

ALL OF AMERICA'S MILITARY support units were out of Vietnam by March 1973 after the Nixon administration finally concluded an agreement to end the war. The departing Americans took home with them what little incentive remained for the press to cover Vietnam. The story fell off the media radar scopes. Newspaper editors and TV news executives had spent millions of dollars on Vietnam. It was the most covered, most controversial war in American history. They were eager to retrench. The news industry was as bone tired of covering the war as the public was of reading about it. Saigon bureaus were closed or reduced. The Vietnam story moved from the top of the network nightly news into the back pages of papers, alongside the Dear Abby columns. The few reporters who remained in Saigon had to appreciate the comment made by a sardonic copy desk editor, "Gooks killing gooks don't make a story."

I was settling down in a new apartment I had rented on the Upper East Side of Manhattan and was trying to disengage from my Vietnam experience and to move on to other topics. But I was still vulnerable to Vietnam's siren song. When AP executive editor Lou Boccardi and the AP's new foreign editor, Nate Polowetzky, asked me to return again in the summer of 1973 I did not refuse. Nina missed her sisters and parents, who were still living in Saigon, so she and the children came along. My assignment was to find out if South Vietnam could survive without American troops or congressional funding. In April, in a speech at the University of Minnesota, I had predicted the fall of South Vietnam "within four years." The strength of the North Vietnamese side continued to increase and the weakness of the south never changed. I described the peace agreement as a mechanism to allow the United States to leave honorably. Henry Kissinger had told his confidants that the stratagem would provide a "decent interval" between American withdrawal and Vietnamese defeat.

Saigon was unwilling to face up to the blackness of the future; the whole city seemed in denial, disinclined to concede that a decade of war and the peace agreements it spawned were inconclusive and flawed.

My friend Ha Thuc Can was building a fine home near the airport in the style of the great Cham temples that studded the southern coastline. He had become an ardent collector and dealer of antiquities, locating artifacts in hamlets and villages previously inaccessible because of the war. Ha Thuc Can was a daredevil, traveling deep into the countryside where no government soldier dared go. He said there was a pause in the war as both sides evaluated their future and this allowed him to move freely.

I had the impression that a political Indian summer had arrived, a false peace like the phony one before World War Two, a last flourishing before the winter's reality. I rented a serviceable Chevy van and driver and headed from Saigon as far north as I could go, with my nine-year-old son, Andrew. For a decade I had chased the news in the towns and countryside all along the way, and I wanted Andrew to see it the way I had, to remember it in the future when the country he was born in no longer existed.

We took our time, departing midmorning on May 10, a hot, hazy day. The crates of soft drinks and boxes of food rattled in the back of the vehicle as we cleared the security posts outside Saigon and headed up Route 1, once known as the Mandarin Road because it led to the old capital of Hue. We passed Bien Hoa and the dismantled American corps headquarters at Long Binh. I recognized the overgrown foxholes at roadside.

As Andrew gulped a Coke, I regaled him with a few war stories and he nodded with mild interest, and I thought he better get used to it because we would be on the road for ten days and I had a lot of stories to tell. We stopped for lunch at a roadside restaurant at the provincial capital of Xuan Loc, where small children milled around us begging for money, claiming they had American fathers. The AP interpreter traveling with us, Tran Dinh Huong, told us the children were saying they wanted their daddies back but would take money from us in the meantime.

We hoped to reach the coastal town of Phan Thiet by nightfall, bouncing along a stretch of highway that snaked between black volcanic rocks and then across expanses of baked sand. There was little traffic. The final miles were marked by a proliferation of government flags, with the yellow banners with three horizontal red stripes hung like gypsy laundry from trees and rocks. President Thieu had been born in Phan Thiet and people were eager to display their patriotism. The town was also the home of the popular pungent sauce nuoc-mam made from fermented fish; it was stored in round, brightly labeled earthenware bottles stacked by the hundreds outside shops and in the marketplace, and the strong choking odor from the seaside factories drifted across the landscape.

I had learned to be respectful of traditional local industries. When I had covered the Wisconsin political primary the year before, I had happened upon the small town of Union Grove and had written what I thought was a witty story about a local debate over the sauerkraut factory and its noxious smell. The next day the angry Union Grove town board declared me persona non grata. I had a feeling that the Vietnamese were similarly sensitive about their favorite condiment.

The next morning, I looked up the American provincial team. In the few months since the peace treaty, 260 advisers and officials had been reduced to three representatives. They were not eager to talk to me, and complained about a gag order placed on them by the U.S. Embassy. They said they knew less and less about what was going on; the Saigon government rarely confided in them anymore even though they administered millions of dollars in U.S. aid to the province.

I asked about corruption, if the local officials were adhering to what used to be characterized as "an acceptable level" of graft, and one of the Americans burst out indignantly, "I'm sick of hearing about an acceptable level of corruption. There is no acceptable level. If they get their chance to take a little money, then they'll take all of it." His colleague added, "I tell the embassy or I write a report about graft and they say basically, cool it, the White House might read it and cause trouble." They suggested that this neglect of responsibilities was the symptom of a greater indifference to the fate of the country, a political disengagement that paralleled the military withdrawal.

The local population was adapting to America's departure, particularly the women who had lived with Americans, had children with them and were left behind. The new foreign participants on the scene were the neutral nations of the International Control Commission, observing the implementation of the peace agreements. With little or no authority to intervene, they had time on their hands and two Polish peacekeepers had each moved a girl with young children into his room at the hotel.

We left the pungent odors of Phan Thiet behind and drove north toward Phan Rang with a stiffening sea breeze blowing through the open windows. The heat shimmered over the salt flats and there was an olive glow to the foothills rising to the west.

I had always loved this stretch of blacktop highway; it crossed a historic locale, the last kingdom of the Champa Empire. The red-brick temple towers still stood sentinel, even though the faithful who built them were long ago vanquished by the Vietnamese peoples in their steady, relentless migration south. My interpreter, Mr. Huong, informed me that one meaning of the province name Binh Thuan was "peace of country, peace of mind."

My reveries were interrupted. Andrew was pointing out the window and shouting, "Look Daddy, tank, tank." We pulled over to examine it. It was a small Japanese tank secured on a pedestal, a memorial to the casualties of the Japanese occupation. I told Andrew it was the wrong war. Further on past Phan Ri Bay we came upon more recent memorabilia, two American-made medium tanks disabled and abandoned in an empty Vietnamese army compound.

At Phan Rang the province chief, Colonel Tran Van Tieu, told me that his forces were unwilling to concede any territory whatsoever to the Vietcong, and that his people were doubtful that the ceasefire would ever be effective. An American official informed me that the South Vietnamese were to blame for a series of skirmishes around the airport and toward the foothills that were jeopardizing the ceasefire. He complained, "The ARVN won't stop fighting; what a monster we have created. We used to complain that the ARVN never did want to fight, now we complain they won't stop."

We pushed on up the coast on Route 1 through sand dunes and rocky escarpments, traveling to the former U.S. base at Cam Ranh Bay where General Westmoreland had decided to anchor his combat supply system for the Central Highlands war. Floating docks had been dragged across the Pacific Ocean to accommodate the transport ships. Thousands of American soldiers had sweated and cursed in the heat as they began and ended their tours of duty in the huge personnel processing buildings at the airport.

The blast of hot wind was still blowing off the burning sands of the Cam Ranh Peninsula as we drove by, but the harbor was empty and the base buildings on the sandy peninsula across the bay were in disrepair. It was like the old ghost towns in Nevada and Arizona. The tarmac where President Johnson had twice been received was cluttered with the debris of buildings torn down for their lumber. There were darkened traffic lights at an intersection named "Times Square." The United States had spent a quarter of a billion dollars on Cam Ranh Bay and some had dreamed it would be a permanent American presence on the Asian mainland.

All we saw that day were a pair of shrunken socks hanging on a line and a love letter tumbling across the sands, its handwriting faded by the sun. A few paragraphs of erotic description concluded, "Destroy this letter when you've read it, please." But the recipient had stuffed it into a garbage can.

At the curving white sand beach fronting the city of Nha Trang a large white painted sign announced in English and Vietnamese that the beach was reserved for the Vietnamese Air Force—"U.S. personnel entry only by invitation." For six years Americans had prohibited the Vietnamese from that section of the Nha Trang beach with a similar sign and now the locals were getting their revenge. I asked the province chief of Khanh Hoa, Colonel Ly Ba Pham, about it, and he just laughed and said his pilots were high-spirited. He added, "The people who really wanted America to leave were the communists; the North Vietnamese goal has always been to fight the south alone, and I think it was very clever of them."

The province chief, in his neatly pressed military uniform, poured us tea and listened as I talked about the disquiet in America over the war and the desire of most people to forget all about it. He responded, "There is no reason whatsoever for the United States to quit totally and not guarantee the South Vietnamese freedom and democracy." We talked on for a while and he finally expressed exasperation with me. "How could the United States give it all up, and leave defeated?"

The route north from Nha Trang wanders along the loveliest coastline in Southeast Asia, rocky bays with coconut palms and thatched-roofed villages where brightly painted wooden fishing boats line the backyard beaches. The highway climbed up and over the leafy Vung Ro headlands; from here the view northward was across the fertile fields of the coastal plain that sweep west to the Darlac Plateau and the highland cities of Pleiku and Ban Me Thuot. In Tuy Hoa I ran into a former American Special Forces officer at the U.S. advisory compound who pointed to a young colleague with blond hair down to his shoulders. "This is what the foreign service has come to. These guys don't do any field duty, they go to the beach, they go to the lakes in Dalat. We know where the bodies are buried, where the corruption and the incompetence is, the new guard doesn't want to know."

The transition from a state of war to a state of uncertainty was most evident at Qui Nhon, a busy commercial center of ugly, unpainted buildings. I began to get a clearer picture of the predicament the South Vietnamese government was in. Thirty Vietcong flags were flying from a small hilltop just seven hundred yards from a government military outpost. American officials told me that Binh Dinh was still a battle zone; the communist side held the foothills and the mountains and were almost impossible to dislodge.

On day nine, we arrived at the old capital of Hue, our vehicle dusty and rattling. We sauntered through once ornate palaces and gardens now overgrown and crumbling. I was trying to show Andrew his Vietnamese cultural heritage, but he was more interested in playing in the old French concrete security outposts along the way and in watching the white-flanneled players participating in the "Northern Provinces Invitation Tennis Meet" at the former French sports club. The city was still at the front line of the war; North Vietnamese troops had spilled across the Demilitarized Zone in the 1972 Easter Offensive and they had not gone home, capturing everything south to the Thach Han River and leaving Quang Tri city in ruins.

I remembered Quang Tri as a prosperous provincial capital. Now it was a moonscape, its buildings leveled and looted. The power and telephone poles were down. A Vietnamese officer drove us to the riverbank, where we looked across at a North Vietnamese tent encampment. A decade earlier, Quang Tri had been the spiritual center of the family of President Ngo Dinh Diem, and Vietnam itself, a problem in counterinsurgency for eight thousand American military advisers. I was thinking aloud about how much misadventure had occurred since then, but the Vietnamese officer just scowled at me. He explained that just to the west bulldozers were in plain sight as the communists improved Route 548, presumably as a wet season alternative to the Ho Chi Minh Trail, which ran south through the mountains.

The communist side had created a "third Vietnam" of interconnecting highways and embryonic towns in the high ground and valleys that stretched six hundred miles inside South Vietnam from Hue, where they were visible, to the Mekong Delta, where they were well concealed. Some of the most famous battle sites of the war were swallowed up in this new entity, including the Khe Sanh firebase, Dong Ha, Dak To, Ben Het, the Ia Drang Valley and so many other locations whose names were inscribed on the battle streamers of American brigades and battalions.

From this vast launching pad the north could deliver the blow that would overwhelm the south, and if I had any reservations about my grim assessments of Vietnam's future, they were dispelled finally when we drove west of Hue to visit a regiment of the South Vietnamese First Infantry Division that was defending a valley approach to the city. The unit commander, Colonel Vo Toan, was brutally candid. He said that if the communists were to attack in strength he had no adequate defenses, and would have to retreat back into the city unless American B-52 bombers and fighter planes came to his rescue. I explained to him that the U.S. Congress was about to stop the bombing for good. The colonel shook his head in resignation.

Back in Saigon I interviewed a U.S. Embassy acquaintance, a perceptive observer of the Vietnam scene named Frank Scotton, who offered a candid appraisal of the crisis. He said that the United States was not trying to win the war anymore, nor prevent the inevitable communist takeover. "Anticommunist Vietnam today is like ice in a river. You can walk across the ice right now, you can spin stones across

it, but the river underneath is flowing swiftly and melting the ice."
His quote anchored my AP series, which began running in American
newspapers on July 15.

The next day, on July 16, President Thieu's press officer, Hoang
Duc Nha, read my story in the Pacific *Stars and Stripes* and called me
in to his office for a dressing down, the first time a Vietnamese official
had ever challenged my reporting. Nha was a nephew of the president,
famous for having shouted at Henry Kissinger during the final negotiations for the peace agreements. Now he was yelling at me: "How
can you write something like this, it is rubbish, it cannot be true, my
government wants to expel you."

I felt I owed him an explanation. I told the press secretary my
methodology and my travel agenda, which had included not only the
drive to Hue but visits to the Central Highlands and the Mekong Delta.
I discussed the American political scene and the Kissinger doctrine,
which I understood to mean that America had no permanent friends
but permanent interests, and that right now Vietnam was not one of
them. My critical mention of Kissinger improved Nha's temper. After
an hour we said goodbye cordially and he didn't bring up expelling
me again.

The Fall of Saigon

ON THE THIRD WEEKEND in March 1975 the ice broke. I read about
it in the *New York Times* as I rode to work Monday morning on the
subway. The headline announced that President Thieu was abandoning
all of the Central Highlands to the communists; the cities of Kontum,
Pleiku and Ban Me Thuot were being given up. I wanted to scream
aloud that the war was finally ending.

I went to the AP foreign desk, on the fourth floor, where the editor
was hunched over the Saigon telex machine. "Look at this, total
chaos," he said, ripping off the latest from George Esper, a story
about a vast, disorganized exodus from the highlands to the central
coast. Thousands of people were fleeing via the backroads. I told Nate
Polowetzky that I felt in my bones that this was the very end and that
I wanted to go to Vietnam right away. He asked only that I clear it
with the boss.

Gallagher was not entirely convinced by my beliefs. He was a year from retirement and had given much of his presidency to the Vietnam story. But he took my hand and said, "Get over there, and we'll need a helluva lot more people joining you if you're right." I was on my way the next day.

Saigon was stunned and angry. The people had preferred ignorance over knowledge, stubbornly supporting a president who had been disregarding the obvious arithmetic of the battlefield. Nguyen Van Thieu's unwillingness to negotiate any reasonable political solution with the communists had doomed the south to military destruction. But ever since the Tet Offensive had been rolled back—only with considerable American combat help—the people of Saigon had acted as though there was no further accounting necessary, that they had won their struggle. Now their country was being wrecked.

Esper met me at the airport and told me the government had just written off the northern quarter of the country, the provinces of Quang Tri and Thua Thien, including the old capital of Hue. The Central Highlands were already gone; South Vietnam had been halved in size in a week. My brother-in-law Colonel Nguyen Minh Chau told me he was hearing talk of a possible coup d'etat against the president, that the Vietnamese leader was being blamed for the battlefield retreats. Old friends asked me where the Americans were, and their B-52 bombers that had rescued them in the past. I tried to explain to them that America's Vietnam policy had been drained of any credibility. Nixon, for reasons entirely unrelated to Vietnam, had been disgraced and driven from office by domestic scandal. The new president, Gerald Ford, was restricted by Congress from using any funds for Southeast Asian combat activities.

Each day, news reports described a country in total collapse. Gallagher ordered in reinforcements, and several AP regional bureau chiefs flew in. In a war where his guys had won five Pulitzer Prizes, Gallagher was determined to maintain the competitive advantage until the end. Other news organizations were also showing renewed interest in the story; on the anxious streets of Saigon and in the French restaurants I began to run into some former press colleagues I hadn't seen in years. Malcolm Browne was back with his wife, Le Lieu, reporting now for the *New York Times;* my old UPI competition Leon Daniels had returned. Each day the roster lengthened. All of us were there to record the death of South Vietnam, all of us with an emotional stake in the story but trying not to let it get in the way.

On March 24, I hitched an early-morning ride on an Air America courier flight to Da Nang, where the retreating defenders from Quang Tri and Hue were regrouping. Da Nang was second only to Saigon in importance, a metropolis of a million people with commercial and residential areas sprawling along the harbor. It was easily defended. Solid fortifications anchored the land approaches and there was a sizeable military supply complex at the airbase with sleek fighter-bombers and helicopters on call to assist the defense forces. The U.S. marines who had waded ashore there in 1965 to fire the first shots in America's ground war had spent half a decade securing Da Nang and the countryside around it. The city was usually described as a bastion, and as we made our final approach for a landing it appeared calm. The picture on the ground was not as comforting; I saw a city on the verge of collapse. Crowds milled around intersections arguing and shouting, and soldiers walked aimlessly on the streets, their weapons at ease on their shoulders, hardly the stance of a defense force preparing for the fight of its life.

The American consul general, Al Francis, was hopeful that a planned airlift would soon move tens of thousands of refugees to secure locations in the south. But the next morning the picture suddenly darkened. Barges and boats carrying the disheveled military evacuees from Hue were pulling into the harbor and unloading their cargoes. The main streets near the docks were soon mobbed with half-dressed soldiers, their weapons discarded or lost, their shoulders bent in exhaustion. These survivors were the remnants of the best two infantry divisions in Vietnam. Those that I talked with told me of the complete collapse of the defenses of the old capital and a chaotic exodus from beaches under heavy shell fire. It reminded me of stories I had heard of the evacuation at Dunkirk in the Second World War.

By late that afternoon rumors had spread through town that the communists were at the gates of the city. The uproar on the streets persuaded me to seek the safety of my hotel where other journalists were staying. Around midnight a young American official summoned us to the consulate. Al Francis now painted the blackest picture of the security situation; he declared he could no longer be responsible for our safety and suggested we leave town in the morning. That was fine by us; we had seen enough.

The thump of exploding rockets woke me, the first shots fired by the communists in their attack on Da Nang. I marveled at the speed of the advance. Hue was fifty miles north and had fallen the previous day and now artillery units had moved across the mountains and were within range of the city. We drove to the airport in a consulate van.

The Fall of Saigon

There were mobs of people hurrying in the same direction and gathering at the airport gates. By midmorning the terminal was jammed with men, women and children trying to leave. The crowd was on the verge of hysteria and mobbed the first plane to arrive, a chartered World Airways 727 we were booked to travel on. Airport security police began shouting and firing their rifles into the air and pushed the crowd back; eventually a somewhat orderly departure was organized. I was just grateful to be leaving safely.

Three days later, George Esper, using his Saigon sources, was the first to report that Da Nang had fallen to the communists. But we soon learned that "fallen" was the wrong word. "Thrown away" was the more accurate description. A Vietnamese stringer photographer arrived at our office that weekend with pictures from China Beach and Marble Mountain that told the truth. Scores of artillery pieces and tanks that had been shipped to Vietnam from American military supply arsenals to defend Da Nang had been abandoned on the yellow sand, their gun barrels pointed not toward the mountain valleys from where the communist attackers were emerging, but nosed down into the rippling waters of the South China Sea, where their crews were swimming on inflated inner tubes to barges waiting offshore. President Thieu had announced a week earlier that the region would be defended to the last man. But his soldiers had given up one of the most powerful military bases in the Pacific without a fight.

We were to hear much worse about the total panic of the Da Nang population. AP correspondent Peter O'Loughlin reported from the American freighter *Pioneer Contender* that refugees had fought to the death to board the ship. Babies had fallen overboard. A woman had committed suicide by leaping from the deck when she realized the child in her arms was dead.

It was not the fall of Da Nang but the way it fell that convinced me that Saigon was doomed. In early April I wrote an analysis that a communist assault on the capital was inevitable and that it could not be resisted. The story was picked up by the English-language newspaper, the *Saigon Post*. The government responded that the battlefield reverses were the inevitable consequence of a regrouping of military forces to defend Saigon and the populated regions around it. Then we learned that Cam Ranh Bay was lost, along with the coastal resort of Nha Trang.

Gallagher called me back to the United States to address the annual membership meeting of the Associated Press in New Orleans. I was making commercial airline bookings when I was offered an alternative way home, aboard a World Airways jet aircraft carrying Vietnamese orphans to their new families in the United States. It would get me back in time and with a news story, too. I had been offered the trip by Ed Daley, the colorful president of an Oakland-based charter airline. He was a bulky, beret-wearing character straight out of the once popular comic strip *Terry and the Pirates;* he wore a pistol tucked in the leather belt around his fat stomach. Daley did not seem in the least intimidated by the crisis; several of his expensive fleet of sleek jet aircraft were parked at the endangered Tan Son Nhut Airport to back up his promises to save as many people as he could. He had already defied dangerous odds by ordering a company plane to Da Nang to pluck refugees from the airport even after the communists had taken the city.

Most of my colleagues wrote Daley off as a publicity seeker anxious to secure new routes for his airline in the United States. They were repelled by his loud, aggressive manner, particularly his habit of backing up dinner table arguments by dumping his pistol on the table. At another time I may have turned away, but the world was caving in and there seemed room enough for a millionaire swashbuckler with a fleet of long-distance cargo aircraft.

We assembled one evening at a warehouse building far beyond the airport terminal where a big DC-8 cargo jet was discreetly parked in a darkened part of the taxiway. Daley and his staff laid wooden pallets across the aircraft floor and piled blankets and pillows for the fifty-seven tiny babies he had gathered. A score of American women civilians came along for the ride to help with the children; they were dependents of American officials and aid workers happy to be going home. The pilot, Ken Healey, told me that the plane had been denied departure clearance because of concern over an expected communist guerrilla attack. Daley brushed aside that complication and ordered Healey to rev up the engines and taxi onto the runway and take off anyway without clearance. Healey obeyed even as the control tower was shouting at him, "Don't take off, don't take off, you have no clearance."

I was in the rear compartment with the babies and watched them roll over on their backs as the big jet soared into the sky and set its course for Yokota air base in Japan and from there to Oakland, California, a twenty-five-hour dash to safety. Daley's dramatic flight made large headlines in American newspapers, and his initiative helped convince American officials to face up to the crisis and begin evacuating at least the most vulnerable dependents from Saigon.

To the newspaper publishers in New Orleans, I explained, "It is not easy to describe in these pleasing surroundings in this lovely American city the total chaos that is enveloping the people of Saigon, who for better or worse participated in America's grand scheme to make South Vietnam a bulwark against the communism that is now overrunning it." I was asked how long Saigon had left. I predicted that the Vietnamese capital would fall within the month. They seemed stunned. So was Nina. She insisted on returning with me to Saigon, where her parents and her sisters were trapped with the rest of the population. I told Tom Buckley that I had decided to do my best to rescue Nina's family. He said, "Peter, you're not heavy enough to do it."

. . .

Back in Saigon nearly everyone we knew wanted to leave and were willing to go to any lengths. The news of the chaos of the fall of Da Nang had traveled south with the desperate survivors. Each day hundreds of Vietnamese lined up for visas at the American Embassy. As South Vietnam diminished, the lines grew larger. Thousands of others were waiting at home with their bags packed, because they qualified for evacuation under a plan to move two hundred thousand Vietnamese whose lives might be endangered by their association with twenty years of American policy.

I arranged for Nina and her parents to fly to Wellington on a special plane hired to evacuate the New Zealand diplomatic staff, and I drove them to the embassy on the morning of their departure. They were allowed only one small bag for their belongings. This was the third time they had lost almost everything. Under a special arrangement with the American Embassy we were able to move out all our AP Vietnamese staff and their families who wanted to leave. I was able to get Nina's two sisters and their husbands to the Philippines on U.S. Air Force C-130s.

One morning soon after, a senior Vietnamese officer was sitting in Esper's office, deep in conversation with him. The military high command rarely sought us out; our adversarial relationship had only worsened over the years. Esper introduced me to Lieutenant General Nguyen Van Minh, the commander of the Saigon garrison, the key man in the defense of the capital. We had met before but I was not prepared for the hug that he gave me or for his effusive compliments on my journalistic abilities.

The general quickly made clear the purpose of his visit. He wanted our assistance in his departure plans: namely to provide him with the coordinates of the U.S. Seventh Fleet vessels off the coast and the carriers' radio ID call signs so that he could make a dash for freedom in his command chopper if the end came too quickly. He explained that for the time being the American high command was unwilling to provide him this information but might make it available when absolutely needed. Minh wanted a safer margin. He did nothing to conceal his certainty that Saigon would be lost. He complained that he had an understaffed division of only six thousand soldiers to defend the capital. His intelligence indicated there were sixteen North Vietnamese divisions grouping to attack the city.

We explained that the military information he desired was classified and therefore not available to us, but that we would advise the American authorities of his needs. The general left promising to keep in touch. I knew we had stumbled on an invaluable source.

There were officials within the American Embassy and the International Commission of Control and Supervision who clung to their conviction that there would be a negotiated end to the war, a solution that would preserve Saigon's status as the center of a neutralist government. I was skeptical when I first heard these reports, because I had witnessed the sudden collapse of Da Nang and the fall of Hue, and the loss of every city down the coast and in the highlands. I could see no reason why the North Vietnamese juggernaut would lay its weapons down at the gates of Saigon. The CIA station chief, Thomas Polgar, was the leading American proponent of this position. From what I could see it took life from the imaginings of Polish and Hungarian diplomats and others who were dealing with communist bureaucrats in Hanoi, bureaucrats who would say anything to divert attention from the true mission of their military forces.

I bumped into Mal Browne and his wife at Givral's coffee shop. I asked why she had not left the country with everyone else. But Mal smiled at me confidently and said, "Peter, there will be no final battle, believe me. I am plugged in better now with all sides than I have ever been in my life." Mal was a journalist I respected and a friend I adored but I thought he was wrong about this one. "Mal," I said, "you taught me to write only what you see and not what you hear, and what I see is Armageddon around the corner."

New York headquarters was becoming concerned about our well-being as the ring closed around Saigon. We were reminded that all American news organizations would close up shop when Ambassador Graham Martin gave the order to pull out on the final helicopter evacuation. We were told to follow the model that had been worked out for the fall of Phnom Penh in Cambodia, where most of the AP staff had pulled out and only a few remained behind. We began scheduling people out of the country.

Around noon on Monday, April 27, General Minh telephoned me with an invitation to visit his home near the Presidential Palace. We sipped warm Chinese tea out of delicate cups, and he explained that the end was near, that his intelligence reports showed that the communist forces were as close as Bien Hoa to the east and Cu Chi to the west and were pressing in from all other directions of the compass. There was heavy artillery lining up to blast Saigon to pieces; communist patrols had already tested the city's defenses. He described what he called "the intoxication of panic" that was overwhelming the Saigon forces. The command structure and leadership they needed so desperately was crumbling, departing in the helicopters of the fleeing commanders.

I assured him I was still trying to get him the coordinates he required for his own journey but he waved that aside and said he knew the general location of the fleet and when the time came he would fly out to find it.

He showed me around his palatial stucco home whose walls were adorned with large, ornate lacquer paintings featuring traditional Vietnamese scenes of beautiful raven-haired women sitting by reflecting pools, and of wild horses prancing across dramatic landscapes.

He shook his head sadly, "It's too late for me to take them now," and he turned to me and declared, "These are all yours, all for you. I know you appreciate art, and this is Vietnam's finest." I assured him that I was no more able to take the paintings out of Vietnam than he was, but he insisted and when I went back out into the courtyard two of his soldiers were tying the paintings onto the roof of a jeep. I told General Minh I had other errands to run and would return later in the day and then I drove off knowing that I wouldn't see General Minh or the paintings again.

In the early hours of Tuesday morning the runways and terminal buildings at Tan Son Nhut Airport were pounded by the big artillery guns that the communists had dragged down from the mountains. The shell fire woke the city. I tumbled out of bed at the Caravelle as the first shells landed at 4 A.M., and ran to the hotel roof, where a few colleagues had already gathered. Aircraft and buildings were burning. As a smoky dawn rose over Saigon's rooftops we saw that many residents were watching, as we were, a few brave aircraft dueling with gunners on the ground, their miniguns spitting sheets of flaming steel

297

as surface-to-air missiles flew up toward them. I saw two aircraft fall from the sky. I phoned Esper from the Caravelle's bar. We agreed that the shelling would probably end the evacuation at the airport and activate Option 4, the final pullout.

The rocket attack also ended further talk of political accommodation. With the airlift terminated, the decision was made to evacuate all essential personnel by helicopter. It would be the last chance to leave. Esper curtly informed New York of the development and that three of us would stay behind, Esper, me and Matt Franjola, an AP reporter who had been covering the region for several years.

Gallagher objected to Franjola remaining behind because he was concerned it would enlarge the risk for all of us, but he agreed when Esper advised him, "Franjola is determined to stay and if we force him he is going to stay for someone else. Request you please reconsider and let me hit this story hardest." I felt I should offer a fuller explanation for my own decision to remain behind because to many it would seem foolhardy, especially to Nina. I had promised to leave when the time came.

I sent a message to Gallagher saying that because I was in Vietnam at the beginning, I felt it was worth the risk to be there at the end to document the final hours. I did not tell him I would contrive to miss the last helicopter if he insisted I leave.

April 30, 1975

BRIAN ELLIS OF CBS, who was coordinating the press evacuation, called the AP bureau around 11 A.M.; the embassy had advised him that the full pullout was beginning. Matt Franjola and I joined Ed White at the bus pickup point not far from our office where our colleagues were arriving on foot and in cars. No one was talking. Those who had watched the war from the beginning were somber. Bob Shaplen of *The New Yorker* was red-eyed and Mal Browne was uncharacteristically uncommunicative. He was an eccentric to the end with an old German steel helmet perched on his head.

Ed White had been covering the war for as long as I had and grown middle-aged in the process. "Jesus I hate to leave this way," he said as he climbed onto the second vehicle. He turned to me, "Are you

sure you're doing the right thing," and I responded, "By God, yes."
A young radio correspondent was darting among the group, microphone in hand, gathering last-minute comment. As he entered a bus
I heard him declaring into his microphone, "The press corps is leaving,
it's all over now."

No, I said to myself, not quite.

Everything I had written about Vietnam had pointed to this day,
and I felt obligated to witness the final reckoning. Franjola and I
climbed in our jeep and followed the buses over to the American
ambassador's house, where they were to wait for instructions. As we
were parked at the curb, a uniformed Vietnamese army officer ran
over to us and begged for a ride out to the airport. I recognized him
as an information ministry official. I told him he would never make
it through the airport gate because the guards were turning back soldiers. He undressed on the street, throwing his uniform behind some
trees and slipping into a pair of trousers and a sports shirt. He introduced a young boy as his son and told me that they were the only
members of the family who would be leaving, that his wife and daughters would remain behind.

I looked over at Matt and we understood what we had to do. The
buses were pulling away and Matt and I told them both to climb in
our jeep. I drove ahead of one of the buses and managed to stop it.
We banged on the passenger door until the driver opened it, shouting
at us, "What the hell do you want?" A chorus of impatient calls came
from those who were eager to get on their way. I pushed and shoved
the Vietnamese officer and his son onto the crowded bus over the
protestations of those inside. I told him to put up a fight if anyone
tried to throw them out.

Matt and I drove through the guarded airport gates behind the buses,
passing dozens of automobiles that had been ditched along the road.
When our colleagues realized that Matt and I were staying behind
they raised a few cheers and then started tossing their car keys at us,
telling us where their vehicles were parked.

.   .   .

The last hours of Saigon were wet. The monsoon season arrived in
heavy downpours. From the roof of the Eden Building I watched as
the dark shapes of helicopters disappeared into the night. Below in
the streetlights a few people were looking into the sky and gesturing,
some with small travel bags in their hands. But it was too late now to
fly away. By late into the night the helicopters were gone, apparently

for good, and I climbed down to the AP office on the fourth floor, where our interpreter, Mr. Huong, and his family were stretched out on the floor.

George Esper had tried to take them to the embassy evacuation site earlier in the day but the crowds had been too unruly to get near the fence. Esper was on the telephone, dialing the embassy even though the officials had stopped answering. He had sat at the same table for a decade pounding out his leads on an old Underwood typewriter. He never got the professional credit he deserved. His coverage had appeared in more newspapers than any other reporter's in recent years. He was still unknown and underpaid and the last to complain. And at 3 A.M., in a city about to die, he was phoning dead switchboards and biting the bits of gristle that passed for fingernails. Esper was worrying whether he had written enough that day and I figured that he had already sent out ten thousand words to New York.

He was gaunt, his eyes were burning with exhaustion. I said to him, "Let's get the hell out of here, George. We've got to get some sleep." He muttered to himself and returned to the string of telexes.

I noticed that some of the messages coming over the wire were from newspaper editors inquiring about the fate of their reporters; others were story requests from our foreign desk and several were from AP bureaus in Europe and the United States with scorecards on the usage of our stories. "Not one of those damned messages is important," I told him. "We're the only ones left here now, no government spokesmen and no press officers to second-guess our stories, no unhappy embassy official waving a denial of what we have written. To hell with New York, they're ten thousand miles away. This one we cover our way, George, they ain't got no choice."

George decided against sleep and typed a nasty note to our New York foreign desk complaining about the message traffic and I hope he sent it. I didn't wait to see. I made my way down the darkened stairwell, and crossed the wet Lam Son Square to the Caravelle. I seemed barely to have touched the bed when I was awakened by shouting in the street below my window. I pulled the curtains aside and the bright sun blinded me for a moment. I could see a commotion in the square: several people fighting over a king-sized bed. I thought I must be dreaming but it turned out to be real. The looting had begun.

I shaved and showered in cold water and selected a gray proletarian shirt for the benefit of the new city masters. I headed upstairs to the dining room, doubtful that breakfast would be served. But I was wrong, the uniformed waiters were on duty as usual. Below, the streets were already busy, with vehicle traffic headed toward the Saigon riverfront, where navy and commercial boats were docked. Sea would be the last avenue of escape. I saw groups of people waiting on the roofs of five tall buildings in the heart of the city, peering into the sky. Don't they know it's over, I wondered, but then came the familiar whine of a U.S. Marine helicopter, circling the twin steeples of the Catholic cathedral on John F. Kennedy Square and settling down on the roof of the American Embassy. A waiter handed me binoculars and I watched a score of battle-garbed marines race from behind sandbagged revetments on the embassy roof and enter the helicopter. In less than a minute they were gone, the last official Americans to leave Saigon.

I telephoned Esper at the office with the story. Even before the last helicopter had cleared the coast, news of its leaving would be in the offices of every major press organization in the world. Franjola joined me at the breakfast table. I had been trying to teach him my New Zealand accent to fake out any belligerents, with little success. We went down to the streets where jeeploads of South Vietnamese soldiers with guns raised were driving frantically through the city. There were no sounds of battle. They were leaderless now, their senior officers had departed. We passed three corner gas stations where pumps had been uprooted and motorists were siphoning gas directly into their cars.

We drove to the American Embassy. The boulevard in front was carpeted with computer paper, torn documents, notebooks and newspapers. A score of vehicles in the parking lot were being stripped by industrious youths. The gates of the administrative building were swinging loose and a laughing Vietnamese soldier pranced along the hallway calling out in English, "It's our embassy now" as he thumbed his nose at us.

When we reached the embassy roof we discovered nearly a hundred Vietnamese still sitting there, waiting. They intended to stay until the helicopters came back to get them and I didn't have the heart to tell them it was all over.

.   .   .

We returned to our office. The stairwells were clogged with Vietnamese hiding behind the thick concrete walls for safety. More people were gathered in the hallway outside the bureau. They had mistaken our activity for authority, and they believed we could provide them

301

sanctuary. Inside the office, Esper was monitoring Saigon radio broadcasts with Mr. Huong and soon the interpreter gave a shout from the monitoring booth. Complete surrender had been announced by the newly appointed president, Duong Van Minh, the same "Big Minh" who had led the coup against President Diem in 1963. He was now officially delivering the country to the communists. Esper typed the bulletin announcement and rushed it to the teleprinter operator. No matter how belated or insignificant, it was concrete evidence to the world that the war was over. The New York foreign desk soon sent us a message that our surrender bulletin had been five minutes ahead of UPI's, proving again that while wars may start and end and leaders rise and fall, the only important determinant in the news business is to be first with the story.

George was delighted with his feat and stood up and stretched and announced that he was going down to the street to see what was going on. He had been at his desk for four straight days and I wished him luck but he was running back to his typewriter within five minutes, ashen-faced. While crossing Lam Son Square, a Vietnamese police colonel in full uniform had accosted him and stuttered in broken English, "It's finished" before walking away ten feet, executing a sharp about-face, saluting a nearby statue, and then raising a .45 pistol and blowing his brains out. For a second George thought the bullet might have been intended for him and he wrote his story with shaky hands.

Franjola came in and announced matter-of-factly, "By the way, they're here." I looked up and asked him, "Who's here?" and he responded, "The VC. I was driving behind the British Embassy when a black jeep came by with this guy sitting on the hood in a white shirt, black trousers and shower shoes. He's carrying an AK-47 and yells at me in English, 'Everybody go home,' and inside the jeep were several other guys all in black shirts. And by the way they were flying the Vietcong flag."

I checked my watch: 11:25 A.M. I told George I was going out to see for myself. A score of South Vietnamese soldiers were running up Tu Do Street, or rather they were hopping and skipping because they were tearing off their boots, jackets and trousers on the run. They were down to their skivvies when they ran by me and disappeared through an alley.

I heard the sharp beep, beep of a truck horn. A large vehicle rolled by toward the Saigon River. My heart stopped: it was a Russian Molotova and riding in the back was a score of young communist soldiers dressed in floppy green uniforms and pith helmets. Their faces were filled with seriousness and wonder as they gazed up at the high-rise buildings at the center of Saigon, probably the first tall structures they had ever seen. The Vietnamese civilians in the streets just looked up in surprise. I saw a couple wave at a truck and then keep walking. A large blue and green Vietcong banner suddenly billowed from the Caravelle flagpole. The staff must have been sewing it in secret for a week.

I started back up the stairs. This was it, this was the end of it all, this was what a generation of Americans had fought against and several presidents had plotted to prevent. And the end had come so quickly and anticlimactically. The people on the stairways were pressing against me, and someone asked, "What's happening?" and I answered, "The VC are outside."

· · ·

I pushed my way through the crowd milling around our bureau door and fell exhausted to my knees. Esper looked over at me. I was totally tongue-tied. George helped me to a typewriter. "Peter, what the hell is wrong?" I heard him asking. I gestured for paper and started to type a bulletin that began, "Saigon, April 30. Vietnamese communist troops occupied Saigon peacefully today, rolling down the tree-lined boulevards in Russian trucks with their flags flying. The people of Saigon watched quietly from the sidewalks. No shooting was heard."

I tottered to the teleprinter room and thrust the page at our beefy Vietnamese teleprinter operator, Tammy. He read the bulletin and gasped and attempted to flee from the room. Esper and I pressed down on his shoulders until he finished punching the tape and then he disappeared out the bureau door and was gone for days.

· · ·

Esper and I were surprised that our communications had remained open, that the fleeing South Vietnamese authorities had not cut the lines. But we knew that any moment our circuit to our New York office could be shut off by the new rulers of Saigon.

Matt and I sprinted down to the streets again and saw the Russian trucks rolling down Tu Do, in great numbers now. The people were spilling onto the sidewalks, their fears of immediate catastrophe gone. A South Vietnamese soldier dressed in khaki trousers and a white T-shirt was ahead of me, and I watched him tear the ID dog tags from the chain at his neck and throw them to the ground. I walked through the open gates of the Defense Ministry in Gia Long Street and into the courtyard, where several uniformed South Vietnamese officers were in earnest discussions with black-clad civilians, presumably communist cadres. As I raised my camera, one of the Saigon officers called to me in English, "No pictures," and held up his hand, and I smiled to myself and continued shooting. "I don't think you're in any position to give orders anymore, are you?"

The Australian cameraman Neil Davis came toward me down Pasteur Street from the Presidential Palace. He'd been in the grounds a few minutes earlier when a North Vietnamese tank had crashed through the main iron gates. He said the crew had dismounted and run to the upstairs balcony where they had unfurled a large Vietcong banner. I was back in the office telling Esper all this when heavy shooting erupted outside our window. A dozen North Vietnamese soldiers were crawling through the bushes and across the grass of the park below us toward the Town Hall, where a few defenders were resisting. The communist soldiers were maneuvering over the park benches, covering one another as they moved quickly forward close to the building and then rising to their feet and rushing it with rifles blazing. The building overlooking the park from the other side of the street was the Rex Hotel, where Barry Zorthian and his band of information specialists had spent years telling us that the Americans were winning the war.

Soon a young Vietnamese named Ky Nhan, one of our part-time photographers, came into the office, and with a bullfighter's flourish he brandished two slightly built North Vietnamese soldiers. This was it, I thought, arrest or at the least internment. I was telling myself that it had all been worth it because we had sent the story out to the world. Esper didn't even look up from the telephone; he was trying to raise the Saigon telephone office for a long-shot call to the United States. A colleague who was impressed with George's telephone tenacity had once suggested he would be on the telephone if the communists ever took Saigon.

I walked over to greet the two visitors. One of them had an AK-47 assault rifle swinging from his shoulder; the other was clearly in charge because he carried a Russian pistol displayed in a leather holster on his belt. As I approached them, Ky Nhan flung his arms wide and exclaimed in English, "I have guaranteed the safety of the AP office. You have no reason to be concerned." I looked at him in surprise because in the years he had been selling us pictures of the war he was a rather passive fellow.

I soon learned why he was so happy. He said he had been a Vietcong agent for ten years and his mission had been to coordinate with the international press corps in Saigon. We never had even the slightest suspicion. The photographer waved toward me and said, "I have told them about the AP, about you, that you are all good people, and they come here to visit you as friends." Our silent visitors were smiling now, and George stood and shook their hands in welcome, as grateful as I that we were not their prisoners. They joined us in a modest snack of yesterday's pastries and some warm Coca-Cola but turned down a shot of cognac from a bottle I kept in my desk for special occasions.

I suggested to Esper that he interview them. They answered his questions. Binh Huan Lam and Tran Viet Ca were both sergeants, both twenty-five, and from Hanoi. They explained they were infantrymen whose unit had successfully attacked Bien Hoa two days earlier, had ridden into Saigon with a tank brigade that morning. They showed us their route on an office map of the area and they were so self-assured I presumed they were intelligence operatives.

George moved into the teleprinter room and began punching directly to New York the first interview with the conquerors of Saigon. The two soldiers followed him in and looked—without understanding—at the incoming AP news wire clacking over a second teleprinter. I tore one of the stories from the machine and asked Ky Nhan to translate, and he read in Vietnamese, "President Ford declared that the evacuation of Americans from Vietnam closes a chapter in the American experience. The president asked all Americans to close ranks, to avoid recriminations about the past, to look ahead to the many goals we share and to work together on the great tasks that remain to be accomplished." Our Vietnamese visitors looked pleased.

Franjola and I returned to the streets to discover that the crowds were out of hiding, mixing with the victorious soldiers and chatting on street corners or sitting together on the sidewalks. An hour earlier the whole population had been cringing; it had recovered its confidence instantly. I met a senior official of the Foreign Ministry, a close friend of Nina's family, walking with his wife on Tu Do Street and he grabbed my sleeve. "Peter," he said, "I don't understand this. I entered Paris with the Free French forces in 1945 and they celebrated by looting a few places. They shot some prostitutes and there were other immediate, brutal acts against collaborators. But these communists, they don't react at all." His wife chimed in, "They're so deferential to us, I just don't understand." My own impression was that the collapse of the Saigon government was so total that the North Vietnamese authorities were encouraging their well-indoctrinated assault troops to mix with the crowds to solidify their victory with an image of calm responsibility.

While driving out to the airport on Cong Ly Street we came upon a communist infantry patrol, jogging right out of the pages of a guide to guerrilla warfare, a hundred men moving in double time along the pavement in their Ho Chi Minh rubber tire sandals. Their baggy uniforms were flopping in the breeze and the point men carried light weapons. Those immediately behind them were hefting heavy mortars and large-caliber machine guns that had been dismantled for transport. These were the cutting edge of the North Vietnamese Army. These were the communist infantrymen who had defied the B-52 strikes on the jungle trails, who had clawed through napalm and the artillery guarding the towns and cities and military bases, who had persisted and finally won the war. Their fortitude had been incomprehensible to a generation of American military planners. I felt no closer to understanding their determination as I watched them pass me by in double time in the blistering afternoon heat in the vanquished capital of their enemy.

The teleprinter was still ticking late that afternoon when I returned to the AP office and George suggested I write a story summing up my impressions. I began, "In thirteen years of covering the Vietnam War I never dreamed it would end the way it did at noon today. I thought it might have ended with a political deal like in Laos. Even an Armageddon-type battle with the city left in ruins. . . . But a total surrender followed a short two hours later with a cordial meeting in the Associated Press office in Saigon with an armed and battle-garbed North Vietnamese and his aide—and over a Coke and pound cake at that? That is how the Vietnam War ended for me today."

I fed the tape into the transmitter and it curled its way through the machine. I began punching again but the machine coughed a couple of times and ground to a stop. I tried the keys again; no response. It was a few minutes after 7 P.M.; the new regime had finally pulled the plug on our communications; the AP wire from Saigon was down and out. I looked at my scrawled notes and figured that the world could do without my philosophizing anyway. I called over to Esper, "That's it, George."

There was nothing to do now but wait for the authorities to decide what to do with us. I was grateful in a way. We were all exhausted. Esper and Franjola and I left the office and walked to the Caravelle.

Numerous European journalists had stayed behind. Many of us would gather each night in the Caravelle dining room to swap information, no longer competing because communications were shut down.

The British press corps had access to the wine cellar of their abandoned embassy, which they raided each afternoon to enliven their nights. I had made friends with a Frenchman who had obtained the keys of the New Zealand Embassy from the departing diplomats; he set himself up in the ambassador's office and began issuing passports and visas to those of his Vietnamese friends desperate to find a legal way to get out. The documents were convincingly stamped and signed with a flourish. I was amused by the Frenchman's enterprise and he offered me the embassy's vehicles. I rode around liberated Saigon in a handsome black sedan with diplomatic plates, the New Zealand flag rippling from the hood.

Most of us were eventually given two days' notice to depart, leaving a handful of wire service people behind for a few weeks, including Esper. After twenty-five days of living under the new communist rulers, we boarded buses for our last trip to Tan Son Nhut Airport and the flight to Vientiane, Laos, and then home. The young Vietnamese soldiers searching our bags were courteous. They allowed us to take all our film but they were less considerate about personal items and even confiscated the souvenir Caravelle ashtrays some reporters had stuffed in their bags. There were eighty-two of us crammed on board the Russian-built Ilyushin aircraft with Hanoi's yellow-starred red flag painted on the tail section. As we taxied out across the airfield we passed the wreckage of transport planes and fighter-bombers and helicopters, a graveyard of war machines and hopes. As we lifted off, a cheer roared through the passenger compartment. We had tempted fate and survived. I passed around a half-gallon jug of Johnnie Walker Black Label whiskey that I had liberated from the New Zealand ambassador's office.

Part III
1974–1990

On the Road

SOME JOURNALISTS WHO SERVED in Vietnam were bruised by the war both emotionally and professionally. And the experience was so consuming they found difficulty in adjusting to normal life. Many quit the news business or took routine jobs in domestic bureaus and never covered the international scene again. Some television correspondents emerged as stars, many others disappeared off the air. A few reporters wrote brilliant books about Vietnam and then branched into other subjects, such as Halberstam and Sheehan and Frances FitzGerald. There were some, like Gloria Emerson, who never let go of Vietnam. They have their places, too, in the conscience of the nation.

Joseph Alsop predicted that many Americans would blame the press for the loss of the war, because we had not slavishly supported American policy. He tried to make his forecast with his own criticism. The debate over coverage was as acrimonious inside the news business as outside.

From the beginning of the war to the end I looked at Vietnam as a news story, not a crusade for one side or the other. I believed that gathering information was a worthwhile pursuit, and truth the greatest goal I could aspire to. We reporters had worked under close public scrutiny, from the controversy over the Ngo Dinh Diem regime during the Kennedy administration, to the fall of Saigon in the time of President Ford.

Our copy was endlessly analyzed. If we had been as irresponsible as our critics suggested during that span of thirteen years, then surely it would be obvious in hindsight. We survived the many investigations by the Kennedy, Johnson and Nixon administrations, all of which endeavored to manage Vietnam reporting by disparaging the press, and were not unwilling to use both the FBI and the CIA to achieve their ends. Only after time did I come to agree with David Halberstam, that it was the wrong war, in the wrong place, at the wrong time.

Still, the passions and blame-placing about Vietnam corroded the standing of war correspondents as it did the soldiers. Friends advised me to move into another branch of journalism. But I was learning that war reporting was what I did in my life. It was my job, not just a place I had been. I could do it not only in Vietnam; I could do it anywhere. I learned that in Cyprus in 1974.

Wes Gallagher called me at home late in the evening of Saturday, July 20, and asked me to reinforce the AP team on the Mediterranean island. Earlier that day Cyprus had been invaded by Turkish planes and troops along its northern coast. The Turkish attack had come several days after Greek Cypriot extremists had tried to force the unification of the island with Greece. In name, the invasion was launched to protect the minority ethnic Turk population, but more significantly, it raised the ugly prospect of a military confrontation between NATO neighbors.

Reporters and photographers on the heights overlooking Morphou Bay and Kyrenia were already filing dramatic stories and pictures. Cyprus had been cut off by air and fighting engulfed the capital city of Nicosia. I explained to Gallagher that I might have to wait some time before I could get in but he brushed aside my objections. "Hire a boat," he said, and hung up.

I arrived in Beirut late afternoon on Monday. Our plane landed in a shimmering heat haze that gave a bluish tint to the backdrop of rocky hills. I took a taxi into the city along the palm-fringed highway past the forest of high-rise apartment buildings recently built by oil-rich Arab speculators, and through the busy business part of town. I checked into the luxury Phoenicia Hotel in the harbor area and from my tenth-floor room I looked out across the sunset-tinted Mediterranean sea, which slapped at the shore two blocks away and stretched to Cyprus beyond the horizon. Being a war correspondent had its bewitching moments.

In the lobby there was a swarm of Americans who had been evacuated the previous day from Cyprus. I interviewed five young women in Bermuda shorts and sleeveless blouses who were members of an archaeological team on a summer excavation of the amphitheater in the ancient city of Salamis when the Turkish invasion took place. They had been visiting Famagusta, and were strolling along the main street when jets strafed the neighborhood. They had hidden in the thick-walled toilet of a Greek Cypriot farmhouse for two days until they could make their way to the nearby British military base at Dhekelia, joining many others who had fled for safety. Soon they were all picked up by U.S. Navy helicopters and transported to the Sixth Fleet frigate that brought them to Beirut. They praised the American rescue effort but showed unrestrained contempt for the Greek Cypriot soldiers, who, they said, had panicked and run away in fear when the air strikes came crashing in.

Early next morning I went down to the harbor to rent a speedboat for a fast crossing, but nothing was available; the British Navy had declared a blockade of the ports along the southern coast of Cyprus until the crisis was resolved. At first, no one wanted to take me.

With the help of the AP bureau in Beirut I was finally able to secure passage on the *Paphos Star,* an ancient ferryboat out of Limassol whose captain had agreed to try a nighttime attempt to run the blockade. I found a place to sit on the smelly deck and we set off in the early evening for Larnaca. My fellow travelers could think and talk of nothing but the crisis. At times tempers flared as our old tub plowed sluggishly through the dark waters of the eastern Mediterranean.

In the early-morning hours the captain ordered all the navigation lights extinguished. If the British Navy discovered his vessel, it would be confiscated. No patrols were sighted and soon after dawn we were off the Cyprus coast and by noon we had pulled into Larnaca.

There were no immigration or customs officials on duty at the docks when we landed. Larnaca was a sunny tourist resort but now its beaches were deserted and many of its shops were shuttered, the air of disaster settling over the city. It prompted me to get closer to the action. It was a different land and a different war but my reactions were familiar to me.

I had trouble finding a taxi to get to Nicosia. Eventually, two students who had been on the *Paphos Star* with me shared their ride. The stony, brown landscape was a contrast to the verdant greens of the jungles of Southeast Asia. There was real beauty in the meadow saffron blanketing the fields with its pinkish white blossoms, the solitary cypress trees lording over sun-drenched slopes and dark ravines, and the lemon and orange groves clustered protectively around stone farmhouses.

We arrived in the capital in the late afternoon. A few soldiers were patrolling the streets. I got off at the Hilton Hotel, where the press corps was assembling, and in the lobby I spotted Joe Fried of the *New York Daily News*, whom I'd known in Saigon. He warned me that the locals were angry at the visiting press. "It's worse here than in Saigon," he said. I presumed Joe was being Joe, a little testy, but then I heard shouting at the reception desk, saw arms flailing and boots flying, and two men wrestling on the floor. One turned out to be a young AP photographer from Paris, Paul Roque. Another former AP Saigon colleague, Max Nash, pulled the two men apart as the hotel staff looked on. Roque later told me that his assailant was a Greek Cypriot soldier who had been drinking at the bar for several days.

The following evening the right-wing radical politician Nikos Sampson walked in and sat on a bar stool glowering at the press corps, one hand on a Scotch and soda and another on a .45. Sampson had been deposed that day after only one week as president of Cyprus. He had been severely criticized by the international press. Few of us were eager to get his views on the crisis.

I felt the same bitterness in the streets of the capital and in the countryside. On this tiny island, neighbors who had lived together amicably for centuries were butchering one another. In Vietnam, the scale of violence was defined by the excesses of the Cold War. Here it was a history of racial and religious differences, not superpowers' egos. I had little insight into the issues but would try to cover the story as I had in Vietnam, simply to write only what I saw myself.

And there was much to see. The drama was being played in a stunning setting. The armies that had spread Western civilization had marched through Cyprus and had left their imprint everywhere—in the Greek and Roman amphitheaters and viaducts, Byzantine churches and Gothic cathedrals. One day Roque and I drove through the old Venetian fortress walls of medieval Nicosia to the Turkish lines, and then across the Mesaoria Plain, where, in 1191, Richard the Lionhearted rescued his fiancée, Berengaria, from the Cypriot emperor, Ducas Comnenos. We climbed up the legendary five-fingered Pentadaktylos Mountains, where the crusader castle of St. Hilarion perched on a rocky outcropping above us, and then we sped downhill to the port of Kyrenia, founded by the Greeks in the tenth century B.C., and overwhelmed in battle a score of times since.

Kyrenia was swarming with its latest invaders, the Turkish military. Many of the shops had been looted, their windows smashed, and doors busted open. A mountain road to Nicosia linked the invaders with the Turkish population in the capital and it was clear to us that control was being consolidated rapidly. The Greek Cypriot population had been rounded up and herded under guard to hotels. In the hillside town of Bellapais, where tourists recently sipped brandy sours and coffee in the cobbled courtyard of the twelfth-century abbey, women and children were being held forty to a room. A Turkish officer claimed that they were being fed and, "We wish them no harm."

In other sectors of the island—territory still controlled by the Cypriots—the Turkish population was being similarly mistreated. One day I drove south toward Larnaca past olive groves and orange arbors to the village of Alaminos. I saw the body of a man in a dry watercourse below Mrs. Feysal Arif's house. She told me it was her husband. She scrambled down the rocky path to chase away the crows feeding on the corpse and told me she was waiting for a Muslim cleric to give her husband a decent burial on the rise above the town square near the recent graves of thirteen other men. I had been led by an old hunchback to a bullet-marked stone wall where, he said, Greek soldiers had executed thirteen Turkish Cypriot village men in retribution for the unexplained deaths of two Greek Cypriots.

The local population was antagonistic to all outsiders and suspicious of the press, but now everyone wanted their stories told since Cyprus was becoming an issue in the United Nations. I saw people in their villages sitting at coffee shops with shortwave radios listening to BBC and Voice of America news broadcasts. Roque and I drove out of Nicosia early each morning, traveling the bumpy roads to the northwestern part of the island where the Turks were attempting to extend their area of control. We flew a white flag from our vehicle, never sure who might stop us because the battle lines were so fluid. Some days we passed through Greek and Turkish lines half a dozen times.

Our favorite vantage point was Lapithos, a tangle of orange and lemon groves and old churches and mosques and eighteenth-century houses that crawled halfway up the foothills of the western Kyrenia Mountains. The last Greek strongpoint on the northern coast was at Cypress Tree Mountain, a rocky pinnacle that rose precipitously from the sea above Lapithos and overlooked the whole northern coast, where the Turks were building up their military forces. On August 2, I watched the first Turkish infantry units moving into the outskirts of Lapithos and interviewed the officers before returning back to Nicosia through Greek Cypriot lines.

The next day as we drove along the coast we heard the artillery roaring again. Small knots of soldiers were walking along the rocky beaches in retreat. More men were half running down the slopes of the sunburned foothills, falling into each other's arms at the roadside, waiting for the occasional jeep or truck to ferry the wounded back to the rear. A young Greek Cypriot officer shook his fist at us as we watched the retreat, holding up an old single-shot Czech-made rifle. "What else can we do but run," he asked. "Do you see what we have to fight the artillery with?"

Their commanding officers had already left for the rear; they were surrendering the whole northern coast and its rich hotels and tourist resorts.

Later that evening Roque told me that he was planning to visit a besieged orphanage in the hills above the northern coast. I counseled him to be careful: the military situation in the region was increasingly volatile.

The next day, as I drove along an empty expanse of the Mesaoria Plain, a rented car raced past and I recognized some colleagues. Soon afterward I was flagged down by another press car carrying several French photographers who told me that Paul had been seriously injured on the road earlier that morning and had been taken to Nicosia for treatment.

I found Paul in the crowded post-operative room at the public hospital. There was little space between the beds and some patients had been rolled out into the hallway. He was wrapped in bandages and he told me his story haltingly: The four press cars had been proceeding up a mountain road when the BBC crew in the lead became concerned about land mines. They had stopped to investigate. The soundman, Ted Stoddard, stepped on an explosive device, which killed him instantly and wounded correspondent Simon Dring. Both lay in the middle of the road. Paul moved up as cautiously as he could to help them, and then he too stepped on a mine. The explosion sprayed him with metal fragments, injuring his left foot, knee and shoulder and inflicting the worst wound in his face. He later lost his left eye. He was waiting to be tranferred to a hospital at the British base of Akrotiri that afternoon, and the following day he was flown home to Paris in a hospital plane chartered by the AP.

The situation was getting worse and the United Nations was unable to stop it. The Turks were clearly intent on expanding their territory. I realized that this was a war that interested the European subscribers of the AP more than the Americans. In the United States the conflict was remote.

After long days and sleepless nights, I was tired and desperate for a rest. Despite the objections of Alex Eftyvoulou, the AP's Cyprus correpondent, I drove to a resort hotel on the Bay of Amathus near

Limassol, where I rented a room and ate a grand dinner and drank a lot of wine. Around five in the morning, the phone rang and through a sleepy haze I heard the voice of Donald Wise of the *London Daily Mirror*. He was a friend of many years who was reputed to have impeccable contacts within British intelligence. He chided me for my excesses and told me to get out of bed and get back to Nicosia. "The Turks are coming in for the kill," he said. There would be air strikes at dawn.

I rushed my rented car through the blackness past security checkpoints where soldiers were fast asleep. The gray dawn lighted my climb up the slopes of the coastal hills to the edge of the Mesaoria Plain just as the sun's rays blinked across the mountains. The Turkish air strikes came with the sun: two pairs of Supersaber jets roared low over the Nicosia airport and dropped bombs on the sleeping city. Other pairs of bombers followed, and black smoke billowed into the air from burning offices. The Hilton Hotel was draped with white sheets painted with red crosses and the lobby was jammed with local residents, shouting and crying and trying to get to the basement air raid shelter. I bumped into Joe Fried again. "This place isn't Vietnam," he warned. I was new here and should be careful.

I nodded to him and went out the door. It was not Vietnam. It was easier to negotiate. I could clearly see what was going on. I drove past abandoned checkpoints toward the airport as the air strikes shifted to other parts of town. I heard the familiar thump of mortar fire and I headed to it. I did not stop until I saw a Greek officer just ahead of me dive into a ditch.

It was only seven but the sun was already blistering hot by the time I joined some soldiers sheltering under the concrete stairs of a new factory building at the edge of the airport. They said Turkish troops were about a hundred yards away and moving toward us in front of tanks. One told me ruefully, "We have already lost the Arkadi bar," a popular drinking place on the airport road.

I returned to the Hilton to phone a story in and then I left the city through the ancient portals of the Famagusta Gate, weaving through narrow alleys and rural lanes for a view of the attack. Standing on a ridge, I could see the Turkish forces stretched out along a line several miles long and advancing rapidly toward me. Tanks were kicking up dust trails and firing at farmhouses and clusters of retreating Greek Cypriot soldiers. The pall of black and yellow smoke almost obscured the craggy Kyrenia Mountains, which form a backdrop to Nicosia.

I drove about a mile further along the old Famagusta road and was stopped by a sweat-stained Greek officer riding a jeep at the head of a column of mobile anti-aircraft guns and armored troop carrier tanks. He called out to me: "Is the road to Nicosia clear, do the Turks have it yet?" I reassured him that the highway was still open. I followed the column back into the capital, where the streets were deserted, the houses shuttered and the Hilton even more crowded. The kitchen staff was serving food on trestle tables in the lobby.

By Wednesday evening, the Turks had pushed the Greek Cypriots out of nearly a third of the island. They expected to keep rolling across the Mesaoria Plain to forge a link with the Turkish enclave in Famagusta in the east. In the morning, I headed there with Spartaco Bodini, an AP photographer who had flown in to replace Roque. We were stuck in traffic for hours as the Greek Cypriot population of Nicosia was attempting to flee in their cars and trucks to the relative security of the southern coast.

In the early afternoon we pulled into the British base of Dhekelia, where thousands of terrified refugees were camped. We drove on to a British military outpost at Four Mile Point that looked across a shallow valley to Famagusta city, where tall white beach hotels gleamed in the sunlight. Bodini and I were chatting with the soldiers when there were explosions nearby, and we saw that we were under fire from a line of Turkish Sherman tanks that were moving across the fields about two miles away. But the tanks did not press the attack. They turned instead toward Famagusta, firing as they went.

I felt as if I was watching a war movie, so perfect were the props. I wanted to witness the end of the battle. I noticed that the highway into the city dipped into a valley out of sight of the tanks and I told Bodini that we could beat them into Famagusta if we drove fast enough. He told me I was mad. I left without him.

I raced down the hill. Three columns of Turkish tanks were moving rapidly in the open ground about half a mile to my left, paralleling the highway for a while and then veering in until I was sure we would collide on the road ahead. I pulled into a side street in a residential area in the outskirts of Famagusta, and as I turned the next corner I almost hit several dozen Greek Cypriot soldiers with their hands held high trying to surrender—to me. I stopped the car, laughed and informed them that they could escape on foot to the Dhekelia base the way I had come.

By evening the Turks, bypassing the modern Greek part of the city, had entered the north gate of the twelfth-century Famagusta fort, where eleven thousand Turkish Cypriots dwelled. The remaining Greek Cypriot residents had figured that occupation was inevitable, and at dusk I saw that even the oldest inhabitants were clearing out of the city. While I was stopping to pick up a blind woman who had begged me to take her to the edge of town, twenty truckloads of police sped by.

In the darkness, modern Famagusta was a ghost town and I had the choice of sleeping anywhere I pleased. I encountered two British correspondents, Will Jones of the *Sunday Times* and Colin Smith of *The Observer,* and we checked out the luxury hotels along Varosha beach, finally settling on the Markos, a high rise with a well-stocked bar and a marvelous view of the city. Like all the hotels, the Markos was abandoned but its lights were still on and the elevators still running. We took keys to the rooms of our choice and I walked over to the bar and gathered up half a dozen bottles of beer. In my room I found the beds neatly made and towels and soap in the bathroom and the shower water hot and satisfying. But I was unable to work the hotel telephone switchboard and had to cross the street to a high school to phone my story in.

At daybreak, as I looked across to the walled fort I saw Turkish soldiers moving out into the Greek side of Famagusta, creeping along the streets with their weapons at the ready. I needed to make contact with the victorious troops and interview their officers, but I couldn't think of a way how. My Brit colleagues were nowhere to be seen. I decided on the reckless approach. I drove to the center of town and entered an abandoned sidewalk café on the main street. I took a bottle of cognac and sat outside on the terrace, sipping a full glass. The scraping and crunching of tanks and the sound of store windows being broken announced the arrival of the Turks. The steel snout of a Sherman tank gun poked around the street corner and zeroed in on me. I told myself that no disciplined gunner would waste an 85mm shell on one lonely civilian.

I had guessed right. The tank rolled past, followed by a squad of infantrymen. They didn't even seem surprised to see me. An officer directed me to the south gate of the fort when I asked how I could get some information, and I drove to a wooden barrier and then walked the rest of the way across the cobbled streets, carrying a white flag on a stick to be on the safe side. A policeman handed my press pass to an official, who came back several minutes later and denied me entry because the pass was one day out of date.

319

I had the road entirely to myself as I drove out of fallen Famagusta and back to Nicosia. Bodini was unhappy: New York was pressing him for pictures and demanding to know why he had not gone with me.

Gallagher called me a couple of days later and told me to come home because the story was winding up. A ceasefire had been worked out at the United Nations. I booked passage by ship to Athens, and I was actually boarding when the purser handed me a message from the AP instructing me to return to Nicosia immediately. The U.S. ambassador, Rodger P. Davies, had been killed by automatic weapons fire during a violent anti-American demonstration at the embassy. I hung around the island for another week. I could see that the story was far from over. The United Nations had cooled passions for the time being but the problem of sovereignty was not resolved. My role had ended, but I was ready to return if hostilities broke out again.

In Cyprus I realized that I was good at covering wars, that Vietnam was not the end of my combat career but the beginning. I was turning forty with a wife and children, but my health was perfect and I had the conviction that what I was doing was important.

Severing the Ties That Bind

I WAS COMFORTABLE WITH THE Associated Press and the people who worked there. I intended to make it my lifetime career. There was a tradition of commitment in the wire services; I was looking ahead to the time when I would wear the thirty-five-year pin and retire somewhere cozy. But the camaraderie we shared in the Saigon bureau was missing in the New York office.

I played the nonconformist. I didn't favor the button-down gray look of AP management; I allowed my thinning hair to grow to near shoulder length. I took the side of labor in an internal struggle between management and the wire service guild, a decision that annoyed my superiors. Wes Gallagher had made sure that I was well paid and I had no personal quarrel with the news organization, but I could not avoid involvement with the guild members who worked alongside me. Some in management were furious because I was the only writer of my rank to join the guild. I further annoyed them by joining picket lines outside 50 Rockefeller Plaza.

A new team of managers took over the AP after Wes Gallagher retired in 1976, led by Keith Fuller, a Texan who had been part of my AP life since he had bought me lunch on my first visit to New York in 1962. Fuller had defended my Vietnam reporting, though I don't think he entirely approved of it. He told me once that the war was a worthy national cause and that we were making too much of the fifty-five thousand American death toll there, "because that many Americans die on our highways each year." I had made little effort to cultivate a relationship with him, relying on Wes to guide my career, which he did with a strong hand, dissuading me from taking job offers from the *New York Times* and NBC News, and dispatching me to distant corners of the world. But Gallagher's era was over and I had misgivings about my future.

The truth was that I was becoming bored. I was tiring of routine assignments. One day the managing editor asked me to do a story on a series of holdups outside a West Side Manhattan McDonald's restaurant where schoolkids were losing their hamburgers to muggers. I declined the assignment on the grounds that it wasn't news. There were complaints about my attitude. My 1977 personnel assessment was the worst I ever had.

I did have some interesting assignments in the late 1970s. I made extensive trips to Canada, Mexico and the Caribbean, assessing the temper of America's neighbors. I was assigned to the Jonestown mass suicide story, and went on a journey around the world with Eddie Adams to observe the plight of the world's homeless people.

I covered school busing stories in Boston and Louisville, and tracked illegal immigration in the Southwestern states. I spent nights in Manhattan tenements with old people besieged by crime, and weekends on mountaintops with armed American families building sandbagged bunkers and preparing for the apocalypse.

I was busy but I was not happy. I was not being sent to the places I really wanted to go: to Nicaragua, where the Sandinistas were fighting to overthrow the Somoza regime, to El Salvador, to Africa, where terrible conflicts were dragging in the big powers, to the civil war in Lebanon.

In April of 1981 I was assigned to Atlanta, Georgia, to cover a story that had attracted the attention of the nation. The great Southern metropolis of Atlanta, with its glass and steel skyline and fancy shops, expensive restaurants and tree-lined streets, had billed itself "A city too busy to hate." But its police officers were hunting a serial killer who had taken the lives of twenty-eight black children. Within spitting distance of the city's shiny commercial towers was another Atlanta of run-down brick housing projects, litter-strewn streets, impoverished neighborhoods and an unemployment rate of 40 percent. I spent a lot of time in that old Atlanta covering the search for the child killer.

I was standing outside a Quality Inn Hotel early one morning, waiting for an official to emerge for an interview, when I saw a former AP colleague, Richard Blystone. He was in Atlanta to renegotiate his contract with the Cable News Network, the communications venture Ted Turner had created one year earlier. Blystone had quit the AP, after a long, successful career, for a CNN job in London.

The three networks, CBS, NBC and ABC, towered over the broadcast horizon, and I wondered at his audacity. CNN was a runty communications organization, with big ambitions and a small audience. Cable technology was not yet available to most of America. But Blystone insisted that he had never had so much fun.

He persuaded me to visit CNN's Techwood Drive headquarters for a look and to meet the executive vice president, Burt Reinhardt. He warned me that his boss could be brusque, and Reinhardt lived up to that billing. His first words to me were, "Just what are you doing here?" I mentioned that Blystone said he was having a lot of fun on CNN, and that I was curious about what was going on. Suddenly, I was conscious of my thinning hair, and my sallow complexion, and I was thinking that Reinhardt must be sizing me up as another hopeful trying to get his face on television. If so, I realized he may have been reading me correctly, even though I had not thought the situation through. I regretted having come.

Still, I listened to Reinhardt describe CNN's possibilities and challenges. It amounted to a video version of the Associated Press—but it seemed like an idea that would come true far in the future. After an hour neither of us was sure who was courting whom. When I made to leave, Reinhardt remarked, "Well, let's have a camera test, anyway," and I figured it couldn't hurt. He gave instructions to an assistant: "Have him look directly into the camera and talk about himself for a few minutes."

When I was placed in front of the camera in a corner of the studio, the assistant told me, "Reinhardt doesn't know what he's talking about. Don't look straight into the camera, look over at me, talk to me." A few minutes later when Reinhardt played the tape back on his VCR and shook his head and said, "Jesus Christ, didn't I tell you to look straight into the camera and talk?"

He called me the next day. "Let's get serious about this." By Monday CNN had come up with a job, the title of national correspondent and a little more money than the AP was paying me. Without hesitation, I accepted. A forty-seven-year-old aging voyager embarking on a new journey on uncharted seas.

My AP colleagues had been aware of my discontent, so no one was surprised at my decision. They saw that I was excited. I went to tell the chief news executive, Lou Boccardi, that I was leaving but it was not easy locating him and I learned that he too was wrestling with his future, weighing a job offer from a major newspaper. When he appeared late in the afternoon, I pushed my way past his secretary into his office but he cut me short. "I'll talk to you about it later."

I was in a hurry to cut the ties. I had my one-line resignation letter hot in my hand and I was determined to deliver it that day. I waited around until I saw Boccardi leave. I ran after him down Madison Avenue as he headed toward Grand Central Station and caught up with him at Forty-sixth Street and thrust the letter into his hand. "I quit," I said. Commuters were pushing past us. He half smiled at me, shook his head and grabbed my outstretched hand and was on his way. Later he wrote me a friendly note that said, "You have mastered the toughest assignments and braved the greatest dangers and for this the Associated Press, journalism and the readers of America are enriched."

My AP colleagues threw a farewell party on the roof garden of a skyscraper near Rockefeller Center, attended by few AP executives but dozens of my newsroom pals who said they were sorry to see me go. Well into the boozy, emotional evening they unwrapped a large photographic copy of an eighteenth-century English print of a courtier pierced by a metal screw of large dimensions. Handing it to me ceremoniously, special correspondent Saul Pett proclaimed: "Arnett, you were screwed by the AP and don't ever forget it," and there was much hissing and laughing and the clink of glasses.

It was not easy to share my true feelings with them or anyone else because I doubted they could understand. I was leaving because of what I had learned at the AP, and what I had learned to love, the thrill of covering wars, for which there was no substitute. I was afraid that wasn't going to happen anymore.

In the Trenches with CNN

I MADE IT CLEAR to CNN that I wanted to be in the hot spots, but I agreed that I first had to learn the new medium. CNN had proved it could stay on the air twenty-four hours each day but it was still trying to define its news philosophy. I presumed that my hiring indicated a desire for the traditional approach to the news. But when I first walked into the newsroom and was greeted by the senior producer, Ted Kavanau, he took me aback by exclaiming, "I'll make you famous on the air. Just remember, if it bleeds it leads." He had pioneered the blood and gore coverage of the successful Metromedia evening Ten O'Clock News in New York City. He explained to me that he wanted CNN to be everything that the traditional TV networks weren't, to bring the excitement and competitive spirit of local news to the national arena. His enthusiasm was hard to contain.

Another view of CNN's philosophy, more akin to mine, came from Reese Schonfeld, whom Ted Turner had chosen to run the company. He told me he wanted CNN to be first at the scene of every major story and show it on the air before anyone, whether it was politics or food poisoning.

Several large satellite dishes were planted like spreading trees in the backyard of the headquarters of Turner Broadcasting, formerly a Jewish country club. From the outside it looked dignified. Inside, the CNN staff was crammed into the basement. The news operation was centered in a sunken control area, called the pit, where technicians manipulated banks of switches and dials, and producers and directors watched the screens and shouted orders and instructions all bent on keeping CNN on the air twenty-four hours a day. Next to the pit were the anchor and national desks, and beyond those were a jumble of tables and chairs pushed together to form larger units where writers and newscasters and editors worked and phones jangled. There was no privacy. At the desk next to mine, anchor Kathleen Sullivan applied her makeup meticulously before each show and tried to ignore interested stares of the men around her.

The place looked put together on a shoestring, which it was. CNN was losing millions each month. There were many young people on the staff, video journalists or VJs as they were called, hired cheap right out of college with the dream of making it in television. I brought

324

a packet of cookies to work one day and offered one to a young woman in the break room who took it gratefully with the comment, "VJs accept food."

The atmosphere in the newsroom was always volatile. Schonfeld had his own table next to the pit. A big, outspoken man, he could be warm and generous but usually he stalked the floor in nervous agitation as important news hours approached. Even though CNN had been operating for a year there were major technical problems to overcome to get material on the air when it was needed.

Schonfeld ruled the news room like a dictator. His noisy outbursts sometimes drowned out the broadcasts. I sat in on a morning news conference where Reese objected to the list of that day's news assignments. The stories were the usual round of press conferences, natural disasters and congressional hearings. "Tell Washington I don't want any of those stories, start from scratch with a new lot," he shouted. "Kill all these stories, come up with another list," he exclaimed to New York, Los Angeles and Chicago.

Upstairs, above the chaos of the newsroom, at the entrance, flew the flags of the United States, the state of Georgia and the United Nations. The unlikely United Nations emblem was a symbol of Ted Turner's philosophy, his resolve to make CNN "a positive force in a world where cynics abound," an organization that would "hopefully bring together in brotherhood and kindness and peace the people of this nation and this world." But in the news room below, desperate to keep the news, any news, flowing around the clock, these lofty aspirations weren't really the issue.

I was first assigned to the New York City bureau of CNN, oddly located in the middle of the lobby of the World Trade Center building. Through the floor-to-ceiling plate glass windows we could watch the crowds passing by. And the crowds could also watch us. The cameras and studio were in full view.

My desk was right next to the window and one noontime a young woman grinned at me as I was typing a script. Then she started licking the glass in front of me, making larger and larger circles with her tongue until my vision was obscured by hazy saliva. One evening a middle-aged man in a beige raincoat stood watching Mary Alice Williams deliver the news for a while, and then pulled his coat open and flashed her while she was on the air. Floor-to-ceiling curtains were installed a few days later.

I had fun wrestling with the new medium. I discovered that my voice was a much more important factor than I had first realized because many people listened to television news even when they were not watching it. It took me some time to get used to seeing my face on the screen. I did not dare admit to former colleagues that I wore makeup.

I was aware of the commanding role that television played in the political life of America, but as a reporter who had labored in print for twenty-five years, I was still startled by its impact. When I was sent to Jacksonville, Florida, to cover a regional meeting of striking air traffic controllers who were risking being fired by President Reagan, a large crowd of demonstrators cheered as the CNN crew walked toward them because we were covering their side of the story. The networks had not found the time to tell the strikers' story as fully as we had.

My first overseas TV assignment was to El Salvador in the autumn of 1981. Some observers worried that it was becoming a second Vietnam, because America was supporting a repressive government against left-wing guerrillas. There was little breaking news at the time. Reese Schonfeld sent me mainly to prove the point he would be making at a national conference of broadcasters in October: that his fledgling network was covering the world's trouble spots.

I was grateful to get back into war coverage. This is what I had been promised. I was excited to be using video and sound to tell the stories, but live coverage was still not possible at that time. We traveled lightly. We had no editing gear and so we shipped all the video back to Atlanta every couple of days with a script that I would write and record on tape. I was working with general guidelines from CNN. Stories were supposed to be three or four minutes in length, and I had difficulty limiting the size of my scripts. I later learned that the edited versions of my stories were running twelve to fifteen minutes, so CNN producers were simply slicing them into three parts to run on successive days.

El Salvador was spectacular, its wooded hills and farms layered in shades of green. The whole country was the size of a Vietnamese province and we could drive around much of it in a day. But the war was hard to find: neither side had sizeable forces, and they were constantly regrouping while we were there.

We did see shocking brutality. Right-wing death squads operated at night under military protection, picking up those who were suspected of disloyalty to the regime. We would drive around each morning photographing the fresh bodies of peasants and students dumped on the roadside. At an old lava slide behind San Salvador Mountain we walked among the skeletons of recently murdered adults and children still clothed in tattered garments, their bones picked clean by fat black vultures who perched in the nearby trees.

As a print reporter I could write descriptions of what I saw and heard, and sometimes I had taken my own pictures. In television news I was only as good as the video that came out of the camera, a complex instrument controlled by someone else. I was discovering that TV news was a team effort, and I had to push hard to get the job done.

My cameraman, Howie Dorf, was a former Miami policeman who had worked with CNN on a few previous assignments. He had invested in the best camera available, a Japanese Ikegami, and he nursed it like a baby. On an overcast day at a National Day parade by the Salvadoran armed forces, Dorf looked up at the sky where rain clouds were lingering and told me that his camera was more valuable than any further video of the parade. I told him to shut up and keep filming, but he laid his equipment down tenderly and shaped up to me in a boxer's stance. My authority challenged, I rushed at him. We grappled on the grass as the army's infamous Atlacatl Battalion marched past us, followed by formations from the National Police. Finally, mud stained and embarrassed, we rejoined our amused news colleagues in the stands.

I phoned the CNN foreign editor, Jeannee Von Essen, next morning for her advice. She told me to hang in: the company could not afford to replace the cameraman. Howie and I made up, though we had problems whenever it rained.

I began to realize that hysterics were part of the birth pangs of CNN, and passion an ingredient in the creative process of all television news. Reese Schonfeld's enraged outbursts around the live anchor desk in Atlanta were symptomatic of a wider frenzy. When I suggested to Schonfeld that I might need some instruction in dealing with the responsibilities of the new medium he laughed, "You're already going to school: the sink-or-swim school of television news."

My growing pains paralleled CNN's struggle to survive. In the United States it was trying to make its mark by pursuing news that could be covered live. Being able to put the news on the air before the networks was its only edge. Congressional hearings and natural disasters were regular grist. Live coverage was also surprisingly affordable because it didn't require the same expensive journalistic and creative skills. All you had to do was be there and turn on the switch. The Reagan White House became the news center around which the whole network revolved; CNN placed more resources there than anywhere else. It would present live reports every hour even if little or nothing was going on. I was offered the job of White House correspondent in 1982, and I tried it out for a month or so but I quickly realized it was not for me.

I told CNN I was available for anything, anywhere, and that I preferred action, that I wanted to cover the little wars spreading across the globe. I doubted that there would ever be another conflict as important as Vietnam, but as long as wars were being fought there would be a necessity to cover them. I didn't see my job any differently than any other beat reporter.

I asked Ed Turner, CNN's vice president for news, to send me to Afghanistan to cover the guerrilla struggle against the invading Soviet military, but he said it was too difficult to get the bulky television equipment inside the country. "You're the kind of guy who'd go to Afghanistan on his vacation," he told me, which is what I did in September of 1982, on a writing assignment from *Parade* magazine. I traveled to the Pakistan border city of Peshawar with freelance photographer Ed Hille and joined escorts from the Jamiat-i-Islami group.

In native attire we trudged thirty hours across a mountain pass into the Kunar valley. The big pebbles on the rutted pathways made the walking hell. We forded the swift Kunar River at midnight on a raft fashioned from inflated truck tires. But they were unable to withstand the punishment from rocks and we were drenched by the time we reached the other side. We spent a week with a band of Muslim mujahedeen fighters whose mission was to ambush Soviet military columns on the Jalalabad road. We ate flat corn bread and red beans and slept in rocky caves.

We waited for the Russians every day at a vantage point on a cliff eight hundred yards from the road. The rock walls around us were pitted with bullet holes and splintered by shell blasts from previous ambushes. The guerrillas said the passing tank columns were difficult to hit, and that there were always immediate counterattacks by Soviet armed helicopters and jet bombers on their hideout. I was told that casualties among the guerrillas were usually high. I was not disappointed that the Russians did not come while we were there.

Covering dangerous stories for television was a greater burden than I was used to since I always needed a crew along. CNN sent me to Iran in 1982 on a government-sponsored visit, and on the way home our crew was assigned to cover the Israeli invasion of Lebanon. My crew members, Vito Maggiolo and George McCarger, held out for pay raises. Vito told me, "We didn't sign up with CNN to get shot at." I argued with them to continue on. I knew the network would not pay them more money and the assignment would collapse if they rebelled. I finally convinced them to proceed on with me to Beirut, and as we flew into Damascus, Syria, on the first leg of the journey I was aware that their well-being was my responsibility.

Being responsible for anyone's safety in that part of the world was a demanding task. We didn't even have Syrian visas, so we spent all afternoon and evening at the airport persuading the authorities to let us in. The next day we hired a taxi and headed overland across the desert plateau toward Beirut.

The Lebanese border post had been destroyed in an Israeli bombing raid, so we didn't have to beg for entry visas. Further inside the country, as we drove over the war-blackened hills into the Bekaa Valley, there were signs of recent military action. Several villages had been destroyed, and burnt-out military vehicles lay in the fields. Our Damascus taxi driver refused to go on, dumping us at the side of the road with all our gear.

Vito and George looked at me expectantly and I tried to appear unconcerned. I suggested we hump our gear toward a small settlement down the hill. We reached a grocery store and the proprietor agreed to drive us into Beirut in his old Chevrolet. We made it into the city but got lost in the jumble of streets, and ended up among the ruined buildings of the port. We checked in at a nearby Christian militia outpost and they directed us to a taxi stand at the Green Line border with West Beirut. I loaded the crew and gear into a car, sent them off to the Commodore Hotel, and followed in another vehicle. I reached the hotel ahead of them and was at the bar when Vito and George arrived, sweating and scared. Their worst fears had almost come true.

"By God we nearly died," Vito exclaimed. Artillery shells had landed near them as they drove across the Green Line. A little later they had been run off the road by a jeep loaded with Palestinian soldiers who had shouted and pointed their guns at them. A British reporter at the bar threw his arm around Vito's shoulder and said, "Hey, cowboy, welcome to Beirut. This stuff happens all the time."

The Commodore was crowded with reporters, including H. D. S. Greenway of the *Boston Globe,* and other Vietnam pals. We tended to cover the war in packs. There seemed to be safety in numbers and that calmed Vito and George. In late afternoons the TV crews would assemble on the hotel roof, their cameras locked on tripods and trained on the horizon as the Israeli jets came in on daily bombing missions.

As the cameras rolled we would retreat under a shelter as metal fragments rained down on the roof.

Two days after we arrived, the Israelis pushed up the coast and surrounded West Beirut with tanks and artillery. We could see their heavy guns in the driveways and in the gardens on the hillsides. We would drive up to their positions each morning to watch them shell the Palestinians. Then we would drive back to West Beirut, check the damage and watch the Palestinians shell back.

Our little CNN team stayed together at all times to help one another. We hired a Mercedes taxi with a dependable driver to get around the war fronts. The PLO leader, Yasir Arafat, had an office in a high-rise building that was under frequent Israeli shelling. When we wanted to interview him we drove to within a block and waited for a shelling spasm to end. Then we would dash along the street into the sandbagged entrance before the barrage resumed.

We made a daily run into the Sabra refugee camp, where a Palestinian military commander who had established his headquarters in a mosque was willing to brief us on the military situation. I went inside one morning, leaving the crew to take pictures. I heard a commotion in the street and ran outside. Vito and George were being driven away in a jeep packed with armed civilians.

Of course, a kidnapping was our biggest fear. My driver threw up his hands in alarm and we careened off on a chase that took us down narrow rutted alleyways and into the slums of the Bourj al-Barajneh district. We arrived at a small apartment building that my driver said was the headquarters of a Shia militia force allied to the Amal organization. The jeep was outside.

I ran into the main hallway but an armed youth pushed me away. My driver, shouting in Arabic, helped me pass and we followed a wall of protective sandbags to the floor below where two more guards barred the way. By now I was convinced that Vito and George were hostages, or worse. I insisted on gaining entry. I had learned that righteous indignation could open doors and break down walls.

One guard shrugged his shoulders and beckoned me to follow him two more levels down the darkened stairway. A uniformed officer was sitting at a desk. Vito and George were squatting on the floor, their hands in front of them. As I approached, Vito turned and grinned. "Hey, Pete, how's Reggie Jackson doing? This guy's a Yankee fan and wants to know if Reggie's streak is holding up." He picked up the cup of coffee in front of him and sipped it. The officer looked at me, seeking an answer to his baseball question. Unfortunately, I couldn't provide it, but he poured me coffee anyway and let us all leave after offering apologies for the behavior of his soldiers. After that, I figured, Vito and George could take care of themselves.

I was lucky and pleased that no photographer or television technician had ever been hurt on assignment with me. Eventually, in Santiago, Chile, in the autumn of 1983 my luck didn't hold while we were covering civil disturbances surrounding the tenth anniversary celebrations of the military dictatorship of President Augusto Pinochet.

Willis Perry from the Atlanta bureau was my cameraman, a tall African-American who towered over the crowd. During a demonstration at a fairground an armada of police vehicles assaulted the crowds. We fled down a side street. Willis turned to raise his camera to his shoulder just as a police bus passed the intersection behind us. Guns blasted from the windows. I heard the whistle of rubber bullets. Willis was standing just behind me and I heard him gasp, "I'm hit," as he slid to the ground, spilling his camera into my arms. He had been struck in the chest and his flesh was gouged in a deep wound. Had I been three inches taller I would have been hit in the face.

I gave a battlefield promotion to soundman Tyrone Edwards because CNN did not have the money to replace Willis, who was sent home to recuperate. Tyrone was in his early twenties and an excellent engineer, but since he was inexperienced in photography I could never be sure if his video would be in focus and of useable color quality. His competence became critical later in the month when we stumbled upon a dramatic news story in El Salvador.

We were out early on the Sunday morning of September 25 when most of the press corps was relaxing. I needed additional videotape for a news analysis on American policy alternatives in Central America, and I was hoping for a few pictures of soldiers in action. The United States was spending millions in military support for the Salvadoran government, but the left-wing insurgents were fighting back.

Our driver was taking us along the Pan American Highway east of the capital. We saw planes dropping bombs beyond a distant range of hills. We drove toward the bombing until we came to a muddy crossroads guarded by soldiers who refused to let us pass. Soon several score of civilians came hurrying down the road, carrying wounded relatives and complaining that they were being shelled by government planes in the garrison town of Tenancingo about ten miles back along the road.

I felt we could not wait at the crossroads and that we had no alter-

331

native but to walk in to get the story. We redistributed the heavy equipment, and went off on foot.

Closer to Tenancingo we saw spotter planes overhead and we hid in the jungle along the roadside. Nearer the town, government A-37 bombers were visible in the sky as they soared and then dove in bombing runs. An armed helicopter came past at treetop level with its guns blazing and we ran into an old stone house that was already occupied by armed left-wing guerrillas. They took us into custody, checked our credentials, and then escorted us through the town.

Near the bombed-out ruins of a corner house on the cobbled main street the bodies of a dozen women and children were strewn across the road. I could see Edwards was shocked, but he photographed the scene. There were scores of guerrillas around. They had captured Tenancingo that morning and taken the government military garrison. The bombing had followed in angry reaction. But clearly the casualties in the streets and inside the destroyed buildings were civilian residents, the people the government was supposed to protect. As we were leaving the guerrillas were pulling out of town. An officer told us, "If we stay there will be more bombing and more civilians will die." The destruction of Tenancingo represented another escalation in the Salvadoran war.

We returned to our hotel in the capital in midevening and looked at our videotape. Some of it was out of focus; some of it had an eerie blue tinge that came from faulty color balancing. But there was more than enough to tell the story. Edwards had passed his test as a cameraman and I embraced him gratefully.

I wrote a script that began, "Death visited Tenancingo on Sunday. It lingered all day in this remote Salvadoran town, snatching at children, at women, at men." Our soundman, Duncan Finch, doubled as tape editor. Though he was exhausted, he sat down at the edit machines and began stitching the tape together over my script. He was a careful technician. When I awoke at dawn he was laying in the last video.

The sun was up as I drove down the coast road to the international airport and shipped the story by the early Taca Airlines flight to Miami. It arrived in the United States around noon and was first played over CNN that afternoon and then repeated many times. The story was the most dramatic I had done for television. A critic in the *Los Angeles Weekly* commented, "The footage was so stark I was astonished it got on the air. Credit to the CNN desk."

The Salvadoran ambassador to Washington, Rivas Gallont, immediately protested that the story was false, blaming the guerrillas for the damage and denying there had been any bombing. The American Embassy in San Salvador initially claimed that the bombing was accidental, but launched an investigation that would lay the blame on the Salvadoran Air Force. The reaction was like Vietnam all over again. I won a journalism prize for the story, my third Sigma Delta Chi Distinguished Service Award.

.   .   .

As a print reporter I might have been tempted to write about the bombing using eyewitness accounts from the survivors, but television news was only as convincing as the picture on the screen. So I was coming to terms with the medium, understanding that I was at most an equal partner with the technology of television. In the Tenancingo story I had leaned on the picture for emphasis and had subdued my inclination toward descriptive prose. The images told their own story. Morley Safer had advised me that the writing was everything, but he was speaking from the vantage of belonging to a television organization that made sure every picture he wanted would be available for his use. CNN did not have that capability; the pictures available for my use were the ones I got.

In El Salvador we were outnumbered four and five to one by the staffs of NBC, CBS and ABC. At satellite centers in foreign hot spots, CNN was sometimes the laughingstock of the others as they watched our often inadequate videotape transmissions. In Guatemala, I had to approach a network colleague I'd known for years to beg for pictures of a coup d'etat that my camera crew had missed. In Beirut, I once borrowed money and tapes from an obliging ABC producer. I even took my then fifteen-year-old daughter, Elsa, to Central America to help out with producing and carrying the gear. I began hearing the insulting "Chicken Noodle News" description of CNN used more frequently. Despairing of ever reaching equality, two of CNN's best young reporters, Mike Boettcher and Jim Mikaszewski, joined NBC.

I tried to compensate for our weaknesses with the hustle I learned at the AP. I stayed with the crew to give guidance on stories. I endeavored to send an edited news package ready for use to our Atlanta headquarters every day from wherever I was, often shipping by air freight to save money. On big stories I saw the major networks wasting thousands of feet of videotape searching for the perfect picture. If I could, I used every inch of our cameramen's shots. The other networks were fickle about their news interests, often passing up good stories as they concentrated on the news flavor of the day. CNN had a lot of time to fill. Everything I sent went on the air sooner or later.

Competition by volume. CNN management tried to get all the bureaus to work that way because it was cost effective. Getting the news on the air first, and in quantity, was more important than making it pretty. The other networks tried to make news an art form, molding it into thirty minutes of programming each evening. They were slick magazines. CNN was the wire service I was used to, the newspaper with a dozen editions, starting with the story from early morning, and staying on it all day. The networks had their stars, but as our executives would declare to anyone who would listen, on CNN the news was the star.

Some TV critics were amused by CNN's brassiness, others were appalled by the unfinished look of the early broadcasts. The rough edges showed in the uneven editing and rambling scripts. Nothing I ever wrote was reviewed in advance by anyone because we didn't have the staff.

Some critics, however, began to notice that the broadcast networks did not have a monopoly on proficiency. In December 1984 the *Los Angeles Times* critic Howard Rosenberg singled out my coverage of the Ethiopian famine: "Arnett and his crew have added to TV's catalogue of powerful images." The volume of information CNN was delivering gathered a momentum of its own. Millions more Americans began signing up for cable.

I was becoming comfortable with gathering pictures and preparing TV news packages. I was finding it more difficult going live. Reese Schonfeld had launched CNN with the promise of delivering live television reports from around the world. In theory this was possible but in practical terms it was difficult to fulfill. Close to home the technological problems could be readily solved. During my brief stint covering the Reagan White House I had stood on the back lawn many a morning delivering live broadcasts without incident. Further afield, it was more difficult.

In El Salvador, in the summer of 1983, covering an upsurge in the war, foreign editor Von Essen had decided that CNN should be the first to beam a live television news broadcast from there. We set up a camera on the roof of the Camino Real Hotel linked by cables hanging down the walls of the building and plugged into a borrowed portable microwave transmitter in our room. As I stood in front of the camera in the blinding noon sun, producer Gerlind Younts was on the phone with our Atlanta headquarters listening to the instructions of the director. I could not hear what they were saying because our young crew did not have the technical ability to transfer the audio to me. I had to deliver three minutes of live commentary on cue. Gerlind tried her best but the telephoned instructions were not clear. She gave me hand signals to start my broadcast too late. I had been standing there several seconds live on air and mute. When I began the director told Gerlind to have me speed up my delivery, and she gave me more hand signals. I was staring at her and the camera and the bright countryside beyond the hotel roof, and I wanted to be anywhere else in the world than Live on CNN.

Over time, I improved. I was sent to Frankfurt, Germany, when the TWA hostage crisis was unfolding in Lebanon in 1985 and I remained live on the air for sixteen hours reporting on the conclusion of the ordeal and didn't miss a hand signal. We were endurance reporters. No one could argue that.

My growing proficiency seemed to impress Burt Reinhardt. He sent me to Japan in the late summer of 1985 to prepare an hour-long live special program on the fortieth anniversary ceremonies of the nuclear bombing of Hiroshima. The early-evening show would preempt two of the network's slickest and most important broadcasts, *Moneyline* and *Crossfire*. Tokyo bureau chief John Lewis advised me that we had so small a budget we would have to depend on arrangements with local TV organizations.

As we approached show time, I felt I was being loaded with extra program responsibilities that would be difficult to fulfill. Our small production crew and I worked through the night to complete the final story requests. I was exhausted when I arrived at our elevated set at Hiroshima's Peace Park. The camera was two hundred feet away because of space limitations, too far to zoom in for a close-up of me or of the panel of experts I would be hosting. To make matters worse, the ceremonies were several minutes late in starting and threw off the CNN schedule. And I was once again unable to communicate with CNN director Bob Furnad in faraway Atlanta.

Gerlind and Elsa tried to help me out by standing in the crowd below, holding up cardboard signs on which they had written cues. When I reached Furnad on the phone he asked me what the hell was going on, and when I answered with a curse he responded sharply, "We all heard that," meaning it had been broadcast on the air.

I was humbled by the whole Hiroshima performance and felt miserable for weeks. Ed Turner and Jeannee Von Essen tried to make me feel better when I returned to Atlanta. They assured me that it hadn't been all that bad. But Reinhardt had the final word. When I walked into his office, the CNN president barked, "That was the worst damned hour of television I've ever seen in my life."

In another place, it might have been the end of a career, but this was the birth of live television news. I just had to try again. I was in El Salvador early in the autumn when Mexico City was struck by a severe earthquake. We flew that night into the capital. Fires were burning out of control and the rubble of office buildings and apartment blocks spilled across main thoroughfares. We joined with the other TV networks in using a newly designed portable television uplink to get our signals back to the United States. We were reporting live at one point from the rubble of a maternity home where newborn babies were being rescued. The CNN correspondents lined up with Tom Brokaw of NBC and Peter Jennings of ABC to take our turns going live.

Watching the chaos of the understaffed CNN operation, Jennings said to me, "I really envy you guys, starting out like this. It reminds me of ABC in the early 1960s when everything was a crap shoot. Now we're so organized, everything is predictable." I offered to swap jobs.

In October, a volcano erupted in a mountain range above the Colombian river settlement of Armero, splashing mudslides and ash down the steep hills and valleys and burying the community in twenty feet of muck. Von Essen handed me five thousand dollars and told me to come back home when the money was spent. I budgeted as best I could, hiring taxis early each morning in the capital of Bogotá and driving several hours down the winding Andean roads until we reached the disaster. We waded two hours through the mud, hauling the camera and sound equipment, until we reached Armero, where twenty thousand people were buried, some with their limbs trapped in the wreckage of buildings and barely clinging to life. It was gripping television.

The other networks covered Armero with chartered aircraft based at the Bogotá airport to fly their numerous crews and producers to a rural airstrip near the disaster scene. They had arranged four-wheel drive vehicles to plow through the Armero mud. We would see them leaving as we were arriving. They would be back in Bogotá in time for their evening broadcasts and a good night of sleep. An ABC producer told me he spent $100,000 on hired planes in the first week of the disaster.

Gerlind and I and the crew came home exhausted when our meager expense money ran out after eight days. I felt burnt out. To be on the road on the major breaking stories was my dream come true, but CNN was demanding superhuman effort. For the first time in my life I was thinking of quitting.

Then I heard that CNN was looking for a new Moscow bureau chief. I applied for the job. Von Essen warned me that there would not be much travel involved because our coverage would be centered on the Soviet capital. That was fine by me.

New Horizons

BEFORE I LEFT FOR Moscow, I became an American citizen. I had been thinking about it more and more. I had come to the United States in 1971, not as an immigrant, but as a journalist. But I had been away from New Zealand for so long that I had forgotten what my hometown looked like.

I had started thinking of myself as a citizen of the world and I demurred when my American friends chided me for not making a more enduring commitment to the country where I lived and in whose currency I had been paid for decades. I looked at the United States through the eyes of a foreign correspondent, not as my homeland, even as my children Andrew and Elsa grew up in America.

Eventually I started thinking like an American. It began to take shape as I was covering the U.S. Embassy hostage crisis in Iran in the winter of 1979. I had been sent to Teheran on Christmas day to help out the hard-pressed AP staff. Inside, fifty diplomats had been held since November 4 by followers of the Ayatollah Khomeini. The fate of the American hostages was uncertain.

The compound fronted a quarter mile of Teleghani Street, which was festooned with political banners that hung like laundry from the trees outside the embassy wall and on the tall buildings across the street. New banners in English were often added, bearing painted slogans such as, "America cannot frighten a nation who has chosen martyrdom from death," and, "The American tradition is murder." Each day, angry crowds, bused in from the countryside, marched along the street, sometimes carrying effigies of President Carter that they burned with roars of approval.

My assignment became a daily vigil, a gesture of support for the captives and a defiance to the Iranian crowds who spat on the reporters

337

gathered at the gate. My stories began to reflect my anger. I wrote of the embassy demonstrations as Teheran's "corridor of hate." Even as I felt my cherished detachment slipping away, I discovered that my emotional stories were striking a chord with American newspaper editors, who were playing them under large headlines on page one.

I was surprised by my own passions, but it was just the beginning of my conversion. I had always embraced American culture. Now I began getting interested even in local politics and in sports competitions. It took only a few years from when I started feeling like an American to becoming one.

The final impetus was the breakup of my twenty-year marriage with Nina, long under stress because of my frequent traveling. I was working with a lot of young people. I had met Gerlind Younts, then an assignment editor for CNN in the Washington bureau. I sensed in Gerlind the taste for adventure that I shared. We moved to Atlanta and she became my field producer. Nina and the children stayed in New York, where Elsa was in high school and Andrew was in college. American citizenship became a logical part of my new horizons.

I was sworn in at a ceremony in Atlanta, Georgia, along with a small group of Asians and Africans and Europeans. Everyone was elated as we raised our right hands and took the oath of allegiance. I felt it was a clean break with the past.

. . .

CNN provided us with six weeks of intensive Russian language instruction, and I made a valiant effort to learn some basics. I had already seen something of the communist world, and had been to Hanoi and Havana, interviewed Fidel Castro, and made a reporting trip to North Korea. The communist world was dour and drab so Moscow did not surprise me.

The CNN Moscow bureau was something more than a news operation. It embodied Ted Turner's dreams of internationalism. His son Teddy Turner, Jr., was working there as a technician.

When I would ask people at CNN about Ted Turner they tended to write him off as an eccentric with a lot of money and a genius for satellite communications and sales. They respected him because he always met his payroll, not for his understanding of news. His internationalism was seen as a naive idealistic indulgence.

I too had my doubts. But as he had learned to leave the running of his sports teams to their managers, Ted Turner left the running of CNN to its news executives and rarely interfered.

Still, his reputation in the Soviet Union made my arrival in early 1986 easy, and the Foreign Ministry officials I was required to meet were helpful as they expressed their admiration.

The cordiality of our relationship with the Soviet authorities was not lost on the distrustful resident Western press corps. The correspondent I was replacing, Stu Loory, was a respected professional of long Soviet experience whose credentials were unchallenged. But I began to hear CNN's objectivity questioned by suspicious colleagues.

The only instruction I had from headquarters was to produce as many stories as possible. I told officials that I wanted to put something on the air every day and they slowly loosened up coverage restrictions that had hobbled the Western press for decades, allowing me interviews with officials as prominent as President Andrei Gromyko and providing access to police and military installations. In the first few months we covered the aftermath of the Chernobyl nuclear reactor disaster. The story was easier than I expected because the Soviet government had been forced into unaccustomed candor by the moral force of Western Europe under the threat of nuclear poisoning.

My Moscow assignment paralleled the ascent of Mikhail Gorbachev. His bold political and social changes kept us working around the clock. I was as busy as I had ever been covering a war.

The Gorbachev era was changing things. The release of the long-vilified dissident Andrei Sakharov marked a new era, but the Soviet authorities continued to violate promises to the Jewish community for more freedom and for more emigration visas.

The refuseniks often took to Moscow's streets with signs and banners for sudden demonstrations. Tipped off, we were often with them as police and KGB thugs rushed the lines, arresting the Jews and pushing them into vans. I was called into the Foreign Ministry one day and lectured by my minder on irresponsible reporting. I replied that the demonstrations represented CNN's definition of news. "But they're only Jews," my interrogator said.

Matters came to a head in February 1987 on the icy cobblestones of the Arbat, a popular recreation street in Moscow. Jewish activists decided to test the limits of Gorbachev's reform policies by sponsoring a week-long series of demonstrations aimed at freeing the dissident Joseph Begun from political prison in Siberia.

His wife, Ina Begun, and the other participants were unmolested for the first few days, but by week's end the authorities were growing impatient. On February 13, a phalanx of beefy KGB operatives attacked the demonstrators and the press, kicking, shoving and punching their way through the lines. Gerlind was carrying the sound equipment and she was thrown to the ground and stamped on. Our cameraman, Gary Shore, barely kept his feet and had to back off to save his gear. I was pummeled and dragged off to an alleyway and dumped on the ground.

After that I noticed that I was being followed around Moscow by security men. Two technicians openly bugged the telephone box outside our apartment door. Police at demonstrations started carrying large garden shears to cut our equipment cables. On Sunday, December 7, the day Gorbachev was flying off to meet President Reagan for their first Washington, D.C., summit meeting, Jewish dissidents gathered to demonstrate at a small park in front of the Moscow Foreign Ministry. The government sent its own demonstrators and a melee ensued. We were in the middle. There was pushing and shouting and cursing. As I tried to help the crew I was pulled to the side by a large uniformed policeman who placed me under arrest.

I showed my press card but I was pushed to the ground by several plainclothes KGB men who dragged me through the crowd and threw me onto a bus, where I was kept under guard by armed security men. A policeman ground his heel on my passport before throwing it in after me. As the bus pulled away I made a resigned gesture to a cameraman who was recording my departure.

I was held at a police station near the Foreign Ministry where an official tried to charge me with public disorder. Eventually I was rescued by the American consul general.

The AP distributed a picture of my arrest and CBS lent CNN video of my being dragged through the crowds. Both the *New York Times* and the *Washington Post* condemned the Soviet action in editorials.

CNN protested to the Soviet government and received an apology. Ed Turner telexed: "Many thanks for taking care of a slow news day here. Soviets ask that you no longer work on weekends."

The December Jewish demonstration was to our knowledge the last one in Moscow that the authorities put down forcefully. By the time President Reagan visited in June, public demonstrations were commonplace.

I had agreed to stay three years in Moscow for CNN, but I got tired of the pressure and asked to leave after two years. I went home soon after Reagan did.

CNN assigned me to the Washington bureau as national security correspondent. It was not a job that got me a lot of television coverage; most of my sources did not want their pictures taken or even be otherwise identified. The beat included the FBI and the CIA, two government agencies not particularly forthcoming to the press in general or to me in particular. My file was thick already.

I didn't mind. The Soviet Union had exhausted me and I needed to recharge my batteries. But as I watched the big news stories pass me by I was unhappy. I was not being called upon to help out in the historic Gorbachev visit to Beijing and the Tiananmen Square massacre that followed it, nor the convulsions transforming Eastern Europe that brought about the end of the Cold War. CNN was using its younger staff and again I worried that my war-reporting days were over but I bit my tongue and suppressed the urge to gripe to Ed Turner.

I promised myself never to lobby too strenuously; I didn't want to tempt fate with overeagerness. I hoped that my track record would speak for me.

Anyhow, I was grateful that I still had my job. Prosperity had changed CNN as sound had transformed Hollywood. Many of the pioneers who had started the maverick cable news company had been let go or had left in frustration. CNN began looking more and more like the broadcast networks, even hiring away their staff.

I did not miss the old days one bit and I was willing to modernize with the organization, but there were limits to what I could do with the years rolling by. When we were chatting on the grounds of the Kremlin during Reagan's visit to Moscow, Dan Rather told me of CBS's staffing policies. They made their first cuts of news correspondents at around age forty, and the second at fifty-five. "If you can get beyond fifty-five in this business you're in for the long haul," Rather had assured me. I was fifty-four.

I was not uncomfortable in Washington. In some ways it was like a last journalist roundup where old globetrotters like myself were put out to pasture, grazing in the grasses of endless congressional committee hearings. Or assigned to stakeouts with mobs of colleagues awaiting the quotes of the day from politicians and designated newsmakers to dispatch them back to the office where more favored staffers got the bylines and the air time.

I enjoyed the company of my old friends but not their eclipse. I lived with my fate, but I did not accept it. There were bright spots. In summer of 1989 I was sent to southern Africa for two months to work on a series on international peace initiatives that Ted Turner had suggested. I traveled to Namibia, Angola, Zaire, Mozambique and South Africa and the journey rekindled my fires.

On the evening of December 19, 1989, I was at home watching CNN, which was covering a crisis in Panama. For several hours it had been broadcasting live telephone calls from residents who were reporting a sudden American military buildup. They were speculating that a U.S. invasion to oust the notorious Panamanian strongman Manuel Noriega, who had fallen out of favor with the Bush administration, was imminent. I had interviewed Noriega several years earlier, when he was an ally of the United States, and I was familiar with the country. The phone rang and it was Ed Turner. He said he wanted to send me to Panama: "You're our first choice to go in." Elated, I left the next morning.

The Panama invasion was short, swift, and the press was shut out from much of it, but it was the first war as media event. CNN matched the other networks in staffing and in equipment, chartering an Eastern Air Lines L1011 jumbo jet out of Miami and flying into Howard Air Force Base in the Canal Zone. We carried editing gear and our own satellite uplink dish. The military sent many of the reporters back home from Panama claiming there was no room for them but I was one of the ten CNN staffers allowed to remain.

We set up our broadcast headquarters at the Quarry Heights officers club for several days. More than fifty male and female news personnel made do with two bathrooms and meager rations and slept stretched out on pool tables and concrete patios. Charles Jaco and I took turns with the other networks' correspondents reporting live every hour from a satellite uplink in the garden.

We went out with the troops when we could and scoured Panama City for stories. The Pentagon had prevented coverage of the initial invasion assaults but we were able to follow up with assessments of damage and casualties. General Noriega, having eluded the initial attack, was in hiding, but when he emerged on Christmas Day at the Papal Nuncio's residence to claim asylum, CNN set up its operation on the fifteenth floor of the Holiday Inn overlooking the compound and began broadcasting twenty-four hours a day.

The military attempted psychological harassment: blasting rock music over the papal compound at deafening levels. The sound was heard around the world on CNN. We stayed live until Noriega gave himself up to the U.S. Army on January 3, 1990.

The Panama story showed CNN just how alluring live coverage of a crisis could be. CNN now had the technology, the skills and the money to go live anywhere in the world.

Part IV
1990–1991

To Baghdad

WE DROVE UP THE winding road from the Jordan Valley looking for action in October 1990. I idly watched a dust storm roll along the desert horizon, through the arid landscape blackened by the sun, but as it came into focus I could see it was propelled by a more predictable force.

"That's no dust storm," I yelled to the CNN crew slumped and sleeping in our car. Mikhail, the soundman, stumbled out of the vehicle onto the road, rubbing his eyes. Yehuda, the husky cameraman followed and rushed to assemble their bulky gear. Tethered to each other like space walkers, they turned toward the swirling sand that was now launching explosions and emitting brilliant flashes of light. I was watching excitedly. We had found our action.

Heavy tanks began wheeling out of the cloud, their guns blasting at targets on a distant hillside. Yehuda was grinning as he adjusted his camera focus. Mikhail's face, covered with sweat, broke into a smile. These men were veterans; they had covered the Lebanon invasion a decade earlier.

For a moment I let myself believe we were seeing the real thing. But the moment passed. What we were watching were Israeli Army tanks training in the Negev Desert. The real action that October was a thousand miles away, across the stony deserts of Jordan and Saudi Arabia, where thirty nations were squaring off against Saddam Hussein. I was stuck in the wrong place and I was unhappy about it.

Later that afternoon we drove home along the Dead Sea shore as the last rays of the sun burned across the rocky parapets of the cliffs and bathed the ancient hilltop fortress of Masada in silvery light. I was enthralled by the drama of Masada. Legend said that the Jewish defenders took their own lives in A.D. 79 to avoid capture by vengeful Roman legionnaires. There was striking evidence of the long siege still clearly visible on the desert floor, a wall of red boulders rolled by Roman slaves to the base of the cliffs to starve out the defenders.

I consoled myself with the legends of the ancient wars of the Middle East because it seemed increasingly unlikely I would get to cover the present one. I had moved to Israel several months ago to be the Jerusalem-based correspondent, and CNN headquarters was insisting that I stay in Israel and follow the crisis from that side. It was an important element of the story, they told me. There was near panic in the country as the Israelis faced the threat of Iraqi chemical attack. But I figured that Israel would just be a sideshow.

My unhappiness grew when, just before Christmas, producer Robert Wiener and correspondent John Holliman arrived from Baghdad for a few days off. They intended to return to Iraq for the countdown to January 15, when the United Nations ultimatum to Saddam Hussein to pull out of Kuwait would expire. Over a drink at Fink's Bar, Wiener could hardly control his excitement: the Iraqis had allowed CNN to install special communications in Baghdad if war broke out. The government had even indicated it might allow them to stay to cover the war. I was impressed with Wiener's accomplishment but I was also green with envy; the biggest confrontation of military might since Vietnam was shaping up and CNN was to cover it live from both sides and I was stuck in a backwater.

I was comforted by Kimberly Moore, a young woman from Lakeland, Florida, I met soon after Gerlind Younts and I had gone our separate ways a year earlier. Kimberly was an intern at CNN, and had come to Jerusalem to join me. She had taken a job with Israeli television's daily English language news program. We canceled our plans for a Christmas vacation in Paris because we didn't want to be caught outside the region if war broke out.

By early January virtually everything CNN put on the air concerned the Gulf crisis. The whole world was counting down to war. Saddam Hussein's intractability was inviting terrible retaliation. Resistance seemed futile. The vast array of American and allied war machines that had been assembled was ready to pulverize him. The allies made it clear that the first target would be Baghdad. Baghdad seemed particularly vulnerable because of the likelihood of bombing raids—of enormous power—if the war started. When I interviewed the Israeli prime minister, Yitzhak Shamir, on January 10, I mentioned that CNN had a reporting team in Baghdad and he looked at me in surprise. "Are they crazy? Do they want to write a book or something?" Many reporters had joined the exodus from Baghdad; the U.S. Embassy was counseling the rest to leave.

When I returned to the office I was told to call the CNN international editor, Eason Jordan, in Atlanta. He told me that the resolve of the CNN team in Baghdad was beginning to crack; some were ready to leave. Would I go there to help out? Baghdad was going to be the most dangerous place in the world in a few days and, yes, I wanted to be there. It was not a question of bravery; I believed that I could do what had to be done, and that I could survive it. Eason asked me when I could leave. "Immediately," I said.

I told Kimberly that I was leaving for Baghdad the next day. She had put up with my griping for months, but now she was a bit afraid for me. She drove with me to Tel Aviv's Ben-Gurion Airport to see me off on January 11, five days before Saddam Hussein had to withdraw from Kuwait or face war.

The airport was on alert and combat troops were everywhere. Many airlines had canceled their flights to the region. Only six hundred miles separated Tel Aviv from Baghdad, but I couldn't fly there directly— I had to go twice the distance through Cairo and Amman, Jordan. The Air Egypt carrier lifted without problem high over the Negev Desert, where a few weeks earlier I'd watched the tanks practicing at war. The Suez Canal was soon below and we landed at noon at Cairo airport. I transferred to a Jordanian Airlines plane to fly to Amman, since Jordan remained Iraq's only friendly neighbor, and Amman had the only international airport still serving Baghdad. CNN had established a forward base there, renting several large suites at the Philadelphia Hotel and installing editing gear and a large bank of high tech equipment that blinked and beeped. A score of technicians and news people were going about their business, reporting regularly to CNN headquarters in Atlanta.

I met Dominic Robertson, a young British CNN technician who was preparing to go into Baghdad with me the following day. He was dismantling a portable satellite telephone and scratching off labels and numbers from the parts. Nic said he was going to smuggle it into Baghdad because the Iraqis had not given their permission to bring it in. The satellite phone could be used anytime, to phone anywhere in the world. It was the newest indispensable information tool.

But Nic wasn't sure he could pull it off. "When I went into Baghdad last September the customs people even took my portable radio," he told me as he began hiding bits and pieces of the phone in a dozen bags and boxes that contained equipment, videotapes and food supplies. But he knew what kind of scrutiny to expect. I watched the resourceful young man with approval as he worked over the equipment, a man after my own heart.

The single-suitcase version of the satellite phone was worth fifty-two thousand dollars; if discovered it would certainly be confiscated. CNN was willing to risk losing the expensive equipment. It had opened its coffers and was spending millions on coverage in order to report the war as fully as possible. The CNN staff in Amman told me the commitment had come only after much internal debate. CNN's engineering department was afraid that the portable "flyaway" video uplink—which would let us report live from Baghdad—included technological breakthroughs that could prove useful to the enemy if it fell into their hands. The half-million-dollars' worth of equipment was now scattered in crates at the Philadelphia Hotel awaiting entry approval from the Iraqis.

CNN had made a far greater commitment to the story than the competition. The next morning at Amman airport I ran into two colleagues from CBS television, correspondent Alan Pissey and producer Larry Doyle. Doyle was a burly man with a reputation for derring-do, but he looked unhappy, sucking fitfully on a beer. I was fond of Doyle. He had once lent me money in Panama to pay my hotel bills. And he was the one who during a coup d'etat in Guatemala in 1983 had allowed CNN to use his video when our cameraman let us down.

"Boy, do I need you guys now," said Doyle. He explained that Pissey and he were being sent into Baghdad without a camera crew. CBS management was unwilling to provide enough insurance to persuade the technicians to make the trip. "This is the network of Ed Murrow and Walter Cronkite and we don't even have a crew going in with us on the most important story of the year," Doyle said. "We'll be knocking on your door for video when the shooting starts."

The plane from Baghdad was late, and it was packed when it arrived, spilling crowds of diplomats and journalists into the lounge. There were not many people in the departure area, just a few Iraqi diplomats and Palestinian and Jordanian businessmen and three television crews from European news organizations. Most everyone was carrying packages of liquor and cigarettes from the duty-free store. Some things never change.

Tracy Fleming, a young CNN video editor, was traveling with Nic Robertson and me to Baghdad after a break. She said she intended to stay for the duration. She looked upon me as a good-luck charm. "They say you're bulletproof," she announced.

Nic was not so determined. He told me that CNN had not been able to guarantee that he could be pulled out in a hurry if he wanted to leave. He was willing to take the satellite phone in, but not to stay indefinitely. Few others from any of the news organizations were likely to remain, he said.

I sat with the young CNN staffers on the forty-minute flight to Baghdad. Below there was only sunlit desert sand and low, bare hills. I had never been to Baghdad, but that didn't matter to me; the landscape of crisis was familiar ground.

When we disembarked, Nic walked ahead of me into the customs area. He was carrying the stand for the heavy satellite dish nonchalantly under his arm, and planned to tell the Iraqis it was a camera mount. We bundled the rest of our gear onto five trolleys and wheeled them over to the waiting customs officials. The control panel was in with the foodstuffs, the handset in a case of electronic gadgets, the aluminum umbrella dish in a bagful of clothing.

The officials were carefully sifting through the gear of a television crew ahead of us, tearing the video cassette boxes apart. Nic paled a bit but he kept his nerve.

When our turn came, a customs official opened the first box and saw the control panel. Nic said it was for editing video. The official nodded and pushed it aside.

The cables got through but Nic lost his replacement shortwave radio. The official placed it behind him on the confiscation table. "I think they use these things to listen to the Voice of America and the BBC," Nic whispered to me.

The customs inspector rummaged around a clothing bag and found the satellite dish, an ingenious device made of silvery wire mesh that collapsed like an umbrella when not in use. Nic explained to him that it was used to shield the camera—"The sun's hot here," he said, as if an Iraqi might not know that. The official did not open it.

By now the search had been under way for half an hour. A big aluminum case was pulled open. Inside was a modem, a device used to communicate signals from a telephone line to a computer. It was a major piece of equipment that could not be disguised and essential for the satellite telephone. When we placed it on the table it looked as big as a tank. Nic had warned me that the Iraqis always confiscated modems.

"This is a voltage regulator," Nic explained to them, launching into a detailed technical description of its use. The inspector listened through it all and then looked Nic directly in the eye. "No, it's a modem," he declared.

Nic stared back. "It's not a modem."

The official insisted. "It's a modem."

"No," Nic responded confidently, standing tall. "This is not a modem. It is a voltage regulator."

There were more minutes of standoff and then the inspector shrugged and let it through.

I thought we had made it. But then the official discovered the telephone handset and smiled with success, calling over another inspector to look at it. Nic protested vehemently. "You can't have that, I need it for my work." This time his protestations failed. The handset was forbidden. It ended up on the confiscation table. In the midst of the confusion our Iraqi driver arrived. He picked up the metal satellite dish stand Nic had been carrying under his arm and took it out to his car. As we loaded up the rest of the gear I congratulated Nic. He'd almost made it; if it weren't for the critical telephone handset.

He laughed in triumph. "Peter, that was the only part of the apparatus that was not vital. I can plug in any phone in the hotel to replace it."

I climbed into the waiting Japanese sedan, buoyed by Nic's success. The airport road led on to the Qadisiya Expressway, a modern six lane highway. There were bungalows and shade trees in the surrounding neighborhood. It looked a lot like parts of Queens, New York, in the middle of the desert.

My joy at being in Baghdad went much deeper than covering the story. From my early youth I had thrilled to the exoticism of the Arabian peninsula. Dried date fruit arrived at my local grocery store in boxes from Basra. I read in my schoolbooks that the hanging gardens of Babylon were one of the wonders of the ancient world. The songs from the broadway musical *Kismet* wove rich tapestries of longing in my imagination. I was now older and wiser, but the magic carpet of journalism had carried me from New Zealand and over thirty-five years to my destination.

Our taxi driver, Omar Hussain al-Aiad, was an elderly Iraqi with a neatly trimmed mustache like all the local men. As we entered the city, he pointed out landmarks: the headquarters of Saddam Hussein's

International Ba'ath Socialist Party, the festival and parade grounds in Zawra Park. We passed the victory monument, two vast steel arches formed by towering crossed swords grasped by bronze hands. Omar told me proudly that Saddam Hussein had allowed his own forearms to be used as models, enlarged forty-eight times in the final cast. The metal for the whole edifice was said to have come from captured helmets and tanks in the war with Iran. Thousands of Iranian helmets decorated the base of the monument.

We turned off the expressway and drove through a concrete underpass, emerging beside a large modern convention center. To the left was the al-Rashid Hotel. Fourteen stories high, it dominated the block. A ten-foot-high metal fence enclosed the compound.

We drove by a large fountain studded with imitation water jars made of brown metal. The structure was topped by a bronze woman reaching into the heavens. It reminded me of the listless totalitarian art of communist North Korea. A circular driveway embellished with flowering shrubs led to the front entrance of the hotel. I stepped out onto white marble steps. The facade of the lobby was made of large slabs of dark gray marble and sheets of beige stone chiseled with geometric patterns.

Manawer, the doorman, introduced himself. He was as tall as a basketball center, his height accented by a crimson turban wrapped around his head. He was wearing traditional Arab garments. When he moved to shake my hand, his outer garments unwrapped, and I saw he was wearing a small beige vest, billowy white pantaloons and pointy-toed shoes. He was straight out of *Kismet.*

Sudanese porters took our bags, and welcomed us in English. On a marble wall I saw a plaque fringed by two crimson velvet curtains tethered by a gold cord. The inscription said the hotel was opened in 1982, "during the era of Saddam Hussein."

The entrance was so dramatic, so glittery. I half expected to see rows of slot machines. Four giant glass chandeliers hung from the ceilings like crystal beehives, and tall glass doors led to garden promenades. But there were barely any furnishings, only a few potted plants and a full-sized picture of Saddam Hussein in a business suit.

The hotel lobby was dark and gloomy. In the distance a sign above a door read "Sheherazade Bar." I walked over to the long mahogany reception desk and was checked in by a man in a black formal jacket, gray vest and striped gray trousers. I figured that the al-Rashid had catered to a tonier crowd.

Nic Robertson pointed to a corner where several Arabs were chatting at a wooden table next to a bank of public telephones and looking over toward us. "They're the minders," Nic said. Iraqi officials had been assigned to escort journalists around the country and watch everything they did outside the hotel.

I entered a dimly lit elevator at the end of the lobby. It lurched up to the ninth floor, where the CNN offices were located. I discovered there was also inside surveillance: an Iraqi security man was sitting in a wooden booth near the elevator and he watched me as I walked down the corridor to the CNN suites.

I heard a familiar voice barking into a telephone in room 906. It was producer Robert Wiener, talking to CNN's Atlanta headquarters. He was using the four-wire phone, a specially installed communications link to Atlanta. He was speaking into a microphone that could be detached from a small black metal transmission box on the table. It was like an international intercom, hooked up to four telephone lines between Baghdad and Atlanta. The extra lines provided a better-quality voice transmission. The four-wire apparatus circumvented the hotel switchboard and other standard switching systems. It was carried directly to a microwave transmitter to Amman, and then by satellite to the United States. Only CNN had worked out an arrangement with the Iraqi government to use the system. It was our ace in the hole. We could talk with the United States any time we wanted and they could talk to us.

Wiener rose and wrapped me in a bear hug. He hadn't shaved in days and he was wearing dark glasses. He thanked me for being there. "I want you to know," he added quickly, "we can get you out of here anytime you want. I've convinced Atlanta to charter an executive jet and keep it on tap in Amman for emergencies."

"Get me out of here, Robert? Hey, I've just arrived."

He took me aside with a conspiratorial air. He told me his grand design for staffing the war coverage was falling apart, that key crew members who had sworn to him in the beginning that they would stay till the end were now changing their minds as the deadline approached. "Promises made before Christmas are being broken in the new year," Robert moaned. He said most of his crew were still in Baghdad only because he had guaranteed that he would get them out in a crisis.

In a strained voice, Robert told me that the melting resolve of the CNN staff matched a growing conviction among the Baghdad press corps that staying behind when the war started would be suicidal. He wanted to cover the story but he didn't want anyone to die trying to do it. He repeated the gossip that had been picked up by journalists in Saudi Arabia who were saying that Baghdad would be bombed back to the stone age when the war began. Pilots with the U.S. Navy carriers in Gulf waters were being quoted as saying that the al-Rashid would be used as a landmark for the bombing campaign because it was the biggest building in the capital city.

"So what," I told Robert. "A smart bomb knows the difference between a strategic installation and a hotel."

"But what if they're one and the same thing," he responded nervously.

Wiener's turmoil was painful. His finest hour had been convincing the Iraqi government that by allowing CNN to stay it could display its war misery to the world. But having made himself indispensable to the network's coverage plans he was inviting the destruction of the whole enterprise by not encouraging the staff to see it through.

I cautioned him that his predictions of doom would not help. "You don't understand, Peter," he told me. "I'm responsible for all these CNN people. You're only responsible to yourself. They have to know the truth, all that's going on."

I didn't argue. Robert was totally sincere. Still, I tried to get beneath the fever pitch of gossip and speculation to the tangible, to find a way to come to understand the situation and weigh it for myself, by my criteria.

I asked him about the security of the hotel. He pointed out of one room to the angled concrete baffles over each window that were supposedly protection from incoming projectiles. The glass windows were several inches thick.

"You have to see the hotel bunkers," Robert said. "A thousand people can hide down there."

He showed me the CNN storage room across the hall from the office. Bottled water was stacked to the ceiling. Foodstuffs spilled out of cardboard containers. There were cartons of cookies, candies, processed cheese, canned meats. There were boxes of candles and matches, flashlights, kerosene heaters, camp beds, blankets, mosquito nets. And cases of Scotch whiskey, Italian wine and rum. It was a general store.

I was astounded. "You should see our electronic safe," he continued gleefully. "That's stuffed with money.

"Whaddaya think, Peter? You've had a quick look at it all. Will you stay?"

"Robert, why else would I be here? Of course I'll stay."

I asked him if he would remain with me. He responded, "I set this thing up. I have to stay. I tied the noose around our necks. We'll swing together."

By nightfall it was clear that few were willing to share our fate. I ran into CNN's main anchorman, Bernard Shaw, in the hallway. He had come in a few days earlier to interview Saddam Hussein and was still waiting to do so. He said he would remain as long as he felt it wise. "I don't want to stay," Bernie said. "But someone should."

At breakfast next morning I met Ingrid Formanek, a CNN producer. Ingrid loved silver tribal bracelets and wore her collection on her arms. She was jangling silver right up to her elbows as she dug into a plateful of fresh figs and ham. Ingrid had helped CNN cover the collapse of communism in Eastern Europe. She was fluent in five languages and knew her way around trouble spots.

She offered to take me on a tour of the city. I had arrived in Baghdad with a sheaf of newspaper clippings and items I had ripped off the news wires, but the story I wanted to report was the usual one, the one I could see and hear for myself.

We were joined by Ala'a al-Ani, from the Information Ministry, a tall, melancholy official who was the CNN minder. Ala'a greeted me pleasantly in hesitant English and then began telling me how remarkable Saddam Hussein was. I listened politely.

I chatted with Ala'a as we drove into town, trying to size him up. He was important to us as our guide and translator. I would be seeing much of Iraq through his eyes. He would never be far away; he told me he had a room in the hotel just down the hall from mine.

The situation had clearly unnerved the business community. Many large stores were closed, their steel shutters pulled down tight to the pavement and secured with heavy metal locks. Some people were loading trucks with merchandise to take out of town. The windows of the stores still open were heavily taped.

We stocked up with six-packs of mineral water. Ingrid bought cans of American peaches and packets of Camembert cheese. A vendor came by with a huge slab of dried dates, maybe twenty pounds in weight, and I bought the whole thing. Dried dates were local hardtack, high-calorie energy food.

Ingrid looked at me as I examined my huge date find. "What are you expecting, World War Three? Our little Götterdämmerung will be over by the end of the week." But Ingrid kept buying despite her prognosis. She stocked up with superior brand whiskey and cognac.

"The minders," she said, "drink like fishes. They're more interested in this than sex." I figured Ingrid would know.

Robert was disappointed that we hadn't found any vodka on the local market. "I suppose we can always get over to the foreign currency store before the balloon goes up," he said. "Who else is buying the stuff but us anymore."

In the afternoon Robert and I went over to the Information Ministry to meet some senior officials. He breezed through the lobby, waving at the security guards as they looked up in surprise. We passed by large, ornate sculptures in an interior conference room. Robert gave the finger to a large portrait of Saddam Hussein in his official robes of office as we entered an executive elevator to ride to the eighth floor.

"Mr. Sadoun," Robert called, rushing up to a burly Iraqi who stood waiting for us. They swept into a tight embrace.

I heard a mumbled "Mr. Robert" from the Iraqi as he kissed him on both cheeks. Neither man had shaved in some days; I could almost hear their cheeks scratching. The Iraqis invariably used the honorific in addressing us.

After I was introduced, Sadoun al-Jenabi looked me over. His big, meaty hand crushed mine.

"Mr. Peter," he said in a booming voice. "You be fair with us, we'll be fair with you. We love Mr. Robert, we love CNN. Welcome."

I was not used to such avowals. I did not expect it from any government official and especially not from a senior official of a country the world was about to go to war with. Robert insisted on seeing Sadoun's boss, Naji al-Hadithi, the director general of the Information Ministry.

Naji was an important Iraqi official who did not normally grant immediate access to the foreign press. He came out and Robert wrapped his arms around him and they, too, traded kisses.

The official smiled at me through his thick glasses. It was a warm, embracing smile. He spoke impeccable English. "We are delighted you are here, Mr. Arnett. We will work closely together." Robert pulled Naji aside and whispered something into his ear. I was reminded of a political candidate getting urgent advice from an adviser, or a gambler listening to odds from a bookie. Robert said he told Naji that CNN felt the Baghdad story was the crucial part of the war coverage. Naji nodded affirmatively and we left.

I was amazed at Robert's confidence, but I was not ready to suspend my wariness. Several months earlier, an Iranian-born journalist, Far-

357

zad Bazoft, had been executed on unsubstantiated spy charges in Iraq. The Information Ministry had approved his visa and had been responsible for his welfare during his visit. These were the same officials who said they loved CNN.

When I asked Robert about it he laughed. "Peter, you do what you have to do. There is no middle ground here. They either love you or hate you." He said he was pressing Naji to allow us the portable television earth station waiting in Amman. Naji's boss, the information minister himself, had promised Robert he would take up the matter with Saddam Hussein, his childhood friend. The satellite equipment would let us broadcast live from Baghdad. If it arrived as scheduled, CNN would make journalism history.

The boldness of Robert's plans floored me. He had clearly won the confidence of the Iraqi officials and had convinced them that CNN should be present during the war. The only uncertainty was the CNN staff's nervousness.

Back at the hotel, Ingrid told us that the White House had announced that the deadline for Iraq's withdrawal from Kuwait would expire at midnight Tuesday New York time. Two days away.

Robert was convinced that the first allied strikes would be crippling bombing assaults on the city; the six Tigris River bridges seemed likely strategic targets. He suggested that we move to the Sheraton on the other side of the river, because the al-Rashid was politically tainted, part of a government construction project.

I was of the opinion that we should remain near the government centers. If war came, the only way we could function on the streets of Baghdad would be with the support and protection of government officials. By remaining in the spacious confines of the al-Rashid compound we would have the minders near at hand, plus a spectacular view of the war from our ninth-floor rooms. Robert agreed that it made sense to stay put.

That evening I filed my first news report from Baghdad, the failure of the last peace mission of United Nations Secretary General Pérez de Cuéllar. When he left he looked glum. In Paris he was asked if there would be war. "Only God knows," he replied.

. . .

On my second morning in Baghdad, I woke up knowing that the war could start the next day. It was 5:30. My room was still dark. I made a mental note of my immediate needs. A flashlight was essential, because when fighting began the power would undoubtedly fail. And candles, and lots of mineral water, and canned food.

I presumed and prayed that the hotel would not be a target of allied warplanes because so many foreigners had taken refuge here. But I wondered about the hotel staff, mostly Sudanese, Indian and Pakistani contract workers. I had been told that the only reason they were staying was because the hotel management had confiscated their passports.

The sun was coming up when I visited the CNN work space. Last night's coffee stained the uncleared cups on the table. Trays of half-eaten food lay around. I sniffed. CNN had agreed to pay for any food consumed on the premises for the duration of the crisis. Few resisted the temptation. Gross consumption plus indifferent maid service equaled mess.

Robert was sitting at a cluttered table with his elbows in a tray of melting ice. He told me tape editor Tracy Fleming was leaving. "I'm getting the charter in for her tomorrow." CNN was sending in a Rockwell Sabreliner, at a cost of fifteen thousand dollars.

I told Robert that it would be better for us all that Tracy left if her heart was not in it. He was not consoled. Tracy had been one of the first few staffers who had pledged to go the distance. Now Tracy was leaving. The rot had set in. Robert was witnessing the disintegration of his bold endeavor. I told him that his plans could be revised, that we could rethink our staffing priorities. He wasn't listening, he was worrying about the safety of the staff. And then there was all that valuable equipment. And there were professional responsibilities to consider. CNN had never handled anything like this. I looked at Robert's furrowed brow and wet elbows and thanked God that I had never moved into management.

As the anxiety intensified, I had concerns I needed to discuss with Robert. First, was being beaten on the story. CNN's competitors in Baghdad included the three other American TV networks, and British, French, Italian, German and Japanese news organizations. CNN prided itself as the network of record. We proclaimed we were the world's most influential news organization. We had a lot to live up to.

I told Robert we had to have at least the minimum in support staff in place if the bombs started falling. I was worrying that headquarters would order us all out of Baghdad if other news organizations pulled their staffs.

I caught up with Robert in the hallway. "In all your talking with Atlanta tell them that not only do I want to stay to cover the war, but that I am convinced that I will survive the experience. Remember, I've got thirty years of experience behind me in arriving at this evaluation."

Who else would stay? The gulf of years between me and the young CNN staff seemed immeasurable, and I had arrived too late to win their confidence. I found Nic Robertson in one of the work rooms cautiously experimenting with the satellite telephone.

We had learned that a few other news organizations had smuggled in phones and could compete with us. As I watched him concentrate on the phone, I knew I needed Nic. In the brief time I had known him he had revealed audacity, ingenuity and integrity.

Nic surreptitiously determined that the equipment was in operating order and he smiled in triumph. I congratulated him and reminded him that its video twin, the portable television earth station, was already packed and waiting in Amman, waiting for Baghdad's approval, which could come anyday.

"Nic, we need you to run this gear. You are the key to our performance here." I smiled at him hopefully.

He did not beat around the bush. "Peter, I know that I'm needed. Anything can happen. You need an engineer. But I haven't decided to stay."

I believed him. When the others made similar assertions I knew they were making excuses and were simply delaying the inevitable decision to depart. I felt I could communicate with Nic. He had an intellectual depth, a detachment from the emotional agitation beginning to swirl around us.

"You know, Peter," he could not resist, "there are people around here who believe you're a crazy war lover who'll do anything for a story."

I tried to explain. "The key to me, Nic, is that I do nothing for fun, and what I do I do carefully. I've weighed the situation here. We can survive it. I will simply be doing what I'm paid to do. If I bug out of here I feel I would have to give my paycheck back because it would be a disservice to my company that hired me as a reporter. If CNN orders me out of here, Ted Turner should give the public their money back because it will be a disservice to them, and the promises that he has made when he signed them up as subscribers to his twenty-four-hour news network. We can't just walk out on the news."

Nic was grinning. "That's all very well, Peter. But what about your personal life? I have a personal life. She doesn't want me here. She worries about me and calls me every day. And frankly, Peter, I'm scared."

He had me there. I had always put the job first, and I wasn't proud of it.

"Nic, you can leave here and no one will ever bring it up again. But you will always know that you have run out on the biggest story there is. If you don't test yourself here where will you test yourself?"

"So you're suggesting that what we do here will separate the men from the boys?"

"No," I responded flatly. "It has nothing to do with being macho. It has to do with being professional. It's taking a clear look at our options here, and our responsibilities. I won't go into the First Amendment and our special responsibilities under the Constitution, because you're not an American, and no one thinks much about those issues anymore, anyway. But needless to say there are a lot of people in this world who are intensely interested in what's going to go down in Baghdad. They will truly appreciate it if we are here to tell them about it."

I detected that I was getting through, so I pushed on. "Nic, the only issue I've heard discussed around this hotel is survival. No one is talking about journalistic responsibility. But if it's survival you're interested in, here is my assessment of what's going down."

I said the al-Rashid Hotel was clearly a superior structure that would be suitable cover when the bombs fell. The shelters in the hotel were well lit and air-conditioned by emergency generators. I told him I doubted that the hotel would be a target, that there was no logical reason to bomb it. There were news staff and civilians living there. Women and children. I'd had my confrontations with the Pentagon over the previous thirty years, but never had I feared that I would be assassinated by the U.S. government.

The air force would be using smart bombs. They would target specific military sites. They had gone on record as saying there would be no carpet bombing of the capital. I told him that anything could happen but that the al-Rashid could probably survive an accidental hit. "It's going to be scary, Nic. But survivable."

Nic smiled at me. "What it gets down to, Peter, is who's going to have my body for the next few weeks. My girlfriend, or CNN?"

. . .

Late that morning I went to the downtown shopping district to get pictures of war preparations. There were now fewer people on the streets. Cars with the roofs piled high with personal possessions were heading out of town.

Iraqi television sent over videotape of the National Assembly cheering Saddam Hussein's policy of confrontation, voting for war rather than to pull out of Kuwait. All males aged fifteen and over were being issued light weapons. War, it seemed, was inevitable.

Later, while we were sitting around in the CNN work space, Bernie Shaw came by in his bathrobe to borrow my portable typewriter. He had interviewed the deputy foreign minister, Nizar Hamdoon, on background earlier in the day. At the time it seemed to him that there was nothing new in the discussion. But Bernie had jumped out of a deep sleep and thought that the Iraqis were telling him something, that it wasn't that they wouldn't make a deal but that they couldn't meet the deadline.

Wall Street responded instantly to his broadcast; the market went up thirty points.

Bernie returned to his room, but within minutes he was rustled out of bed by a concerned Atlanta headquarters. Did we or didn't we have peace?

Bernie went on the air again to emphasize the fine print of his report, that concessions, if any, should be made at an international peace conference. The allies had emphatically rejected such a conference.

Wall Street retreated.

Still, the incident showed me that CNN was being watched by the whole world and was believed. We had to get the story right and get it clear.

. . .

The nineteenth-century clock tower on the Baghdad railway station was barely visible in the dense early morning fog, but I could hear the bell chiming. One, two, three, four, five, six, seven, eight. It was January 16. The deadline for withdrawal had passed and Saddam Hussein had not budged.

CNN cameraman Mark Biello strained to capture a clear image of the old wooden clock tower. Nic Robertson adjusted the microphone on his audio pack. I looked up to the gray skies and listened intently. The echo of footsteps at the train station was all I heard.

I returned to the al-Rashid to broadcast. I was told that President Bush had signed a national security directive authorizing war unless there was a diplomatic breakthrough. I described what I had seen in the streets, the calm passersby, clusters of uniformed youths awaiting transport to who knew where. I quoted an Iraqi who said that Saddam Hussein and George Bush were both stubborn men bent on mutual destruction.

With the deadline for withdrawal passed, the press corps began leaving. Larry Doyle of CBS bounded into our room. "We're outta here," he proclaimed. Doyle said most would try to make an overland dash for the Jordanian border. His home office was persuaded that Baghdad would be bombed that night.

CNN president Tom Johnson wanted me on the phone. He said he understood that I wished to stay, but he was concerned. When he had been president of the Los Angeles Times Company, he had to retrieve the bodies of two of his favorite staff correspondents from battlefields in the Middle East and Central America; he didn't want to have to do it again.

I assured him I had no intention of becoming a statistic. I pointed out that Baghdad had a population of four million people, and if I stayed it would grow to four million and one.

Robert Wiener had been listening to the conversation. His distress was palpable and he wrestled with the moment of truth that all his planning had brought him.

The staff gathered around us. They were told again that they could leave anytime they wished while management made up its mind about whether to cover the story. Saddam Hussein had invaded Kuwait the day after Tom Johnson had taken over CNN. He had already spent millions preparing for war, and sent more than a hundred staffers to the Middle East. His options were to pull everyone out of Baghdad, to relocate to safer positions in the outskirts of the city, or leave us be. During the week, White House spokesman Marlin Fitzwater told Johnson, "Your people in Baghdad are in grave danger." He had spoken with Vice President Dan Quayle, who had told him Bush was worried. The president himself expressed concern about his friend Bernie Shaw's presence in the Iraqi capital and had urged Tom to "Get him outta there."

CNN wavered and then Ted Turner put his foot down in an instruction to CNN's executives: "We are an international network and we have an obligation to report the story from Baghdad if we can. We should give our people the opportunity to do so. But we should give them the choice to leave if they so desire. I don't want my views countermanded by anyone."

I couldn't have said it better myself. He resolved the dilemma for management. Now it was just a matter of making it work.

By the evening of January 16, there were forty-five Western journalists left in Baghdad. Wiener decided to stay. For Nic Robertson, CNN triumphed over romance. That would leave three of us to handle the story. The six other staffers planned to depart by chartered jet first thing next morning. They thought they could get out before the war started.

Late that night, Walter Cronkite came on the air from CNN's Washington bureau. The grand old man of television was in a philosophical mood as he chatted about the handful of American correspondents who had stayed in enemy capitals in the earliest days of World War Two. "I don't think the danger in Berlin or Tokyo, either one, was particularly imminent as it is for Baghdad today," he observed. "I think the decision to stay in a place that is clearly a major danger zone where one's mortality has to be considered on the line is probably the toughest decision any newspaperman ever had to make. And it's tough on his management as well."

He also predicted that propagandists in the United States would not be happy if our coverage evoked any sympathy for the Iraqis.

Cronkite gave me some friendly advice over the air. "Peter, you're a very valuable asset to courageous reporting around the world. You've proved that. Don't grandstand this one. If you take all those things into consideration. Why, you know, save your skin, boy."

For a moment I stared blankly into the four-wire microphone. I did not expect to hear this from Walter Cronkite, one of my role models. Why did everyone want me to retire?

I told him I had nothing left to prove. "This is just the greatest story in the world at this time and I'd like to cover it as much as I can."

Day One, January 17

WE WERE TOO RESTLESS to sleep. Sometime after 2 A.M. Mark Biello began to set up cameras at the windows just in case something happened outside. Nic was chatting with me.

I was looking out the window. There was no moon in the skies over Baghdad, a "bombers' night" someone had once told me in Vietnam, when warplanes could sneak in unnoticed.

Nic inclined his head a little, did he hear planes? I told him he was dreaming. He walked across the hall to a room with open windows. Then he ran back, his face flushed.

"The dogs in the entire neighborhood are going crazy. They're barking like they're deranged," he shouted.

Dog radar?

In the next instant, a huge flash lit the southern sky. Nic looked like his insides had dropped into his trousers. I shook my head in disbelief. Conventional wisdom said that President Bush would wait a few days before he ordered the bombers in.

The staccato crack of guns firing into the skies confirmed that the war had begun. I glanced at my watch for history's sake: 2:32 A.M.

In my wire service days, minutes made the difference between a scoop and being second. In live television, seconds made the difference.

I lurched toward the work space. The four-wire phone was humming its invitation to broadcast. Nic was already on the move, disappearing down the hallway. He had propped open every doorway between his room and the safety of the bomb shelters ten floors below.

Bernie Shaw was kneeling, gazing out the ninth-floor window as he groped for the microphone. "Come to Baghdad, come to Baghdad," he was shouting, his fingers stabbing at the control button. "Something is happening, something is happening."

My heart skipped a beat. Bernie was first with the story. But my competitive disappointment evaporated as I looked beyond him out the windows.

The glow was so red it seemed as though the sun had returned to set again. Chains of yellow lights swung across the sky as though suspended from a giant chandelier and I assumed they were tracer bullets from the anti-aircraft guns.

365

Mark Biello was moving cautiously to reset one of his cameras. There was no video broadcast at this point. The camerman was trying to get the video for later use. I was going over to help him when I heard Bernie call, "Peter Arnett, join me here." Atlanta was taking us live, interrupting an interview with former Defense Secretary Caspar Weinberger.

Bernie began, "The skies over Baghdad have been illuminated. We're seeing bright flashes going off all over the sky. Peter?"

As I pressed my face to the mike, I stuttered my own observations and talked of the "tremendous lightning in the sky, lightninglike effects."

Outside, the lights were still on in the building and the streets. The alert sirens began sounding for the first time across the city, but every Iraqi was already awake.

As John Holliman walked into the room the hotel lights went out and so did our four-wire communications signal. I thought, Damn. All the planning. All the debate. All the money. All down the tubes. As the world beyond our windows exploded we were helpless bystanders.

I found Biello in the room next door and helped him set up small cameras at several windows before he left for the shelter. When I returned to the work space I saw Holliman crouched at the window, staring at the fiery night and talking into the four-wire microphone, which he had attached to a long cord.

"Hello, Atlanta, Atlanta. This is Holliman. I don't know whether you're able to hear me now or not, but I'm going to continue to talk to you as long as I can." Holliman had placed new batteries in the four-wire to revive it. The yellow pilot light was glowing but Atlanta was not acknowledging the signal.

Holliman placed the microphone out the window to pick up the sounds of the night. Our windows rattled. We opened the doors to connecting rooms to get a panoramic view of the landscape.

Then, during a break in his monologue, Holliman heard a response from Atlanta. They'd been listening to him for ten minutes, waiting for him to stop talking so they could break in.

John danced in exhilaration as a large bomb blast crashed three blocks away and shook the room. I supposed it was Saddam Hussein's Ba'ath Party headquarters.

"David, this is a remarkable night. How nice it is to be with you." Holliman was chattering on, live from Baghdad, to anchor David

French. We passed the microphone back and forth to each other like a relay baton.

The executive producer in Atlanta, Bob Furnad, came on the line. His voice was animated.

"Go for it, guys. The whole world's watching."

. . .

By 3 A.M. the first raids were over. A white emergency vehicle raced along the tree-lined avenue below us, its blue lights flashing and siren screaming. Nothing else seemed to be moving. The southern skies were dark again, but to the east, over the Presidential Palace, nervous gunners were firing at random, the tracer bullets arching through the sky.

One of the CNN video editors, Kris Krizmanich, looked up at me with apprehension. She was squatting on the floor against the wall, coughing quietly. She soon made her way to the shelter with Wiener.

I handed the microphone back to Holliman. As he took his listeners on a visual tour of the early-morning cityscape, the heavens began falling in again.

"Oh, oh. Now there's a huge fire that we've just seen due west of our position. And we just heard—whoa. Holy cow. That was a large air burst that we saw. It was filling the sky . . ." Holliman's eyes were bulging like his prose. The roar of technological warfare engulfed us.

It was my turn again. I leaned close to the microphone. The hotel was shaking with shock waves. I peered out the window and my voice died in my throat. "I think, John, that air burst took out the telecommunications center." The roar of exploding bombs rolled across us.

I tried to speak steadily but there was a high-pitched timbre to my voice that I couldn't repress. "You may hear bombs now. If you're still with us you can hear bombs now. They are hitting the center of the city." I closed my eyes and held up the microphone. Let the world hear what war sounded like. I crouched under the windowsill. The reverberations from multiple explosions were rattling my teeth.

I passed the microphone to Holliman, who was speculating that our communications link with the United States was finally blasted out. "I'm going to ask if you can still hear us in Washington and Atlanta. Are you still able to hear us?"

Anchor David French's voice over the crackling speaker reassured us. "John, we do still hear you. Continue. We do hear you."

Holliman explained, "You know, when you see your main com-

367

munications link to the outside world hit with a bomb you have to keep checking to make sure you're getting out."

French interrupted with confirmation from U.S. headquarters in Saudi Arabia that the war had begun. "I suppose that information may be superfluous to you. You're watching it," he commented laconically. We had scooped the Pentagon's press office by twenty-seven minutes on the start of the Gulf War.

I shook Holliman's hand. John repaid me with an on-air tribute and concluded, "I'll tell you that my experience in being under attack is very limited, I'm proud to say. But I think by the time the sun comes up tomorrow, my experience will be much improved in this regard."

When the sun came up. That was still nearly four hours away. We could expect no letup in the bombing or in CNN's requests for live commentary. My throat was scratchy from the endless nervous chatter. My head ached and I felt painful bumps on my upper arms and upper back. By God, I was breaking out in a nervous rash. I tentatively explored the eruptions on my skin and briefly wondered at the drama of the human circulatory system. At least I hadn't fainted.

We were settling in for the long haul. The communication link seemed secure. The war was roaring over our heads like a long predicted hurricane making its end run into our backyard.

My biggest concern was to avoid appearing stupid to a worldwide audience. I vowed to abstain from chatter, sentimentality and guesswork—to report only what I saw. Superficiality is one of the perils of live television but hesitation is a mortal sin. Still, it is not easy to speak before you think.

There was a swish outside the window. Holliman leaned over my shoulder toward the microphone. "Oh, that sounded like a rocket. That was pretty close." I reassured him, "The rocket I think was going up, not coming down at us, John." He laughed good-naturedly. The roar of the warplanes became constant, and thick black palls of smoke were rising from government buildings a mile and a half away. The bombing was intensifying and getting closer to the hotel. There were a lot of targets in our vicinity.

All the lights in Baghdad were out except in our room, where an emergency lamp was glowing on the ceiling. When he noticed it, John turned to me, "Peter, why don't we see if we can make that light go out. If we have to smash it, let's do it. Let's get that light out." The glowing light was crucial to our movement around the room, to find the mineral water, to control the four-wire communications, to avoid banging into chairs and equipment boxes.

I told John not to worry. It seemed to me that the stealth bombers and cruise missiles were striking at predetermined targets. The al-Rashid would be a target only if the Pentagon had so decided, and if we were on the bombing list no darkened room would save us.

The next flash was to the southeast, and it was followed by ten more explosions. They were going for the oil refineries on the Tigris River. Those sturdy symbols of modern Iraq were gone in the flash of a second. The hot breath of the fires fanned through our open hotel window.

It was my turn again at the open mike. I said that all the bombs seemed to be hitting directly on target. I tried to qualify. We could see a lot from our ninth-floor perch but certainly not everything. We didn't know what was happening out there. I knew that in the critical first moments of the war, public opinion could form on our report. We had an open line to the world; there was no censorship at either end. The Iraqi minders had taken off for the bunkers.

Bernie Shaw rejoined us. He had been down in the hotel bomb shelter and was panting from the exertion of climbing nine flights of stairs in the dark. He reached for the mike, but Holliman held it back from him.

"Bernie, you and I have a rule from the days that we both anchored. You always warned me, don't ever go on television out of breath. I'll give you another moment to catch your breath."

The room phone rang suddenly and we jumped. Bernie took the call as John hollered across the room, "Is that something our viewers need to know about?" Holliman seemed determined to let the world eavesdrop on our every move.

It was the hotel switchboard urging us to leave our rooms and go down to the shelter. I thought our cover had been blown. From the time the bombing started I had been waiting for security to walk in and close us down. According to Bernie, all our media colleagues had been herded into the basement shelters and were restrained from leaving by burly armed guards. Those with transistor radios were tuning in to the BBC, which was carrying our live commentary. The competitive antagonism was reaching explosion point.

I was counting on the confusion of the first hours of the war to keep our broadcast window open. I doubted that the Iraqi government ever intended to allow the three of us reporters to spill our unsupervised observations to a worldwide audience at such a critical time. Every step outside the hotel and every interview during the whole Gulf crisis had been supervised by Iraqi minders. The raw information we were relaying was of vital military significance. If our colleagues in the bomb shelter could monitor it, I presumed the military officials in Baghdad could also.

We heard a CNN broadcast from Tel Aviv. A reporter was saying that the Israeli Foreign Ministry was watching CNN, and that Israeli state radio was broadcasting our commentary. CNN executives confirmed it.

Holliman offered Bernie a tunafish sandwich. There was a breeze blowing in through the open window and Holliman mentioned that even so we were all still sweating. Everything we said was being transmitted live on the air. Thank goodness Wiener wasn't there with his colorful vocabulary.

We had hours to kill on the air. The raids were coming in every fifteen minutes. We compared the bombing to a million fireflies, to Fourth of July fireworks shows, to hurricanes, to shooting stars, to a space shuttle launch. Shaw said it was like the center of hell.

We rarely contradicted one another, but one time Bernie challenged Holliman's description of a bombing strike as "beautiful." He commented sharply, "John, that was not beautiful to me."

We ran from one side of the hotel to the other checking the landscape. The avalanche of bombs and missiles was picking off anti-aircraft batteries, radar sites, government ministries, industrial targets and the communications links to the Kuwait battlefield. But we could see that the bridges were still standing over the Tigris River.

There was a sharp banging on the door. I looked at Bernie and John and suggested they hide. I would handle the interruption. Holliman slipped into an adjoining room and squeezed under a bed. Shaw went into another room and hid under a table.

I turned off the telephone switch and its yellow light and unlocked the door. Three flashlights lit my face and I was pushed into the room. They were security guards, all much bigger than I. One pinned me against the wall while the others ran through our suite of rooms, opening closets and slamming down the windows. They took our cameras off the stands and carried them into the hallway. And they ordered me down to the bunkers.

There was no way I was going downstairs. I simply sat down in the doorway. I announced that I was claustrophobic. I demonstrated with my arms flailing the fear that came over me in enclosed spaces. I said I had spent ten years in Vietnam and the bombs outside did not bother me, but that in a closed room I was maniacal. I protested, I think I wept.

The security men made a limp effort to drag me off and then gave up, marching off with our cameras. I watched their flashlights disappear into the stairwell and then ran back into the room.

Atlanta thought they had lost us. David French had told viewers, "I don't wish to alarm anyone," but that contact with us had been lost. Wolf Blitzer reported from the Pentagon that electronic jamming had finally put us off the air.

I turned on the four-wire and told Atlanta we were back in business.

Bernie announced that he was concerned that we not be summarily picked off all at once. "I'm going to yield the microphone to you, John, and to you, Peter, and I'm going back to hide under this table, not because I'm fearful of what's happening outside in the air but I want to be sure that if there's another sweep, if you two get picked off, at least one of us will be here."

By now the anchors were calling us the "Boys of Baghdad." Bernie was on the air when there was a sharp rap on the door again and it shut him off in midsentence. He whispered, "We've got to hide" and thrust the microphone at me.

I signed off to check the door and heard David French announce, "Thank you very much, gentlemen. We assume that's not the Fuller Brush salesman."

It was Wiener. He had managed to talk his way out of the shelter. The four of us listened over the four-wire to President Bush's speech, in which he laid out his minimum demands for the bombing to stop: that Saddam Hussein's forces leave Kuwait, and that he comply with United Nations resolutions.

A roar of explosions punctuated the president's speech. When Bush said, "This will not be another Vietnam," I was thinking about a series of American raids against the outskirts of Hanoi when I visited in 1972. The United States had delayed its heaviest raids until the end of that war. In this one they were coming at the beginning.

Ingrid Formanek, who also succeeded in sneaking out, came up from the bunkers and told us there had been a "down with Bush" demonstration as hotel security people walked around the shelters with automatic weapons and gas masks.

We tuned in to a press conference being given by Defense Secretary Dick Cheney. A reporter asked if he were worried that the bombing in Baghdad had killed civilians. He responded, "The best reporting

I've seen on what transpired in Baghdad was on CNN. And it would appear, based on the comments that were coming in from the CNN crew at the hotel in Baghdad, that the operation was successful in striking targets with a high degree of precision. At least that's the reporting according to CNN."

When dawn arrived it was quieter. We had the pleasure of being able to sit in a chair for a change after lying on our stomachs and crawling on our knees. I reminded the audience that the lull did not mean the end of anything. "Only the first shots in the war have been fired."

There had been no indication of Saddam Hussein's reaction. I thought he would hang tough. "He had made it clear in the past week that he welcomed this war and was prepared to fight. His battle cry was the slogan Allah Akbar—God is great."

The fog was beginning to roll back in. There were signs of traffic on the eight-lane highway that ran in front of the hotel. The morning commuter buses were on the road. We saw a hook-and-ladder fire truck go by. But the horizon was curtained in thick black smoke.

We were exhausted and our thoughts were wandering. The three of us had been awake for thirty hours. Bernie said bravely, "Let's just hope that our minds will continue to serve us and our senses, and further our abilities to continue reporting to the world what it is we are experiencing and seeing here."

I was bone weary and my eyes hurt. Our CNN colleagues were arriving from the shelter below. I heard someone ask when they could leave the hotel for the border. I gestured to Wiener that I was going to my room. I collapsed fully dressed onto the bed.

· · ·

When I awoke around noon, I made a personal discovery about the efficacy of the overnight bombing: my toilet wouldn't flush. There was no running water in the bathroom taps, either. I washed my face in bottled mineral water.

The power had not come back on in the hotel. Holliman was tapping out a script on my portable typewriter because the computers were down, and I grinned to myself. Everyone had made fun of me when I had brought it to the hotel several days earlier. Didn't I know we were in the computer age?

The four-wire telephone was still in business but because it was early in the morning in the United States there was little call for live reporting. The work space was in disorder as the crew packed up to leave. The hotel suite had been home to CNN and media colleagues for five months. Open bureau drawers revealed the debris of long residence: half-empty bottles of booze, music cassettes and girlie magazines. I noticed an unfamiliar cardboard box on a table and on closer examination saw that it was a half-empty case of condoms, and I realized I was even less attuned to the activities of young reporters than I had thought.

I looked out the hotel window. In the distance, beyond Baghdad University, black smoke billowed from the Dora oil refinery on the Tigris River. More black smoke wreathed the horizon to the south, where much of Iraq's chemical and nuclear industry was located. Brown dust and smoke were rising from the old part of the city where direct cruise missile hits had destroyed the three wings of the Defense Ministry. But despite the barrage of bombs, the skyline of Baghdad had not essentially changed. The high government ministry buildings were undamaged. Traffic was moving lightly on the broad city thoroughfares.

Saddam Hussein was not cowed by the violence of the initial raids. Nic Robertson had seen him earlier at the telecommunications center on his way to broadcast a message of defiance to his people that "the mother of all battles" had begun. Nic said Saddam, impeccably uniformed, looked "very resolute, there was determination in his step." If the allies had been hoping for a one-time knockout punch, it was not to be.

I took my broadcasting turns with Holliman as Bernie slept, describing the bombing raids as they came over every half hour or so and chatting about Baghdad and the closed stores, and the restrictions placed on cameras. I learned that we were no longer exclusive with the story, that some other news organizations had unveiled their own satellite telephones and began reporting under the supervision of Iraqi officials.

I was becoming aware that we had become part of the story. The CNN anchors asked persistently about our welfare. Molly McCoy picked up a comment I had made earlier, that I had felt "relatively safe" in the al-Rashid. She asked how the others felt and I answered that they didn't share my confidence, a comment that brought a murmur of assent from the assembled CNN crowd.

It all ended at seven in the evening as Holliman was broadcasting live. Our minder, Ala'a, came into the work space and tugged at my sleeve and whispered that we had to shut down. Then he turned to Holliman and sliced his finger across his throat.

Holliman hammed it up, raising his voice as he said, "Mr. Ala'a, what do you want me to do, sir? I don't understand. You've got to talk to me." The official would not go to the microphone but at our insistence he gave a reluctant explanation: the Telecommunications Ministry had ordered us shut down.

Wiener came into the room and announced that he had been informed that military censorship had been decreed, live news broadcasts were prohibited, and we had to shut down immediately. Wiener said into the microphone, "This is something we desperately don't want to do."

Wiener and Holliman were not ready to yield their ground. CNN had gotten favorable attention during the Tiananmen Square massacre when the producers had resisted the demands of a Chinese official to shut down the broadcast. I figured that my colleagues were trying the same tack.

I wanted to close up shop. My feeling was that we had made the most of our unique window of opportunity. We had reported live for seventeen hours without a second of censorship. We had watched the enemy capital come under intensive attack. We had identified every target that we knew had been hit, and speculated on many that hadn't. We had said everything and anything we wanted to about the war and Saddam Hussein, right in his own backyard. We had a thorough scoop over our competitors the night the war began. And we all needed sleep.

I pulled rank. I took the microphone from Holliman. "So, John, I will make the decision to cut the communications because I am the senior reporter here."

The anchor in charge in Atlanta, Bob Cain, was responding as I moved away from the four-wire that the Boys of Baghdad had "broadcast the first reports, they may have just broadcast the last reports from Baghdad. We will keep you posted."

We made our way down to the bunkers as a rumor swept the hotel that it was on the evening's bombing list. I didn't argue with Wiener's beliefs, that there was imminent danger, as he led the way, his flashlight bobbing ahead of us down the hotel stairwells. I fought the panic that I saw around me. I was arguing to myself and to the others that there would be no reason for the allies to bomb the hotel, particularly now that our presence there was so established in the public eye. Even if the hotel were bombed, I thought the shelters were strong enough for us to survive.

The bunkers were crowded and dimly lit with emergency generator power. The toilets were starting to stink. The CNN crowd had tried to cordon off our own sleeping corner with blankets from upstairs, but others had spilled across it. Now there was only the floor to stretch out upon.

I ended up lying next to an Information Ministry official, Jalil al-Sekh, who had brought his whole family to the shelter: his two teen-aged daughters, Rand and Reem, his wife, Ishraq, and his mother-in-law, Saffia. They were friendly. They talked about surviving Iranian attacks during the war that had only recently ended. They passed around a bottle of mineral water and some oranges. They had nowhere to go; they were stuck for the duration and they were making the best of it. I was starting to feel at home.

Day Two

MOST OF THE CNN staff, except for me, Nic and Robert, left mid-morning in taxis for the long journey to the Jordanian border. Because of air strikes against traffic on the highway, the cost of the trip had gone up to five thousand dollars in cash per car.

"And then there were three," Nic commented as we walked back inside the hotel lobby. I had mixed feelings. We were without a cam-eraman and an editor, which virtually crippled us as a television team. I would have to continue voice reporting on the four-wire while NBC and the BBC remained in Baghdad with full television crews.

The positive side was that we had cleared the decks of all those who did not want to stay. It would be easier to function without the anxiety and agitation governing every decision we made. Wiener was shocked when I said that, but I didn't mean any disrespect to those who left. I just wanted to get on with the job.

By now the press corps had dwindled to a handful, even though the Iraqis had encouraged all to stay. Wiener moved the CNN operation to the Sheherazade Bar in the lobby, because the elevators were no longer working. The hotel staff began carrying down the boxes of gear. The management did not object because the lobby was now a war zone, the plate glass windows taped and the reception desk closed.

Nic relocated the four-wire. We were losing our panoramic view of the city but the lobby was closer to the action and to the shelters where we were herded whenever the sirens sounded, which was every half hour or so. And the leather banquettes were more comfortable than the floor.

We were beginning to get the first official reaction to the air strikes, and I was anxious to start filing stories again. As sirens screamed outside and the chandeliers shook in the lobby, information director general Naji al-Hadithi read to us from the first communiqué of the general command of the Iraqi armed forces, ridiculing President Bush and praising Baghdad's air defenses. Later, we drove to the Information Ministry several blocks away for another briefing with Minister of Information Latif Jassim, who reiterated the government hard line. Afterward we discovered our taxi had driven off because of an air strike a few blocks away. We quickly hitched a ride back to the hotel.

Latif Jassim had patted Wiener on the cheeks at the briefing and encouraged him to stay "because you are welcome here." Wiener had a way with the locals, and converted it to our advantage. The relationship of trust reminded me of Ted Turner's links with Soviet officials in Moscow, which had given me room to maneuver through the thickets of press restrictions.

I hastened to capitalize on CNN's edge. I told the officials that it was imperative that we start filing stories again to justify our being there. News blackout only gave rise to negative speculation back home. They were willing to listen to me but unsure how to function. None of them had ever faced such a crisis before.

We were finally told we could use the phone that evening. I crouched in the stairwell writing a dispatch with my typewriter on my lap during a long air raid as Robert held a flashlight over me. Ala'a sat beside us, watching intently. When he had announced that he would be our official censor I was pleased. I had feared that we would be assigned military officials. Compared to the official examiners I had dealt with in Ngo Dinh Diem's Saigon, in Hanoi and on other restricted stories around the world, Ala'a was agreeable. He had a calm manner, and puffed contentedly on Gold Coast cigarettes. Tall and slim with closely cropped hair and a neat mustache, he was a bachelor with an eye for the hotel receptionists, and they for him. The CNN staff had fun with Ala'a's courtly ways. But to me, he was the hurdle between my reports and the outside world.

My news dispatch was a straightforward account of the briefings we had received from Information Ministry officials plus a few comments about life under pressure in the al-Rashid Hotel. Ala'a cut nothing out. Initially we had been told to tape the report, but he let me read it live on the phone in the Sheherazade Bar. He sat beside me through the dispatch. The flash of explosions was reflected in the wall mirrors. Sirens squealed. When I finished, Bob Cain, the anchor in Atlanta, came up with some questions, but I had to tell him that under the guidelines I was not permitted to answer them. I heard him tell his audience, "Arnett's entire report has been cleared by Iraqi censors and he's not able to add anything unless and until it has been cleared by the censors."

It was not a wholly satisfying experience. I was happy to have resumed reporting but concerned about the restrictions. I told Robert that we had to convince the Iraqis to allow us to expand our broadcasts to meet the expectations raised by our earlier eyewitness reporting.

Day Three

WE WERE STILL denied permission to explore beyond the hotel grounds but you didn't have to travel far to see what was happening: the skyline of Baghdad was changing before our eyes. Late that morning the telecommunications center, one of the larger buildings in the city, was reduced to rubble. It just disappeared from the southern horizon.

Our four-wire link with Atlanta died along with the center, and with it our instant communications. But we still had the satellite phone, its shiny metal case hidden behind the canned tuna boxes in the supply room. It was time to reveal the existence of the phone to the Iraqis even though we risked losing it. They did not protest we had it, but insisted we use it only under supervision.

We dragged the large case to the lobby bar. With evident glee Nic began assembling the high-tech contrivance. But my first report an hour later carried disappointing news: the Western press corps had been ordered out of the country. We were packing our bags.

I raged at Wiener that we should fight the order but he went racing off to arrange taxis, "just in case we need transportation."

Our TV colleagues were as depressed as I was, but we were not pulling together to improve things. Our relations with them had become awkward. CNN's initial broadcasting marathon had been so startling and had such an impact that everyone felt in our shadow. There was more sense of combativeness than camaraderie among those who stayed behind. They had their satellite phones in place, and their camera crews ready. They were finally in a better competitive position and eager to press their advantage.

The passions would soon heighten dramatically when the Iraqis decided CNN could stay while the others would have to leave. The Iraqis cleared the news battlefield of all our competition. Wiener's months of planning and politicking had paid off.

Day Four

OUR DEPARTING COMPETITORS resisted but were hurried out of the hotel by impatient officials. Nic and I ate our breakfast discreetly in the CNN supply room on cheese and crackers. Wiener ran around the hotel pretending to be among those leaving. No one was fooled.

A freelance photographer, Jana Schneider, found our hideaway and banged on our door, demanding that she be allowed to join the CNN team because she was an American. She was mad as hell that we were staying and she was being forced to leave. I couldn't blame her, but I looked at her blankly. This was new to me, to be so privileged.

Later in the morning I found Robert in the lobby with Sadoun, the senior Information Ministry official at the hotel. The Iraqi exuded confidence. Robert had told me Sadoun was popular with the press because he was jovial and liked to party. Since he was allowed to be a drinking buddy with Western reporters, he must have been trusted by the regime. Robert had forewarned me that Sadoun had accompanied him on a botched assignment to occupied Kuwait in October that reflected badly on CNN. Nonetheless, Robert had very good relations with Sadoun.

Sadoun told me that with everyone now gone he had the time to take "personal care" of our needs. I asked him what the rules would be and he ticked them off on his fingers in flawless English. No logistical information, no military information, no travel without permission. I asked him what the hell would be left and he smiled at me and said, "No comment." I hoped he was kidding.

I was taking an afternoon nap in the CNN suite when a large explosion rumbled through the hotel and shook me awake. As I glanced out the window I saw two elongated projectiles sail over the conference center across the street and pivot around the hotel above me, heading toward downtown Baghdad. Anti-aircraft weapons on the roof of the building behind us opened up with shattering fire. I presumed the arriving missiles were Tomahawks; I had seen pictures of them, but never the real thing. They had passed so close to the hotel that their long shapes had filled the windows of the room. I felt I could have reached out and touched their round noses.

The explosion downstairs had probably been a third missile. I ran down to the lobby and saw that the thick glass walls of the Sheherazade Bar had caved in. Masonry and debris were spilled over the floor. The furniture was upturned. Dust drifted through the air. Black smoke was curling up from the garden beyond the swimming pool.

I was relieved that neither of my CNN colleagues were in the wreckage, but when I found them downstairs in the bunkers they were convinced they had narrowly escaped death. Wiener hollered at me, "I knew the hotel would be hit sooner or later." He had been chatting with Nic in the bar and had been thrown off his feet by the blast in the garden outside.

When we checked the grounds it turned out that only part of the missile had plowed into the empty hotel staff quarters, probably after it had been shot down by anti-aircraft gunners. Neither Nic nor Robert was hurt, but the experience had unnerved them. The Iraqis informed us we would have to leave the hotel indefinitely "for a safer location" in the countryside, but that didn't make any of us feel safer.

I was intrigued by the prospect of driving around Iraq with a satellite telephone in the trunk of my car, but Wiener worried that leaving the hotel would cut our moorings, leaving us adrift in a hostile environment. Nic observed that we would have to jettison our considerable supply cache. Rather than argue the point with the Iraqis, they decided that they would leave the next morning for Jordan.

I was worried that headquarters would order me out with them. I assured Tom Johnson that I could function professionally in the constrained environment. Contrary to my fears, Johnson offered "the fullest support." I was greatly encouraged; the network was behind me.

That evening in the hotel bunkers, an Iraqi television broadcast flickered across the monitor above our heads. Interviews with captured American and Allied pilots were shown to those in Baghdad who still had electric power. Iraqi and Jordanian families, crammed for safety into the shelter, cheered at the screen as the subdued, uniformed prisoners of war haltingly condemned their governments in responses to an unseen interrogator.

I knew this would be a controversial story. I had been through it with American POWs in Hanoi. I took notes and scribbled out my script in longhand because my portable typewriter had been stolen or destroyed in the ruins of the bar. I had to read my account to Sadoun because my writing was nearly illegible. He approved it.

Now Sadoun came out to the lobby to monitor my telephoned account. I listed the names of the pilots and their criticism of allied war policy. I quoted Saddam Hussein as promising to treat them humanely when the war ended in his victory.

I kept on talking beyond what Sadoun had approved and began to answer anchor Reid Collins's questions. Sadoun was chatting to Robert. I said that one pilot had a bandaged hand and that two others had bruised faces. I compared the filmed confessions to communist practices during the Vietnam War, when American pilots were paraded around Hanoi and forced to criticize the war. We chatted on for a while.

I knew that CNN had been labeling all my reports restricted by Iraqi censors. The presence of Sadoun was indeed somewhat inhibiting, but the questioning by CNN's anchors began to pay off. I realized I could convey nuances about the situation in Baghdad in casual conversation that were impossible in my censored scripts. I was feeling more comfortable about the possibilities.

Later that evening the Iraqis gave us the interview tapes and Nic sent the audio to Atlanta via the satellite phone. With no competition to worry about we took our time.

The information director general, Naji al-Hadithi, asked me if I wanted to interview the POWs the following day. The reporter in me wanted to, the old campaigner in me was not so sure.

I got Ed Turner on the satellite phone and told him of the offer. I reminded him of the controversy when journalists were excoriated for interviewing American POWs in Vietnam. I said I understood how sensitive CNN's position in Baghdad was now that we were there by ourselves. I said I would understand if he passed up the opportunity for the interviews.

"Damn it, Arnett," Turner said. "Do the story."

Day Five

NIC AND ROBERT LEFT at daybreak for the border. "And then there was one," Nic quipped as he shook my hand and got into the taxi. As I waved them goodbye I thought of Robert's farewell comment in the emotion of the moment, that I was the "last of a dying breed" of correspondents because I was staying behind. I knew he was mistaken; there were younger journalists who felt as I did. Not enough of them were on CNN's payroll.

I walked back into the hotel lobby stuffing money into my leather jacket lining. Robert had passed me forty thousand dollars; we had to pay all our bills in cash. The previous evening I had cut into my jacket lining and hidden another sixty thousand because I did not trust the hotel safe. The layers of hundred dollar bills made me two sizes bigger.

I ran into Sadoun in the lobby and he congratulated me for staying behind, showering on me the kisses normally reserved for Robert. I did not kiss back; I tried to keep my distance. It was not my style to buddy up to officials. As far as I was concerned, when Robert left he took all his relationships with him. Now we were playing by my rules— and Sadoun's. His manner quickly changed. He said I should start packing to move to another location.

I dug my heels in. I insisted on knowing why, and he admitted the government was concerned about the safety of the al-Rashid Hotel. Along with the conference center next door, it was a showplace of the regime.

I wanted to stay to enjoy what little comfort remained because I doubted it would be any better anywhere else. I pulled arguments out of my hat. I told him that I believed the only reason the hotel had not been hit was because the press corps had made it famous. I told him the truth that I knew General Norman Schwarzkopf from the early years of the Vietnam War, and I invented a bit more: Schwarzkopf would never turn his bombers loose on a friend.

I said my decision to stay was contingent on my remaining at the hotel. We were talking in the lobby and hotel staff wandered in and out of the discussions. Sadoun's boss, Naji al-Hadithi, arrived and we continued our conversation at a higher decibel. They finally agreed to delay the move.

381

The reception desk manager, Mrs. Nihad, came to me later and thanked me for guaranteeing the safety of the hotel. I accepted her appreciation with a rueful grin. I knew if I were wrong, no one would be left to argue the point. And if Israel decided to retaliate against Baghdad for the Scud missile attacks on Tel Aviv, I doubted that they would give any special favor to the al-Rashid.

As I settled in again, I discovered that I was not the only journalist who had been allowed to stay in Baghdad. Three Russian reporters were stuck there with no money for the trip home to Moscow, along with several Jordanian journalists and a Spanish reporter. Still, I had an unassailable advantage, the only communications link with the outside world.

In the late afternoon I tried to assemble the satellite telephone. I had watched Nic and had scribbled out his instructions in a note pad but I was no cyberpunk.

Tom Johnson had given me specific instructions about the telephone: no one could use it but CNN; I should call only Atlanta and nowhere else. He said he had guaranteed the Pentagon that we would be the sole users of probably the only voice link out of the country.

I understood clearly. One purpose of the air strikes of the first two days was to close down all Iraqi communications. We were in effect opening them up with our telephone. I was not eager to give the U.S. military an excuse to knock us out of business.

Assembling the phone was proving difficult. Sadoun and Mohammed, the World Television Network cameraman, one of the several Jordanian journalists who stayed, helped me out. We dragged the heavy suitcase to the edge of the garden. A cold wind was blowing and our fingers were freezing.

First, we had to start up a small gasoline generator for power, and then line up the dish with the distant Indian Ocean satellite positioned to handle such transmissions. A small keypad charted our progress.

Then, through the modem, we talked with a ground station in Norway that patched us through to CNN's international desk in Atlanta. It was now early evening and dark. Nearly a minute passed before I heard ringing and Eason Jordan was on the line. I pounded Mohammed on the back. We had done it.

The air raid sirens began blaring about the same time we were connected. Anchor Jonathan Mann came on the line. After my report, he asked me if the Iraqi government was trying to cover up panic and disarray, "that people in Iraq are losing faith in Saddam Hussein, that the hypnotic spell this man has been casting over them is now being pierced by the bombs that are now landing down on Iraq?"

I glanced at Sadoun. He was smiling at me genially, unable to hear the incoming setup. I told Jonathan that the Iraqis had had eight years of preparation for the bombing during their war with Iran, and that there seemed to be more quiet confidence than panic in Baghdad, but that the picture might be different elsewhere.

Sadoun brought the Spanish reporter, Alfonso Rojo, to the phone and asked whether he could call his office in Madrid. I reminded Sadoun of my restrictions, and offered to pass on a message through Atlanta. Rojo stamped off.

The other journalists came by. They were eager, notebooks clutched in their hands. A Jordanian woman, Leila Dhib, started listing the organizations she worked for and they included a major news agency on almost every continent. Then the Russians wanted to use the phone.

I got Ed Turner on the line and explained the situation. He responded clearly, "Nobody uses that telephone but CNN and you are responsible." I got the impression he was more concerned about scooping the world than worrying about me, but either way, the instructions were clear.

When the call was concluded I dismantled a piece of the modem and put it in my pocket, just in case Sadoun, with his newfound knowledge of technology, might be tempted to use the phone himself.

Sadoun insisted that for my security I spend each night in the bunker, but I think he wanted to keep an eye on me. Jalil's family kept me a place near them on the hard floor. I brought blankets from the CNN supply room for the whole family. The shelter was crowded but only the youngest children seemed able to sleep. The worsening bathroom stink and the tension kept most people awake.

Those in the bunker were becoming familiar faces. Next to me was the Tawfieq family, a mother and two daughters who passed around a thermos of hot Iraqi tea and usually offered me sweet biscuits and kebab sandwiches. The mother would burst into tears when the air raid sirens sounded, burying her head in her quilt as the building shook. Her older daughter, Laheeb, a dental technology teacher at the Baghdad Medical Institute, would comfort her as best she could.

Sadoun and his cadre of minders were sprawled out in a nearby group. They all spoke fluent English and in the months of the crisis had gotten close to many visiting journalists. They laughed a lot about my colleagues' foibles. I continued Robert's practice of bringing down bottles of Scotch and cognac and handed them around until they were gone. I drank to be sociable and it helped me to get to sleep.

When they got over their initial fears, Sadoun and his minders took pleasure in baiting me about the bombing. Since I was sharing the dangers with them they seemed to absolve me from responsibility. Sadoun was convinced that America had launched the bombing prematurely and could be persuaded to stop once it understood the Iraqi position. He argued that Iraqi's historical claim over Kuwait was legitimate, but that details could be negotiated "between friends." He was not a subtle man. He made it clear to me the only reason CNN was asked to stay was because our reports would be valuable for the Iraqi cause. I encouraged him in his thinking because I believed that his needs and mine could be mutual.

Sadoun also played up the Palestinian cause, which Saddam Hussein had been trumpeting for some time. I name-dropped unashamedly, making the most of my familiarity with the Palestinian leadership, whom I had gotten to know during my year in Israel—just before I was sent to Baghdad.

The bunker population included a dozen Europeans from an international peace delegation who identified with the Iraqi cause. A larger number of them were at a primitive camp at the Iraqi-Saudi border, where they hoped to form a human shield. I found greater stress conversing with the activists than the Iraqis because they opposed the war stridently and brooked no debate. Sadoun told me his government was paying all their expenses and would send them home soon because their mission had failed.

Day Six

A YOUNG BRITISH freelance journalist had been brought to the hotel during the night, and Sadoun introduced me to him at breakfast. His name was Bruce Cheesman and he looked thin and frightened. I had asked Sadoun about him the previous evening after a CNN producer told me that he had been reported missing. Sadoun said he had found him in jail; he had been arrested the night the war began, wandering around Baghdad looking for a telephone. He had been mistaken for a downed American pilot. Sadoun described him as the victim of a "misunderstanding." I fudged the rules a bit and let Cheesman phone his parents and he indicated to me that his incarceration had been brutal. He was broke and had lost his passport. I realized that Sadoun and his minders were all that separated me from a similar fate. I gave Cheesman the key to the CNN supply room and told him to eat up.

Naji, the information director general, came to the hotel with startling news. His government had decided to allow CNN to bring in a portable TV satellite uplink, giving us the ability to relay pictures and news reports live from the battlefield. The heavy equipment was still in Amman and would have to be trucked across the bomb-endangered desert. I worried that CNN could not find someone to risk the trek. But they did.

My entreaties to see more of the war paid off. Ala'a took me on a drive through western Baghdad. He started lecturing me about indiscriminate allied bombing, but the prosperous Mansur district we were driving through showed no signs of damage at all. The shops and businesses were closed but we passed several busy vegetable and fruit stalls. Cars were lined up at open gas stations. Water trucks filled up cans. Vehicles were returning to the capital laden with luggage. The first shock of the war seemed to be wearing off.

The poorer suburbs were also intact, but as we crossed an overpass in the industrial agricultural complex at Abu Garib I saw in the distance the remains of a sizeable building. We drove alongside the main Jordan highway to reach it, pulling into a dirt road past a large, faded poster of Saddam Hussein comforting a distressed child. The small signpost at the entrance bore a crudely lettered sign, "Baby Milk Plant," in English and Arabic. The structure was barely recognizable as a building. The sheet aluminum walls and roof had been ripped off and scattered across the yard, reflecting the noonday sun harshly into our eyes. The steel roof girders were twisted and blackened. The machinery underneath was a tangled, molten pile.

Ala'a spread his arms in a gesture of confirmation. This was the evidence of indiscriminate bombing, the only baby milk plant in the country, he told me. Its purpose was the well-being of the children of Iraq. "Your President Bush said he would not bomb civilian targets, yet look at this."

Ala'a introduced me to several officials as the World Television News cameraman, Mohammed, and his producer, Michel Haj, moved freely around the wreckage. The officials claimed that the factory produced twenty tons of infant formula powder each day, and had been destroyed in raids the previous Sunday and Monday. They said no one had been injured because the three hundred workers had finished their evening shift. They pointed to the ruins of what they said had been large drying towers. They showed me the plastic spoon-making machines with the output strewn by the thousands on the floor. There were iron wagons packed with milk powder along a wall. I saw carbonized incinerated packets.

There were documents lying all over the place. I surreptitiously picked some up and put them in my bag. One was a full schematic plan of a structure called "Baby Milk Plant Iraq" drawn up by the builders, Sodeteg Industries of France. The milk product was described in other documents as a powder of sugar and malt extract. A barbed wire fence circled the grounds. A solitary wooden guard tower sat at one corner. It looked like an innocent production plant to me. I gathered up an armful of powder packages to distribute to the children back at the hotel because they were complaining there was no milk.

At 8:30 that night, January 23, I broadcast my first report on the factory's destruction. I gave details of what I had seen and quoted officials as saying it was the only source of infant formula for Iraqi children. I had seen no evidence that the factory had been used for any other purpose. CNN anchor Patrick Emory asked me no questions about the story. He was more concerned with the Iraqi Scud missile attacks on Tel Aviv.

Day Seven

I WOKE UP FREEZING cold after spending the first night in my own hotel room since the war started. Sadoun let me stay upstairs because the bombing seemed to be moving away from the hotel. I enjoyed the soft, springy mattress of the single bed but the blankets I had thrown on to keep me warm had fallen off, and through the open windows came the roar of distant bombing and a cold winter breeze. I lit a candle in the bathroom and poured bottled mineral water into the sink and shaved in the flickering light. I vowed to keep clean every day whatever happened. That entailed stepping into the empty bathtub and soaping down and pouring more icy jugs of water over myself. As the only person on the whole hotel floor, I felt free to shout my lungs out.

I had raided all the open rooms for clean towels but someone had beat me to it. There was still no maid service. My sheets were grubby. I was running out of clean clothes. I rinsed my socks and underwear with mineral water and also flushed the toilet with my diminishing supplies. The most dreaded request from a room visitor was, "You don't mind if I use your bathroom a moment, do you?" I ran out of shirts and replenished my supply with some flashy ill-fitting garments from the dwindling supplies of the government's dollar store. We also had to contend with the constant pilfering of our flashlights. As I looked out the window I saw that other hotel guests were gathering drinking water from in the ornamental pools in the hotel garden and washing their clothes in the swimming pool. Great idea.

I went into breakfast. The dining room had been relocated to an inside chamber for safety. The Muzak had also survived the move, unfortunately, and endless renditions of the same songs floated through the corridors, stringed instrumental versions of "Danny Boy," "Killing Me Softly with His Song" and "You've Lost That Lovin' Feelin'."

Several nervous Pakistani waiters in unpressed white jackets attended the dozen or so tables. There was no menu. Food was laid out on a sideboard: boiled eggs, slices of stale bread, a few wizened oranges and jars of guava jelly. The waiters poured thin coffee from a metal pot. I had CNN's vast storehouse of junkfood at my disposal and supplemented the meager breakfast rations with cheese, crackers and cookies. I shared a table with Said, a Palestinian businessman from Jordan who had stayed behind to care for his fertilizer plant in a Baghdad suburb. Said knew the city well and had connections at the Zulal water company. He sold me forty cases of drinking water. He also came up with several drums of French goat cheese marinated in olive oil that gave zest to our meals. My new driver, Sabah, brought me flat, circular loaves of chewy unleavened bread that his wife baked freshly each morning. The hotel's lunches and dinners were as Spartan as breakfast. The main courses were thin stews of unrecognizable meats, the desserts pale imitations of flan.

The war was a week old. A CNN producer told me over the phone the Pentagon had conceded there would be no quick end, that the bombing campaign would go on indefinitely. I toured Baghdad with Ala'a, who translated for me the day's government military commu-

387

n’qué. It complained of more attacks on industrial installations, and lamented the loss of the baby milk plant.

People were moving around the main marketplace near the Khazmir shrine, buying fruit, vegetables and slabs of fresh meat. The population had settled down to the crisis and no longer seemed in fear of being targeted. When an air raid alert would sound they barely stirred. A bomb blast from across the river shook the market but the people seemed no more startled than if a car had backfired.

Sadoun took my report of that outing and began censoring it. His mood alternated between the flip and the severe. He was reading the account of my visit to the city center. I had written that the water system "is beginning to fully function again."

He turned to me, his pen raised. "You expect me to pass that?" I protested it was harmless.

"It's not the security, it's the grammar," he reproached me. "You have split the infinitive." He corrected it with a flourish. I remembered that Sadoun was proud of being an English literature graduate of a Scottish university. The previous day he had removed a reference I had made to Israel as "the Jewish state" as being racist, although such usage was commonplace in the West.

Even though Sadoun came down hard on military information, blue-penciling references to Baghdad's air defenses and the general estimates I was making of the bomb damage to the city, I felt I had reason to be contented with my work. I had mastered the satellite telephone and was reporting regularly to CNN. And I was stretching the limits of censorship with my more informal responses to the questions from Atlanta.

Day Eight

I TUNED IN TO THE BBC at daybreak, and heard White House spokesman Marlin Fitzwater call me a liar. The president had watched my report on the baby milk plant and, Fitzwater said, they were not pleased. He said the installation was a "production facility for biological weapons."

Fitzwater claimed that the infant formula production at the installation was a front; he described CNN as "a conduit for Iraqi disinformation."

CNN's first reports of the attacks against Baghdad had generally met with the approval of the U.S. government because our observations on bombing accuracy were helpful to American policy. Now that I was seeing the negative side, the White House was obviously changing its tune.

I saw Sadoun at breakfast and he grasped my hand in pleasure. "You have made the Americans angry, no?" he laughed. I told him that CNN would be on me to produce hard evidence that the plant was what I said it was. He asserted, "Everyone in Baghdad knows that's a baby milk plant. The French built it and ran it for years."

My breakfast companion, Said, chimed in. "Peter, I have been there several times. It produced milk powder." The previous evening I had given him one of the milk packets I had found at the factory. He tore open the corner and poured it in his coffee and took a sip.

I told Sadoun that the pictures we sent were not enough. It was getting down to my word against the word of the White House. My credibility was on the line. I needed convincing documentation on the history of the factory.

I also used the opportunity to demand greater flexibility to report. I needed freedom on the telephone to respond to questions from the CNN anchors, unlimited time to state my side of the story. I said I had to see more of what was going on in the city and the countryside because the bombing campaign had been proceeding for more than a week and I had to settle mainly for Iraqi radio handouts.

Sadoun grasped my shoulders. He smiled warmly. I was reminding myself of the old Arab saying that an enemy of my enemy is my friend. He hated the White House, the White House hated me, therefore I was accepted. He said, "Peter, the Americans claim they are experts at pinpoint bombing, right? They claim they have destroyed only military targets. Well, today we'll take you around Baghdad and show you otherwise."

I drove with Ala'a and the other journalists to the Iwadhi district in the northwest where a block of small businesses were in ruins. There was a fifteen-foot-deep crater in the sidewalk. Glass windows were broken in a nearby mosque but local residents said there had been no injuries.

We visited the Suma district in the north where the headquarters building of the Civilian Defense Directorate was said to have taken two direct hits. Half a mile from the al-Rashid we were driven down an alley where three private homes had been demolished, according to people standing in the street. Several residents were said to have been injured.

In two hours, we saw only these three examples of civilian damage. We had driven past several ministries and communications buildings that had been destroyed earlier in the war, but we had already reported their destruction. It seemed to me that the air raids had been more accurate than Sadoun wanted us to believe.

When I came up at noon for my first report of the day, anchor Rick Moore mentioned the ongoing White House complaints about the baby milk plant story and asked, "Are you being misled?" I maintained that I could report only what I saw, but that we had been permitted to walk around the destroyed premises and examine them thoroughly. I said I would be concerned if chemical and biological substances had been produced there because I would have been contaminated.

I reminded him that we had been permitted to take extensive videotape of the destruction, which was on its way back to Amman, Jordan, and could be examined by experts.

When he asked how reliable the information was about the baby milk plant, I said we questioned everyone we met but could not guarantee the veracity of their answers. I told him, "I learned in Vietnam to believe only what my eyes had seen. I have an inborn skepticism because I am a journalist. I can confirm only what my eyes can see."

Rick pressed. He asked me if I was being told what to say, that there was a feeling by some that I was being instructed to report the Iraqi line. I said that was not the case. The Iraqis were mostly concerned that I not report information that would aid the allied cause.

Rick signed off by saying, "We ask our viewers to keep in mind that Peter's reports from Baghdad are based on official statements by the Iraqi government, and whatever personal observations he is able to make. His movements are, of course, restricted by the Iraqi government and he has no access to outside independent sources of information."

At the end of the session I felt that even my own news organization was doubtful about my ability to assess the facts. I worried that political pressure from the U.S. government could undermine what I was doing. I had experienced similar attempts in Vietnam and Central America.

Sadoun had been listening to me and seemed puzzled by the exchanges. He said, "They want proof? Tomorrow I have a trip for you, we will go somewhere to show you wanton destruction. You will have your proof.''

Day Nine

WE LOADED UP FOR a long trip north, "beyond Samara," as Sadoun explained. Samara is an important archeological site, a center of ancient Mesopotamian civilization. It was also known to be a major center of Iraqi's chemical industry.

As usual, Ala'a came along. We had become friends of sorts after I acted as his go-between with a pretty al-Rashid receptionist whose wealthy family disapproved of their relationship. Ala'a was trying to improve his English and was quick to pick up on any unfamiliar phrase. The previous day I had added "kicked butt" to his vocabulary.

The route north took us out of Baghdad's sprawling suburbs and along the Tigris River toward Mosul. It was a wet, overcast day, happily not ideal for aerial attacks. We passed many small roadside communities in the first hour; none showed any signs of bomb damage. There were people trading at fruit and bread stalls, and portraits of Saddam Hussein in uniform, in various Arab dress and in Western suits, in the squares and streets.

At first the countryside was flat with scattered farms and trees. At one intersection I watched a truck convoy of Scud missiles and their launchers speed west toward launching regions closer to Israel. Ala'a touched his finger to his lips in silent warning. Tanks and military trucks roared past us toward Baghdad and I presumed the capital's garrisons were being reinforced by units from the north. Again, it was indicated that this was military information I was forbidden to pass on.

After two hours, the land became sand, though I could see rolling hills in the distance. When we passed Samara there were archaeological digs, miles and miles of mounds and excavations and crumbling ancient walls and fences. Beyond them, black smoke billowed across the eastern horizon.

We were soon in stony, semidesert scrubland. A large complex of buildings along the road to our west was smoldering. Ala'a described it as a "technical institute."

Several miles in the distance I saw a residential community sprawling up a sloping, barren hillside. It was the town of Al Dour, Ala'a said, the bedroom community for the technical institute's work force. We pulled into the center of town. The houses were constructed of gray concrete bricks and looked relatively new.

We drove to the southwest and turned a corner. Several city blocks were leveled as though by an earthquake. The streets were impassable.

I walked past houses with splintered roofs, whose walls had caved in. The trees were uprooted. I counted twenty-three homes totally destroyed before I stopped. There was a bomb crater outside of each. In front of a badly damaged mosque there was a hole thirty feet deep and about sixty feet across. At one intersection there were four craters quite close, as if grouped together. They were so deep they looked like an excavation for the foundations of a skyscraper.

Ala'a rounded up groups of local people who claimed to us that twenty-four civilians had been killed in the bombing. They shouted out the names of families who were lost. And they looked hostile. If I had arrived in Al Dour without my minders I might well have been set upon.

The local officials said the bombing had taken place in the early morning hours of January 21, the fifth day of the war. There were no bomb shelters in the town because it was believed the settlement had nothing to fear. We were taken to a local cemetery where there were twenty-four fresh burial mounds. The officials insisted that there were no military targets in Al Dour, and one told me, "Look to the horizon. You will see nothing." I did see the smoke from the "technical institute" several miles to the south. It seemed to me that possibly Al Dour had been bombed accidentally by allied planes attacking the installation.

In the wreckage of one home I found a torn paperback copy of Thackeray's *Vanity Fair*. The frontispiece was inscribed with the name Raeda Abdul Aziz, who had been killed in the raid, his neighbors said, a nineteen-year-old who was attending the University of Baghdad, and had majored in English literature.

He had made numerous margin notes and on a separate piece of paper he had written, "Rebecca Sharp was not a kind, forgiving person. She said all the world treated her badly. But the world treats people as they deserve to be treated. The world is a mirror. If you will look angrily back at it, it will look angrily back at you. If you laugh at it . . . and with it . . . it is a warm, kind companion."

I took the battered novel back with me as a souvenir but I did not plan to mention it in my broadcast. I knew I would take a great deal of heat by reporting a controversial bombing of Iraqi civilians in the existing climate of disapproval.

Sadoun made no changes in my story even though I had written that truck traffic on the road was heavy. Holliman was anchoring the evening report and I gave as full a description as I could of the damage and the accounts of the survivors. In his first comments, he told me that many Americans thought I was being duped. Viewers would have to get used to hearing reports like that of Al Dour, I responded. You couldn't unload thousands of tons of bombs on a country with seventeen million people and not expect civilian casualties. I said that in 1966 Harrison Salisbury of the *New York Times* had been taken to places in North Vietnam where communities had been bombed and civilians injured in American air strikes. He had been widely criticized for reporting the destruction.

I said that I hoped now that we were all more aware of the nature of war, but Holliman broke in, "There's no way that this was just a staged event for you to look at? I mean, it really did happen, right, Peter?"

I wanted to punch him on the nose, but that was impossible. I wanted to scream a profanity at least, but broadcast discipline restraining me, I spoke slowly, "There's no way this could have been a staged event, John. I've seen bomb damage in seventeen wars in the past thirty years and this is just typical. It filled all the qualifications, all the appearances of a bombing. The residents confirmed it. This was not a setup."

Holliman asked me if I had any new thoughts on covering the war from the enemy's side. I responded that I hoped Americans would be sophisticated enough to know that innocent civilians were going to get hurt in the war, and that the White House could justify that within the larger picture of the war. "I think this little piece that we are providing here is valid."

He asked me then for an assessment of the larger war effort, but I could not provide it. I told him that I had no sense of how the war was going beyond my limited vantage point. I could not confirm Pentagon claims that the allies had air superiority and were defeating the Iraqi forces. From the local newspapers I quoted Saddam Hussein as saying that the destruction the country had sustained could only be justified by total victory. I supposed that meant his losses were considerable.

As Holliman asked question after question, the rain leaked through Sadoun's umbrella wetting his shirt, and I was getting hoarse. I was also hungry. I told John the communications were breaking up, and that the generator noise was overwhelming and signed off. One advantage of being alone on a story was that there was no one around to contradict such decisions.

Day Ten

ATLANTA TOLD ME Bob Simon of CBS and his crew were missing in the Kuwaiti war zone, believed captured by the Iraqi Army. I had run into Bob in Jerusalem a month earlier and he had told me that press restrictions were so tight in the Saudi Arabian theater that he would have to outsmart them to cover the story. I took up his case with Naji and pressed for confirmation. I told Atlanta to keep asking me about Simon on the air.

I also pressed Naji to rescue the CNN truck with the portable TV uplink that was stuck at the Jordanian border in heavy snow. The crew that CNN had rounded up were calling Atlanta, saying they were freezing and frightened. Naji had sent two emissaries with official authorization to bring them in but they couldn't find them. I urged the officials to try again. Tom Johnson had told me the truck would have CNN painted in bright red on its roof and assured me the officials would be safe. They looked dubious, but took off, anyway, after I loaded them up with food supplies from the storeroom and gave them several hundred dollars in traveling money.

Today Naji was unshaven and tired. He said I looked like I was enjoying the war. He was right. I was reporting every day, with the story pretty much to myself. WTN was sending out videotape by courier every morning for CNN to use, and the pictures backed up my phone dispatches. I told Naji that CNN wanted me to interview senior officials of the government, to get past the propaganda agencies. "Who do you want, Saddam Hussein himself?" He burst out laughing. I asked him why not.

"Be lucky to have me," Naji said. "The leader has much more important things to do."

He offered me a trip south to An Najaf, a Muslim holy city, the third most important Islamic center after Mecca and Medina. He claimed that An Najaf had been "savagely bombed."

For the fourth day in a row we were taken to residential areas damaged in the war. I did not complain because each place was a dramatic story. That's what war is about. I asked to visit damaged military sites but my requests were turned down on security grounds.

I was not concerned that my reports covered only one side of the story. Each day the allied high command in Saudi Arabia announced lists of destroyed Iraqi military targets, even distributing warhead camera videotapes of the successful strikes to the media. But they were not acknowledging civilian casualties. I knew that Iraqi officials believed their interests could be served by an emphasis on the innocent victims of the war. I felt my reporting outweighed their propaganda gain.

As the criticism of CNN, and of Arnett, grew, the minders became more amenable and they loosened their grip a bit. I knew I was skating on thin ice.

On the hundred-mile journey to An Najaf, I noted that the truck traffic was heavy and also that Saturday shoppers were busy in the markets and farmers were working in the wheat fields and date plantations. Despite the bombing, downtown An Najaf was lively.

Sitting in the back seat of the car on the drive home, I wrote out my report on a large note pad, balancing a flashlight under my chin. Night had fallen, and just as we approached the southern outskirts of Baghdad, a massive air strike began against an industrial complex to the left of the highway. It was so close that our driver turned off his lights and steered by the glow of the anti-aircraft fire. Ala'a urged him on, as anxious as I to get away from the danger. But even in the city center there was the thump and dazzle of bombing—another attack on the Dora oil refinery and renewed strikes against the government's Muthand Airport, which was near the hotel.

The lobby of the al-Rashid was dark and deserted. Sadoun was in the bunker, and he signed my dispatch without changing any of it. He told another minder to supervise my call to Atlanta, saying he was "too tired."

We dragged the heavy phone case outside to the garden. In the cold, I had trouble fine-tuning the settings. The WTN cameraman, Mohammed, had to rescue me. Bobbie Battista was at the anchor's desk and she kept me on the phone for fifteen minutes with questions, much to the annoyance of the minder, who wanted to get back to the shelter. Because he was listening to the bombing more than to me, I was able to talk more freely than usual. Bobbie asked if I was hearing any talk of peace from the people we met. I told her there was evident unhappiness with the war, a view I had heard in conversations with civilian Iraqis in the hotel and on the streets. A carpet merchant outside his shuttered shop in the old city had quietly cursed the day that Saddam had invaded Kuwait becuse business was so bad. I told Battista that many Iraqis were listening to the views of the allied coalition over shortwave broadcasts, from the BBC and the Voice of America.

She asked me whether I was "developing a relationship, so to speak," with my minders.

"You mean something like the Stockholm syndrome," I laughed, "when captives identify with those who are holding them?" Perhaps Atlanta thought I had lost my marbles. Hadn't the producers been listening to my broadcasts and figured out otherwise? I hoped my critics would not equate my amiability with the minders with disloyalty. If I was really trusted by the Iraqis I would not have needed minders at all.

That night Sadoun told me he had received the first word from his pregnant wife and her mother. When the bombing began, they had fled to a relative's house in a distant village. They were safe. Naji, too, had sent his family into the countryside and was worried because he had not heard from them. Jalil's family was content to be with him in the bunker. They passed food around and sang songs in the early evening, and laughed a lot when the bombing was distant.

After some of my Scotch and cognac, the minders grew boisterous. Sadoun said he was puzzled by the American response to Iraq's invasion of Kuwait. He acted genuinely hurt. "For ten years we looked upon America as our friend, and see what you do to us now," he protested. "America will never be trusted in Iraq again."

I tried to break through Sadoun's self-righteous pose. I said America and the world were furious at Saddam Hussein and he had only himself to blame. Now all of Iraq was paying the price for his brinkmanship and it was a shame. He listened without too much indignation. At one point, one of the younger minders called out, "Sadoun would censor you if you tried to say that on the air." Sadoun wagged his beefy finger at me and laughed. "Don't try, Mr. Peter."

I asked them how they felt about Saddam Hussein. They responded with enthusiasm. He was the ruler, the supreme authority, as simple as that. Some had seen him in parades. None of the minders had met him; they were too low on the pole. I got the impression that few were even in the socialist Ba'ath Party, the political organization through which Saddam ran the country.

One minder, Nasir, told me that he had fought in the war against Iran, which had lasted through most of the 1980s. He was proud of his service, he said; it was a just war. I told Nasir that this time it was different, this time they were against the wall. There was no way that Saddam Hussein could prevail against the coalition. They didn't say much. Whether by my arguments or by the liquor, they were finally subdued. They turned over to sleep.

On the way to my room I wandered across the lobby. The skies were clear. I pulled open the front doors and saw the bulky outline of a large vehicle parked across the driveway. As my eyes got accustomed to the tricky light I realized it was a Scud missile on a launcher, in our front yard. If the Pentagon knew about that then the al-Rashid was a goner. I closed the door and tiptoed to my room.

Day Eleven

SADOUN BUSTLED UP TO ME in the lobby in the late afternoon of the eleventh day of the war, and said I must prepare to interview a "VIP." He declined to be specific, hurrying me to change my sports shirt and leather jacket for more formal garb. I settled for a pair of dark woolen slacks and a gray sports jacket. I had not brought a suit to the war. I presumed the interview was with Jassim, the information minister, who had not been around for a week but had promised me one. I jotted down a few questions to ask him.

When I returned to the lobby I was accosted by four men in dark suits with close-cropped hair who frog-marched me back up the stairs. I appealed to Ala'a for assistance and he indicated I shouldn't worry and followed along at a distance.

Inside an empty room the four men told me to undress. I was to be strip-searched. I doubted that anyone but Saddam himself would require such security measures. As my mind raced, they took each piece of my clothing and examined it thoroughly, running their fingers along the seams of my jacket and turning out the pockets of my trousers and peering at the inseams of my underwear. They tapped at the soles of my shoes and dismantled my ballpoint pen and peered into my wallet. They studied my naked body.

After I dressed, they insisted I wash my hands in disinfectant in the bathroom sink and I figured it was because I would be shaking the hand of their leader. I was not required to use mouthwash, which led me to believe I wouldn't have to kiss him. They put my notebook, wallet and pen in a plastic bag to be returned later, and took me back down to the lobby.

While I was waiting, I heard familiar voices from the lobby entrance. I recognized the beaming face of Vito Maggiolo, a CNN producer from Washington whom I had worked with in Lebanon and elsewhere, and Nic Robertson. They had been escorting the CNN TV uplink from Jordan. I knew it must have been a hellish journey and I wanted to greet them, but I had been warned to remain silent, not to talk to anybody, so I called out, "Don't come near, don't talk to me." Vito looked at me as if I was crazy.

One of the guards tugged at my sleeve and led me away. At the hotel entrance a black late-model BMW was waiting, the rear right door open. I stepped inside and greeted the driver, who didn't respond. He pulled out immediately and turned into July 14 Street.

I settled back in the plush comfort of the car and enjoyed the moment. An interview with the most feared man in the world. We drove across the Republic Bridge and onto the Qadisiya Expressway, and north past the wrecked telecommunications center. There were no other vehicles on the road. We took the exit onto Palestine Street and the driver began looking over his shoulder to see if we were being followed. There were few cars abroad. Soon we were in a residential area in the northwest part of the city I had never visited. From road signs I saw it was the Cairo district.

In the dusk I could see that the streets were lined with neat two-story wooden bungalows with flowers and plants in their front yards. We pulled up at one. A more innocent atmosphere could not be imagined. The driver opened my door and a figure came toward me and directed me inside without a word. I walked through a darkened corridor and into a large room bright with television lights. Three video cameras were aimed toward a richly decorated section of the room. It looked like a Hollywood movie set. The white wall was decorated in gold trimmings, large vases were in the corners. On a lush carpet bearing the official Iraqi seal were two comfortable chairs covered in white damask.

Several men were in the room, including minister Jassim. One identified himself as Saddam's private secretary, another as his cousin. They were subdued. They were all dressed in military uniform. I recognized the interpeter from videotapes I had seen of interviews. He mentioned that they had been watching me on CNN.

Saddam Hussein was expected momentarily, but after half an hour he hadn't arrived. To break the silence, I asked Jassim about Bob Simon, who was still missing, and he exploded in anger, accusing me of being more interested in a handful of Americans than I was in the fate of Iraq. Jassim, who had a quick temper, refused to comment further.

Saddam Hussein, I had heard, was even more unpredictable. But I was not intimidated. I presumed I had been summoned for a reason, and that I would survive the encounter. Psychologically, I had an advantage. He was on the run. He was the target of the bombers, not I. I felt I could push him.

The door opened and Saddam Hussein walked in alone. He was wearing a dark blue suit, a light topcoat and a gray wool cap. He towered over the aides who gathered around him. He soon excused himself and went out to prepare for the interview. The interpreter went with him to change into civilian clothes.

When Saddam came back he walked over to me and thrust out his hand. He had a firm handshake. He looked at ease. His mustache was neatly trimmed and his thick black hair was impeccably styled. I was reminded of the old Hollywood images of Latin lovers. He could have auditioned for a role, maybe as a stand-in for Cesar Romero. His suit was superbly tailored and he wore a fashionable scarlet floral tie.

Through the interpreter, Saddam asked why I had stayed in Baghdad. I told him I did that sort of thing for a living. He smiled broadly. That's a dangerous business, he said, maybe this will be the last time you'll have to do it. I remembered that he had said this was the mother of all battles.

I told him the world was eager to hear what he had to say.

"Did you bring a long list of questions with you?" he asked. I told him I would ask him what the world wanted answers to. It was a pompous remark and I immediately regretted it, but he didn't seem to mind. He took my arm and led me toward the set. "Ask me what you like," he said.

I knew that interviewing Saddam Hussein in the middle of this war was going to be controversial. Those who had already criticized CNN's decision to stay in Baghdad and were angry that we had chosen to show the results of the allied bombing would be further outraged. I vowed to be as uncompromising with Saddam as possible. CNN would surely run the entire interview on air. Every word I uttered would be scrutinized. I did not address Saddam with an honorific title. I launched directly into each question, or at most offered a "sir." I learned later that the interpreter had prefaced my questions in Arabic: "Your Excellency," "Honorable Leader" or "Great One."

I observed that the bombing had plunged Baghdad into darkness, and that the U.S. high command had announced that it was winning the war. Saddam replied that the brightest light was still shining, the light in the souls of the people, and that the allies were not reaping victory from the bombing, but shame for launching the attacks in the first place.

His answer was wordy and roundabout. I knew I couldn't afford to pause, to consider different strategies, but I also knew I had to get more newsworthy answers out of him. I remarked that in just a few days of bombing, more damage had been inflicted on Iraq than in its eight-year war with Iran. Saddam shrugged that off. His people and military remained determined to fight. I wanted to know the fate of his air force, which had flown off in its entirety to Iran, and his use of oil as a weapon in Kuwait. He dissembled in his answers. The translation delays made it difficult for me to press him too exactly.

I tried to provoke him by asking about his decision to use captured allied pilots as human shields at strategic installations, pointing out that even though he himself would cite the Geneva Conventions, his behavior didn't square with those agreements governing conduct in war. Saddam turned the question around, accusing the West of a double standard in restricting nationals of Iraqi descent in their countries when the war began, then complaining about his treatment of prisoners.

I could sense that my pressure was having some effect. Saddam complained that President Bush had called for dialogue to resolve the crisis only as a cover for his war buildup. He asserted with a bitter tone that he had been tricked into releasing the five thousand Western and Japanese foreign "guests" that the Iraqi authorities had held in Baghdad for several weeks while the crisis was developing. "What did the political hypocrites in the West say at the time? They said keeping

400

the foreign guests would in fact lead to the war—will cause the war to happen. They said letting them go will prevent war from happening. We don't regret letting them go. But had we kept those five thousand individuals from the West and from Japan here, would Bush have still attacked Baghdad?"

I felt I was making some headway. Saddam was getting mad. He was sheltering less behind rhetoric, revealing more about himself. I pushed him on his war plans. That would be the crux of the interview. I told him there was much speculation about the upcoming ground war and fear of his legendary arsenals, and of his potential for destruction. How long did he think the ground war would last? How many casualties did he expect to inflict on his enemy?

Saddam seemed to enjoy that question, but in answering it, he revealed a little more that would make it easier for those who would hear it to hold him in contempt. He bragged, "The Iraqis are going to fight in a manner that is going to win them the admiration of even the human being inside the individual American fighting man." But he threatened Armageddon. "Lots of blood will be shed, lots of blood." He thrust out his arms to suggest its measure and he warned, "We're referring to blood on every side—American, British, French, Saudi and, of course, Iraqi blood. And let not fickle politicians deceive you once again by dividing the battle into air and land parts—war is war." He smiled. "Didn't they say this would be a war of only days? They were wrong in that assessment, and they'll be wrong again."

I brought up the greatest fear of those who opposed him, his weapons of mass destruction. The previous year he had threatened to lay waste to half of Israel with them, yet he had not used such warheads in his Scud attacks on Tel Aviv. Coalition forces in the Gulf were prepared for chemical and biological attack. Would he finally unleash his potent arsenal?

Saddam paused. "We shall use the weapons that will be equitable to the weapons used against us. We have shown you how true we have been to our word. You have tested us, we have responded as we promised."

He was equivocating, so I pressed. "The multinational forces have said they would not use chemical weapons against you. Does that mean if they don't use them, you won't?"

"What I said was that we should use the weapons that shall equate the weapons that are used against us," he replied. It seemed to me he was backing off his threats, so I pressed some more. He claimed,

401

I said, that Iraq's souped-up Scud missile called the El Hussein could carry chemical, biological and nuclear warheads, "Yet you have only used conventional weapons so far?"

Saddam hesitated a moment. "We are a people who follow traditional values. All this air superiority that you see now has failed to dislodge us from the path of balanced combat. We have maintained our balance. We have used the missile with its conventional warheads."

Was he dissappointed that Israel had not responded directly to his missile attacks, averting further polarization of the Arab world. Saddam answered with his old refrain, that it was "the Zionists in the corridors of the American administration that led to the war being waged."

Had his nuclear production facilities been destroyed, as the Pentagon claimed? I asked. He feigned indignation and delivered me a little lecture on security. "You want me to talk of this, even though the American authorities have imposed restrictions on even the simplest news about the individual soldier in Saudi Arabia? They have restricted the simplest details about their military operations. And they say they are a democracy. You describe Iraq as a dictatorship, so how do you expect us to give you details of this gravity, of this serious nature?"

Having brushed aside my question, Saddam volunteered a soliloquy on Iraqi morale. "What is important is for the Iraqi individual to remain intact, sound in faith, sound in self-confidence, sound in conviction. Whatever the aggressors destroy, as long as the people of Iraq remain intact, sound and alive, then they can rebuild even greater what has been destroyed."

I felt I had held my ground. And Saddam had been mostly calm and smooth. The only stress he betrayed was in his rapid blinking. (According to *Time* magazine, whose reporter counted, he blinked forty times a minute compared to his normal twenty-five.)

I said to Saddam that it seemed that every field commander throughout history had doubts about the battle ahead. "Do you have any doubts whatsoever?"

"Not even one in a million," he replied. Saddam's aides were fidgeting. I checked my watch.

For my last question, I asked what Saddam Hussein hoped the impact of the interview would be on the United States and the world. He considered for a moment, and then he grandstanded to "those people who are coming out onto the streets, demonstrating against this war." He thanked them for "countering a war that has been waged unjustly against our people." I was sure it would be seen for what it was.

The interview had lasted ninety minutes and it could have gone on longer. It was I who called a halt. Saddam rose and smiled broadly and shook my hand. He seemed pleased with his performance. He had stonewalled part of the time, and propagandized. He had gotten his message out, he thought. I felt he had betrayed his intransigence and hypocrisy.

Saddam beckoned a photographer who had been snapping away during the interview. We stood together against the gold-trimmed wall and smiled into the camera. The Iraqi leader spoke a few words to his aides and then was gone.

The TV crews stacked up the nine videotapes from the shoot. One camera had been focused on Saddam, one on me and the third on a wider view. As I gathered the tapes, Jassim touched my shoulder and told me to put them down. He said they would be delivered to the hotel in the morning. I objected strenuously. The Iraqis had been accused of tampering with tapes of meetings with Saddam. We compromised. Jassim would deliver the tapes to me by midnight. I figured that would give him just enough time to copy them but not enough to edit.

When I got back to the hotel the lobby was dark. I went down to the bunker to find Vito and the CNN gang and was met by Sadoun, who pumped my hand and smothered me in kisses. He shouted in Arabic to the crowd that I had met the president. The bunker erupted in applause. I was mobbed by the other minders. Families came up to me, smiling, touching my arm, asking questions.

Vito said in surprise, "By God, you're a hero here." I said I needed to tell Atlanta about the interview, that we could satellite it over the uplink in the morning.

Nic Robertson quickly set up the phone. I got Tom Johnson on the line, and he said he wanted a story that minute, that he was switching me over to the anchor for a full report. I protested that I did not have my notes together but he insisted and within seconds I was live.

I said it had been a chilling interview, because Saddam Hussein had betrayed no emotion other than supreme confidence even as his country was being blown to pieces. He had justified his invasion of Kuwait and offered no compromise. But he had indicated he would not use weapons of mass destruction. Saddam had come across as a stubborn, uncompromising man, I said. If anything, I felt that the interview would reinforce the West's determination to proceed with the war.

I was asked where the interview had taken place. In a private bungalow at the edge of town, I responded. Sadoun was shaking his fist at me. "You'll get him killed with those details," he stage-whispered.

The videotapes arrived around midnight as promised. The courier had an additional package, a folder with pictures of the interview printed by the presidential photographer.

Around daybreak, an aide to Sadoun banged on my door and told me to send the interview tapes to Jordan with the courier car because they had not received permission to set up the TV video uplink. I was worried. I had realized there was probably a debate within Iraqi circles about allowing live coverage of the war. If they were not even prepared to transmit tape of an interview with their own president, they might be backing out of the deal altogether.

I decided that if we couldn't go live, we wouldn't send the interview. I strung Sadoun along all day, telling him the tapes were on their way to Jordan for transmission to the world via our uplink in Amman. When it was too late to send the interview overland, I visited him in the bunker and told him he had no choice if he wanted the interview to air. We had to go live.

Sadoun accused me of treachery. He said he was in deep trouble. He sent an aide to bring his boss Naji to the hotel. Naji explained the problem. The government was convinced the transmission of the interview from Baghdad would invite retaliation against the hotel, that the Americans would do anything to silence Saddam.

I argued that the Americans wanted to hear what Saddam had to say. Eason Jordan, the international editor in Atlanta, had told me on the phone that CNN was getting hundreds of calls about the interview.

Naji was unhappy. Sadoun was morose. They left together. But by midevening, Naji returned. "Okay, Mr. Peter. We'll do it your way this time."

Nic and engineer Jay Ayer jumped to the task of assembling the uplink in the al-Rashid garden. In an uncertain glow from flashlights and storm lanterns, they pieced together the large pie-sliced shapes of the dish. They dragged the large power generator off to the far side of the garden to reduce the noise level, and erected a tent to house the transmitters. The squeal of air raid sirens was unnerving. There was more bombing than on previous nights and the vibrations shook the ground. The sky was lit with anti-aircraft fire.

The engineers finally fixed on the communications satellite twenty-three thousand miles in the sky, and got the signal through to Atlanta.

We were ready to roll with the first video when a close bombing raid sent everyone inside. As we took shelter in the stairwell, Nic brought up something that was worrying him. He had heard that signals emitted by a powerful transmitter, the kind we were using, could attract guided bombs. It was possible that a cruise missile, or one fired from an aircraft, could lock on to our signal and fly its path to the source. He said that if we transmitted for any length of time we would be endangering ourselves and the hotel. He recommended against it. Margret Lowrie, a CNN correspondent from Amman, backed him up. Vito reminded them that we had used the similar technology of the satellite telephone without incident. I urged that we go ahead.

We started rolling the interview at one o'clock in the morning. Eason Jordan told us over the phone that the CNN newsroom in Atlanta had cheered when it came in.

I was to go live at 4 A.M. Baghdad time to open the evening news program with anchor Bernie Shaw. Dave Rust set up his camera under a concrete-covered walkway. Then I was on, the bright camera lights glaring in my eyes and Bernie's familiar voice in my ear. As if on cue, distant bomb blasts grew to a roar, our background music.

Shaw wanted to know all about the interview, and he asked a lot of questions. As we talked, Ala'a grew alarmed about the bombs falling. He wanted us to stop broadcasting. We were the only lights on in Baghdad, with bombers in the sky. He insisted we turn them off. We continued broadcasting in the dark, the camera picking up the bright patterns of anti-aircraft fire behind me. Bernie said my daughter, Elsa, was watching in Boston, and I said, "I love you, darling, and keep looking." He asked what it felt like to be on worldwide television, reporting from an enemy capital under attack. I said that I remembered filing AP dispatches by Morse key from Jakarta. "Would you believe, from Morse key to speaking live to the world in thirty years? Well, that possibly sums up my career, Bernie."

I stayed tuned in to Bernie's broadcast for a few minutes after my report. Bill Moyers was recalling that he had been in the White House "when Lyndon Johnson used to shake the foundations over Peter Arnett's reports out of Vietnam. Johnson actually said, 'You know he must have communist sympathies,' only he said it worse than that."

Shaw replied, "And, of course, there is the present-day situation of the Bush White House and the Bush Pentagon and its negative reaction to some of the reports filed by CNN's Peter Arnett."

I pulled out my earpiece. I was tired. I hadn't slept for thirty-six hours.

"Baghdad Pete"

AT THE END OF January the Iraqis began letting more journalists in to cover the war. There were no American journalists in the first group of twenty to arrive, and I lobbied Sadoun to let in the main news organizations. He said CNN was enough, but I argued that my credibility would be strengthened if other Americans saw and reported what I was seeing and reporting.

Some of the news crews complained that CNN was receiving privileges from the Iraqis. Some suggested that we had made a deal to share our satellite facilities with the government. I had allowed Sadoun to call the Iraqi Embassy on the CNN link to authorize the visas for the journalists. He had agreed to speak in English, and I had listened in. Sadoun, some colleagues said, could have easily used the telex in the Information Ministry to relay his visa approvals. I told them he was too scared to leave the hotel but they didn't believe me. At a briefing where the visitors were complaining about press restrictions, Sadoun said, "If you have any problems just ask Peter Arnett. He's our supervisor." His joke got me into a bit of hot water.

The al-Rashid garden was turned into a communications center; several satellite phones were now in use, their shiny umbrella antennae unfolded, their power generators humming. CNN agreed to allow the Iraqi Voice of America reporter to use our phone, and at my own discretion I let other reporters call home. I was no longer worried that the hotel would be bombed.

But because we had the only TV uplink, and because our Atlanta headquarters insisted on a substantial advance payment before we would transmit video for the other TV organizations, we had to contend with angry correspondents unable to send their pictures until their home offices came up with the money. Instead of being slapped on the back or even acknowledged with a pleasantry, I was the focal point of a lot of discord and grumbling.

The pressure was getting me down. Even after the CNN crew arrived I was lonely at night and sometimes felt depressed. The bombing always seemed closer in the darkness. I proposed to Kimberly over the satellite telephone and was elated when she accepted. Mr. Sadoun, who was listening as usual, congratulated me.

Now, with a complete crew in town, I was able to achieve more effective news coverage. We moved everything down from the upper floors of the hotel, and set up a studio in the lobby bar. Cameraman Dave Rust was eager to get out in the field with me. While visiting the wreckage of the baby milk plant one day, six cruise missiles came flying overhead on their way to downtown Baghdad. After he photographed the missiles, we raced after them into the city and found two civilian areas where the Iraqis said two missiles had hit. Smoke from the Dora power station nearby showed that the other missiles had been on target.

Rust's presence allowed me to portray more fully the texture of life. We attended services at a Christian church. We wandered through the legendary copper market, where people were buying lamps and containers for water. We showed children playing on the banks of the Tigris River, and their mothers washing clothes in its flowing waters.

I kept asking Naji for permission to visit the battlefield in Kuwait, but he rejected all such requests. On February 6 he allowed us to visit An Nasiriya, forty miles from the southern city of Basra. The highway we were driving was under attack from allied coalition war planes. I saw a small passenger car a mile ahead of us hit with a missile. There was a flash of flame. As we passed it I saw that its roof was torn and the passengers inside were injured, but our minder did not allow us to stop.

An Nasiriya's two main bridges had been destroyed in the bombing and for the first time we were allowed to photograph them. The Iraqis had previously categorized such targets as military, and off limits to our cameras. I had been trying to persuade Sadoun for weeks to broaden our coverage list. Earlier that day he had said we could not visit damaged banks and post offices.

We got back to Baghdad late that night. We went live at midnight but there was an air raid alert during the broadcast and a new minder, Mahmoud, stepped in front of the camera to try and stop the broadcast. He was worried that our bright lights would attract the attacking aircraft. We continued with flashlights bobbing on my face.

The next day, we were allowed to get closer to the battlefield. We traveled to Basra, the city from which the invasion of Kuwait had been launched. It was almost within sight of the border. We drove along the back roads and country lanes to avoid the air attack, but we passed the wreckage of many oil tankers and trucks.

We crossed into Basra on a barely negotiable span of the only bridge still passable, and found a city in the middle of war. Attack aircraft were visible in the skies above. The sun glinted off their bodies as they dove on bombing runs, and maneuvered around the missiles firing from the ground. Everyone scurried for cover at the whine of constant alert sirens.

Basra was a major target with its port and extensive military installations. Consequently, there was more damage to civilian installations than in Baghdad. We visited a damaged hospital and a flattened mosque. We stayed at the Sheraton Basra, a once handsome hotel that had been turned into a bunker, its lobby and corridors sandbagged and its windows boarded up. At dinner that night the table shook so much that our knives and forks fell to the floor.

I was eager to provide variety in our coverage, but the first guest I chose to interview live in Baghdad was probably a mistake. He was Anthony Lawrence, an American member of the Gulf Peace Team who had just returned from a three-week vigil at the Saudi border after failing to prevent hostilities from breaking out. The soft-spoken Washington bureaucrat was transformed on the air to an emotional advocate demanding that all Americans join the peace movement, before the conflict "turns into a holocaust." Though I tried to balance his diatribe with pertinent questions, I got the worst of the exchange. Many of his sympathizers had gathered in the hotel garden to watch and applaud him. The CNN producers were not amused.

. . .

The first group of journalists to join us in Baghdad left on February 8; they had only been issued visas for one week. Another group followed, including the first Americans since the war began, an ABC television news team lead by correspondent Bill Blakemore. CNN, absolved of visa requirements, stayed put.

The Americans arrived with mail and messages, and now I became fully aware of the controversy surrounding my reporting. My numerous calls to CNN headquarters in Atlanta had been devoted almost entirely to delivering the news from Baghdad. I had received sporadic accounts of negative reaction in the United States and elsewhere in the world, primarily from phone conversations with my daughter, Elsa, who was working as a reporter at the *Boston Globe*, after graduating from Harvard University. Now I learned that I had been denounced on the floor of the Congress. Representative Lawrence Coughlin of Pennsylvania had charged, "Arnett is the Joseph Goebbels of Saddam Hussein's Hitler-like regime." Tom Johnson had gotten a letter from thirty-four House members who complained that my coverage "gives the demented dictator a propaganda mouthpiece to over one hundred

408

nations." Conservative members of the British Parliament had compared me to turncoats of World War Two. Political cartoonists enjoyed teaming me up with Saddam Hussein as a "video Benedict Arnold." An extremist right-wing organization nicknamed me "Baghdad Pete" and picketed CNN bureaus to get me off the air. Charlton Heston depicted me as something approaching a traitor.

CNN was still labeling my reports as "censored" as it kept up the daily interrogations from the anchors. But it was doing much more: three times each day, the network was running on-the-air letters and faxes of complaint from viewers who were angered that I was reporting from the enemy side. Calls, letters and faxes to CNN were coming in at a rate of two thousand a day, three to one against. CNN used my stories and Q&A often, but it also brought in a retired air force general who pushed the Pentagon view and regularly trashed my coverage.

On February 7, Republican Senator Alan Simpson of Wyoming told reporters at a Capitol Hill luncheon that I was "what we used to call a sympathizer. . . . He was active in the Vietnam War and he won a Pulitzer Prize largely because of his antigovernment material. And he was married to a Vietnamese whose brother was active in the Vietcong. I called that 'sympathizers' in my early days in the Second World War." In response to a call from the *Washington Post,* Simpson said he had been given the information "by an AP man who was involved in reporting the Vietnam War. A man of great repute. A friend I've known for thirty years. He said he didn't know the brother-in-law's name or the nature of his supposed Vietcong activities."

Neither did I. One of Nina's three brothers had died in the 1950s. A second, a medical doctor, died in North Vietnam in the 1960s. The third was a math teacher who lived in Hanoi and was not politically active.

Simpson was a powerful figure on Capitol Hill, then the Senate minority whip and a close friend of President Bush. Early in the 1980s I had interviewed him, and had worked with his staff on a story for CNN on an immigration bill he was drafting. I had last seen Simpson in Jerusalem in April when he was returning home from a meeting with Saddam Hussein in Baghdad. At a press conference, he had criticized the insensitivity of Western reporters to the Iraqi leader. It was later revealed that he had said to Saddam Hussein, "Your problems lie with the Western media and not with the U.S. government. As long as you are isolated from the media, the press—and it is a haughty and pampered press—they all consider themselves political geniuses. That is, the journalists do. They are very cynical. What I advise is that you invite them to come here and see for yourselves."

Friends supported me. David Halberstam told the *Washington Post* that he liked the senator but not "the ugliness of him even mentioning someone like Nina and connecting Peter's extraordinary coverage, as if he'd been sympathetic to the other side. He's dead wrong. I know the family, and that charge is particularly painful to them."

The *Washington Post* scolded Simpson, "If Peter Arnett had been anywhere near as bootlicky and obsequious with Saddam Hussein as Alan Simpson was in a visit with the Iraqi dictator last April, we could understand why the CNN correspondent was being assaulted for his interviews and coverage. But compared with what Senator Simpson and some of his colleagues on that visit did to butter up Saddam Hussein and make themselves beloved of him, Mr. Arnett looks downright surly. . . . Peter Arnett is standing up straight over there in Baghdad. Here at home, Alan Simpson has slipped into the slime."

And CNN did resist the calls for my removal. On February 12, Ed Turner issued a statement: "Some of the words and pictures are painful, but so is war. The censorship is onerous but so are the restrictions in other countries, including the United States." He concluded, "Arnett and CNN are there so that all our viewers can be there, as imperfect, restricted and dangerous as the conditions are."

Anger in Amiriya

IN THE EARLY MORNING of February 13, the rumble of explosions disturbed my sleep. Later, I was sitting eating breakfast with Vito and Dave when Sadoun came to us, tears streaming. "By God, this is the worst, this is the worst," he gasped, wiping at his face.

He said a civilian air raid shelter had been bombed that morning and that some of his friends and his secretary may have been killed. There was a government bus heading that way.

We raced to the parking lot. Other reporters had been alerted, including Bill Blakemore of ABC. I told our driver to follow us. We drove down Yafa Street toward the Amiriya district. It was a middle-class residential area that I had not been to before. Military jeeps passed us on Jordan Street, their sirens blaring. An ambulance swung out a few blocks ahead of us.

We pulled into a side street. There was thick smoke coming from the roof of a squat concrete building just ahead. A large crowd blocked our way. I saw a sign on a power pole with the traffic sign symbol of a running person, the word "Shelter" written in English and Arabic. I pushed my way through to a chain link fence that surrounded the smoking building. There was frenzied activity in the yard inside. Firefighters were pushing a water hose up a ramp and into an open steel door in the building. Others were hacking at another entryway, which was jammed. Uniformed military officers were shouting orders. A truck was backed up to the ramp and firemen were carrying down bundles wrapped in blankets and Iraqi flags, and loading them into the vehicle. The crowd murmured in anguish whenever they emerged carrying the bodies. There was a sign in Arabic on the building. Ala'a translated it as, "Department of Civilian Defense Public Shelter No. 25."

Dave kept his camera running. We worked our way around to the main entrance. I saw Jassim talking with the mayor of Baghdad. I pushed in between them as Dave began shooting over my shoulder. I asked Jassim what had happened. He said two precision-guided bombs had penetrated the shelter at around 4:50 that morning. He insisted it was a civilian shelter.

I asked if Dave and I could go inside and he ordered a firefighter to accompany us. We walked down a sloping concrete entranceway through a foot of water and then up a dark stairwell. I choked on the smoke and slipped on the steps. The heat was so oppressive I could barely breathe. There was a terrible stench of seared flesh. With his camera light shining ahead of him, Dave was more sure-footed and led the way.

We scrambled over debris and entered the foyer of the upper level. Lamps illuminated a hellish scene. Firefighters were crawling across the debris. The insulation had peeled off the walls. A fire was burning in a pile of bedding and clothing. Dave edged forward. My foot slipped in something soft, a charred body. Two firemen pushed me aside, another body in their arms. Further in, daylight streamed through a large, round hole in the concrete roof that looked nearly fifteen feet thick. The steel reinforcing rods were twisted and bent.

I made my way back outside. The shelter manager, Hassan Janadi, met me at the entrance. As Ala'a translated, an agitated Janadi estimated that more than four hundred civilians had been in the shelter, mostly women and children. Some had been trapped behind steel doors jammed shut by the intense heat. He said local people brought

411

their own bedding and food to the bunker. This was one of twenty similar shelters around the city constructed in 1984. Ala'a was weeping. "How could America do this?"

I left Vito with Dave and Ala'a and found our driver in the crowd and sped back to the hotel. I ran through the lobby, calling out to Sadoun, "Send me a minder." The overnight editor of the CNN international desk came on the line. I told him I needed to go live immediately. As I waited, Sadoun approached. "No censorship today. Say what you like about this. We have absolutely nothing to hide," he said.

When the anchor asked me what was happening, I responded, "There's been a major disaster here, a tragedy, a civilian air raid shelter has been hit."

A producer came on the line. "Just cool down," he instructed. I finished my report.

The video we sent of the bombing contained the most gruesome pictures of the war. But Sadoun said, "The Germans are sending worse pictures than you." I told him we didn't run body parts on CNN.

When Reid Collins came on the air a few hours later I quoted the shelter manager as saying that two hundred bodies had been discovered, mainly women and children.

Reid broke in, "Peter, the U.S. command in Riyadh says it wasn't really a bomb shelter, but rather was a command-and-control military bunker." The Pentagon claimed that the shelter had been reinforced for military use.

Later that evening I heard the official White House statement explaining the shelter attack, alleging that military instructions had been fed "directly to the Iraqi war machine" from the destroyed shelter, and that it had been painted and camouflaged to avoid detection. It was not known why civilians were there.

By then I had been back to the bunker twice. I had crawled over and through part of it and climbed to the roof with a dozen other journalists. We saw no paint or camouflage. Civilians I met at the scene said they had been using the shelter since the war began. I saw an antenna about ten feet high but no other evidence of a high-tech command center. The shelter was located at the center of the suburban community, surrounded by a mosque, a school and a supermarket.

It was not my job to argue with the U.S. government; it had an array of spy technology and special sources of information beyond my reach. I did not for a moment believe the Iraqi claim that the shelter had been targeted by the Pentagon to kill civilians. The whole bombing campaign up to that time indicated otherwise. All the damaged civilian areas I had seen were near military targets.

Still, some targets—such as dual-use installations where officials and civilians worked together—enlarged the potential for innocent casualties. The Amiriya shelter could have been in that category, suspected of being both a military command center and a civilian shelter. Several government ministries handling administrative affairs had been destroyed or damaged in the previous week. Three post offices had been bombed in Baghdad. Two of the Tigris River bridges in central Baghdad used mainly by civilians had recently been destroyed even though nearly all military traffic was routed across the large, modern overpasses to the north and south of the capital that had not been bombed. Just the previous night while I was reporting live, three missiles had slammed into the large conference center across the street from the al-Rashid Hotel and had burned all night.

The upshot of the publicity over the shelter bombing was that fewer raids were directed at Baghdad. But even so, the attack altered the nighttime habits of many people in the capital. The al-Rashid staff showed a sudden preference for their outside dormitories. When I interviewed PLO president Yasir Arafat at his embassy, he said the Iraqis had shown him an air raid shelter he could use but he preferred to fend for himself. The Independent Television News correspondent Brent Sadler told me he had visited a large shelter near the July 14 Bridge that was empty. Some people said they even stopped sleeping in their basements.

As long as there were bombers in the skies overhead, no one could feel safe. The price for the invasion of Kuwait was that everyone's lives were put at risk. At a large rally in Amiriya the next day, several hundred angry relatives and friends marched and shouted anti-American slogans and chased off the foreign press. It was the first large, open assemblage of people we had seen since the war began. They did not seem to care that they made an easy target.

It was only a brief display of defiance. Baghdad's mood became one of fear, intimidation and resignation. My press colleagues told of unexpected encounters with passersby who complained about Saddam Hussein. A young man came up to us one day in the street as we were interviewing shopkeepers and shouted that he hated the government, and ran off. Ala'a said if we used the video he would be forced to investigate the youth so I edited him out.

When the *New York Times* quoted military sources as alleging that the al-Rashid Hotel housed a major military communications center in a secret sub-basement the whole targeting issue suddenly became personal. The Pentagon had said the destruction of the Amiriya shelter was authorized on grounds that it was a military command center. Would we be next? There were nearly 150 civilians living in the hotel including journalists and diplomats. I hurried to check it out. I found the hotel general manager, Gahzi Ali Ismail, and insisted that I be given an immediate, complete tour of his whole establishment. When he brought Sadoun into the discussion, I added an additional requirement, that I be allowed full access with my cameraman through any door I wanted opened.

They agreed without quibbling. Dave and I headed down into the basement and through the bunkers; the manager opened storage rooms and closets. We came to a large room that he said was the base of the hotel's internal communications system. I thought we had found something: two men were working there at a switchboard. It was only the hotel staff. We looked for tunnels connecting the basement to other buildings, and trapdoors in the floors. After an hour I reported no visible evidence of the existence of a command center. The next morning's *New York Times* quoted American officials in Washington saying that the hotel "might now be the main Iraqi command post," but confirming that it would be spared bombing because of the presence of civilians. It seemed like a bad joke to me but I wasn't sure. I may have been confusing the propaganda war for the real one.

I was never entirely certain about who stayed in the hotel rooms and what all of them were used for. The hotel was enjoying a special status and I knew the Iraqis would not hesitate to use it to their advantage if it fitted their purpose.

The CNN engineers told me they were worried about a room on the eighth floor overlooking the garden. A line ran up there from one of the many generators powering the press satellite phones and TV uplinks. At night, lights were on in the room, yet it was in a part of the hotel that was closed off to guests. The engineers said their video signals were indicating interference that may have been coming from that room, maybe from a radio transmitter. I thought about the British colonel in the movie *The Bridge on the River Kwai* who attempted to thwart an Allied commando assault on the structure he had built for the Japanese military. I asked myself if the hotel was important enough to our operations to tolerate a blatant abuse of its neutral status? What could I do about it, anyway? Could I, in good conscience, keep functioning knowing that we were a cover for a clandestine Iraqi operation?

I was considering what to do when a French television correspondent asked my help. She said some of her press colleagues had persuaded three of the maids to sell them sex, and they needed a large supply of condoms. Could I help? I asked her where this setup was and she said it was on the eighth floor, giving a number that I knew corresponded with the room I was worried about. I relaxed: what was being transmitted in the room was certainly not radio signals.

The debate over the Amiriya shelter bombing shifted attention from my credibility to the Pentagon's. The pictures had been so shocking that people did begin to question policy. Few argued that the consequences of a bombing raid that had taken over three hundred civilian lives should be ignored, particularly in a high-tech war where such mistakes were not expected to happen. The public had naturally believed military briefers and their assertions of technological perfection and absolute accuracy. Now, CNN producers told me, mail to the network was beginning to run in my favor, with fewer calling me the voice of Saddam Hussein, and more addressing the need for the public's right to know.

By mid-February in Baghdad, a month after the bombing began, the Iraqis were talking compromise. Scores of military and industrial targets had been destroyed inside Iraq. The army in Kuwait had been pulverized. Yevgeny Primakov, an emissary sent by Soviet leader Mikhail Gorbachev, sought to convince Saddam to leave Kuwait before the ground war began. When we spoke with him at the al-Rashid, he said he was confident of peace. The Iraqi government even announced it was ready to withdraw from Kuwait, clear evidence that Saddam's will was faltering. But the offer was loaded with so many conditions that it wasn't acceptable to President Bush.

However, the withdrawal offer that was announced over Baghdad Radio revealed much about the mood of the population. They wanted the war to end. We photographed people firing guns in the air in the center of the capital. They mobbed us as we walked down Jamouri Street. They ignored our minders and came right out with their feelings. One man said in English, "The world left us no choice. We must leave Kuwait." Another said it made no sense to continue resistance. "No food, no medicine, no electricity. So what can we do?"

A minder pulled me aside and told me that Bob Simon and his crew were in captivity in Baghdad. He even drove me by the intelligence headquarters where he said they were being held, and I identified it on the air. I suspected the Iraqis were trying to send a signal to the

Pentagon not to target the building, but if they were, it didn't work. A few days later it was bombed, without injury to the CBS staffers who survived in the basement cells.

On February 19 I was joined by CNN correspondent Christiane Amanpour, and we shared reporting duties, going live morning, noon and night. We made some more trips to the countryside, but accidental bombings were making less news than the last-minute efforts for a peace before the ground war would commence. In trips to Samawa and Kebala in the south and Kirkuk in the north I noticed there were fewer bombings; the coalition planes were concentrating on destroying Iraqi forces in Kuwait. Highway traffic was heavy, mainly laden military trucks, a fact we were not permitted to mention. One night on the air, Bob Cain asked me if the bombing campaign had succeeded in stopping military traffic on one major highway I had traveled. I told him, "There was a lot of traffic on the road, and not much of it civilian." That slipped past the minder.

The efforts to achieve a negotiated peace became the focus of our coverage. The Kremlin sought a compromise; Foreign Minister Tariq Aziz made a well-publicized visit to Moscow. A few days later, on February 21, Iraq announced, through the Soviets, a willingness to begin "the full and unconditional withdrawal" from Kuwait. It was followed by a belligerent speech from Saddam Hussein, who said that if the offer was rejected then Iraq would fight, as he had called it before, "the mother of battles" to victory.

President Bush gave Saddam forty-eight hours to withdraw all his forces from Kuwait City, and to complete a full withdrawal from the country in a week. Saddam rejected the ultimatum. On Friday, February 23, Bush announced the beginning of the ground war.

Last Broadcast

THE LAND WAR WAS BRIEF and brutal. The Iraqi forces in Kuwait caved in and fled. For journalists in Baghdad, it was anticlimactic because the capital was cut off from the battlefield and all our news came from international radio broadcasts. The minders listened right along with us. The Baghdad population seemed stunned. They were listening to the same accounts of the swift collapse of their armies.

On the morning of February 26, the government made an announcement: Saddam Hussein officially called on his forces to withdraw from Kuwait. The minders at the hotel cheered and embraced. I saw no hand-wringing over defeat, no regrets for the loss of Kuwait, just relief that the ordeal was ending.

I watched dispirited soldiers straggling into the city from the battlefields in the south. They had been disarmed at the edge of Baghdad. We were not allowed to photograph or interview them. Baghdad looked wide open to attack. I woke up each morning during the ground war and looked out my window, wondering if armed helicopters would appear over the horizon, if General Schwarzkopf would push his tanks all the way to the capital. There was nothing to stop him from advancing to Baghdad from his forward positions on the Euphrates River if Bush ordered it. But the orders were never given. It turned out that Bush, too, was eager to get out of the war.

The last bombing of Baghdad occurred in the early hours of February 28 against targets in the southern suburbs, less than an hour before Bush announced that the war was over. The attacks had gone on for forty-three days. Baghdad Radio declared Iraq had won. I went downtown in the early afternoon and the streets were filling up with people who had been hiding for weeks. Youths were playing street soccer, disabled people were being wheeled around and enjoying the sun. I could find no one who regretted leaving Kuwait. But even though the bombing was over, the industrial sites south of Baghdad continued to burn for days, belching black smoke into the sky.

A primary provision of the ceasefire was the immediate release of all military prisoners of war, which was done. Bob Simon and his crew were also freed, and stayed the night at the hotel before leaving for home.

The end of the war was followed by civil insurrections among the Kurdish peoples in the north and the Shias in the south, but we were not allowed to visit. Over international radio, we heard that the populations had risen up in their thousands and occupied government buildings and barracks, taking advantage of the weakness of the central authority. But Saddam still had enough military forces in reserve to counterattack. The information ministers in Baghdad offered us few details. We were broadcasting live each day but we had less and less to report because we were not allowed to travel to either of the troubled regions.

I was exhausted and coughing a lot. I had lost weight. I wanted to leave Baghdad. Sadoun frustrated my plans. He told me that once again all news organizations were going to be expelled in a few days. Only CNN could stay, and only if I remained behind. I felt like a hostage. I was lonely. But I felt I had no choice but to remain, even though the story had shifted to liberated Kuwait and the embattled Iraqi cities where civil war raged beyond our reach.

Sadoun was uncharacteristically severe, insisting we report nothing but the official government story. I protested that the news of Iraq's suppression of its minority peoples was being broadcast internationally from the new war zones, and it was so at odds with what his government was telling me that I was starting to look ridiculous. The Iraqis claimed that nothing was going on, but businessmen I met in Baghdad, and Arab diplomats, were passing me information about the ferocious crackdown on the Kurd and Shia populations. But I could not use it. I even had valid reports of rioting in the Shia sections of the capital and their ruthless repression. And the few correspondents still there also chafed at the restrictions. Lee Hoffstader of the *Washington Post,* who was using CNN communications, tested Sadoun's patience by submitting pages of copy that included criticism of Saddam Hussein. The minder was furious. Hoffstader told me Sadoun tore up one page into hundreds of pieces.

The CNN anchors would not let the matter rest. Whenever Christiane or I came on the air, they peppered us with questions about the insurrection. Sadoun grew irritated. He demanded not only that we not respond, but that I inform CNN that these questions should not even be asked. That was too much. I told him we could not do business that way. Not even at the height of the war had such demands been made. Sadoun responded, "This is much more sensitive than the war." I supposed he was under greater pressure.

I made a pest of myself. I complained to Naji that we couldn't go on in such a manner, that we needed a regular flow of information. So they decided to end my misery. Sadoun came to me as I was having a late dinner to inform me that CNN would have to leave in the morning. We were getting kicked out at last.

I was relieved. The story had come to a dead stop. The only news left was our impending departure. I summoned Dave and we set up the satellite telephone and called Atlanta. I went ahead and broadcast live without waiting for a minder. For the first time, I had nothing to lose. Atlanta was not satisfied with just the phone interview. They wanted me on camera.

Sadoun agreed to a last broadcast and sent a young minder I barely knew to supervise me. He didn't seem to care what I said. He stood in the shadows in the hotel garden out of earshot chatting with Christiane as Dave fastened a microphone to my shirt and adjusted the light.

Frank Sesno was anchoring out of Washington. I spilled everything I knew. I talked for half an hour. I said Saddam Hussein would probably remain in power because his political base was intact and he still had a large security force to suppress all opposition. I said the Iraqi people were well aware of the battlefield defeat but were in no position to force a change of government. The minder was still talking to Christiane. I did not want to go too far; if senior Iraqis were watching me with their satellite dishes, the young minder's future could be in jeopardy. I told Sesno I was saving more comment for Amman, "Where I don't necessarily have to embarrass any local official."

Sesno asked me to reflect on my two months in Baghdad, and on the criticism of my reporting. I said the whole world had signed off on the bombing of Baghdad and I was its eyewitness. I was proud to be there.

Sesno asked me if I knew I was famous. I told him a reporter from Ankara said that women in Turkey were naming their children after me, even the females. A Vatican reporter said the pope wanted to meet me. I said I didn't feel any different from when I had first arrived in Baghdad two months earlier, just more tired.

We spent all the next day packing and left early the following morning for the border. Sadoun embraced me for the last time. He was unshaven again and his bristles scratched my cheeks. "I have learned a lot from you, Mr. Peter," he said with seriousness. Sadoun was always so emotional, so melodramatic. I think he did like me a little. We had shared much, an unlikely pairing in the age of the global village. I knew I would miss him. But I had never doubted where his loyalties lay.

Our convoy wound its way across the desert, past destroyed communications towers, burnt-out oil tankers and bomb craters. The Iraqi border post had survived the war. Officials checked our exit papers and waved us through. The Jordanians were equally expeditious, and invited us for tea.

Vito and I shared a taxi to Amman. It was after midnight and we were fourteen hours into our journey from Baghdad when the taxi broke down in the desert an hour from our destination. I walked onto the dark road and a little while later I flagged down a truck. It caught me in its headlights and stopped. I heard a voice shout out my name from the cab. I wondered who I could possibly know in a truck in the

419

middle of the Jordanian desert. The turbaned Palestinian driver climbed out and started pumping my hand. He was a fan. He had watched my broadcasts on Jordan TV. "Peter Arnett, CNN, welcome," he said.

I called to Vito and we climbed into the truck. I was amazed to be recognized, but I was more grateful for the ride. When we got to our hotel a crowd of press colleagues were waiting and they crushed around Vito and me, taking pictures and shouting questions about Baghdad. Upstairs at the CNN bureau I was hurried into the live studio and was interviewed first by Frank Sesno and then by Larry King. There were no minders around. I almost missed Sadoun.

At five in the morning, CNN finally left me alone. The bedroom was warm. The toilet flushed. There was hot water. And the sheets were clean. The al-Rashid seemed far, far away.

deen, the resistance fighters. The secret aid operation was
ng when I had traveled to Peshawar a decade earlier to walk
hanistan with a guerrilla force. I felt then the excitement in
ts, and I sensed that the war was becoming not only an Islamic
against the invading Russians but also a critical conflict of the
r. American officials I met there talked with satisfaction of
"Vietnam in Afghanistan," expressing the belief and desire
cow would pay dearly for its military support of the com-
vernment it favored in Kabul.

mericans were correct; the Russians eventually quit Afghan-
efeat. But Peshawar's dusty bazaars and steamy slums and
ssociations were perfectly cast for its role as a center of
e activities, and the city had since become a nightmare for
States. Islamic radicals from Arab lands that had supported
istan struggle were using their wartime connections to plan
ampaign on an international scale. The World Trade Center
uspects had connections in Peshawar and reportedly had
ely to and from the city.

ve nature of Western involvement in the war against the
d also allowed drug traders to flourish. They were using
n of obscure overland routes from Afghanistan to bring
opium and hashish to the region, turning Peshawar into a
r for the international drug trade. Narcotics and terrorism
ly combination.

on the notice board at the American Club cautioned
ing anywhere after dark. American officials and their
prohibited from visiting even the historic Khyber Pass,
ve away, because of the threat of abduction. The danger
emed pervasive. When I checked into the first-class Pearl
otel I saw a large sign in the lobby that read, "Arms
ught inside hotel. Gunmen must deposit weapons with
."

ited for the plane to Kabul, I talked with influential
eshawar who blamed the chaotic situation on a mercurial
ign policy that had wholeheartedly supported the Af-
ebels while they fought the Russians, but abandoned
d. "The chickens are just going home to roost," was
of a newspaper editor on the bombing of the World
"All you cared about was destroying communism, and
extremists to the struggle and trained them to kill. But
eople don't like you either, and you're the next target."

Part V

1993

Kabul, Afg[

THE DAY AFTER I finished writing
ways jet in Washington, D.C., en r
break from war reporting was over
CNN. I settled into the long ov
through London to Islamabad, Pa
was exhilarated to be on the roa
team looking into Afghanistan's
February 1993 bombing of New ˈ
spectacular terrorism that Ame
wider conspiracy by Islamic radi
United States. Some of the A
Afghanistan's war against the
1980s, a conflict I had covered

My CNN colleagues had flc
videotapes, bottled water, food
ern reporting team—a satelli
helmets. We planned to prod
ghanistan but were also prep
veloped. There was only one
Pakistan, and that was frequ
the airport. I waited in Pes
Northwest Frontier province
Afghanistan's Russian invas
terminded by American a
operatives funneled weapo

mujahe
beginni
into Af
the stre
crusade
Cold Wa
Russia's
that Mos
munist g
The A
istan in d
sinister a
clandestin
the United
the Afgha
a terrorist
bombing s
traveled fr
The furt
Russians h
the profusi
harvests of
major cente
were a dead
A warnin
against walk
families were
an hour's dri
of violence se
Continental
cannot be br
hotel security
While I wa
Pakistanis in F
American for
ghan Islamic
them afterwa
the comment
Trade Center.
you welcomed
many of those

A businessman complained that America had benefited from the collapse of the Soviet Union that the Afghan war helped bring about, and that Pakistan was "left holding the bag—the refugees, the drug trade, the instability. We got nothing out of it. The least we expected was to get a new trade route into Central Asia but even that hasn't come about because of the insecurity."

It was suggested that I see for myself what had resulted by taking a taxi to the badlands town of Darra thirty miles inside the tribal areas, a semi-autonomous border region, where guns and drugs were in abundance. There I was offered a kilogram brick of plastic-wrapped hashish for fifteen dollars at a roadside shop near a nineteenth-century British fort. There were bags of heroin under the counter, scarcely more expensive. But Darra was better known for its gun making. When I drove into the ramshackle town, salesmen were standing on the roofs of their stores test-firing automatic weapons into the air. A shopkeeeper offered to let me shoot a shoulder-fired rocket launcher from his backyard for seventy-five dollars. He showed me a captured Russian flame thrower. I could buy both of the weapons for less than a thousand dollars. After visiting Peshawar and Darra I felt I was ready for what Kabul had to offer.

The plane left on schedule, an Ariana Airlines 727 jet run by an immaculately uniformed Afghan crew. About twenty other passengers were on board, mainly Afghan officials and aid workers. A tasty snack was served. I was pleasantly surprised. I would remember it fondly because it was my last indulgence for several weeks. I had embarked on the trip with no illusions. By all accounts, Afghanistan had degenerated into a chaotic, lawless land after the Russians had deserted the battlefield in 1989. The American Embassy staff in Kabul had been evacuated, their lives at risk. They had not returned. And the State Department was warning American citizens against travel there, cautioning about politically and criminally motivated attacks and violence that included robbery and hostage taking.

History was repeating itself once again in Afghanistan. Stability had always been a scarce commodity there because of its location at the crossroads between Central and South Asia. Alexander the Great and later Genghis Khan subdued the Afghans on their way to greater glory in India and Persia; Great Britain in the nineteenth century and the Soviet Union in the 1980s failed to conquer the mountain-locked country. Even in peaceful times when no invasion was under way, political control in Afghanistan was of necessity loosely administered from the capital of Kabul, the tribal groups always indifferent, often hostile to supervision. But what made Afghanistan's instability now so dangerous was that the remote land was being recast into the Lebanon of the 1990s. It had no national security force capable of maintaining order. It was becoming a hub of international terrorism and narcotics production.

Our plane touched down at Kabul airport after a thirty-minute trip and we taxied to the terminal. I recalled my fear when I had flown in from Moscow in 1988 on a press trip organized by the Soviet government. Then, there was a danger that the guerrillas would fire Stinger anti-aircraft missiles at us. Our Antonov aircraft had spiraled down from a great height, firing salvos of flares from pods under its wings to deflect attack. We had been joined in our descent by armed Russian helicopters also firing flares to help us land. This time I saw at the edge of the airfield the rusting wreckage of Russian aircraft that had not made it down safely.

A hot wind was blowing and thick dust stung my face. I sucked in the gritty air because the Kabul plateau was nearly six thousand feet high and I needed the oxygen. The bright afternoon sun reflected off the enormous sienna-colored mountains that ring the plateau. Not far to the northeast beyond the mountains of the Hindu Kush were the Himalayas. The CNN team was approaching across the terminal to meet me. They introduced me to a young Afghan official, the government's chief of security, who had spent a year in the United States during the war recovering from stress, some of the time living in the basement of the Silver Spring, Maryland, house of Richard Mackenzie, a veteran reporter of the war who was helping us with the story. Afghans value friendship. The official had come out to help me through customs, and Mackenzie said he would be indispensable in getting us around the country. All the Afghans at the airport were carrying guns. On our short drive into the city we were stopped at a dozen roadblocks by soldiers who poked rifle barrels into our taxi as they checked our identities and cadged cigarettes and money. It was authorized robbery. Even the traffic cops were armed. CNN producer Peter Bergen said, "People wear guns here like they do wristwatches back home."

I could hear shooting as we drove to our guest house in the New City district. My colleagues did not seem perturbed as bullets and rifle grenades echoed through the streets. "Wedding celebrations on the other side of town," Mackenzie joked, pointing to the southwest of Kabul across two craggy hills topped by ancient walls. Several armed militia groups were vying for control of that part of the city and

Part V
1993

mujahedeen, the resistance fighters. The secret aid operation was beginning when I had traveled to Peshawar a decade earlier to walk into Afghanistan with a guerrilla force. I felt then the excitement in the streets, and I sensed that the war was becoming not only an Islamic crusade against the invading Russians but also a critical conflict of the Cold War. American officials I met there talked with satisfaction of Russia's "Vietnam in Afghanistan," expressing the belief and desire that Moscow would pay dearly for its military support of the communist government it favored in Kabul.

The Americans were correct; the Russians eventually quit Afghanistan in defeat. But Peshawar's dusty bazaars and steamy slums and sinister associations were perfectly cast for its role as a center of clandestine activities, and the city had since become a nightmare for the United States. Islamic radicals from Arab lands that had supported the Afghanistan struggle were using their wartime connections to plan a terrorist campaign on an international scale. The World Trade Center bombing suspects had connections in Peshawar and reportedly had traveled freely to and from the city.

The furtive nature of Western involvement in the war against the Russians had also allowed drug traders to flourish. They were using the profusion of obscure overland routes from Afghanistan to bring harvests of opium and hashish to the region, turning Peshawar into a major center for the international drug trade. Narcotics and terrorism were a deadly combination.

A warning on the notice board at the American Club cautioned against walking anywhere after dark. American officials and their families were prohibited from visiting even the historic Khyber Pass, an hour's drive away, because of the threat of abduction. The danger of violence seemed pervasive. When I checked into the first-class Pearl Continental Hotel I saw a large sign in the lobby that read, "Arms cannot be brought inside hotel. Gunmen must deposit weapons with hotel security."

While I waited for the plane to Kabul, I talked with influential Pakistanis in Peshawar who blamed the chaotic situation on a mercurial American foreign policy that had wholeheartedly supported the Afghan Islamic rebels while they fought the Russians, but abandoned them afterward. "The chickens are just going home to roost," was the comment of a newspaper editor on the bombing of the World Trade Center. "All you cared about was destroying communism, and you welcomed extremists to the struggle and trained them to kill. But many of those people don't like you either, and you're the next target."

Kabul, Afghanistan

THE DAY AFTER I finished writing my book I boarded a British Airways jet in Washington, D.C., en route to Afghanistan. My two-year break from war reporting was over and I was again on assignment for CNN. I settled into the long overnight flight that would take me through London to Islamabad, Pakistan, for connections to Kabul. I was exhilarated to be on the road again; I was joining a reporting team looking into Afghanistan's ruinous civil war and its links to the February 1993 bombing of New York's World Trade Center, an act of spectacular terrorism that American officials charged was part of a wider conspiracy by Islamic radicals to launch attacks on the mainland United States. Some of the Arab bombing suspects had fought in Afghanistan's war against the Russian occupation army during the 1980s, a conflict I had covered from both sides.

My CNN colleagues had flown into Kabul ahead of me, hauling videotapes, bottled water, food supplies and the requisites of the modern reporting team—a satellite telephone, flak vests and protective helmets. We planned to produce an hour-long documentary on Afghanistan but were also prepared to report news stories as they developed. There was only one scheduled flight a week into Kabul from Pakistan, and that was frequently canceled because of insecurity at the airport. I waited in Peshawar, the bustling center of Pakistan's Northwest Frontier province, once the headquarters of the war against Afghanistan's Russian invasion force, a jihad, or religious war, masterminded by American and Pakistani intelligence agencies whose operatives funneled weapons across the mountainous border to the frequently traded gunfire, he said. We pulled up in front of our guest house and I noticed children playing soldier in the roadside dirt. They aimed their plastic rifles at each other and shouted what sounded to me like "tac, tac." Peter Jouvenal, a cameraman, said it was the local equivalent of "bang, bang." It was not the sound of bullets leaving the gun that children in the West imitate, but the noise the projectiles make as they fly over your head. It was a sound every Afghan child had gotten used to.

Our lodgings were near the old Round Hill Fort at the German Club, once a popular watering place. Its foreign patrons were long gone. The large pool hadn't seen water since the spring rains. The garden was overgrown. A set of children's swings had rusted. Power was intermittent. My first shower was with bottled mineral water because the pump had failed. As I sluiced the cold water over me I remembered Baghdad's al-Rashid Hotel. But we were grateful for the German Club because it provided the only decent guest rooms in the whole city. The leading hotels, including the luxury Intercontinental, had been put out of commission in the fighting.

The hotels were not the only losses from the wasteful civil war. Kabul and its ancient monuments had managed to survive the decade-long conflict against the Russians because the insurgents could rarely get their big guns close enough to attack it. When the Soviet military pulled out, the guerrillas had come from the mountains to conduct a bloody squabble over the spoils of victory. The capital was sliced like a pie into opposing armed camps. Each faction found reason to attack the other, and large sections of the city had been destroyed. The handsome century-old carpet bazaar where I had shopped on my last visit was in ruins. The sounds of battle I was hearing indicated the destruction was continuing.

As we explored the city on my first few days there I was astonished at the checkerboard pattern of military occupation. The main highway near the Kabul customs house was in the hands of militia of the moderate Jamiat-i-Islami faction, but a stone fence paralleling the road a cornfield-distance away was controlled by an arch enemy, the fundamentalist Hezb-i-Islami. A similar pattern existed throughout most of the city. Roads to and beyond the Kabul zoo were in the hands of opposing factions, while a third faction, the National Islamic Front, held the zoo with a large detachment of soldiers. When we entered the compound we saw that its main purpose had become a military strong point. The few animals that remained were thin and bedraggled. A lean tiger nervously prowled its cage. A large black bear hurled itself at me as I peered through the steel bars, and I slapped away its reaching paws with my camera. I saw what I thought was an attendant in one of the cages but cameraman Jouvenal said he was probably a prisoner.

We drove along Jade Darulaman into southwest Kabul, an area controlled by the fundamentalist Hezb-i-Islami faction. The whole district had been laid waste in a year of fighting. Only crumbling walls remained of businesses around the first traffic circle. We drove past a high school in the next block that had been the scene of heavy fighting several hours earlier. The gates of the large abandoned Soviet Embassy compound further on were padlocked, the walls and guardposts pockmarked with bullets and rocket holes. We looked inside from a nearby building and saw that the extensive complex had been looted and burned. At the end of the road stood an ornate government building known as the Darulaman Palace, which had been shelled earlier in the year. We went inside to take pictures and found that soldiers were industriously stealing the building's lead and copper roofing and loading it into trucks.

The once renowned Kabul Museum was in shambles across the street, its upper floors in ruins from bombing and shelling. I kicked at stone fragments of a second-century Buddhist statue in the rubble. Shards of ancient pots were strewn on the floor near the ashes of the museum files. The soldiers downstairs claimed that many of the valuables had been locked inside a storeroom on the ground floor, particularly the historic gold and silver coin collection. But when I peered through a crack in the door all I could see were broken timbers and pieces of furniture. Jouvenal led us to the museum garden where the automobile collection of the late King Ammanula was housed. A magnificent Rolls-Royce Phantom from the late 1920s had bullet holes in the door. The seats had been torn out by soldiers who were using them to sleep on. The engine had been cannibalized. A worse fate had overtaken the two vintage Daimlers and a Cadillac First Edition sedan, and they were unsalvageable.

Most diplomats had fled Kabul when civil war erupted after the departure of the Russians, and no Western embassies remained. When we visited the empty American Embassy in the Karte Wali district to videotape my commentary on the anarchy in the country, we met the local embassy staff, who told us they were irregularly paid and felt aggrieved at being neglected by the U.S. government. When Jouvenal complained that a small tree beside the main entrance door behind me was impairing his picture, an embassy gardener obligingly uprooted it and threw it aside before we could deter him.

As we drove around the city we were stopped by gun-toting militiamen at every intersection but they waved us through when we gave them cigarettes or explained we were journalists. We were benefiting from the generally positive impression left by the Western press's coverage of the war. Jouvenal had walked across the border into Afghanistan with guerrilla fighters seventy-one times during the decade-long struggle and he was familiar with their foibles. Mackenzie had also been a frequent visitor and trumpeted with authority the few words he knew of the local language, Dari. When our press passes failed us our taxi driver, Amir Shah, weighed in. He persuaded one stubborn militiaman to let us through by describing Jouvenal as the brother of British Prime Minister John Major. At one time I was portrayed as a relative of Maggie Thatcher.

At the end of the second day we were tired and thirsting for something more to drink than canned Pakistani orange juice. Richard Mackenzie had spent the summer of the previous year in Kabul and knew his way around and he ordered our taxi driver to purchase some "German petrol," a code name for beer because all alcohol products had been officially banned when the communist government had collapsed. We traveled to the western suburbs of the city to a district controlled by the Ismaili sect, which condoned drink, and purchased a case of canned German beer from a roadside black-market shack, chilling it in the refrigerator at the guest house.

The banning of beer was about all the belligerents could agree on. Afghanistan did have a government of sorts, with a president and a prime minister and a cabinet. But the political arrangement had no practical significance. Power was in the hands of the armed factions of the seven major political groups. After the Russians quit and the communist government was defeated, the factions divided up Kabul and split the rest of the country into baronies. President Burhanuddin Rabbani's Jamiat-i-Islami party was supported by the guns of the most successful of the military commanders, Ahmed Shah Massoud, who was a sworn enemy of the prime minister, Gulbuddin Hekmatyar, an autocratic Islamic fundamentalist. The prime minister had never even entered his office in the capital or dealt with the president because he apparently feared for his life, preferring to stay at his heavily defended encampment fifteen miles to the southwest. The other factions had shifting alliances with the two major groups.

The inability of the war victors to resolve their political differences subjected Kabul to the endless misery of shelling and fighting. The hit song while we were there was called "Kabul Is Burning," and Amir Shah would sing along on the car radio. The song was a lament to a city destroyed by a civil war that was killing thousands of civilians. One verse went, "Kabul is burning and smoking, Kabul once had wonderful fresh air and gardens, Kabul once had wonderful clear weather, now Kabul is burning and smoking."

President Rabbani gave us an interview at the former Kabul Palace, a once handsome building now pockmarked with shell fire. I had met him a decade earlier while he was in exile in Peshawar and forming an alliance with competing political leaders that had long been rent asunder. Rabbani is a soft-spoken theologian with a flowing white beard who describes himself as an Islamic moderate. The ornate interview room had a large bookcase with a thirty-six-volume edition of the writings of George Washington, and the United Nations yearbook for 1953. An antiquated Russian telephone occasionally jingled. The president complained that his government was unable to function because it had no funds. He appealed for the return of Western embassies to Kabul, and the resumption of economic aid. And he blamed the Islamic fundamentalists for the continued civil war.

Next day we drove north to the Kunduz region, where a border crisis was flaring up with neighboring Tajikistan, a section of the former Soviet Union that was embroiled in civil war. We crossed the massive Hindu Kush via the Salang Tunnel, which had been drilled through the mountains at the breathtaking height of twelve thousand feet. In several fertile northern valleys beyond, the destruction of the Russian war was evident. Villages were totally destroyed, the houses crumbled, the fields overgrown, the farmers and their families still in refugee camps in distant Pakistan because they feared to return. Only near Kunduz was life coming back to normal, and fields were yellow with delicious jintor melons, the famous late-summer crop of the region.

It was a religiously conservative region and we saw few women. They were rarely allowed to leave the walls of their compounds. When they did, the adult women wore the burqa, a black or purple garment that totally covered them, with tiny slits for the eyes. A woman carrying a child nearly walked into our vehicle. Our interpreter explained that women were frequently in accidents because of the inadequate vision of the burqa. He said the garment was so hot in summer that some women fainted in the marketplaces or vomited on the crowded buses.

We stayed at Taloqan, a flourishing market town an hour's drive from the northern border. Without much trouble we found the head-quarters of the Tajikistan Islamic Front, the rebel organization fighting the country's communist government. There was a large sign announcing their presence on the gate of the former headquarters of Ahmed Shah Massoud, the Afghan Tajik whose military forces were backing President Rabbani. Armed soldiers were going to and fro but declined to be interviewed. Taloqan reminded me of Peshawar a decade earlier when the Afghanistan war was gearing up in neighboring Pakistan.

On our way back to Kabul, we passed a bare promontory that thrust down from the mountains. Our interpreter turned in his seat. "This is the Girdan area. It's famous for robbers." As if on cue I saw two armed men running hard down the barren slopes toward the road, waving and shouting for us to stop. We sped on, but a United Nations vehicle behind us was not so lucky and the bandits pulled it over at gunpoint. We had no weapons or other symbols of authority to actively intervene so we drove off without offering assistance.

The dusty, rutted roads of Kunduz made our journey seem endless. I was relieved when we merged with the repaired Kabul highway in Baslan province and drove into Pul-e Khumri for lunch. Peter Jouvenal had promised us an amusing diversion, a meeting with a friend of his, the province governor. The official, Said Jaffer Naderi, measured up to our cameraman's promise. A plump young man, mustached but otherwise clean-shaven unlike most other Afghans, Naderi was an Ismaili, a member of the prosperous religious sect headed by the Aga Khan, and known for its more liberal social attitudes. He had a hangover. "I had some friends down from Mazar-e Sharif and they partied all night," he complained when we were introduced in his ice-cool office, the only place other than Kabul's presidential palace that we found air-conditioning. The red-eyed governor opened a small fridge in his office and handed us cans of German beer. He apologized for not joining us. "I'm on Alka-Seltzers right now." Naderi used colloquial American slang in his conversation, picked up, he told us, in New Jersey, where he had spent his early twenties spending his father's money and running around with a biker gang. "If they could see me now," he laughed, producing his business card in which he was described as governor of Baslan province and "commander of the 80th Division." His card listed both his office and home phones. He talked nostalgically about his New Jersey days. "I'd like to suit up and take a spin right now but I can't wear a leather jacket up here, it wouldn't look right on the governor."

Naderi looked deceptively guileless. When he returned from New Jersey to take over the family mandate in Baslan province in the late 1980s, he worked first with the Russian occupiers and then with the communist government in Kabul until its overthrow in 1992. He had kept his feet in the slippery political shoals that followed, and now Naderi was aligned with President Rabbani's faction, but not too closely. "Rabbani recently sent up two judges he'd appointed. I told him we already had a judge and sent them back. And the other day the minister of communications couldn't hear me on the telephone and turned me over to an assistant. Imagine, a deaf minister of communications?"

Naderi's stronghold of Pul-e Khumri straddles the main north–south road, and his military forces control territory far to the east and west. He said he would fight to prevent any of the factions taking over his domain. "Frankly, I'd wish a plague on all their houses," he commented as we were departing. "In this city we have a functioning cement factory and power plant and other small industries, and people are working and happy. Nowhere in Afghanistan can equal that."

We returned to Kabul to find that Richard Mackenzie had gone off to Ahmed Shah Massoud's encampment at Jabal al-Saraj to try and finally nail down our interview with the legendary warrior. Next morning Peter Bergen impatiently headed off by taxi in pursuit. Time was running out. We were already behind schedule and Bergen needed to hurry things along.

Near Charikar he was stopped by a group of soldiers intent on getting more than just his ID. One stood in front of the taxi with his automatic weapon aimed at the driver. Another, a long knife clamped between his teeth, reached into the vehicle and searched through Bergen's pockets and clothing. He rifled Bergen's leather briefcase, removing several hundred dollars' worth of local currency and a handful of credit cards. But the case was so jammed with schedules and briefing notes and clippings that the thief missed the main prize, several thousand dollars' worth of cash and traveler's checks buried in their midst.

When I arrived at Jabal al-Saraj early in the afternoon Bergen was shaken up but undaunted. He told Massoud's embarrassed elder brother that he had trained for Afghanistan in the streets of New York. Because the incident had taken place in their security zone, our hosts offered to immediately replace the stolen money. They suggested sending out a military patrol to apprehend the thieves but the taxi driver objected, explaining that he traveled the route frequently and

432

would be subject to reprisal. Massoud's brother told me it could have been worse. "Just the other day in that area a taxi drove onto the road shoulder and was blown up by a mine buried there years ago by the Russians."

We met Massoud in a carpet-bedecked room over the east gate of the crumbling old Royal Palace. A strong wind rattled the windows, blowing away the heat of late summer and hinting at the severe winter ahead. Massoud is a man of slight build and modest bearing. He wore a black waistcoat over his loose-fitting white cotton robes, and a pakol perched on his head, the traditional woolen hat that had become his trademark. Massoud has the narrow features and light skin of the Tajik people who dominate northern Afghanistan. I was eager to talk with him. He had generated more ardor among my journalistic colleagues than any revolutionary soldier since the North Vietnamese general Vo Nguyen Giap. Just as Giap had frustrated America's designs on Vietnam, Massoud had humbled the Soviet superpower by defying the massive forces mobilized against him and capturing his country's capital. Richard Mackenzie, who had covered Massoud's campaigns during the war, admired him and had worn a dark suit and tie for the meeting, frequently brushing the dust off his lapels as we squatted on the cushions.

Massoud's brother stood guard outside the door during our meeting, which lasted well into the evening. He spoke French well but preferred to converse in Dari through an interpreter. I asked him to compare Afghanistan's struggle with Vietnam's and he laughed. "We had the more decisive victory. After Afghanistan there was no Soviet Union. But after Vietnam there was still the United States of America." He told me he had watched CNN's coverage of the Gulf War via satellite dish, and asked, "Why didn't the Americans kill Saddam Hussein?" I responded that Saddam had hidden amongst his followers in Baghdad just as Massoud had escaped repeated Russian assassination attempts in his Panjsher valley hideout.

I asked Massoud why he hadn't taken total power when his forces swept down from the north and captured Kabul in April the previous year. Traditionally in Afghanistan the most powerful military figure became master of the country. He said he willingly relinquished governing responsibility to the movement's political leadership because it promised democracy. At war's end, from their base in Pakistan, the politicians had organized a unity government. But the promise of democracy had collapsed in civil war. Although the leader of his Jamiat party held the presidency, Massoud agreed that the politicians had

433

failed and he regretted that he had not been more assertive. I got the impression Massoud was just biding his time before he took over the government in Kabul and moved against his enemies.

Massoud was anxious to present himself as a leader the world could deal with, a moderate eager for close relations with the West. He said he differed from his former ally and now principal enemy, the Islamic fundamentalist Gulbuddin Hekmatyar, who Massoud said was "made into a Frankenstein" by receiving preferential CIA weapons shipments during the war, which allowed him to turn against the United States.

While criticizing his enemy's support for Islamic extremists, Massoud played down his own involvement with the Islamic revolution in neighboring Tajikistan, blaming local commanders for the presence of the armed Tajik rebels we had seen at his old headquarters in Taloqan. He grew more animated as our meeting progressed, promising that with political stability and Western aid his forces could move against Afghanistan's drug trade and the terrorist training camps. We ended our interview with enthusiastic handshakes and embraces. But I did not forget the chaotic situation in Kabul, and Bergen's assault earlier in the day almost within sight of our interview room. I figured Massoud's goals were far distant.

That he had accomplished much became clear the next day. Massoud lent us a Russian-built helicopter to fly into his home base, the nearby Panjsher Valley, the springboard from where he had taken over much of Afghanistan after defying years of determined Soviet attempts to subdue his forces. Peter Bergen coaxed the pilots with a handful of local currency to fly low and fast for dramatic pictures, and we set off on a roller-coaster ride over precipitous mountains and through narrow gorges, skimming across slivers of silver blue water and roaring over tiny cornfields as farmers fled for their lives.

I have a rule never to do anything dangerous for fun and I thought of that rule as our pilots defied the laws of aeronautics, bucking and bouncing in air drafts as they negotiated windswept ravines and straddled sharp mountain ridges at 180 miles per hour. A few months earlier the AP bureau chief had been killed in a neighboring valley in just such a helicopter outing. To calm my beating heart I reasoned that the risk was worth it. In contrast to the magnificent scenery and the timeless way of village life there was the visible detritus of war, the scores of tanks and trucks and jeeps left behind by the Russians, their rusted wreckage pushed to the sides of the roads, or nose deep in the rushing river waters. The remains testified to the tenacity of the ill-equipped mountainmen who beat them back.

Mackenzie had a friend living at Jishta village ninety miles up the valley, a farmer who had sometimes guided him through the mountain passes to the Panjsher and who had once saved his life. Mackenzie had taken him and his crippled sister back to the United States a few years earlier, where she had received successful medical treatment. Now they were back home. For another handful of currency our helicopter pilots flew us to the tiny village, inadvertently flattening a ricefield as we landed, requiring Bergen to fork out money to the irate farmer who had been harvesting the crop. Mackenzie's friends greeted him with embraces and kisses. I noticed that even though the afternoon was quite warm the villagers were dressed in heavy clothing and they exuded strong body odors. Jouvenal said the mountain people rarely washed, even though the river was only a few steps away, because it was cold much of the year. We stayed to sip hot tea before returning home. That evening Mackenzie started scratching his arms and chest and I saw that his body was red with welts and bites. "They've left me a lasting reminder of our close friendship," he laughed as he searched for bug spray to kill the fleas and body lice he'd picked up on his reunion.

Mackenzie's friendship with Massoud's organization helped him through a dispute with a former landlord who had rented him a house in Kabul the previous year that had been robbed. The landlord was demanding that Richard pay for the cost of furniture and carpets stolen from the house though Richard himself had been robbed by the thieves at knife point. I heard him bellowing in rage one morning as he was unexpectedly arrested by burly policemen who dragged him off to headquarters. A senior police officer, who was presumably bribed by the landlord, demanded he pay a considerable amount or go to jail. Before being taken before the commanding general Richard managed to call Massoud's chief of security. His friend told him, "Don't worry about the general, Richard, he's ours," and the case was soon dropped.

Mackenzie's enthusiastic advocacy of Massoud was in contrast to his contempt for the competing leader, Hekmatyar. He was convinced that Hekmatyar's fundamentalist forces had deliberately killed Western journalists during the war. His criticsm got the reporter labeled an "enemy of Islam" by Hekmatyar at a press conference in Peshawar several years earlier.

We had been trying since we arrived to interview the fundamentalist leader but had difficulty coordinating with his staff. Local phones rarely worked. The principal leaders had satellite telephones in their headquarters but these were often not functioning for various reasons including power blackouts and equipment failures. Massoud's phone was cut off while we were there because he had an unpaid bill of $55,000. He complained to his aides, "But I thought the Arabstans paid for it," using the popular term for Saudi Arabia, which had poured millions into the Afghan struggle.

We tried to coordinate an interview with Hekmatyar through the skeleton staff at the vacant prime minister's office but were put off. It was only on his return from a brief visit to Pakistan and Iran that we had our chance. Along with a few resident Kabul correspondents, we were invited to a press conference at Hekmatyar's headquarters at Charasayab south of Kabul on the Logar road. We traveled there late one afternoon.

Charasayab is almost within sight of Kabul but it may as well be a different country. It is the sharp end of a sizeable wedge of territory that Hekmatyar's Hezb-i-Islami forces control to the south and west. It is like a stick poking into the heart of the capital, aggravating the open wound of civil war. We reached its first outposts by driving across a no-man's-land over a dusty, rutted highway garnished with empty oil drums, rusting cargo containers and abandoned wooden shacks. The green pennants of the Hezb-i-Islami were fluttering from the first sandbagged checkpoint where guards waved us through. Kabul's second and third lines of defense during communist times ran through this area. I noticed that the artillery pieces and rocket launchers in the bunkers and outposts now had their barrels pointed at the city and not away from it. At regular intervals these weapons would pound the capital with thousands of shells as Hekmatyar turned up the screws in the civil war. Earlier in the year he had tried to capture Kabul but failed. Many of his own forces had died in the counterbombardments. We saw many simple cemeteries dotting the hillsides, with sheafs of commemorative green pennants flying from poles shoved into the graves.

Hekmatyar's headquarters is in the foothills in a former government military camp. In the last mile or two we followed a jeep carrying several Arab soldiers that drove on past our turnoff. Another Arab soldier on a motorcycle roared by while we were parking. These sightings confirmed accounts that Hekmatyar harbored fighters from outside Afghanistan, but when he appeared at his press conference he emphatically denied that any Arabs remained with him. Hekmatyar blamed the CIA and "other Western intelligence agencies" for the political instability in Afghanistan. And he praised the help he was receiving from neighboring Iran, whose Islamic fundamentalist government was the model for his vision of Afghanistan's political future. The Hezb leader ended his press conference quickly but I stood up and appealed to him for a private interview. He turned me down but a few minutes later an aide came to tell us we could have half an hour with him after evening prayers. The aide said they were familiar with CNN, and followed our news reports via satellite dish. Another aide startled me by complaining about critical remarks he said he'd heard Ted Turner's wife, Jane Fonda, make about Islam. I assured him that he must have been mistaken but he wanted a retraction and I gave him CNN's home address to write for an explanation.

On his return Hekmatyar was more relaxed. He adjusted his tightly wound turban and flowing robes and pronounced himself ready to begin. If Massoud is the warrior of Afghanistan and Rabbani the statesman, then Hekmatyar is the adroit politician, autocratically wielding control over his centralized, dedicated Hezb-i-Islami movement. He is a Pashtun, the majority race in Afghanistan, which has long enjoyed good relations with Pakistan. This helped Hekmatyar win preferential treatment over Massoud and other leaders during the war when billions of dollars in American aid was being distributed by Pakistani intelligence operatives. He has learned passable English and used it during the interview. I was anxious to get his ideas on the World Trade Center bombing and the aborted plot to blow up other New York facilities because some of the Muslim suspects served in his military units during the war. He denied knowing any of them. But Hekmatyar did admit meeting in Peshawar with the most notorious of the suspects, the blind Egyptian cleric, Sheik Omar Abdel Rahman. He expressed sympathy for the sheik and predicted "he will be exonerated."

Hekmatyar has never hidden his distaste for Western society, despite his willing acceptance of weapons from the CIA to fight the Russians. In a visit to United Nations headquarters in New York during the war, Hekmatyar refused to meet with his most influential patron, President Ronald Reagan. His hostile attitude to the West remains. He looks to neighboring Iran and other "brother Islamic countries" to help Afghanistan rebuild, and blames the West for siding with his enemies in Kabul. And why had he not occupied the prime minister's office in the capital? "They will kill me if I go there. I will not step foot in Kabul until every gun is gone from the city," he said, blaming Massoud and Rabbani for the continuing civil war. "Their planes bombed me here, my house, and endangered my wife and children." It was clear to me that Hekmatyar was determined to keep fighting the civil war and that Afghanistan's long night of turmoil was far from over.

With his interview on tape we could return to Kabul and leave for the last part of the story early in the morning. We were assigned a van of soldiers to escort us to the last Hezb checkpoint. It was well after dark when we drove out the gate past the security guards sitting at a candlelit table. The nearby mountains were gray shadows against the blackness of the night. Outside the gates we saw taxi driver, Amir Shah, in our headlights, signaling for us to stop. He handed Bergen a hastily scrawled note from Mackenzie in Kabul warning us not to drive back to the capital. "On no account come back tonight. It is too dangerous. Your lives are more valuable than leaving early in the morning," Mackenzie had written. Was he serious or was it the "German petrol" he had been drinking? Jouvenal, impatient to leave the uncertain security of the war zone, insisted we proceed and climbed into Amir Shah's taxi. Bergen briefly considered the alternative, which was bedding down with a platoon of unwashed soldiers and using nature's toilet in the trees. The German Club was only forty minutes away. We drove off behind our escort.

The danger was not in Hezb territory but beyond, the two-mile stretch of no-man's-land that separated the belligerents in the outer suburbs of Kabul, an expanse rarely traversed at night. There were three layers of sentinels to pass, the first a mercenary force based at the old fort of Bala Hissar. We drove slowly beyond the last Hezb checkpoint with the vehicle lights our only illumination. A soldier materialized at my window with a submachine gun. He was a Hezb and waved us on. Further on in the glow of the headlights of the taxi ahead I saw the snout of a rifle grenade bobbing toward us past some overturned cargo containers. I heard Jouvenal's voice shouting loudly in Dari, "Foreign journalists, foreign journalists." The rifle grenade was joined by an automatic rifle and pistol in the hands of three soldiers who peered into our vehicles and let us proceed. Jouvenal walked back to our car. "I think they were Dustan's men, but I'm not sure," he said, naming the local warlord. "Just go very slowly and listen for rifle shots and stop when you do."

We slowed down to three miles an hour. I could have walked faster. A match flickered in a building to my right and I could see the outlines of a soldier at a machine gun lighting his cigarette. To our left appeared the bulky outlines of Bala Hissar. Ahead was a checkpoint where the soldiers asked Amir Shah for money before we drove on. Now we were in the three city blocks controlled by the Kabul garrison. The city power was off again. I could barely make out the gaunt remains of businesses destroyed in the civil war. Finally we reached Jamiat lines, who controlled the center of town. They waved us through. I thought we had made it safely. But even here, relatively early in the evening, there was no traffic in the streets, no movement whatsoever. I remembered Massoud's brother telling me, "Don't ever go out at night. After dark, everyone in Afghanistan is a bandit."

We left Kabul late the next morning for the long drive to Jalalabad and the Pakistan border. It was the last part of our assignment. We had been two weeks in country. Bergen and I crammed our gear into a small Japanese-made taxi whose driver, who spoke no English, delighted in showing us how in reverse gear a recording announced in a squeaky voice, "Attention please, this car is backing up." The highway was a war museum. Heading toward one checkpoint we saw that the road divider was a long row of empty artillery shells. Further on, our way was blocked by a stack of long, gray-painted 122mm rockets, the unscrewed fuses piled nearby. Soldiers checked our papers before pushing the rockets aside to let us pass.

As we drove off the Kabul plateau we were stopped at a water well by armed men who belonged to no identifiable political faction and who were demanding money from passing buses. Grudgingly they let us pass untaxed. Further on we saw two dozen trucks loaded with United Nations food aid that had been hijacked the previous week by a local warlord and were parked behind his military compound. The route off the Kabul plateau was famed for its spectacular beauty. The road descends down precipitous gorges and follows bubbling streams. But it was a death trap for the Russian military convoys that were required to negotiate the highway to supply border garrisons. In one mile-long stretch I counted forty-three destroyed tanks and trucks, their rusted carcasses pushed off the road or lying in the ravines below, victims of daredevil guerrillas who scaled the surrounding mountain peaks to blast the convoys with rockets. On some canyon walls were the outlines of painted graffiti in the Russian alphabet, Cyrillic.

Nearing Jalalabad, we made a rest stop at some roadside restaurants where the Kabul river disappeared over the spillway of a power plant. I walked across the highway for a closer look at the surging waters and noticed the strong smell of human excrement. The riverbank was evidently a favored rest room for passing travelers who had no other choice. I didn't recall every having seen a public lavatory in Afghanistan, and could find few private ones. The smell of human waste was often in the air. Jouvenal came up beside me, sniffing. He laughed. "There are those who say the whole of Afghanistan is a toilet, a toilet with a national flag."

We arrived in Jalalabad early evening, dusty and tired, drinking in the lush landscape. We had entered an oasis fed by the Kabul and Kunar rivers, with towering palm trees and green, wooded farms. The luxuriant portrait was framed by a surrounding horizon of gaunt, rock-bound mountains. Jalalabad is the principal city of Ningrahar province and was once the royal winter capital and a center of ancient Buddhist culture. But we were told by the desk clerk at the cavernous Hotel Spinghar to avoid the streets after dark. He said the city was more dangerous than Kabul.

The perils in Jalalabad were more pernicious than the open warfare of the capital. The city's community of international aid officials were being targeted by Islamic fundamentalists resentful of what they saw as outside interference. Five United Nations workers had been brutally murdered on the main road east of town earlier in the year. Most Westerners fled the region when it was learned the suspected assailants were a dozen Arab militants who were receiving terrorist training within Afghanistan to fight for international Islamic causes. After their arrest the militants had been quickly released, and further inquiries dropped. Western aid officials presumed that the weak local authorities had abandoned the case to avoid a confrontation with the Arabs' influential benefactors. A few weeks later, another several hundred militant Arabs had entered the province after being expelled from neighboring Pakistan. They were believed to have joined fundamentalist terrorist training camps.

Jalalabad was also a hub of a rapidly expanding narcotics industry that was flourishing in the turbulence. The stony upland soils of Ningrahar had long been devoted to opium poppy crops. Local mothers traditionally put their teething babies to sleep by rubbing raw opium on their gums. But now, productive farmland was being used to grow vast crops of poppies. The bulk opium was being shipped to border areas for processing into heroin destined for the streets of Western cities. The Afghan resistance leaders who had fought the Russians with sizeable U.S. help were now becoming the world's biggest opium producers, who, according to American drug enforcement officials, harvested more than two thousand tons in 1992 for conversion into heroin.

Our CNN team had neither the contacts nor the desire to probe too deeply into the sinister side of Jalalabad. We talked with the province governor, who had once spent a summer as a guest in Jouvenal's London home. He served us tea and polite conversation. He professed to know nothing of drugs or terrorism. He offered an armed escort to the Pakistan border when we left town and we decided to leave before he changed his mind.

Mackenzie had a young Afghan friend named Nasrat who had joined us on our journey. Richard wanted to take him to Pakistan for a few days to see what the outside world looked alike. Nasrat had been unable to obtain a passport but it didn't stop him. He walked past the Torkham frontier post unchecked, confirming our suspicions that the border was a sieve.

I left Afghanistan feeling none of the excitement of my visit a decade earlier when I had first been with the mujahedeen fighters, caught up in the fervor of their unequal struggle, buying into their dream that the defeat of the Russians was a goal whose realization would bring peace and reconciliation. This visit had punctured that illusion. The collapse of the Soviet empire, the end of the Cold War, had not brought harmony to Afghanistan, merely conflict and criminality. And the United States would reap a bitter harvest from the seeds of the Islamic revolution it helped sow.

Peter Bergen suggested one last standup at the crest of the Khyber Pass. We drove up the winding road beyond the watchtowers and forts the British had built in the previous century to hold back the Afghan tribes. Jouvenal had to hurry to set up his camera. The sun was beginning to set over the western ranges, casting its last glowing yellowness across the ancient valleys and craggy mountaintops. A few Pakistani soldiers were standing around. I glanced at the notes I had scrawled in my pad and stared into the camera in a suitably sincere pose. "For centuries, the Khyber Pass has been the gateway between central and southern Asia," I intoned. "Today, it is the gateway for drugs, Islamic radicals and terrorists." We packed up our gear and climbed into our taxi. I was glad to be leaving Afghanistan but I knew that the story was not over. I would probably have to go back.

Index

Index

Index

460

Lightning Source UK Ltd.
Milton Keynes UK
UKOW04f1807111213

222849UK00001B/21/A